The Transport Amphorae and Trade of Cyprus

Edited by Mark L. Lawall
& John Lund

Aarhus University Press |

THE TRANSPORT AMPHORAE AND TRADE OF CYPRUS

GÖSTA ENBOM MONOGRAPHS

General editor:
Bodil Bundgaard Rasmussen.

Gösta Enbom Monographs is a peer reviewed series.

Published with support from The Foundation of Consul General Gösta Enbom.

Graphic design:
Nina Grut, MDD.

Printed at Narayana Press.

Typeset with Stone Serif and Stone Sans.

ISBN 978 87 7124 213 3
ISSN 1904-6219

Aarhus University Press
Langelandsgade 177
DK-8200 Aarhus N

White Cross Mills
Lancaster LA1 4XS
England

70 Enterprise Drive, suite 2
Bristol, CT 06010
USA

www.unipress.dk

Front cover:
A White Painted IV jug. London, British Museum i.n. 1926.6-28.9. Courtesy the British Museum.

Back cover:
Amphora in the National Museum of Denmark, Collection of Classical and Near Eastern Antiquities, i.n. 9707 from Tomb 80 at Marion; Late Roman 1 amphora *in situ* from a wreck at Cape Zevgari. Photo by courtesy of Justin Leidwanger.

NATIONALMUSEET

Amphora attributed to the painter Syriskos, Athens 500-470 BC, Collection of Classical and Near Eastern Antiquities, The National Museum of Denmark, i.n. Chr. VIII 320.

Table of Contents

Preface

BY PER KRISTIAN MADSEN
DIRECTOR GENERAL
THE NATIONAL MUSEUM OF DENMARK
MEMBER OF THE BOARD OF THE FOUNDATION
OF CONSUL GENERAL GÖSTA ENBOM

Transport amphorae, the more or less standardized ancient ceramic containers primarily used for the shipping of agricultural products, offer a great potential for elucidating important aspects of the economic history of the Mediterranean in Classical antiquity. This is probably the main reason why they have been the focus of many studies in recent years, a situation reflected by this volume. Earlier versions of some of the chapters were read at a workshop on *The Transport Amphorae and Trade of Cyprus* held at the Danish and Canadian Institutes at Athens in 2007.

The contributions gathered here are also symptomatic of a growing awareness of the societal and economic aspects of ancient pottery. The latter constituted one of the main themes of the research programme "Pots, Potters and Society in Ancient Greece", which the Danish National Museum launched in 2008 thanks to a substantial grant from the Foundation of Consul General Gösta Enbom.

The focus on Cyprus in this volume may be perceived as a natural consequence of the special place of pride Ancient Cyprus holds in the Danish National Museum, where a new gallery of Cypriot antiquities was inaugurated in 2002, thanks to a large donation by the A.G. Leventis Foundation in Nicosia. Moreover, in the early 1970s, Dr. Vassos Karageorghis, then Director of Antiquities in Cyprus, had invited Danish students of classical archaeology to participate in his excavations at Kition, and this led to a Danish involvement in a Canadian landscape survey around the city of Palaepaphos (modern Kouklia) in the 1980s. Between 1989 and 1992, the University of Aarhus organised a landscape survey and excavations in the Akamas peninsula, and the University of Copenhagen investigated from 1992 to 1999 a rural settlement at Aradippou in the Larnaka area. After the turn of the millennium, Danish archaeologists returned to the island to participate in the Troodos Archaeological and Environmental Survey Project organized by the University of Glasgow.

Consul General Gösta Enbom (1895-1986).

The Transport Amphorae and Trade of Cyprus thus bears witness to former and present Danish engagement in the archaeology of Cyprus as well as the international collaboration in the archaeological exploration of the island, which the Department of Antiquities in Cyprus has promoted for several decades.

I wish to conclude by expressing my gratitude to of the contributors to this volume and to all other individuals who have helped in one way or the other, in particular the anonymous reviewers and the editors Mark L. Lawall and John Lund. Last but not least I thank the Foundation of Consul General Gösta Enbom, which made it all possible by its generous support.

Introduction

BY MARK L. LAWALL & JOHN LUND

Placed as a stepping stone on the sea route between Europe and the Near East, Cyprus has always been a meeting place of many cultures. Though rarely united politically through many millennia of history – and for extended periods subject to foreign rule – the island nonetheless managed to maintain specific and unique identities.[1] This publication focusses on aspects of the economy of Cyprus between c. 700 BC and AD 700, a crucial millennium and a half of her history. True, several generations of scholars have elucidated many aspects of the Cypriot economy and trade in these centuries,[2] not least the important role played by the copper mines throughout history.[3] But gaps remain in our knowledge of the role played by the island's export and import of agricultural products at the regional and interregional level.

The aim of this volume, *The Transport Amphorae and Trade of Cyprus*, is to throw new light on these questions. The title was chosen so as not only to cover the transport amphorae produced in the island but also the imported amphorae manufactured in other parts of the ancient world. Both categories need to be taken into consideration if the potential of amphorae as a source for the economic history of Cyprus is to be fulfilled. While the shipping containers, the transport amphorae, are our focus, it is important to recognize that amphorae (like any other type of archaeological and historical evidence) can only further our understanding of parts of the picture. Indeed, all relevant classes of material need to be taken into account in our quest to arrive at a better understanding of the ancient economy. Still, the amphorae remain a prime source for the ancient trade in agricultural products and other foodstuffs, even if other types of containers were also used – in particular for overland shipments – for this purpose.[4]

A good deal of new information has emerged in recent years about transport amphorae manufactured in and shipped around the Levant in general. But we are far from having a comprehensive understanding of Cypriot amphorae, and in fact the present volume is the first monograph devoted to this subject. Scholarly interest in the amphorae of Cyprus may be traced back at least to the final decades of the 19th century, when Luigi Palma di Cesnola and his brother Alessandro Palma di Cesnola conducted extensive excavations in the island.[5] They shipped many of their finds to Great Britain and America, where they subsequently became scattered between public museums and private owners. Some of the transport amphorae – in particular the Rhodian ones – were published,[6] but there was little understanding of the pottery of Cyprus until Einar Gjerstad and his collaborators in the Swedish Cyprus Expedition (1927-1931) imposed an archaeological methodology developed in Sweden on the Cypriot material.[7] They established an overall chronological framework of the island, subdividing the centuries of concern here into the (Cypro-)Archaic, Classical, Hellenistic, Roman and Late Antique periods – a division which is still often used.[8] Yet, as far as transport amphorae were concerned the results were somewhat inconclusive. In many cases, no distinction was made between amphorae produced in Cyprus and imported ones, and the classification of fabrics was notably generic. Virginia R. Grace, in a series of trips to Cyprus, did make a detailed study of finds from the Swedish Expedition, and her notes, now in the archives of the American School of Classical Studies at Athens, include suggestions of which jars are imported and which are local Cypriot.

Jean Deshayes' study from 1963 of the Late Classical and early Hellenistic amphorae found at Ktima, the predecessor of Nea Paphos,[9] remains the most comprehensive treatment

1 See for instance Mikrakis 2012.
2 Karageorghis & Michaelides (eds.) 1995; Mehl 1995; Papacostas 2001; Leonard 2005; Coureas 2005.
3 Kassianidou 2000; Kassianidou 2004 and forthcoming; Given *et al.* (eds.) forthcoming.
4 See the contribution by Tønnes Bekker-Nielsen to the present volume.
5 For the activities of Luigi Palma di Cesnola, see Marangou 2000.
6 Cesnola (A.P. di) 1881; 1882, and Cesnola (L.P. di) 1903; Hall 1885.
7 Houby-Nielsen 2003. For critical assessments of the legacy of Gjerstad and his associates, see Nys 2008 and Smith 2009, 220-233.
8 Gjerstad 1948, 427: Archaic I from 700 to 600 BC, Archaic II from 600 to 475 BC, Classical I from 475 to 400 BC, Classical II from 400 to 325 BC; Westholm 1956, 71: Hellenistic I, 325 to 150 BC, Hellenistic II, 150 BC to 50 BC, Roman I, 50 BC to AD 150, Roman II, AD 150 to AD 250, and Roman III, from AD 250 onwards. These dates are retained by Karageorghis 1982a, 9, except for the beginning of Archaic I which is dated to 750 BC.
9 Deshayes 1963, 210-212; Salles 1993b, 270-271.

of the unstamped Cypriote amphorae of those periods, but their stamped counterparts have been studied in some detail by Grace, Yves Calvet and Henryk Meyza.[10] Moreover, Zosia Sztetyłło, Calvet and Ino Nicolaou have investigated the imported stamped Hellenistic amphorae found in the island even more extensively.[11] The unstamped transport amphorae of the later Hellenistic and Roman periods have received less scholarly attention, but John W. Hayes' publication of the pottery from the House of Dionysos retains its fundamental value,[12] together with the indispensable communications to be found on the pages of the Report of the Department of Antiquities, Cyprus. In the last decades, our knowledge of the Late Antique amphora production of Cyprus was significantly advanced by the publications of evidence from amphora kiln sites by Stella Demesticha and Demitrios Michaelides.[13] There has nevertheless been little collation, interpretation, or synthesis of the data until recently. But this situation is rapidly changing, thanks in no small part to the contributors to the present volume, who are actively engaged in new studies of transport amphorae from shipwrecks, surveys and excavations. Moreover, the Hellenistic transport amphorae of Cyprus are the focal point of an ongoing Ph.D. project by Agata Dobosz at the Instytut Archeologii Uniwersytetu Jagiellońskiego, Kraków, and Anthi Kaldeli initiated a major new research programme in 2010 on the "Roman amphorae from Cyprus: interpreting Production, Trade and Exchange in the eastern Mediterranean".[14]

The time seems appropriate, therefore, for the present volume, which has the following goals: 1) to gain a first overall view of both the Cypriot production of transport amphorae and their distribution around Cyprus and beyond, 2) to gain a better understanding of the trends and patterns in imports to Cyprus and 3) to begin coordinating the amphora material with evidence of the trade routes, harbour facilities, and, within the island itself, the overland routes that made this trade possible. We have deliberately chosen a long time frame with the expectation that trends, models, or interpretive ideas from one period may prove useful for others. These goals, however, may ultimately lay the foundation for achieving the wider aim: to start a discussion about what the evidence of amphorae can tell us about the fluctuations in the economy of Cyprus from the Archaic period through to Late Antiquity.

The starting point for the chronological range of this volume roughly coincides with the capture of Cyprus in 709 BC by the Assyrian empire.[15] This is seen as a period of considerable autonomy as well as fragmented political structure with ten kingdoms attested in Esarhaddon's list of 673 BC.[16] This period sees considerable prosperity with both Greek and Levantine influences being seen at many sites and plenty of imported goods from both sides. Even if such influences, likely via trade contacts to at least some degree, were engendered by the need to provide tribute to the Assyrians, Cyprus shows no lack of foreign contact in this period.[17] Perhaps the best illustration of this dynamic period is illustrated on the cover of this volume: the Bichrome IV jug from Karpass showing a merchant ship with two, possibly Phoenician, amphoras perched on the deck. The recent studies of Archaic shipwrecks with mixtures of Cypriot and Greek cargoes off the southwestern coast of Turkey, reported here by Elizabeth Greene, Justin Leidwanger and Harun Özdaş, both provide vivid examples of Cyprus' connections to the Aegean world and begin to explore the institutional frameworks underlying this exchange. K. Levent Zoroğlu's paper highlights the intensity of activity in the area between the Cilician coast and Cyprus already in the 7th century and continuing into the early Hellenistic period.

Cyprus' contacts and trade with the broader Mediterranean world show little negative impact from the collapse of the Assyrian empire in 612 BC. The brief period of control by Egypt *c.* 560-545 BC (Hdts. 11.182) is seen as a time of increased Egyptianizing elements in Cypriot material culture, but contact with the Aegean world continues.[18] It is difficult to specify illustrative details of the amphora record for such a relatively narrow chronological window, but various Chian white-slipped, bobbin-shaped amphorae from Cypriot tombs might well date to this period of Egyptian control.

Persian domination, starting *c.* 545 BC (Hdts. 3.19) under Cyrus and continuing with substantial administrative reforms under Darius, brought with it both developments of economic practice (e.g., the emergence of coinage *c.* 520 BC) and an apparent intensification of Aegean-Cypriot interaction.[19] Some of the Cypriot kingdoms (though not Salamis or Amathous) joined the Greek cities of Asia Minor in the Ionian Revolt albeit briefly (Hdts. 5.116), but Cypriot ships are then attested on the Persian side at both the battles of Lade and Salamis.[20] Persian control of the island began to fragment after 480 culminating in the expanding power of Salamis under Evagoras I starting in 411 BC.[21] Persian control was re-established with the King's Peace of 386 and further strengthened throughout subsequent decades.[22] In 332 BC, the Cypriot fleet shifted its allegiance to Alexander the Great during the siege of Tyre.[23] Despite the volatile political history of the island with respect to both the Aegean and its nearer neighbours in the Levant, Cyprus remained a significant crossroads in the later Archaic and Classical amphora trade. Mark Lawall's chapter in this volume offers a preliminary attempt to characterize this trade with consideration of the Aegean amphora forms imitated locally on Cyprus as well as the regional variation in imported amphoras.

After Alexander's death, the island's cities were variously aligned with Ptolemy I and Antigonos Monophthalmos with Ptolemy gaining the upper hand in 312.[24] This state of affairs reversed when Demetrios Poliorketes captured Cyprus in 306. In 294, however, Ptolemy regained control of Cyprus, and the island remained a fundamental part of Ptolemaic maritime power with only brief interruptions all the way down to the period of Rome's intervention in Ptolemaic affairs in the early 1st century BC culminating in Octavian's victory at Actium in 31 BC. The connection between Cyprus and Ptolemaic Egypt plays a significant role in a number of papers in this volume. Kristian Göransson reports on rare fragments of Cypriot basket-handle amphorae, from an early 3rd century BC context, found in excavations at Euesperides in Cyrenaica. The marine 'landscape' shaped by prevailing winds and currents, together with prevailing Ptolemaic political alliances, must have significantly shaped the dominant presence of Rhodian amphorae in Hellenistic Cyprus already at the very beginning of the 3rd century. The papers by Craig Barker and Agata Dobosz provide various perspectives on the Rhodian record on Cyprus. The same Rhodes-to-Alexandria trade corridor, with Cyprus as a key nodal point, may also be indicated by the frequent discovery of Cypriot amphorae amongst the otherwise Rhodian-dominated amphora record of Alexandria as is documented here by the work of Gonca Cankardeş-Şenol and Ahmet Kaan Şenol. The further circulation of Cypriot amphorae of the Hellenistic period is also attested extensively at sites in Israel, and these finds are presented here by Gérald Finkielsztejn.

Once Cyprus became part of the Roman Empire,[25] the connections evidenced by the amphora record multiply considerably, yet the regional importance of the island remains clear. Anthi Kaldeli's paper on the amphora records of Nea Paphos and Amathous the 1st century BC to early 3rd century AD highlights the increased geographical range of Cyprus' imports, now with direct imports from the Western Mediterranean at Nea Paphos while Amathous shows a continued dependence on circulation and re-circulation of goods within the Eastern Mediterranean. Complementing Kaldeli's paper, Henryk Meyza and Dobiesława Bagińska's paper on the amphorae from the Polish excavations at Nea Paphos illustrates this mixture of Mediterranean types present at the site and continues the account into the late Roman period. While sites such as Nea Paphos and Amathous show various imports from the Aegean basin, the ceramic evidence for shipping from Cyprus towards the Aegean can be surprisingly sparse as Tamás Bezeczky's paper notes for the case of Roman Ephesus. Amphora production on Cyprus and nearby coastal regions is discussed in papers by David Williams and John Lund (the "pinched handle" amphorae, predominantly from Rough Cilicia, 1st - 4th centuries AD) and Stella Demesticha (Late Roman 1 amphorae, 4th - 7th centuries AD, with production appearing to spread from Cilicia to Cyprus and, only in the latest periods, up into the Aegean). Demesticha's paper also tracks the changing

10 For the Cypriot-produced stamped amphorae see Grace 1979; Calvet 1986, 509; Meyza 2004.
11 Sztetyłło 1976; 1984; 1985; 1991 and 2010; Barker 2002a; 2002b; 2004; Nicolaou 2005.
12 Hayes 1991; see also Papuci-Władyka 1995.
13 Demesticha 2000; 2003; 2005; Demesticha & Michaelides 2001.
14 This project continues and expands Kaldeli's Ph.D. thesis (2007).
15 Karageorghis 1982b, 57-64; Grayson 1991a, 90 and 1991b, 107; Reyes 1994 focuses on the 8th through 6th centuries; see too, Iacovou 2008; Cannavò 2011.
16 Karageorghis 1982b, 57-59; Grayson 1991b, 127; Iacovou 2008, 632-633; Reyes 1997, 308.
17 Karageorghis 1982b, 60-64.
18 Karageorghis 1982b, 64-68.
19 Karageorghis 1982b, 69-70; Maier 1985; 1994; Wiesehöfer 1990; Pouilloux 1989; Raptou 1999.
20 Maier 1994, 306-308; Georges 2000; Raptou 1999, 238-243.
21 Maier 1994, 308-312; Costa 1974; Raptou 1999, 250-261.
22 Maier 1994, 312-317; Ruzicka 1999.
23 On the period after the King's Peace down to the treaty of the Diadochoi in 311 BC, see Maier 1994, 326-336.
24 A recent overview of the Hellenistic history of Cyprus is found in Gordon 2012, 70-90; see too Will 1984a; 1984b; and Heinen 1984.
25 Gordon 2012, 279-302.

extent of distribution of LR 1 amphorae through successive typological developments. While the geographical extent of such production of Cypriot-related amphorae was expanding in the Late Roman period, however, Cypriot amphora commerce appears to have become more intensively regional in scope. Justin Leidwanger's survey of maritime sherd scatters along the south coast of Cyprus shows a dominance of amphora types from the Eastern Mediterranean; even the Aegean is more often represented by Hellenistic types instead of Late Roman pieces. On land, Marcus Rautman's report on patterns identified in the Vasilikos Valley likewise highlights the dominance of LR 1 amphorae with far lesser percentages of other Eastern Mediterranean types. Kristina Winther-Jacobsen's paper comparing finds from the Troodos mining region with surveys of other contemporary regions, Methana in Greece and the Eastern Desert mining regions in Egypt draws attention to the ways that amphora types (present and absent), alongside the record of non-amphora ceramics, can begin to fill in the historical developments of broader commercial practices, in this case the extraction of mineral resources.

Taken as a whole, then, the contributors throw new light on a variety of relevant issues and in particular on the emerging patterns of regionalism in Cyprus – islands being particularly well suited for regional studies of this kind.[26] They trace an outline of a pattern (or patterns) of exports from and imports to the island through time of amphora-borne agricultural products. It may well be that wine constituted the most important of these commodities, but scientific residue analyses are urgently needed to ascertain the contents of the amphorae.

It is easy to form the impression that Cyprus was largely self-sufficient in olive oil and wine – with the exception of years of crop failures – and that her considerable import of wine was mainly due to a thirst for more exotic vintages than those produced locally. But the verdict is still out on this and many other issues, because the evidence gathered here underlines more than anything the need for new research aimed at helping us distinguish more clearly the amphorae produced in Cyprus from the imported ones - new discoveries of kiln sites in the island will surely contribute to solving this quandary in the future. Also, more publications of quantified amphora material from Cyprus and the surrounding areas need to be made available. In the absence of such analyses it is well-nigh impossible to determine the scope of the island's import and export trade in amphora-borne foodstuffs and hence their importance to the economy of the island. Therefore this volume cannot (and does not) claim to provide definite answers to the involved issues, but we hope that it may constitute a new point of departure for the future study of the transport amphorae and trade of Cyprus.

26 For recent discussions of "island archaeology" with reference to Cyprus see Knapp 2008, 13-30 and Kopaka & Cadogan 2012, 18-24 and 28-29.

Transport in Ancient Cyprus

BY TØNNES BEKKER-NIELSEN

Transport in Ancient Cyprus

BY TØNNES BEKKER-NIELSEN

Over the last two generations, the systematic study of amphorae has provided insights into the extent, scope and organization of trade in the ancient Mediterranean that no other category of source material can offer. It needs to be borne in mind, however, that the goods transported in amphorae form only part of a much larger picture of ancient commodity flows, most of which have left little or no trace and can only be reconstructed in very general outlines.

WAYS OF COMMUNICATION

Land and water

In classical antiquity as in other pre-industrial societies, land transport was expensive: the resource input required to produce a ton-mile of overland transport was five times that required for transport by barge on an inland waterway, and twenty-five times greater than that required to move the same quantity over the same distance on the high seas. The cost of transport by coasting vessel has not been calculated, but would lie somewhere between that of river and sea transport.

For non-perishable goods, water was generally preferred over land transport. For travellers and couriers, on the other hand, road travel had the advantage of predictability. A sea traveller might have to wait days or weeks in port for a ship and a favourable wind.[1]

In Cyprus, sea transport predated road transport. The Neolithic colonists who were able to cross the sea from the mainland to Cyprus will have had little difficulty navigating the coastal waters of the island and in the 2nd millennium BC, the Uluburun wreck, laden with some ten tons of Cypriot export wares such as copper and ceramics, testifies to the sea trade between Cyprus and the mainland coasts.

Most of the ancient royal cities – the exceptions being Idalion and Tamassos – had ports. In the Ptolemaic and Roman period, every *polis* of Cyprus was a port city. Karpasia (Rizokarpaso/Dıpkarpaz) had two harbours, one on either side of the Karpas peninsula.[2] Some port cities were located in bays, facilitating the transport of raw materials from the periphery of the *chora*. For instance, Marion (Polis tou Chrysochou) was supplied with building stone from a quarry at the water's edge near Agios Nikolaos on the western shore of Chrysochou Bay. The importance of coastal shipping for goods transport in Cyprus is attested by the port and emporium at Dreamer's Bay, formerly thought to have been only a Late Roman trading settlement but now known to have been in use throughout the Hellenistic and Roman periods.[3] Since the port at Dreamer's Bay is not tied into the highway network of the island, its primary function was apparently as "a transshipment port through which local and regional trade goods (many contained in amphorae) passed bound for other destinations and markets",[4] linked to the other ports of Cyprus by coastal shipping. Less exclusive imports and staple export goods (such as timber and grain, to which we shall return below) will also have passed directly to or from the *poleis* and local ports.

ROADS AND VEHICLES

Compared to that for sea transport, our evidence for roads and wheeled vehicles is both later and sparser. Horse-drawn war chariots were among the grave goods deposited in one of the royal graves (tomb 79) at Salamis in the 8th or 7th century BC, and a terracotta model of a quadriga or four-horse chariot was found in the sanctuary at Agia Irini (7th century BC) at the opposite end of the Mesaoria. With their wide wheelbase and large wheel diameter, light vehicles such as these were able to range over the central plain of the island, independently of roads.

A terracotta model from Tamassos of c. 500 BC shows a covered two-wheeled vehicle (Fig. 1). Carts typically had a narrower wheelbase of c. 1.4 metres and were drawn by mules, donkeys or, more rarely, horses or oxen, yoked in pairs. The two-wheeled cart is simple to construct and maintain, can be easily controlled on a descent and is capable of turning in a narrow circle, which was important on switchback roads. Its chief limitation is its load capacity, which rarely exceeded 300 kilograms. Light two-wheeled vehicles would normally be drawn by mules or donkeys.[5]

The four-wheeler was a heavier vehicle with a correspondingly greater carrying capacity, up to 800 kg, and requiring greater tractive capacity: teams of up to ten mules are recorded[6] but for heavy work, oxen were generally preferred. In its simplest form with two fixed axles, the four-wheeler required good roads without excessive gradients or narrow curves. More complex versions with a movable front axle and brake gear are known from other parts of the ancient world,[7] but there is as yet no evidence that these were used in ancient Cyprus.

Like sea transport, the land transport network within ancient Cyprus must be conceptualized as operating on two levels. At one level, it served the needs of local and inter-urban trade, connecting one farmer with another, connecting the *polis* with its *chora*, or two *poleis* with each other. At another level, land transport links formed part of long-distance trading networks, but in a secondary and ancillary rôle in relation to sea transport.[8] This dualism is reflected in the development of the Cypriot highway network.

Recent fieldwork suggests that much of mainland Greece was criss-crossed by man-made roads as early as the Archaic period,[9] but there is no good evidence for a similar network in Cyprus. By the end of the 4th century BC, however, long-distance roads were in existence, forming two sub-networks: a somewhat rudimentary western road system connecting Palaipaphos, Marion and Nea Paphos,[10] and a more developed network in the east, branching out from Salamis to link up with the central Mesaoria, the Karpas peninsula and the *poleis* of the southeastern coast. Under Ptolemaic rule, the road system was extended from the new administrative capital at Nea Paphos into the city's *chora*, but there is nothing to suggest that the early Ptolemaic *strategoi* had any overall road policy. The western and eastern sub-networks were not joined up; there was no road connection between the capital at Nea Paphos and the Mesaoria, and a traveller going from central Cyprus to Rhodes had to embark at Kourion.[11] Only shortly before, possibly after, the Roman annexation were roads built along the north and south coast to link the Salamis and Paphos networks, creating the peripheral highway that is a striking feature of the island as depicted on the mediaeval *Tabula Peutingeriana* (Fig. 2). This route and the highway from Salamis into the Karpas peninsula are the only Roman roads in Cyprus from which milestones are known. These testify to major renovations of the coastal highway in AD 198 and again in the late 3rd and the early 4th centuries. On the first occasion, the work included the construction of a direct link between Coral Bay and Arodes on the west coast highway,[12] eliminating a detour via Drepanon (Agios Georgios Pegeias) and shortening the journey by twenty stades (4 km), an impressive feat of road engineering (Fig. 3).

Fig. 1. Terracotta model of a covered two-wheeled wagon from Tamassos, c. 500 BC. Height 13cm, length 16cm. Cyprus Museum, Nicosia. Reproduced by the permission of the Department of Antiquities, Cyprus.

1 Cf. the travel diary of Rutilius Namatianus, who left Rome in mid-October AD 417 hoping to reach Gaul before winter, Rutilius spent two weeks in Ostia waiting for a favourable wind (*De reditu suo*, 1.205-7) and four weeks after his departure from Rome, he had progressed no further than Pisa (*ibid.* 1.630-32). Had he gone by the *via Aurelia*, the journey would have taken no more than two weeks.

2 Strabo, 14.6.3.

3 Leonard & Demesticha 2004, 197-198.

4 Leonard & Demesticha 2004, 202.

5 Landels 1978, 173.

6 *Codex Theodosianus* 8.5.8 (AD 357).

7 Greene 1990, 37-38.

8 Metal exports from the mining areas (Kalavasos, Skouriotissa) form part of a similar land-sea transport chain, but because of its specialized and localized nature, metal transport will not be discussed in this paper.

9 Pikoulas 2007, 79.

10 Bekker-Nielsen 1993, 186-188.

11 Bekker-Nielsen 2004, 106-107; Strabo, 14.6.3.

12 Bekker-Nielsen 2004, 112 and 126-130; 1995, 107-110.

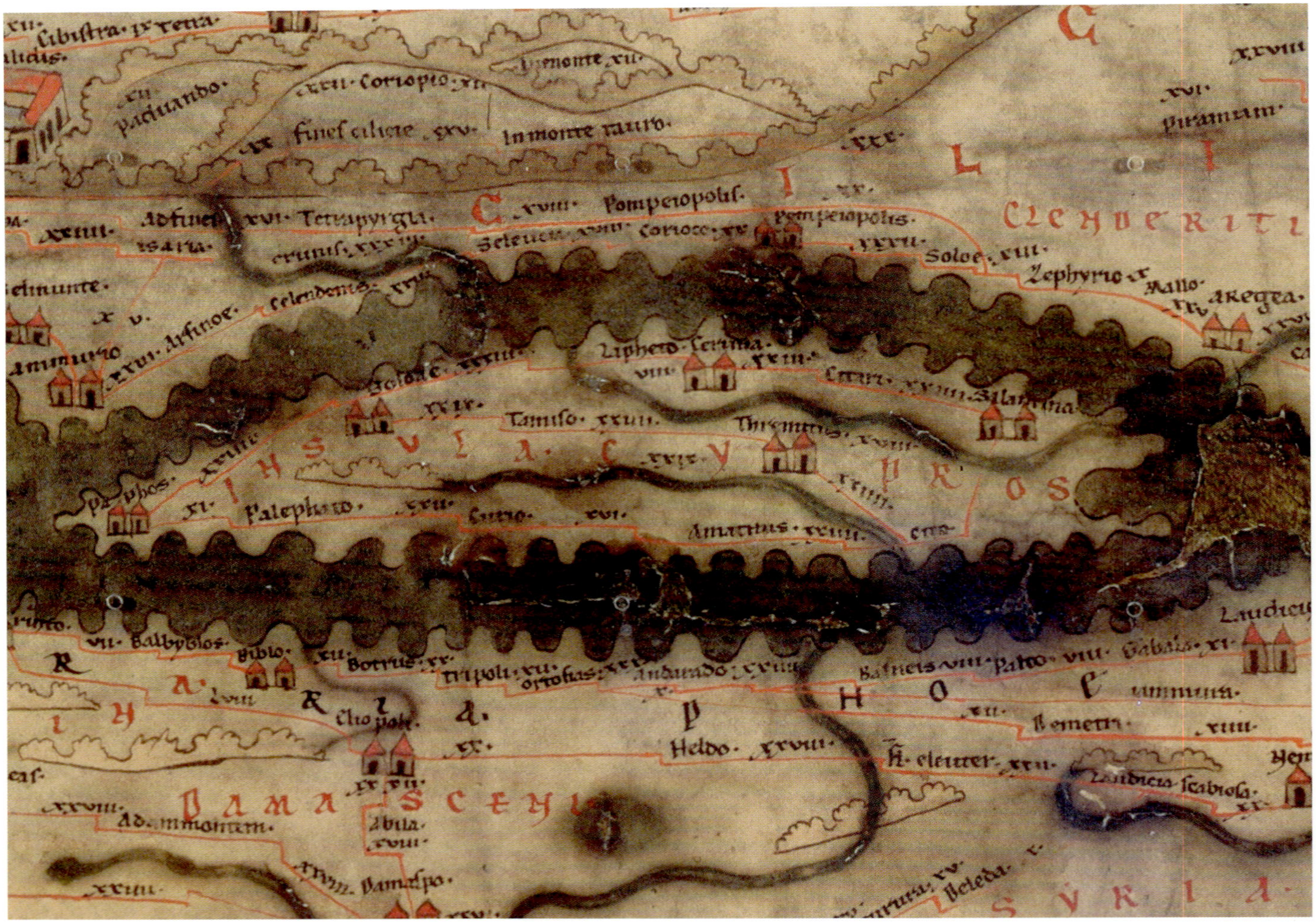

Fig. 2. Cyprus as depicted on the Tabula Peutingeriana, *Codex Vindobonensis 326, Österreichische Nationalbibliothek, Wien.*

The other main road shown on the *Tabula*, the trans-island highway from Soloi via Tamassos to Kition, was created at an unknown date by running a road from Morphou Bay into the southern Mesaoria, where it linked up with an older road towards the east.[13]

In the comparatively unimportant island province of Cyprus, we find few roads to match the Roman highways that we know elsewhere. There was no overall attempt to upgrade the road system of the pre-Ptolemaic or Ptolemaic period to Roman standards, and many routes included steep and narrow sections that were more suited to pack-animals than to wheeled vehicles (Fig. 4).

The mule or donkey carrying a pack-saddle has been a mainstay of land transport in the Levant since time immemorial, and remains in use even today. It has a limited carrying capacity (90-120 kilograms for a mule, 54-90 kilograms for a donkey[14]) but has the advantage that it is to some degree independent of roads. Thus a pack train could take short cuts across level country, for example in the Mesaoria, saving time and effort. As late as the 1990s, it was still possible to encounter pack trains on the byways of western Cyprus.

COMMODITIES

What types of goods were transported on the roads of Cyprus, and how? Let us consider some examples.

Salt

In the *History of Animals*, Aristotle notes that the shepherds of his time "give the flocks salt every five days in summer, to the extent of one *medimnos* to the hundred sheep, and this is found to render a flock healthier and fatter".[15] That works out at six *medimnoi* or 312 litres of salt per month for a flock of a hundred sheep (or goats), or 3.75 kilograms per animal. In recent history, the population of sheep and goats in Cyprus has been large, about one per each head of population. We have no reliable estimates for the human, nor for the animal population of ancient Cyprus, but for the present purpose, absolute numbers are not important. Whether the sheep and goat population numbered 20,000, 50,000 or 100,000, we are talking about a significant transport operation.

Since Cyprus possessed neither salt mines nor inland salt springs, all salt had to be transported from salines on the coast to the grazing areas, which in summer would often be in the high hills and inaccessible to vehicles. As it happens, one *medimnos* of salt is about equivalent to one donkey load.[16] Taking, for the sake of argument, the middle figure as our point of departure, 50,000 grazing animals would require 500 *medimnoi* every five days, that is 100 donkey-loads per day. Assuming that on average a donkey made one return trip per day, a hundred donkeys – perhaps twenty donkey trains of five animals each – would be working the roads and byways of Cyprus in order to keep the inland and upland pasturing areas supplied with salt.

Forestry products

In the ancient Mediterranean world, there was a constant demand for timber of good quality and large dimensions, suitable for constructing ships and houses. As not every region possessed tall forests, there was a lively maritime trade in timber and in other forestry products, such as pitch.[17]

In the Classical period, the Cypriot kingdoms, led by Salamis, had maintained large navies and shipyards.[18] Writing in the 4th century BC, Theophrastos[19] specifically mentions the use of Cypriot pine for shipbuilding; he also notes that the tall stands of timber in the mountains of the island were not exploited commercially because transport was difficult at a times when roads had not yet been built into the upland forest areas.[20] Seven centuries later, Ammianus Marcellinus remarks that Cyprus was so well endowed with nature's gifts that she could outfit an entire cargo vessel, from mast to keel, from her native resources.[21]

Fig. 3. Overgrown switchback ascent on the road between Coral Bay and Arodes, on the highway from Nea Paphos to Marion. This section was built at the end of the second century AD and engineered to Roman standards. Author's photo, April 1991.

The island's timber resources were concentrated in the upland areas, and whether intended for shipbuilding, for export as raw planks,[22] or as prefabricated boats,[23] the timber had to be hauled down to the coast, presumably after being rough-trimmed on location. Since it would be impractical to load the long timbers required for masts, spars and rafters on a vehicle or on a train of pack animals, these must have carried by teams of workmen or slaves. Shorter pieces of timber could be loaded on carts or dragged on sledges.

13 Bekker-Nielsen 2004, 179 and fig. 37.
14 Landels 1978, 172. For carrying capacities of ancient pack animals and the somewhat contradictory evidence of the ancient sources, see Bekker-Nielsen 2004, 74.
15 Aristotle, *HA* 596a.
16 A *medimnus* of salt weighs c. 62.5 kilograms. See also note 15, above.
17 Hannestad 2007, 92-96.
18 Raptou 1996, 254-255, with references.
19 *HP* 5.7.
20 *HP* 5.8; cf. also Bekker-Nielsen 2001.
21 *History* 14.8.14.
22 Cf. the "40,000 cubits of squared pine planking" donated to the citizens of Rhodes in 227/6 BC by Ptolemy II Euergetes (Polybios 5.89): much of this presumably came from Cyprus.
23 Strabo. 16.1.11.

Grain

In the Ptolemaic as well as the Roman period, Cyprus was subject to a land tax that was in effect a tithe on grain and other agricultural products, such as olives.[24] On the analogy of other provinces, we may take it that the tithe was assessed on the threshing floor or in the barn, but that it had to be delivered to a central collecting point in the city – that is, on the coast. For this purpose, vehicles could be used, since the network of tracks and roads in the island converged on the *poleis*. From some areas, however, water transport may have been preferable: this would apply to some districts in the *chorai* of Marion, Soloi, Salamis, Kition and Kourion. The extent of the island's grain production is no easier to estimate than its goat and sheep population, but by any reckoning, moving one-tenth of the grain harvest over an average distance of at least 10 km would represent a considerable transport chore.

If we take a human population figure of 100,000 – a conservative estimate[25] – as our point of departure and the estimate of Foxhall and Forbes (1982) of 212 kg/year as the average grain consumption of an adult, we may, very roughly, estimate the gross harvest at 27,000 metric tons and the tithe at 2,700 tons. At most, one-third of this could have been transported by water, leaving 1,800 tons of tithe grain to go by road. Loaded on two-wheeled carts carrying an average load of 250 kg, this adds up to 7,200 cart-loads and 144,000 vehicle-kilometres (including the empty return journeys) annually. Assuming that each cart could make thirty return trips between the end of the harvest and the deadline for delivering tributary grain to the *polis* (an entirely arbitrary assumption, since the date of neither is known), no less than 240 carts and mule teams would be required during the season.

CONTAINERS

So far, we have considered examples where transport must have taken place on an extensive scale but has left no trace in the archaeological record, because no transport containers have been preserved: either the commodity was not packaged at all (forestry products) or it was shipped in containers made of organic, perishable materials, probably sacks (salt and grain). This is a useful reminder how much ancient trade and transport remains "invisible" to the modern eye, and confirmed by the pictorial evidence for goods being loaded in bales, bundles or nets as well as the description of a mixed cargo that was – or so at least it was claimed – lost at sea in the 4th century BC: "jars of Koan wine, *bales* of wool, jars of salt-fish, *bundles* of goat-skins".[26]

From the point of view of this conference, however, these commodities are less interesting than liquids, which could not be transported in sacks or in bulk: wine, olive oil and fish sauce, all of which required a container.

Amphorae

The amphora is too well-known to require any introduction. It was an extremely versatile container that came in a wide range of shapes or sizes, reflecting local traditions as well as functional considerations. It was the maritime transport container *par excellence*,[27] but less suitable for land transport because of its high tare weight. The last century BC witnessed several innovations in marine transport with a view to obtaining better tare:weight ratios. One was the wine tanker with permanently fitted *dolia*,[28] another was the wooden barrel (see below).

Skins

Animal skins were used as liquid containers in Greece and the Levant from an early date until recent times. The smaller, easily portable skin bottles were made from the skins of lambs or kids, larger containers from sheep, goats, hogs or oxen. Skins of even larger animals are recorded in the ancient literary sources but were hardly suitable for everyday use.[29]

A skin container was made by flaying a quadruped, keeping the skin as intact as possible, sewing it up and closing all orifices except the neck where a tube-like spout with a stopper was inserted. The process is simple enough, but care has to be taken throughout: for a good result, unnecessary perforations must be avoided; the skin must be cleaned well on the inside (whereas the outside is left more or less in its natural state); the edges and leg orifices must be sewn and sealed carefully to achieve a sturdy, watertight seam. The resulting "bottle" is light, unbreakable and portable. We are told that when Odysseus set off to meet the Cyclops, he decanted some of the wine carried in amphorae aboard his ship into a "large skin bottle" made from the skin of a goat.[30]

Animal skin is not entirely impermeable and there will be a small amount of evaporation though its pores; furthermore, if the skin container is placed against a surface such the floor of a wagon or a ship's deck, it will leak at the edges and the points of contact. For this reason, small

Fig. 4. The northern ascent to the pass at Melounda/Mallıdağ where the road from Aphrodision to Salamis passed through the northern range. (Author's photo, October 2012).

skin bottles are often carried in a rope sling attached at the ends and hung over the shoulder or from a hook. In Gaul, a number of inscriptions were set up by, or in honour of, *utricularii* or their professional corporations. So far, we have no parallels from Cyprus or the eastern part of the empire. The functions of the *utricularii* have been much debated. Since skins (*utres*) were also used for flotation,[31] some researchers have interpreted the *utricularii* as masters of river vessels supported on air-filled skins, and inscriptions recording *utricularii* are often found on sites that were river ports in the Roman period. It is more likely, however, that *utricularii* were artisans producing skin bottles, for which there would be great demand in river ports where shipments of wine, oil or *garum* arriving in large containers (amphorae or barrels) were repackaged in smaller units. Did this also take place in Cyprus?

To my knowledge, we only have one ancient image depicting wine transport in Cyprus: the "wine drinker" mosaic in the so-called house of Dionysos at Nea Paphos.

24 Bagnall 1976, 109; Hadjisavvas 1996, 135.
25 Michaelides 1996, 143 estimates the island's population in the 2nd century AD at 200,000.
26 Demosthenes, 35.34 (*Against Lakritos*).
27 Maarleveld 2010, 268-269.
28 Heslin 2011, 162-163.
29 Marlière 2002, 21-23.
30 *Odyssey*, 9.196; 212.
31 E.g., Suetonius, *Divus Julius* 57; Zosimos, *New history*, 3.89.

The scene is based on the sad story of Ikarios, whom Dionysos rewarded with a gift of wine. Ikarios shared this with his neighbours; when they felt its effects, they suspected Ikarios of being a poisoner and killed him. On the left stands Ikarios, to the right are shown two of his stupefied neighbours, and for good measure the legend informs the observer that this pair are "the first wine-drinkers". In the centre is a schematic depiction of a two-wheeled vehicle loaded with wine-skins: a box-like superstructure resting on a single axle with solid disc wheels and drawn by two oxen. The mosaicist's intention was presumably to depict a heavy farm cart.

Transporting a load of wine in the way shown on the mosaic would not really be practical since the skins would rub against each other, causing them to leak, and the load pressing down on the skins at the bottom of the pile would rupture them.[32] More significant for our purpose is that when the mosaicist wanted to depict a load of wine, he chose skins, not amphorae. It would appear that to his audience, a skin bottle was a more familiar sight, and/or more directly associated with wine, than an amphora.

Barrels

Barrels make their appearance in the archaeological and pictorial record much later than skins and amphorae; they are not attested until the last century BC and seem to have been especially popular in the western and north-western provinces. Barrel-making may have been introduced to the Romans by Celtic craftsmen who were known for their joinery skills, which they used, *inter alia*, in the manufacture of wheels and war-chariots. Barrels could be made to any capacity from 3 up to 1,300 litres. The largest examples so far known have been found on the Rhine frontier and were presumably used for military supplies of wine. Unlike skins and amphorae, barrels did not need to be carried but could be rolled, thus easily transferred from boat to shore and vice versa, which may account for their popularity in river-borne shipping. Sturdier and lighter than amphorae, and well suited to transport on carts, the barrel became a popular container in the west and in Italy itself.[33]

ROADS, VEHICLES, CONTAINERS

Our knowledge of land transport routes and overland trade in Cyprus is essentially based on two categories of archaeological evidence: routes (roads) and containers (amphorae). With both, we face a series of problems of interpretation.

The ancient road map of Cyprus shows many radial roads converging on the ports that were also the *poleis*. This may reflect the dominant position of the ports within the pattern of commodity flows; it may also reflect the dominating position of the *poleis* within their territories and that major road construction projects within the *chora* presumably required the approval and financial support of the *boulê* of the *polis*. Thus it remains an open question to what degree the road system reflects the economic geography of the island (i.e. commodity flows and trading patterns) as opposed to the *political* geography. Did the transport network (roads) created by political factors shape commodity flows and trading patterns, or vice versa?

The distribution of amphora finds across the island might provide some pointers to flows of imported liquid or semi-liquid commodities such as pickled fish, fish sauce, wine and olive oil. It needs to be kept in mind, however, that the point at which the empty amphora is discarded will not always be the point of its contents' final consumption. Liquid goods coming into Cyprus would pass several "break of bulk" stages.

Let us try to imagine a consignment of amphorae from a single producer arriving in Cyprus from overseas – coming into Salamis, Dreamer's Bay or Nea Paphos by ship. Part of it would be acquired by one wholesaler, another part by another; some customers would buy a dozen amphorae, others less. Some of these sub-consignments would be sent onwards by coastal shipping to minor ports and landing-places, where they would be sold to local retailers. Eventually the contents of the amphorae would find their way to the end-users, either through retailers in the city or through itinerant merchants. But only a few wealthy householders (who would be found in the *polis* itself) would buy a whole amphora of imported wine at one go, and even fewer would require a whole amphora of first-class olive oil or fish sauce. At the retail stage, the contents were presumably resold by measure and taken home in the customer's own container (as is still the case today in many parts of the Mediterranean world).

If this reconstruction is correct, we should expect to find the largest concentrations of amphora remains at the points where the contents were either resold in smaller quantities, by measure, or transferred to other containers for onward transport by road. This would be not unlike the distribution patterns found in other parts of the Roman Empire, where large concentrations of amphora fragments are typically found in cities, in ports and in military camps.

From the viewpoint of road studies as well as those of economic history and amphora studies, it would be useful to correlate the evidence for roads and transport routes in Cyprus with that for transport containers. Unfortunately, at present the Roman amphora material from Cyprus does not permit statistical or geographical analysis at the macro level;[34] it is not possible to draw a reliable distribution map for comparison with our map of the road system. For the time being, we have to limit ourselves to some general observations.

CONCLUSIONS: LAND AND SEA TRANSPORT

In ancient Cyprus, land and sea transport formed complementary systems. Land transport of goods was primarily radial, i.e. between ports/*poleis* and inland settlements, while shipping offered a more economical alternative for goods transported along the coast. These could travel in the vessels of local shippers, or in the incoming ships from the mainland which might call at several ports in the island before returning.[35]

Import goods entered Cyprus through major *emporia* (e.g., Salamis, Dreamer's Bay) as well as minor landing-places (e.g., Kioni, Thronoi). Liquid goods may have been repackaged for resale or for onward transport into the interior by pack-animals. The nature of the containers used for secondary transport of imports (after repackaging) so far remains conjectural, but skins may have played a significant role; in an island rich in goats and sheep, the material for skin bottles will have been readily available.

Goods for export (metals, timber, tithe grain) were probably taken from the interior to the coast using pack-animals or light two-wheeled carts. Since the first two required no packaging and grain would have travelled in bulk or in sacks, these exports would not leave traces in the archaeological record in the same way that imports of amphorae did.

---

32 Marlière 2002, 22.

33 In AD 238, a Roman army approaching Aquileia from the south had no difficulty in collecting enough empty wine barrels to build a pontoon bridge, Herodian, *History of the empire* 8.4.4.

34 Cf. Jacobsen 2004, 144 for an overview of the problems involved.

35 Cf. the ship in Demosthenes' *Against Lakritos* (note 26, above) which called at several ports in the Crimea before returning to the Aegean.

Expanding Contacts and Collapsing Distances in Early Cypro-Archaic Trade:
Three Case Studies of Shipwrecks off the Turkish Coast

BY ELIZABETH S. GREENE, JUSTIN LEIDWANGER & HARUN ÖZDAŞ

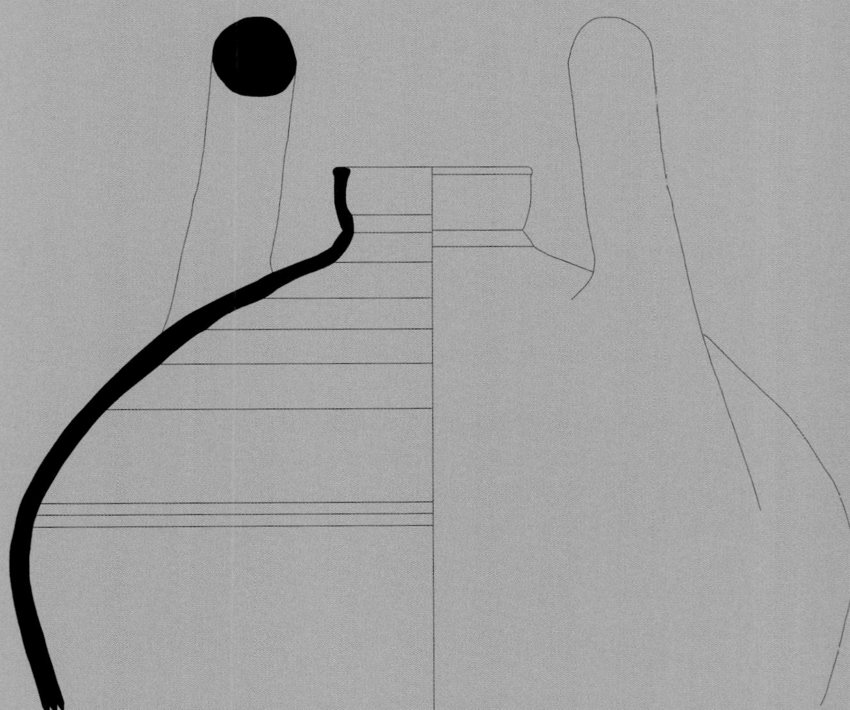

Expanding Contacts and Collapsing Distances in Early Cypro-Archaic Trade: Three Case Studies of Shipwrecks off the Turkish Coast

BY ELIZABETH S. GREENE, JUSTIN LEIDWANGER & HARUN ÖZDAŞ

In his discussion of Archaic Greek identity formation within the context of expanding Aegean and Near Eastern contacts, Alexander Fantalkin draws attention to what he considers a brief but crucially transformative period around the late 7th century BC. Over the course of perhaps just a quarter century BC, he argues, East Greece broadened its horizons and "rediscovered" the larger eastern Mediterranean world through the movement of goods and people.[1] What Ian Morris describes as a "collapse of distance", influenced in part by new shipbuilding technology, facilitated the drawing together of certain peoples around the eastern Mediterranean closer than ever before since the Bronze Age.[2] If seaborne trade went hand in hand with these expanding cultural horizons, the distribution of pottery should provide some index of emerging contacts. How to interpret the presence of concentrations of East Greek ceramics along the coasts of the eastern Mediterranean and where to assign agency for this exchange remain contentious issues: does the distribution of East Greek pottery signal direct East Greek-led trade, commerce through some intermediary, or rather the physical presence of Greek populations – like mercenaries or early emporia – abroad?[3]

Comparative insights are sorely needed for evaluating these nascent connections, but firm evidence to substantiate the actors and distribution networks within the early Archaic economy is scarce. The underwater material record of shipwreck cargos often provides primary evidence for such patterns and mechanisms in antiquity, yet the relatively few Archaic shipwrecks known across the Mediterranean world (in particular from the eastern Mediterranean) leave us with a poorly representative sample.[4] Each new discovery and investigation offers the possibility of significantly deepening our understanding of mechanisms of exchange and the economy more broadly. Building economic models that span the Greek world and the Near East on the basis of few examples – or at times even a single shipwreck – may be an enterprise fraught with conjecture, but it also provides a framework for productive speculation.

In the case of the overseas trade of Cyprus, we are in an unusually fortunate position for this challenging period. Although no Archaic shipwrecks have yet been reported in Cypriot waters, three sites have come to light during surveys off the coast of south and southwest Turkey, directly between the Aegean world and the Near East. All of the sites can be dated between approximately the mid-7th and the turn of the 6th century BC, spanning Fantalkin's critical point of transformation in seaborne contacts around the eastern Mediterranean.[5] Each of the cargos presents a new facet to these seaborne networks, yet the overall picture appears rather consistent: cargos dominated by Cypriot basket-handle amphorae but exhibiting strong material connections to East Greece. From the standpoint of distribution within an emerging agricultural economy, these assemblages offer solid archaeological evidence for expanding relationships between the Greek world and the broader eastern Mediterranean, a sphere of interaction somewhere between the local links that tied together single islands or coastal regions, and globalization or "Mediterraneanization" models proposed for the Iron Age.[6] They allow us to explore the role of commerce and the possible agency of different groups within a model of developing cultural exchange, and in particular offer insight into the role of Cyprus within this world of collapsing socioeconomic distances.

BACKGROUND

A series of underwater surveys by the Institute of Nautical Archaeology (INA) since the 1970s brought to light two of the three shipwrecks examined here: located at Kekova Adası and Kepçe Burnu. The third site was located only recently, by the Dokuz Eylül University (DEU) survey team in 2008 at Çaycağız Koyu. Over the past few years, the sites have been the focus of systematic survey by collaborative teams from DEU, Brock University, and INA.[7] Renewed studies of these sites aimed to achieve more comprehensive

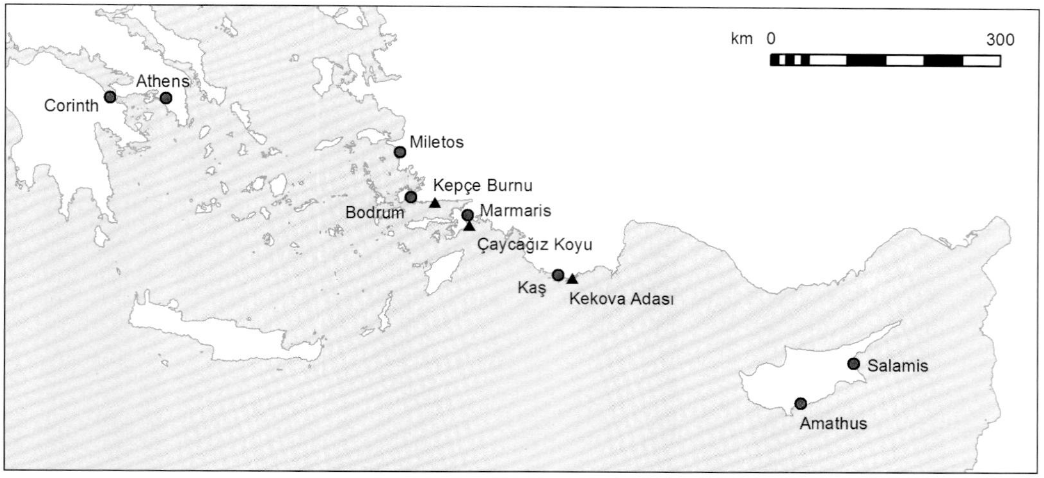

Map of the key Archaic sites in the eastern Mediterranean showing the Kekova Adası, Kepçe Burnu, and Çaycağız Koyu wreck locations. Map by J. Leidwanger.

photographic documentation and artefact counts, along with selective sampling to gauge the range of materials at each site and to contextualize better the finds raised by the initial INA surveys and currently housed in the storerooms of the Bodrum Museum of Underwater Archaeology. Better dates can now be offered for each of the wrecks in light of detailed studies of the pottery completed over the past few years. Compositional analysis of selected samples was undertaken at Brock University in Canada. The results provide more secure evidence for the origin of the different cargo components as well as the scale of production and the number of workshops that may have contributed to these shipments.[8]

KEKOVA ADASI

Located along the Lycian coast just east of Kaş, the shipwreck at Kekova Adası (Kekova Island) rests inside the channel behind the long narrow island after which it is named (Map). This protected area may have offered opportunistic shelters that served as stopping-points for coastal sailors plying these waters between the Aegean and the eastern Mediterranean even before the Archaic period.[9] The extensive assemblage of perhaps 130 cargo amphorae along with other remains lies strewn from approximately 8-24 m of depth across the sloping topography of a reef, the tip of which today rests less than a couple of meters from the water. In antiquity, this reef may have broken the surface and presented the danger that claimed the unsuspecting vessel, whose trail of ballast begins near the top of the reef.[10] Within

---

1 Fantalkin 2006.
2 Morris 2000, 257-261.
3 E.g. East Greek pottery at the site of Meẓad Ḥashavyahu: see Na'aman 1991; Fantalkin 2001. On the proto-history of East Greek mercenaries, see Luraghi 2006; Hodos 2009a, 225-228 offers an overview of "pre-colonization activity".
4 Parker 1992 fig. 3 represents numbers only as of the publication date, but still remains the most up-to-date account of diachronic shipwreck data across the Mediterranean. Shipwrecks dating to the Archaic period may be slightly more common, at least in the literature, in the western Mediterranean, though the sample is still small: see generally Dietler 2007, 267-270.
5 Fantalkin 2001, 202-204.
6 Globalization, Hodos 2009a; Mediterraneanization, Morris 2003.
7 Greene *et al.* 2011, 60-65 with bibliography on earlier surveys at Kekova Adası and Kepçe Burnu. Recent work at Caycağız Koyu is noted in Leidwanger *et al.* 2012, 401-402; Özdaş *et al.* 2012, 272-273.
8 For a preliminary note on the fabric analysis of finds from these shipwrecks, see Leidwanger *et al.* 2012. The Institute for Aegean Prehistory and ASOR's Harris Grant program supported the study of these samples. Additional support was provided by the Social Sciences and Humanities Research Council of Canada and Brock University, where debts of gratitude are owed to John Menzies and the Department of Earth Sciences.
9 E.g. for vessels like those which sank at Uluburun and Cape Gelidonya, just to the west and east respectively, while traveling along this stretch of the Lycian coast.
10 Flemming has suggested a localized coastal subsidence of between 0.9 and 1.0 m per millennium for this region during the Holocene era, a relative sea level change that would place the reef, now submerged some 2.4 m, virtually at the water's surface in antiquity. See Flemming 1978, 412-413.

this assemblage dominated by transport amphorae, several additional ceramics and finds hint at life on board the ship.

Among the scattered fragmentary ceramics that mark the site on the seabed, the distinctive massive handles and bulky sherds of basket-handle amphorae are the most numerous and conspicuous (Fig. 1). Although no intact jars of this type were recorded, quantification of the fragments reveals evidence for 90-100 examples, fully three-quarters of the total assemblage by number. The basket-handle amphorae from the Kekova Adası wreck are characterized by a wide biconical body with slightly convex shoulders and a maximum diameter above the midsection, thick and high looping handles, a simple base with a flat resting surface and circular recess underneath, and a low cupped rim that terminates in a rolled lip (Fig. 2). Most of the rims raised for study exhibited a diameter of around 0.123-0.125 m, although another group of rims shows a diameter of only around 0.11 m, raising the possibility that either some range of jar sizes was employed in the shipment or details like rim size were highly unstandardized.[11] A variety of better preserved samples allow the reconstruction of overall dimensions for an amphora at the larger end of the spectrum: diameter of 0.53 m and height of around 0.70 m. Three-dimensional modelling based on a composite line drawing provides an estimate of the volume at 69.1 l.[12] Petrographic analysis of seven samples revealed that the fabrics all belong to a single broadly defined and rather plain calcareous group that should probably reflect manufacture confined to one general geographical region. Though the fabric group is not particularly distinctive, the most likely candidate seems to be Cyprus, probably eastern Cyprus, due not only to the geology of the area but also to the general consistency between the mineralogy of these samples and *comparanda* that are almost certainly local products studied from among the finds in the early Archaic necropolis of Salamis.[13]

Amphorae of this type are well represented in Cyprus, and it seems likely that the primary origin of the type, at least during its early production, is also to be found on the island. The first well dated examples come from tombs at Salamis, where they appear to have been produced locally from the late 8th century BC onward.[14] It is only in the 7th century BC – the latter part in particular – that the type appears consistently outside Cyprus: at sites in Cilicia as well as the northern and southern Levant and as far south as Egypt.[15] Beyond this narrow corridor,

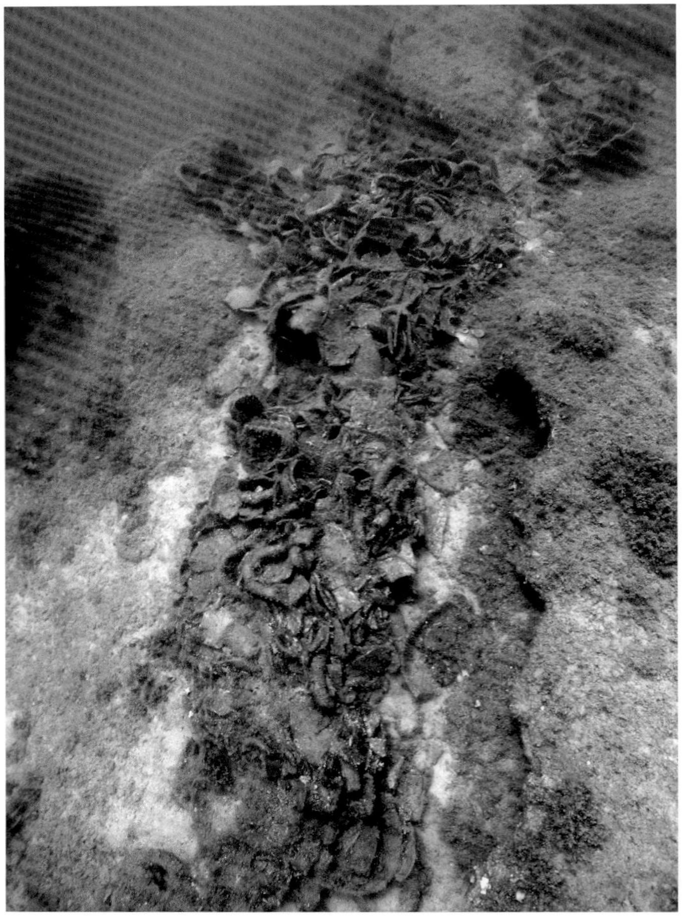

Fig. 1. General view of the wreck assemblage scattered on the sloping seabed at Kekova Adası. Photo by H. Özdaş.

11 Visual analysis and preliminary measurements by the authors of the larger basket-handle amphorae from Tomb 79 in the necropolis of Salamis suggests that the rims could range considerably in size independent of any similarity in overall dimensions between jars.

12 Thanks to Toby N. Jones, Newport Medieval Ship, for undertaking the three-dimensional reconstruction and providing the volume calculation.

13 Samples were obtained as *comparanda* from several of the Archaic tomb assemblages at Salamis. Thanks are due to the Department of Antiquities Cyprus for permission to undertake that part of a larger project on basket-handle amphorae.

14 Karageorghis *et al.* 1973, 115.

15 See generally Sagona 1982, 106-108; Lehmann 1996, 443-445 Form 421. Cf. also the contributions by Zoroğlu and Göransson in this volume.

Fig. 2. Upper (Sur10-004) and lower (Sur10-006) fragments from Cypro-Levantine basket-handle amphorae, raised and re-deposited during the 2010 DEU survey. Drawing by L. Radloff.

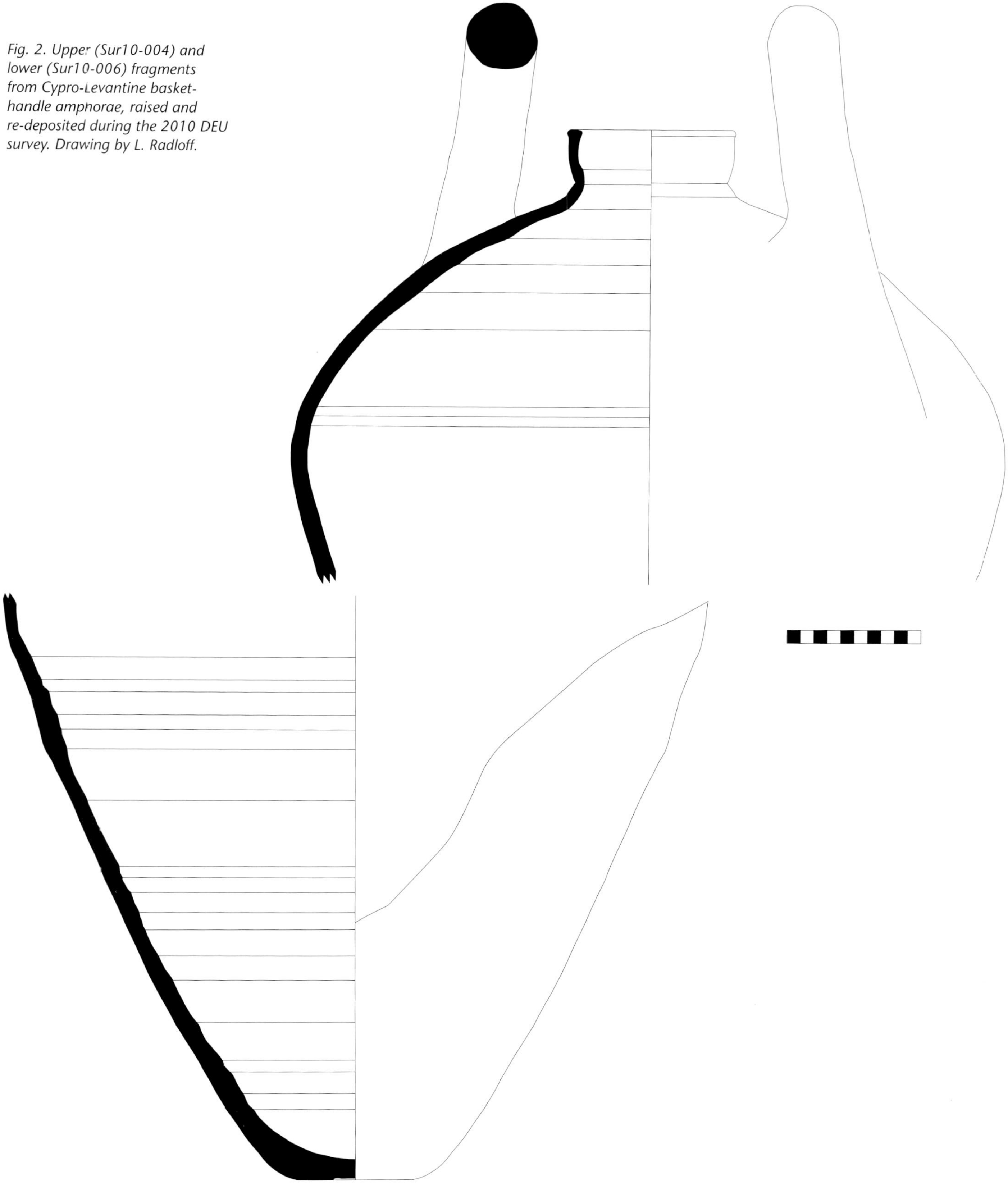

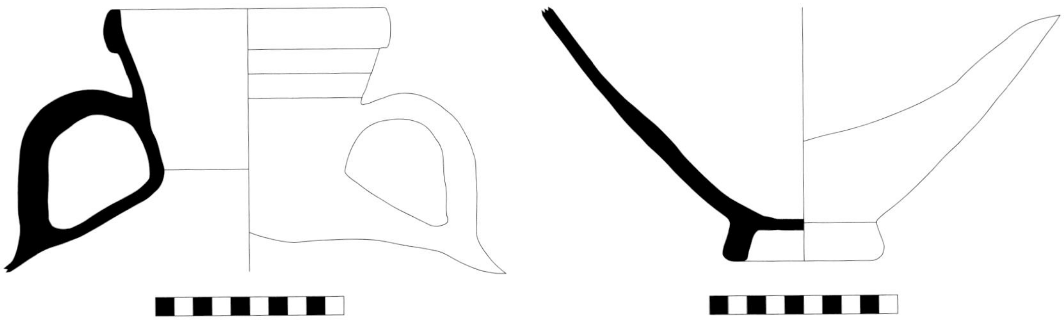

Fig. 3. Top (K83-24) and base with ring-toe (K83-22) of southeast Aegean amphorae, raised during the 1983 INA survey and currently stored in the Bodrum Museum of Underwater Archaeology. Drawings by N. Jago & C. Carss.

basket-handle amphorae are comparatively rare, with few examples appearing in the material record of just a handful of sites around the Aegean or further west, and none seemingly in contexts that can be dated to the 7th century BC.[16] The typology of this long-lived amphora is hardly straightforward or well understood, but the forms at Kekova Adası appear to belong quite early in the series. Among the best *comparanda* to date are a series of jars from a mid-7th-century BC level at Tell Keisan in northern Israel, where compositional analysis suggests that they were imported from Cyprus.[18] Inscriptions indicate that this amphora type was at times intended to contain oil, but no direct evidence is available for this or any other agricultural product among the Kekova Adası jars.[19] Nor can it be securely established whether these jars were in primary or secondary use, and different jars may well have contained different products.

The remaining cargo is comprised of two amphora types that together amount to less than one-quarter of the total assemblage. Only 20 fragmentary examples were recorded on the seabed for the more numerous of the two, a type that belongs generally within the southeast Aegean family of amphorae (Fig. 3). This group includes the production of several different Ionian centers – Miletos, Samos, and no doubt others – whose jars are difficult and sometimes impossible to differentiate reliably on the basis of morphology or even composition.[20] The examples from Kekova Adası have a simple bulging rim and a wide flaring neck marked by one or two overhanging ridges. The curved handles meet the rounded shoulders at a low angle, while the ovoid body tapers to a small ring base. Three samples analyzed to date exhibit similar geological origins but also certain differences that likely point to the involvement of multiple producers within the greater southeast Aegean region. This should not be surprising in light of the morphological variants noted even among the few amphora tops raised for detailed study.

Archaic southeast Aegean amphorae travelled comparatively widely throughout the Mediterranean and eventually the Black Sea. The best parallels for the Kekova Adası rims, necks, and bases come from early to mid-7th-century BC Miletos itself, where local production is suggested from the end of the 8th century BC.[21] Other East Greek *comparanda* from contexts on Crete, as well as at several sites around the western Mediterranean, further support a date broadly in the 7th century BC.[22] Incomplete preservation prevents direct measurements or estimations of volumes from the Kekova Adası amphorae, and good parallels are generally only fragmentary for jars this early in the southeast Aegean series. Three-dimensional models of Samian and Milesian examples from slightly later (late 7th and early 6th century BC) contexts provide volumes close to 29 l.[23] Amphorae from the southeast Aegean have at times been assumed to have transported oil, although the agricultural produce in this corner of the Aegean was hardly limited to olive cultivation during the Archaic era.[24]

Seven to ten examples of Corinthian Type A amphorae comprise the final cargo component and provide some of the best evidence in establishing a date for the assemblage (Fig. 4). The Corinthian jars from the wreck exhibit a wide cylindrical neck, broad heavy rim, and thick arching handles situated below the rim. The base, no example of which was raised, extends from the slightly concave lower walls of the jar to a simple flat resting surface. Of the three samples analyzed to date, all are likely products of Corinth itself. Two of the samples compare well with the coarse fabric identified as the most common local Corinthian

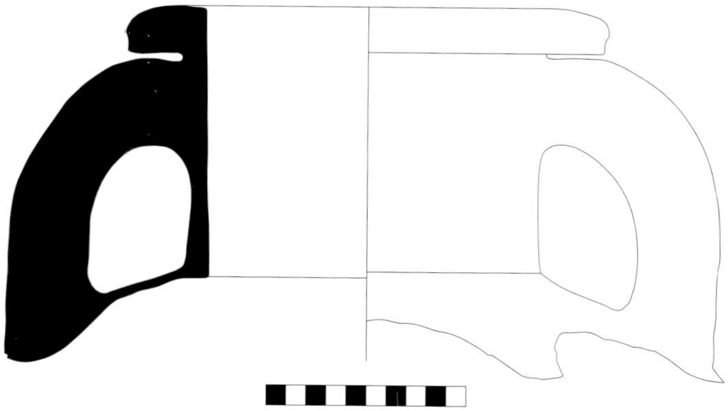

Fig. 4. Top (K83-20) of a Type A Corinthian amphora, raised during the 1983 INA survey and currently stored in the Bodrum Museum of Underwater Archaeology. Drawing by C. Carss.

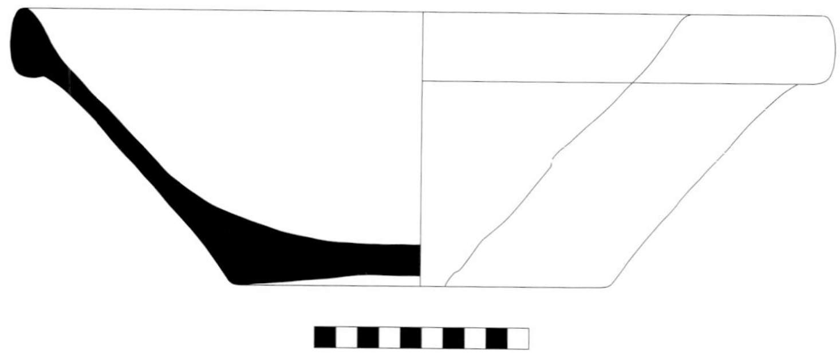

Fig. 5. Mortarium (Sur10-001) from the Kekova Adası shipwreck, raised and re-deposited during the 2010 DEU survey. Drawing by L. Radloff.

Type A production.[25] The final example is finer and rather difficult, but is not wholly inconsistent with other fabrics published as local to the area of Corinth.[26] The involvement of multiple workshops is to be expected in light of the prevalence of Type A amphorae and Corinthian overseas trade more broadly during the early Archaic period.

Like the southeast Aegean jars, Corinthian Type A amphorae traveled over considerable distances, yet along the shores of the eastern Mediterranean they still represent relatively exotic finds.[27] The morphological characteristics of the Kekova Adası amphorae point to a date early within the series. The best parallels come from contexts Carolyn Koehler has dated as early as the late 8th or early 7th century BC through the mid-7th century BC.[28] Various 7th-century BC assemblages on Crete and throughout central to south Italy and Sicily have yielded jars that are similar.[29] A jar of the first half of the 7th century BC at Metaponto is quite close.[30] This date coincides well with the chronology for the basket-handle jars and overlaps with the less well dated southeast Aegean jars, allowing the shipwreck to be situated with reasonable confidence in the mid-7th century BC or even a bit earlier. No direct measurements of volumes are possible for these jars due to their fragmentary and incomplete nature, and Koehler's measurements demonstrate well the drastic differences in capacities among these early jars. A rough comparison between the dimensions of the necks of the Kekova Adası jars and those of early amphorae in this series, however, suggests that a volume of approximately 30 l is probable.[31] What these

16 In the Aegean, only a few examples have been reported, primarily on Rhodes as well as at Kommos and Miletos: Jacopi, 1929 pl. IV; Jacopi 1931 pl. VIII; Johnston 1993, 370; Johnston 2005, 358 and 372; Niemeier 1999, 389-392.
17 See generally Humbert 1991.
18 Salles 1980, 136-141; for the analysis, see Courtois 1980, 358-360; Gunneweg & Perlman 1991.
19 Masson 1967, 132-133. Organic residue analysis may prove useful here if new samples can be raised from the site.
20 On the problem of regional styles of East Greek amphorae, see generally Dupont 2000.
21 Naso 2005, 75, 79 and 80 fig. 2 n. 3-4.
22 Johnston 1993, 365-368; 2005, 367-370; Cavagnera 1995, 46-47; Docter 2000, 65-77.
23 Three-dimensional reconstructions of Samian and Milesian jars were completed by Toby N. Jones, Newport Medieval Ship, on the basis of figures provided by Dupont: see 1998, 166 fig. 23.6b and 171 fig. 23.7a.
24 Dupont 1998, 175.
25 Whitbread 1995, 268-270.
26 Whitbread 1995, 272-273.
27 Koehler 1979 Vol. 1, 9-13. A few examples have been recovered from Cyprus, including in the necropolis of Salamis: Karageorghis 1970, pl. 44 n. 26 and pl. 202 n. 266.
28 Koehler 1979 Vol. 1, 89 and 91; Vol. 2, pl. 1 n. 2 and 6.
29 Crete, Johnston 1993, 370; Callaghan *et al.* 2000; Johnston 2005, 364; Italy and Sicily, Panzeri Pozzetti 1986, pl. 35; Rizzo 1990, figs. 41 and 54; Berlingò 1995, 422-430; Cavagnera 1995, 41-43; Pelagatti 1995, 411-416; Olofsson 2003, 73-74.
30 Koehler 1981, 451 and pl. 98b.
31 Koehler 1979 Vol. 1, 92-94; Vol. 2, 31.

jars contained and whether they were in their initial or some secondary context are impossible issues to resolve with confidence on the basis of survey results. Koehler has argued for oil, but other products remain possible.[32]

The Kekova Adası shipwreck cargo appears to have been carried in three amphora types representing the agricultural produce of Cyprus, the southeast Aegean, and Corinth. The nature of the site's relief raises the possibility that additional materials, especially smaller finds, may have trickled down into the sandy pockets and reef topography. Nonetheless, several additional finds on the seabed provide context for interpreting the maritime cultural life of the merchants and crew. Situated among the main concentration of amphorae were two *mortaria* exhibiting thickened triangular rims and slightly concave bases. These could have served to facilitate the preparation of food on board or associated with the transported products upon arrival at their destination, or assisted in some mercantile activity linked to the measurement and distribution of dry goods (Fig. 5).[33] At least one fragment of a thin-walled (cooking?) pot was observed on the seabed, along with a single large bowl or cup with a small close-set loop handle. Several broken roof tiles were recorded throughout the site; such fragments may hint at the ship's galley or reflect later deposition. The only other remains visible on the surface and certainly associated with the shipwreck were more than 80 ballast stones found mixed among the ceramic remains, particularly in the shallow end of the reef. The stones are of diabase, commonly associated with ophiolite outcrops such as those of the Troodos on Cyprus and across in the northern Levant.[34] A Cypriot origin for the ballast fits well with the origin of the major cargo items. No estimate can be offered for the ballast weight, but these stones certainly would have added somewhat to the ship's overall tonnage.

KEPÇE BURNU

A second shipwreck with a similar cargo lies strewn across the shallows at the headland of Kepçe Burnu ("ladle point"), near the modern town of Çökertme just east of Bodrum (Map).[35] Local subsidence in the Gulf of Gökova would suggest that the reef on which the wreck foundered, currently only 1-2 m deep in places, would have rested even closer to the surface during the Archaic period.[36] A second shipwreck around the opposite side of the reef dates to the Hellenistic era and underscores the continued danger presented by this promontory.[37] The remains that can be attributed to the early Archaic wreck extend down a gentle slope from approximately 5 m deep into the sea grass beyond 10 m. Given the location, shallow depth, and present condition of the site, it seems likely that the ceramics have been badly disturbed by wave action as well as perhaps by more recent casual removal of materials from the site. The assemblage is dominated largely by highly fragmentary transport amphorae. The state of the ceramics, the extensive concretion of the finds, and the overgrowth of sea grass toward the deeper end of the site prevented detailed counts from being undertaken and a fully representative range of samples from being raised.

The large looping handles and heavy body sherds of basket-handle amphorae are immediately apparent among the remains and clearly constitute the vast majority of finds on the seabed. Amphora fragments from Kepçe Burnu are less well preserved but can be compared with those from Kekova Adası. They exhibit a generally similar rim, but with a slightly greater diameter, a lip that is rolled on the interior, and more inward curve that produces a less open shape to the mouth (Fig. 6). The bases show the same wide rounded recess underneath as on the Kekova Adası jars, but with a slightly narrower resting surface. One body sherd raised for measurement yielded an estimated maximum diameter of approximately 0.61 m. Such figures suggest that these jars should be at least as large as, if not even a bit larger than, those from Kekova Adası. It remains difficult to establish the detailed chronology of finer trends in the early development of basket-handle jars, particularly on the basis of small fragments available for study. The broad typological characteristics and general proportions of the Kepçe Burnu jars place them easily within the 7th century BC.[38] Nine samples were raised for analysis from the site. All share a generally uniform mineralogy that is similar to the Kekova Adası amphorae as well as to the slightly coarser Salamis jars, though with some unevenness evident in the clay mixing and overall production. This group of amphorae is again consistent with an origin on Cyprus, perhaps in the eastern part of the island.

One or two Southeast Aegean amphorae provide the only other visible evidence of cargo on board the Kepçe Burnu shipwreck, although their numbers suggest they played a limited role. Extensive concretion made it impossible to raise a diagnostic sample of this type, but observations on the seabed of one top belonging to this type reveal that the neck terminates in a similarly tall

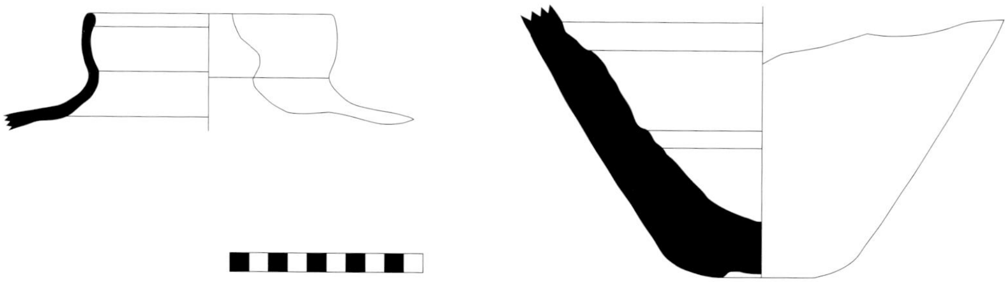

Fig. 6. Diagnostic fragments of basket-handle amphora rim (Sur10-020) and base (Sur10-017) from Kepçe Burnu, raised and re-deposited during the 2010 DEU survey. Drawings by L. Radloff.

rounded rim as the Aegean jars from Kekova Adası, and the handles attach just below the midsection of the conical neck. A small sample was raised to facilitate compositional analysis. This sample compares well with one of the Southeast Aegean jars from Kekova Adası and exhibits a fabric consistent with a geological origin in the same general region.

The only other remains brought to light at Kepçe Burnu include a single mortarium and a small bowl. The mortarium exhibits the same general shape and style as those from Kekova Adası, though with a thicker walls and a less pronounced triangular rim (Fig. 7). Analysis of the sample shows that it shares its fabric with the basket-handle amphorae from this same site. The bowl, raised during the 1973 survey, is largely intact and has not been analyzed to date. If it does properly belong to this early Archaic assemblage – and is not intrusive or from the second shipwreck on the other side of the reef – then it could provide evidence for food consumption on board the vessel.

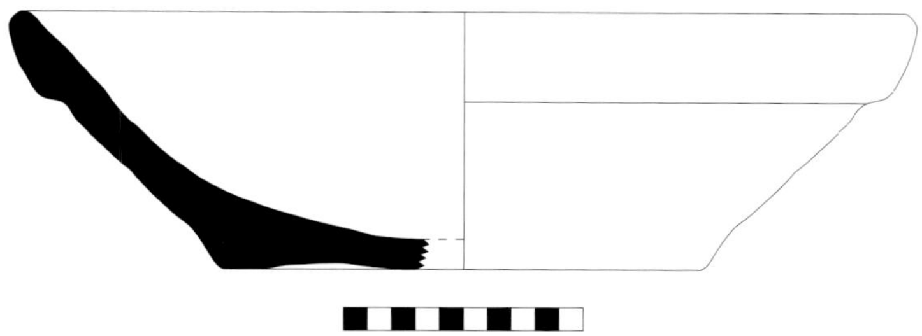

Fig. 7. Mortarium (Sur10-021) from the Kepçe Burnu shipwreck, raised and re-deposited during the 2010 DEU survey. Drawing by L. Radloff.

ÇAYCAĞIZ KOYU

The recent discovery of a shipwreck at Çaycağız Koyu near Marmaris adds a third facet to the pattern of Cypriot contacts with the Aegean world (Map). Again the cargo is badly broken. Its location in the shallow waters (approximately 5-12 m deep) of a small but busy inlet popular for day swimming excursions and overnight *gulet* mooring suggests that modern disturbance of the site is likely. All ceramics observed are badly broken and scattered across the rocky seabed and reef near shore, and many are heavily concreted. Diving survey recorded artefact counts and raised a number of samples for documentation and analysis.

The largest part of the cargo is comprised again of fragmentary basket-handle amphorae. At least 50-60 examples of this type were documented among the surface

32 Koehler 1978, 231; Koehler 1979 Vol. 1, 5-6. Koehler's suggestion is based primarily on the assumption that similar characteristics (density, hardness, decreased porosity) between the fabrics of Corinthian amphorae and those of oil lamps and jugs favor a shared content.

33 Villing 2006; Villing & Pemberton 2010, 602-624; Greene *et al.* 2008, 705.

34 Thanks to David Williams for sharing his thoughts and expertise on this sample from the ballast. A more detailed study of this ballast is to be included in the larger analysis of the finds currently being prepared.

35 This shipwreck has been reported on two separate occasions and therefore erroneously listed as two separate sites with contrasting details and even distinct coordinates in Parker's catalog: the "Çökertme A" wreck (n. 324) and the "Kepeç" wreck (n. 542). Parker correctly notes that Rosloff's published coordinates are incorrect: see Parker 1992, 148 and 226. In light of common naming conventions, which call for shipwrecks in Turkey to be associated with nearby topographic features, the modern Turkish spelling of "kepçe" is adopted over the older "kepeç".

36 Flemming provides no estimate for this specific location, but the general trend of subsidence along this coast argues that the reef may have been shallower in antiquity. The figures Flemming provides for Bodrum (-0.4 m / millennium) and Cedreae near the head of the Gulf of Gökova (-0.2 m / millennium) give some sense of the probable magnitude of this change. See Flemming 1978, 412.

37 Rosloff 1981, 279-280.

38 Salles 1980, 136-141; Humbert 1991, 580-583.

Fig. 8. Surface scatter of basket-handle amphoras at Çaycağız Koyu. Photo by H. Özdaş.

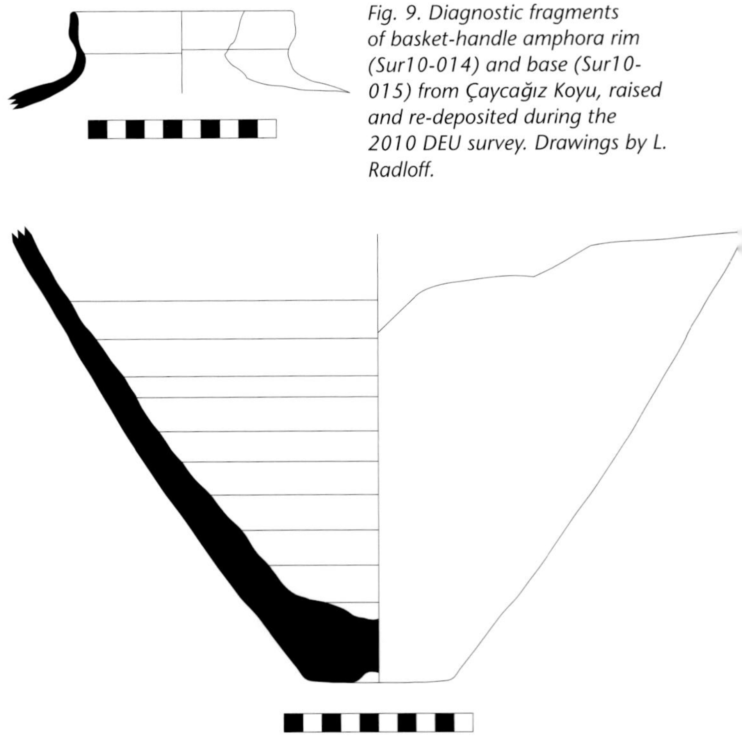

Fig. 9. Diagnostic fragments of basket-handle amphora rim (Sur10-014) and base (Sur10-015) from Çaycağız Koyu, raised and re-deposited during the 2010 DEU survey. Drawings by L. Radloff.

scatter (Fig. 8). The jars from Çaycağız Koyu present a delicate rim, which follows in the tradition of the rim forms seen at Kekova Adası and Kepçe Burnu but displays a more vertical shape and lacks a significant rolled lip. The base is narrower, with a smaller resting surface, a rudimentary finger indentation on the underside in place of a shallow rounded recess, and slightly steeper lower walls on the body indicative of a more attenuated shape (Fig. 9). This type of base seems to represent an early phase in the slow transition from a wider base with a carefully cut shallow recess underneath toward a narrower flat resting surface lacking any recess, a form that eventually narrows further into the peg toe that characterizes later jars.[39]

With a typology only broadly defined for the early basket-handle jar series, it is not surprising that relatively few well dated *comparanda* are available for these specific morphological traits. Several examples come from Tomb 3 at Salamis, dated to around 600.[40] Both Tel Kabri and Ashkelon provide one or more jars with similar proportions from strata probably closed toward the end of the 7th century BC,[41] along with a jar from a late 7th- or early 6th-century BC burial at Tell Sukas in Syria.[42] Various other undated finds from Salamis provide additional parallels, as do finds from Tell Kazel in Syria.[43] In light of the tentative dates and limited *comparanda*, it seems best to date this group of amphorae to the late 7th or early 6th century BC. Petrographic analysis undertaken on nine fragmentary basket-handle amphorae from this cargo suggests that the jars all belong to a single broad group. While the comparatively plain calcareous fabric again is not so distinctive as to be attributed easily, it is also not so different from that of the other basket-handle jars as to necessitate a wholly different origin. Without better comparanda that might suggest a different location, it seems most likely that this basket-handle

Fig. 10. Fragmentary ceramic mortaria mixed with basket-handle amphora sherds on the seabed at Çaycağız Koyu. Photo by H. Özdaş.

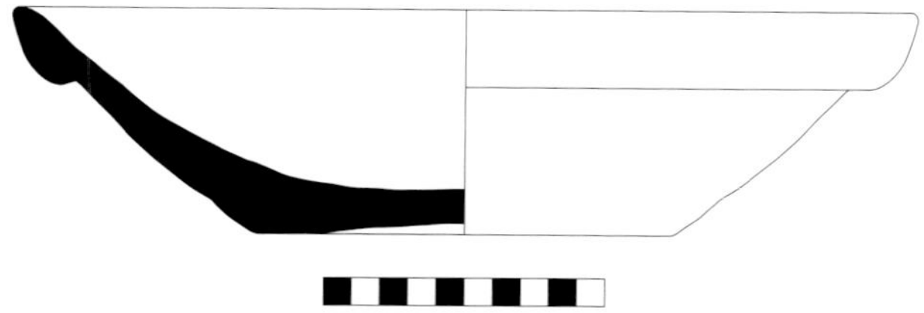

Fig. 11. Mortarium (Sur10-013) from the Çaycağız Koyu shipwreck, raised and re-deposited during the 2010 DEU survey. Drawing by L. Radloff.

amphora assemblage, like the others, was manufactured on Cyprus, perhaps even in the eastern part of the island. Unfortunately, no clues are available for what these amphorae may have contained other than the standard possibilities raised for the Kekova Adası and Kepçe Burnu jars above.

Although no other amphora types are visible at the site, the other major component of the assemblage consists of at least 30 ceramic *mortaria* (Fig. 10). The examples raised for analysis as well as those observed on the seabed all appear similar in basic form, proportions, and dimensions, each exhibiting a slightly overhanging triangular rim and concave base (Fig. 11). One concentration revealed at least 10 nearly intact *mortaria* and associated fragments. The number of these vessels argues that they formed part of the cargo, rather than shipboard cooking utensils or measuring devices for exchange as may more plausibly be the case for the one or two examples recorded in the Kepçe Burnu and Kekova Adası assemblages. Analysis of the fabrics of two *mortaria* sampled showed that they share a common composition with the basket-handle amphora group, suggesting that both cargo elements should be assigned to the same general origin on Cyprus.

No other remains can be attributed to the Archaic shipwreck site at Çaycağız Koyu with certainty, although survey in another part of the bay revealed a large stone anchor stock approximately 1.5 m in length and generally similar in form to those used on ships during the Archaic period, such as the example recovered from the mid-6th century BC Archaic shipwreck at Pabuç Burnu.[44] Fragments of a large pithos and a single conical base probably belonging to the long-lived series of Levantine torpedo jars were discovered not far away, although these – like the many fragments of later amphorae recorded in the inlet – may also represent the standard debris associated with anchorage traffic in antiquity.

In the case of the three wrecks discussed above, particularly the shallow sites at Çaycağız Koyu and Kepçe Burnu, it is difficult to determine whether modern disturbance

39 Humbert 1991, 583-586.
40 Karageorghis 1967, 38 and pls. XLI and CXXVI nos. 97, 99 and 101.
41 Ashkelon, Barako 2008, 441 fig. 23.11; Stager *et al.* (eds.) 2011, 114 and 115 fig. 7.57; Tel Kabri, Lehmann 2002, 213 fig. 5.84.1-2.
42 Riis 1979, 20 and 21 fig. 52 n. 26.
43 Salamis, Karageorghis 1970, 17-18 and pl. 118 n. 13, 215 n. 110, and 219 n. 218; Tell Kazel, Badre & Gubel 1999-2000, 128 fig. 3e-f.
44 Greene *et al.* 2008, 687 note 15.

has reduced the number of visible ceramics. The counts at Kekova Adası may be most reliable, since the site lies in a protected marine zone where diving is prohibited. Estimations of cargo capacities are tentative, but help to provide some sense of scale to these maritime endeavors. The numbers of visible amphorae at Kekova Adası are relatively small – no more than 130 or so – even if these reflect only the uppermost layer of jars on the seabed and do not include those that may have tumbled into the crevices of the reef or the deeper sand at the lower levels of the site.[45] Yet with a potential volume of around 70 l for each basket-handle amphora, the cargo size grows considerably: this component could carry at least 6300-7000 l of liquid cargo. Factoring in the weight of the containers themselves as well as the volumes of the smaller southeast Aegean and Corinthian jars, the visible remains account for more than 10 t of cargo weight. Lower counts of basket-handle jars at Çaycağız Koyu and Kepçe Burnu may still suggest capacities of 5-10 t, the size of a modest merchantman. For each of the wrecks, additional cargo not signaled by surviving material record is a possibility, but cannot be confirmed without more detailed analysis of the sites and their contexts. Such basic estimates, however, give a sense of scale and underscore the importance of considering amphora capacity along with numeric counts in the estimation of ship sizes.

COMMERCE IN A SHRINKING EASTERN MEDITERRANEAN

The three shipwrecks at Kekova Adası, Kepçe Burnu, and Çaycağız Koyu share similarities in their major cargos of basket-handle amphorae and the concurrent appearance of ceramic *mortaria*, both likely of Cypriot origin. The southeast Aegean jars at Kekova Adası and Kepçe Burnu, as well as the Corinthian amphorae from Kekova Adası, speak for a wide network of eastern Mediterranean contact visible as early as the 7th century BC. The nature of this exchange – in processed agricultural goods and coarse wares – reflects a movement of goods beyond precious metals and fine painted pottery. While scholars frequently propose a system of exchange by Greeks and Phoenicians for the 8th and 7th centuries predicated upon Homeric-style aristocrats in pursuit of adventure and gifts,[46] these three wrecks offer insights into somewhat less lofty facets of exchange. Who was behind these ventures and what sorts of interactions are suggested by these assemblages?

Elite traders, who sought wealth and luxury goods as sources of symbolic capital that could be used to reinforce status and power, may be associated with the Iron Age burials of Salamis. In Tomb 79, alongside ivory furniture, a chariot, a bronze cauldron, and engraved metal bowls were approximately three-dozen basket-handle amphorae and at least as many ceramic *mortaria*.[47] While the bronze and ivory items speak for the conspicuous display of wealth in metals and imported luxury, the transport amphorae and *mortaria* assert control over regional agriculture and food production on an impressive scale. The capacity to export agricultural products is a marker of surplus; receipt and enjoyment of such processed agricultural goods, like the wine and olive oil stored in amphorae, are markers of consumption of a commodity whose worth comes not only from extrinsic value, but from the very nature of its transport and the status connection it symbolizes. Certainly, the combination of luxury materials and physical markers of land ownership and agricultural control serves as a means of identifying the wealth and status of the occupants of the Salamis tombs. The circulation of both types of goods suggests Cypriot participation in the mobility of people and products during the 7th century BC.

Recently both Fantalkin and Nino Luraghi have suggested the role played by mercenary activity in the movement of goods and peoples in the 7th-century BC eastern Mediterranean. Citing finds of East Greek pottery in the vicinity of major military bases along the southern Levantine coast, Fantalkin argues for "Greek mercenary activities in these areas rather than pottery trade", and "East Greek mercenary garrisons rather than trading emporia".[48] Luraghi details the literary evidence for such activity in the 7th century BC, noting the example of Alcaeus' brother Antimenidas, who appears to have fought in the army of Nebuchadnezar II that defeated Ashkelon in 601.[49] Arguing that the mercenaries who served Egyptian, Babylonian, and Phoenician armies were not solely members of an aristocratic elite, Luraghi broadens the category to those land owners who could afford hoplite armor, neither the richest nor the poorest factions of society.[50] The presence of Greek hoplites alongside Cypriot and Assyrian warriors on a Phoenician silver bowl from late 8th- or early 7th-century BC Amathous would seem to support the notion of a military community that linked the eastern Mediterranean.[51]

While nothing in the cargoes of the three wrecks would suggest a military association,[52] the elite and middling social status of Fantalkin's and Luraghi's mercenaries fits well with that of the traders who shipped luxury items and processed agricultural goods between Cyprus, the eastern Aegean, and the Greek mainland. These goods – including wine and olive oil, the commonly identified contents of the jars found on our three shipwrecks[53] – have been described by Lin Foxhall as "semi-luxuries", exchanged neither through elite reciprocity nor for need of scarce commodities, but within the framework of preferential consumption or the exchange of processed agricultural goods that become fashionable, despite being unnecessary in the sense of basic availability.[54] Sappho's brother Charaxus (Strabo, *Geog.* 17.1.33) stands as an example of the import of Lesbian wine to Naxos, conducted by a member of the *aristoi*, with the desire for profit at its root. The Phoenician or Sidonian trade networks of Homer's *Odyssey*, in which the Greek Odysseus takes part when it seems convenient, generally involve luxury commodities, but wine is exchanged between Greeks at *Iliad* 7.467-75, suggesting the participation of Homeric warriors in both forms of exchange systems.[55] For the nature of trade in the 7th century BC from the regions of Samos and Corinth, Herodotus (4.152) tells of Colaeus, the Samian whose travels to the west gained him sufficient profit to dedicate a six-talent bronze cauldron at the Heraion. What goods Colaeus traded are unclear from the literary tradition, but likely included wine, olive oil, wool, textiles, and leather.[56] For Corinth, Dionysius of Halicarnassus (*Rom. Ant.* 3.46) recounts the tale of Demaratus the Bacchiad who made his fortune through transporting Corinthian pottery to Etruria.[57]

Members of elite families might be best equipped to initiate ventures of international trade, forging horizontal bonds of friendship between elites of different regions through the exchange of luxury materials alongside consumable agricultural semi-luxuries, the latter transported not out of strict necessity, but out of preference for such social markers of status and power. This multifaceted exchange reveals the larger-scale mobility of people and customs along with commodities, as well as a network of relationships between those who had a sufficient agricultural surplus to export, capital to fund a venture, and desire to forge connections. Social bonds may have been created through food preparation, feasting, and drinking, as visible in the transport amphorae as well as vessels such as *mortaria* that may have been involved in the preparation of specialized foodstuffs, including sauces, cakes, soups, and gruels.[58] Alexandra Villing proposes the utilization of *mortaria* for *myttotos* – a mixture of garlic, grated cheese, herbs, olive oil, and vinegar, used as a sauce for tuna – and suggests the concurrent transport of *myttotos* and *mortaria*.[59] While identifiable sauce boats or other small closed containers are not readily visible on any of the three wrecks, it would not be surprising if the practices associated with the preparation of new food items were exchanged alongside other social rituals involved in commercial interaction. As has been proposed for the ritualized drinking, feasting, and other ceremonial activities facilitated by the transport of Greek ceramics to the western Mediterranean, social status could be demarcated by preferential consumption, and the preparation of consumables in vessels that signaled status through their foreign nature.[60]

The material links between Cyprus and the southeast

---

45 On the 8th-century BC Tanit and Elissa wrecks found off the coast of Ashkelon, nearly 400 amphorae were visible in the upper two layers of cargo; see Ballard *et al.* 2002, 158.
46 For different scholarly approaches to Greeks and Phoenicians, see Tandy 1997; Gubel 2006, 86; Hodos 2009a.
47 Karageorghis *et al.* 1973; Rupp 1988.
48 Fantalkin 2006, 202.
49 Luraghi 2006, 23; Alcaeus fr. 48 and 350 L.-P.
50 Luraghi 2006, 22-24.
51 See Luraghi 2006, 36-38 and pl. 1-2.
52 The suggestion that *mortaria* were used to measure soldiers' rations measured from basket-handle amphorae is not widely accepted; see Salles 1985, 207.
53 For oil content of basket-handle jars, see Karageorghis 1967, 40; Masson 1967, 132–133; Rupp 1988, 130-131 notes the suitability of the Salamis region for cultivation of olives, grapes, and cereal.
54 Foxhall 1998; 2005.
55 Tandy 1997; Greene *et al.* 2008; Hodos 2009a.
56 Shipley 1987, 42-48.
57 See Salmon 1984, 106, 114 on the archaeological evidence for Corinthian trade with Etruria.
58 For these foods and other items prepared in *mortaria*, see Villing & Pemberton 2010, 612-620.
59 Villing 2006, 35-37; Villing & Pemberton, 2010, 616. The analysis by Spataro and Villing (2009) of *mortaria* from Miletos, as well as sites in Syria, Israel, and Egypt, reveals Cyprus to be a major production center for these items.
60 Dietler 1999; 2005 has discussed the ritualized consumption of alcohol utilizing Greek pottery shapes in Iron Age France, while Hodos 2006; 2010 discuss the use of the trefoil oinochoe and other drinking vessels adopted by local populations in Archaic Sicily.

Aegean visible on the three shipwrecks discovered off the Turkish coast indicate a direct exchange between these regions centering on processed agricultural goods alongside coarse ware ceramics. For Fantalkin, the second half of the 7th century BC represents a key period of increased mercenary and commercial interaction between East Greece and the Near East, and a resultant "crystallization of an East Greek identity, dictated by geography".[61] To such a model, the role of Cyprus in the mobility of goods and people, ideas and identity should not be overlooked, especially during its earliest phases in the mid- to late 7th century BC. The consumption of particular commodities provides an index of local identity in the context of a global Mediterranean world linked, according to Tamar Hodos, "by sets of practices, or bodies of knowledge, that transgress national or cultural ideas".[62] Through the exchange of common goods, individuals and communities are connected; through the particularized use of these commodities and products, local diversity is enhanced. By the 6th century BC the role played by Cyprus in the establishment of cultural contacts between the Greeks and the Near East is visible in finds of basket-handle amphorae and *mortaria* in religious and habitation sites in both regions, and we might look toward the island as an intermediary – and perhaps facilitator – in these renewed cultural contacts. The collapsing distances between the eastern Mediterranean worlds can be recognized in the physical movement of artefacts and the intellectual exchange of ideas and knowledge. Further research on these three and other early Archaic shipwrecks may shed light on the association between the archaeological remains of ancient trade and the sociocultural and economic interactions that marked the Iron Age eastern Mediterranean.

61 Fantalkin 2006, 203-204.
62 Hodos 2009b, 23; Hodos 2010, 82.

ACKNOWLEDGEMENTS

The authors are grateful to George Bass, Cemal Pulak, and Faith Hentschel, who kindly shared reports, photographs, and notes from the various Institute of Nautical Archaeology (INA) surveys conducted between 1973 and 2004 at the sites of Kekova Adası and Kepçe Burnu. For permission to undertake the more recent Dokuz Eylül University (DEU) investigations of these sites as well as that at Çaycağız Koyu, thanks are due to the Turkish Ministry of Culture and Tourism. The Bodrum Museum of Underwater Archaeology kindly facilitated permissions for export of the samples analysed here. Financial and logistical support from DEU's Institute of Marine Science and Technology, the Scientific and Technological Research Council of Turkey, the Social Sciences and Humanities Research Council of Canada, the Canada Foundation for Innovation, Ontario's Ministry of Research and Innovation, Brock University, the American Schools of Oriental Research, and INA made the present study possible. Mark Lawall provided helpful suggestions and lent his expertise throughout the course of the project and artefact study. Finally, thanks to the editors for their interest and assistance in the preparation of this contribution, and to the anonymous reviewer for comments.

Cypriot Basket-handle Amphorae from Kelenderis and its Vicinity

BY K. LEVENT ZOROĞLU

Cypriot Basket-handle Amphorae from Kelenderis and its Vicinity

BY K. LEVENT ZOROĞLU

INTRODUCTION

The so-called basket-handle amphorae were a kind of storage and transport vessel of which the most prominent feature are two handles rising to various heights from the shoulder on either side of the mouth of the jar.[1] The loop handles allowed the jar to be carried both by hand and by a pole passed through them. Research into the provenance, distribution and date of the basket-handle amphorae has conclusively shown that this type of vessel was first produced in Cyprus and used between the 7th and 3th centuries BC. Even so, surprisingly few examples are displayed in museums or found in excavations in Turkey, even if a not inconsiderable number of finds have been made in shipwrecks off the Turkish coast.[2] Therefore, the finds from Kelenderis and its vicinity provide very important evidence for the town's relations with the outside world.

Kelenderis is located on the Mediterranean coast of Turkey, in ancient Rough Cilicia (see Map).[3] The land where the town is located is mountainous and covered with trees (mainly pine, oak and cedar) whose timber was the main product and export from the region in antiquity. As Pliny the Elder pointed out,[4] Kelenderis was not only the name of the town, but also the name of the area surrounding it. The economy of the *region celenderitis* was likely directed by Kelenderis, to which all production materials were transported and from which export materials were shipped. The town was connected to the hinterland by paths, most of which stretched up to the central Anatolian Plateau where agricultural activity was the prominent occupation of the people. Thus, Kelenderis was not only the main harbour in the area, but was also one of the most important export and import ports on the Mediterranean coast of Asia Minor, from which other overseas regions, especially Cyprus, could be reached easily.

Archaeological finds at Kelenderis, where excavations began in 1987, may help answer questions about the relationship between Kelenderis and Cyprus, the north coast of which is located roughly 40 miles south of the town.[5] One of the most important relevant groups is made up of basket-handle amphorae, the study of which enables us to confirm the cultural proximity between the two regions, especially in the late Archaic and Classical periods.

THE BASKET-HANDLE AMPHORAE OF KELENDERIS

Basket-handle amphorae come from two areas of excavation in Kelenderis. One group was found in the settlement area in a test trench in the Lower City. A second group is constituted by those used as burial gifts in the cemeteries of the town. Both excavation areas allow the amphorae to be dated by associated artefacts. The other vessels published here were found in the sea. Two were discovered during the underwater survey off the shores of Kelenderis conducted by our team, and the rest were brought to the Amphora Museum in Taşucu near Silifke by local fishermen.

The first group of basket-handle amphorae (Nos. 1, 3, 4 and 5) was found in the Lower City, as a pile of more than six basket-handle amphorae from destruction debris associated with the first settlement level along with fragments of Protocorinthian, East Greek and of Cypriot painted pottery. The basket-handle amphorae discovered here was probably originally situated in the depot of a house. The datable pottery found in this destruction level corresponds well with the Persian invasion that occurred in the mid-6th century BC, and the preceding activity period during which time the amphorae were in use should date to roughly the 7th through first half of the 6th centuries BC – in other words, to the pre-Persian period of the town.

Two base fragments with pointed toe, one of which is listed in the following catalogue (No. 12), were found in the same trench, in the Persian Occupation Levels. And since a few fragments of Attic black and red figured vases were found in the same levels, these two base fragments may be dated roughly to the late Archaic and Classical periods.[6]

The second dateable group from Kelenderis (e.g. Nos. 9, 10, 11, 14 and 15) comes from the necropolis. The first three vessels (Nos. 9, 10, 11) were excavated illegally and are now on display in the local museums of Silifke and Anamur.[7] Nos. 14 and 15, on the other hand, were found together in 2006 in the chamber of an underground rock cut tomb in the East Necropolis. This tomb was clearly used several times. The earlier period of use, to which Nos. 14

Map. Find places of the basket-handle amphorae in Cilicia.

and 15 belong, can be dated to the late 5th and first half of the 4th century BC.[8]

TYPES

According to their shapes and dates, the finds listed in the following catalogue may be arranged and discussed under the three main types.

Type 1: Biconical – broad body and flat base (Nos. 1, 2, 3, 4, 5, Figs. 1-4, 13).

As mentioned above, Nos. 1, 3, 4 and 5 were found in the test trench; they were all broken and only one example (No. 1) was restored. In addition to this restored example, we also catalogued three more pieces here: a fragment of the neck and shoulder, a handle with an incised upper part, and a base in order to describe the form better. No. 2, which is almost intact, was found by fishermen in the sea.

The fabric of Nos. 1, 3, 4 and 5 is creamy white and has a yellowish white surface with a light red core. The inner

---

1 For a general description and classification of the basket handle amphora, see Sagona 1982, 89-91 fig. 4; Humbert 1991, 580-590; Lehmann 1996, 443-445 Form 421 pls. 79-80. Further references are given below.

2 See the contribution by Elizabeth S. Greene, Justin Leidwanger & Harun Özdaş in the present volume.

3 On Kelenderis, see Hild & Hellenkemper 1990, 298; Zoroğlu 1994.

4 HN 5, 27; regio celenderitis cum oppidum.

5 The ongoing excavation in Kelenderis began in 1987. On relations between Rough Cilicia and Cyprus see Zoroğlu 1994, 26-27.

6 It must also be mentioned here that various Attic vases were found as burial gifts in the underground rock cut tombs; for a group of these see Zoroğlu 1994 figs. 57-64; see also Zoroğlu 1999, 141-145.

7 The earliest date of burials in the necropolis of Kelenderis began in the second half of the 6th century BC and continued to the end of Roman period; for the necropolis and grave types in Kelenderis see Zoroğlu 1994, 32-36 and Zoroğlu 2000, 121-125 pl. 22 fig. 3.

8 The second period of use in this tomb contained a Rhodian amphora with stamped handles (a rose and an inscription which probably refers to Demokrates I) and unguentaria of the late 3rd and first quarter of the 2nd century BC.

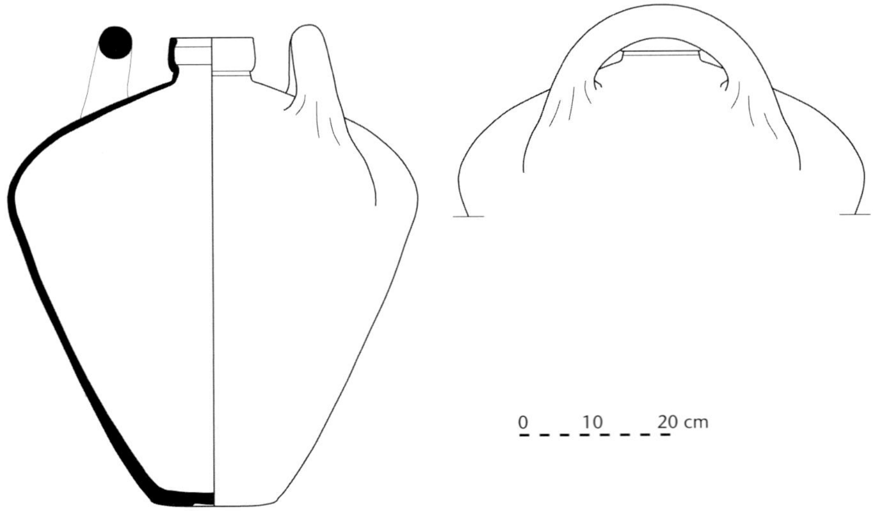

Fig. 1. No: 1 (K.92 AG 01; 2987).

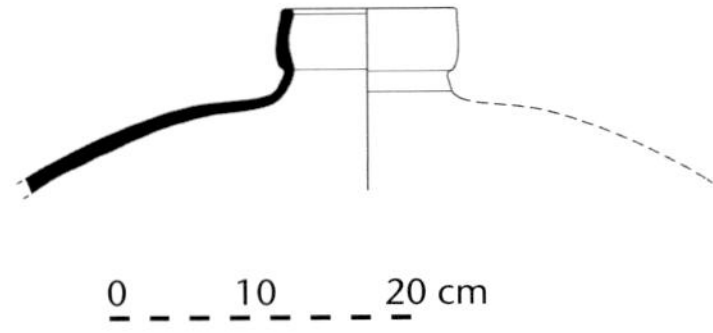

Fig. 3. No: 3 (K.92 AG 002).

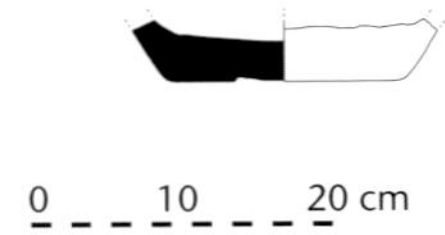

Fig. 4. No: 5 (K.92 AK 019).

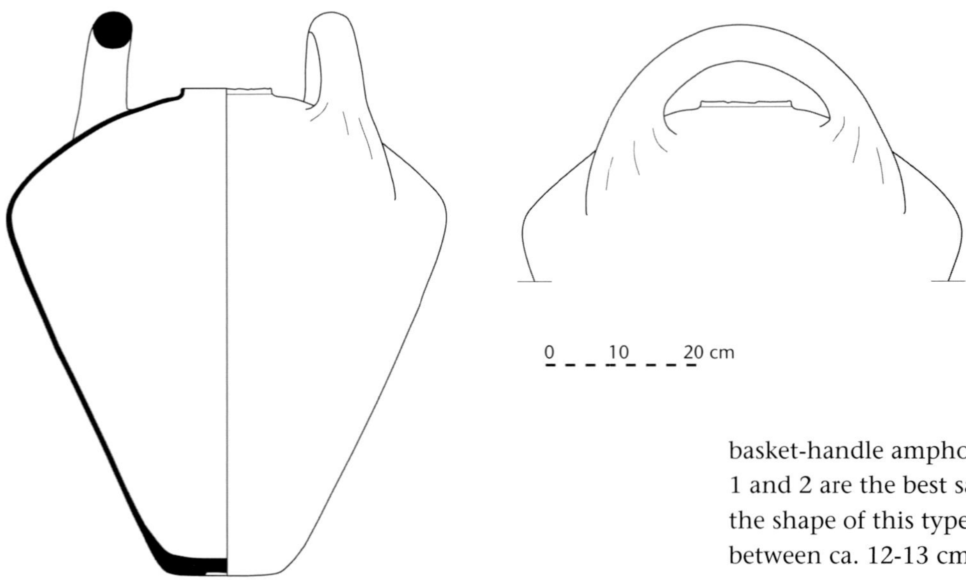

Fig. 2. No: 2 (13-252).

surface is also light red. No. 2, on the other hand, has grey and dirty buff clay, perhaps due to the salty seawater, in which it was found, and to various organic materials that cover the vase. All vessels also have quite big inclusions of limestone and small particles of mica and sand.

With regard to the shape, this is the broadest of the basket-handle amphorae and, as mentioned above, Nos. 1 and 2 are the best samples to describe the features of the shape of this type. The diameter of the mouth varies between ca. 12-13 cm and seems to be quite narrow – if compared with the broadness of body. Nos. 1 and 3 have a plain rim, and the exterior of the mouth is thickened so as to give the illusion of a collar around the neck. This part of the mouth has a convex profile on the exterior and is concave inside. Below this, the neck joins to the shoulder after an offset.[9] The broad and bi-conical body, ca. 50 cm wide and ca. 60 cm high, is comprised of a convex profiled wide shoulder, which slopes gently down to the widest point of the body, and a conical lower part, which narrows down to the flat base. The base of this type, which is ca. 15-17 cm wide, is also narrow and it has a depressed underside

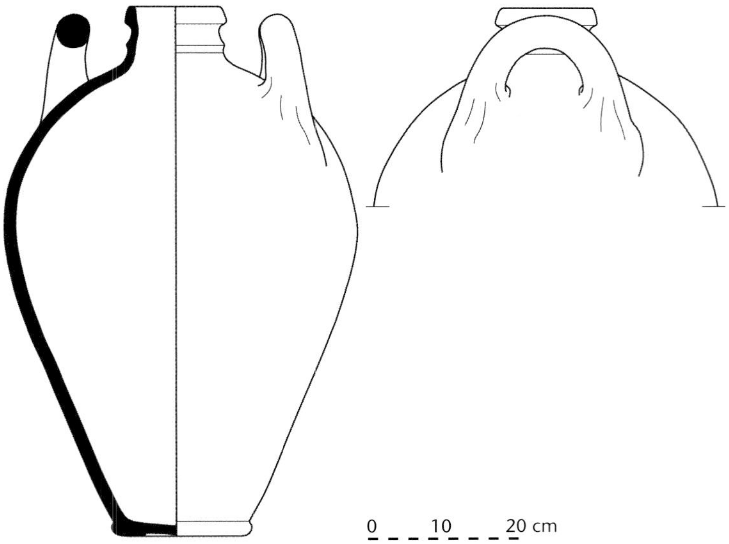

Fig. 5. No: 6 (9-251).

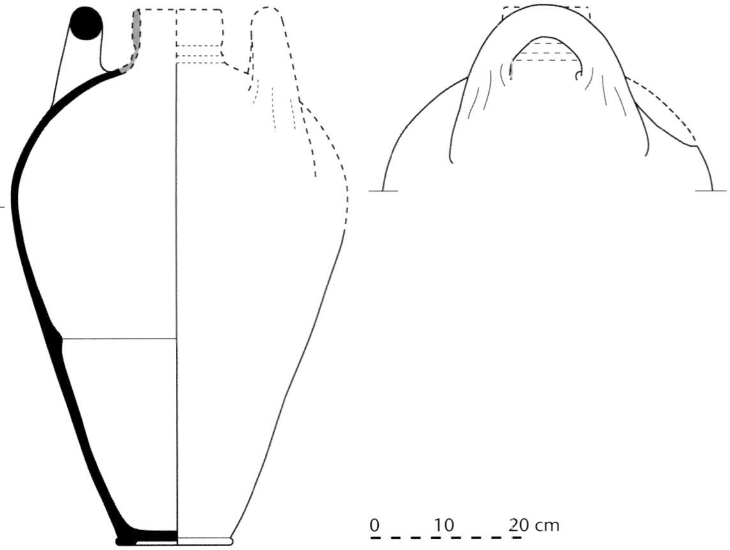

Fig. 6. No: 7 (K.02 Y. Ada BL 013).

(see No. 5 in Figs. 4 and 14). Two loop handles placed in the middle part of the shoulder are thick and have a round profile. They are vertical and attached to the shoulder in the shape of a bow; both ends are broader and traces of smoothing are clearly seen. The handles of No.1 are not higher than the level of the mouth, so the vessel may have been carried by means of holding the handles instead of by use of a pole.

Two handle fragments from Kelenderis, one of which is catalogued here (No.4, Fig. 13), bear six short incisions, probably marking the weight of its content.

Because of the organic materials that cover the vessel, the profile of mouth of No. 2 is not evident; it is not clear whether its rim and neck were broken or if it had a plain short mouth joined to the shoulder without the neck. In both cases the body form of this vessel is close to No. 1, so the mouth form may have been more or less a similar to Nos. 1 and 3.

As noted above, the examples from Kelenderis were certainly used for storage purposes, especially for liquids like olive oil and wine, or semi-liquids like honey and sauces. Although the vessel displayed in the Amphora Museum in Taşucu is from the sea – which reveals that the amphorae belonging to Type 1 were also used for transporting purposes – their broad body form is not

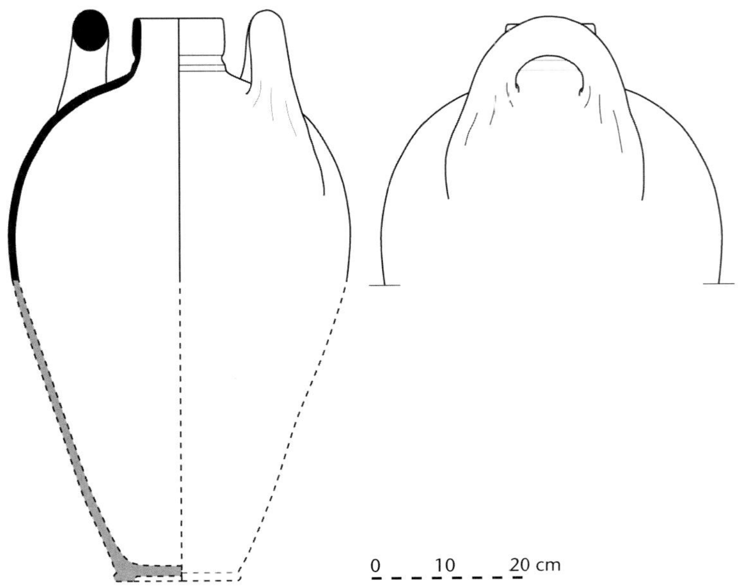

Fig. 7. No: 8 (K.07-E 001).

9 The profile of the mouth of this type is repeated on the mouth of No. 8 of Type 2 (see below).

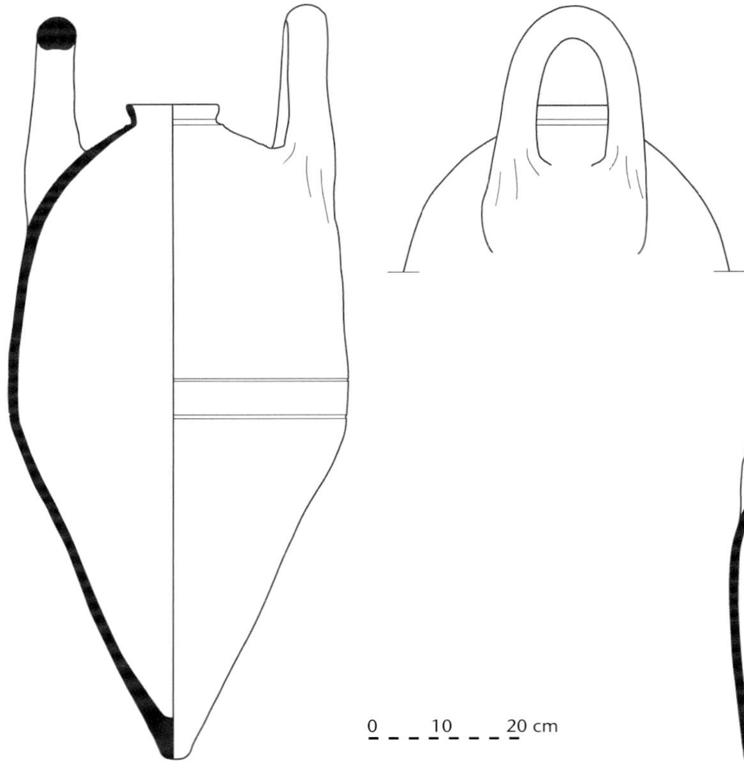

Fig. 8. No: 9 (288).

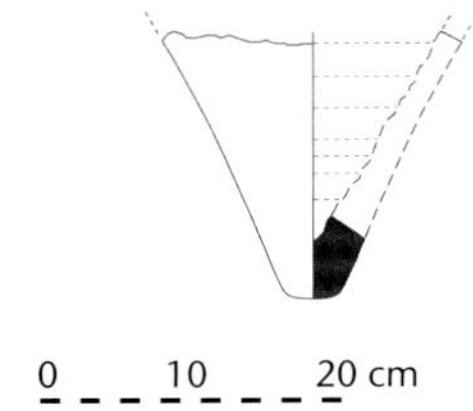

Fig. 9. No: 12 (K.92 BB 030).

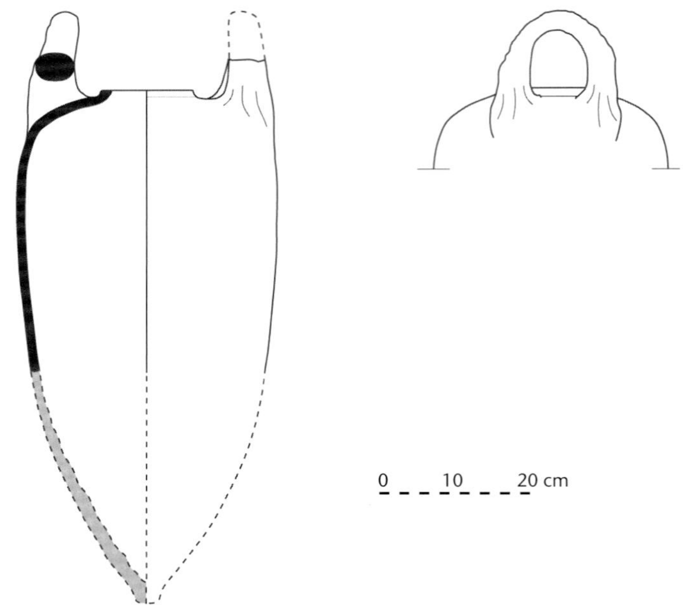

Fig. 10. No: 13 (130-250).

suitable for stacking in the cargo of a vessel.[10] On the other hand, the closest parallels found in Salamis in Cyprus, were placed in the dromos of a tomb, which reveals that they were also used as burial gifts.[11] The form of its mouth indicates that it was certainly covered with a skin, which was attached with a string on the lower part of the neck where there is an offset to prevent the cover from sliding off.

Type 2: Oval body and flat base (Nos. 6, 7, 8, Figs. 5-7).

There are two intact examples of this type displayed in the Amphora Museum in Taşucu, both of which were brought to the museum by local fishermen. Only one of these is catalogued here (No. 6). In addition, two amphora fragments were found in the sea near Kelenderis (Nos. 7 and 8).

The clay varies from light buff to grey, and there are

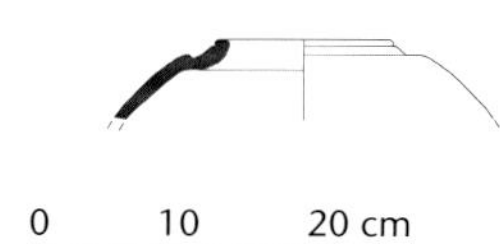

Fig. 11. No: 14 (K.06 DN-A V BG 001).

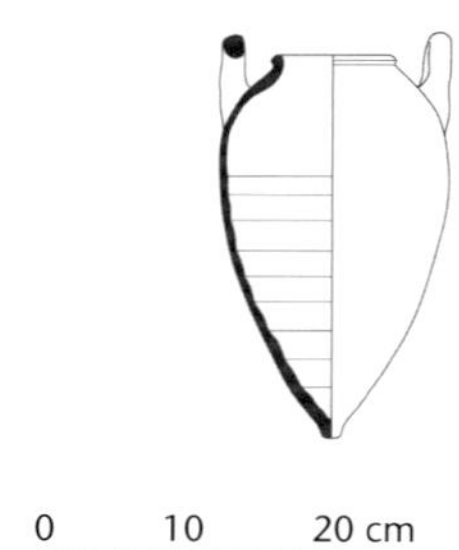

Fig. 12. No: 15 (K.06 DN-A V BE 001).

quite large inclusions of limestone and sand. However, it must be pointed out that the colour of clay may vary as it depends greatly on the conditions in which it was found and as salty water may damage the fabric.

When the shape is compared with that of the first type, the striking feature of this type is the oval-shaped body. Its height (ca. 0.68 cm) is more or less equal to Type 1, and the diameter of the mouth is also close. The rim of No. 6 is thickened on the exterior; the neck is higher and has a drip ring on the lower part. The mouth form of No. 8 (Fig. 7), on the other hand, is close to Nos. 1 and 3 of Type 1. After the narrow and convex shoulder, the body tapers down gently and gains its oval form. Its base, which is more or less 17.5 cm in diameter, is also flat and has a slightly projecting torus edge. The underside is also depressed like the base of the first type. The handles, which are placed on the lower part of the shoulder, are quite vertical with both ends fixed to the shoulder in a way that puts them closer to each other in comparison to the bow-shaped handles of the first type. As a result, the handles here gain a more or less u-shape. Another important feature is that the handles are now lower than the level of the mouth, making it possible for the vessel to be carried by holding the handles instead of using a pole.

As noted above, two examples (Nos. 7 and 8) found in the sea probably belong to Type 2. One of these (No. 7, Fig. 6) is a body fragment, of which the neck and one of the handles are missing.[12] The shape of the body is quite similar to that of No. 6 and No. 8; No. 8 is a fragment from the upper part of the vessel and may also belong to this type as reconstructed here in Fig. 7.

As noted above, the vessels belonging to Type 2 shown here are underwater finds, and this situation may allow us to conclude that they were used mainly for transport purposes, especially of liquids, e.g. olive oil and wine. The form of the neck and mouth make it possible to cover them in the same method as Type 1.

I have not seen any close parallels of the type described here in other publications. So, it may be suggested as a local version of the basket-handle amphora which may have been developed from Type 1.

Type 3: Oval body with pointed toe (Nos. 9, 10, 11, 12, 13, 14, Figs. 8-11, 15, 16)

Two base fragments belonging to this type were found in the Persian Occupation Levels of the trench in Kelenderis; only one of these is catalogued here (No. 12, Fig. 9). Other examples, except No. 13 (Fig. 10), which was found in the sea, are from the cemetery of the town.

The amphorae are made of buff clay with quite large inclusions of limestone and sand, including very little mica; the clay of Nos. 9, 10, 11 and 12 are hard, and the lower part of the body is thick.

The shape corresponds to the well-known and widespread type of basket-handle amphora, which is also known as Zemer 24.[13] The common feature of this type is the almost slender and tapering body form with a pointed toe. Some of our examples (Nos. 9, 10, 11) have a flaring mouth and a concave profiled neck, whereas others (Nos. 13 and 14) have a mouth with a plain rim which was joined directly to the shoulder without a neck.[14] The body is narrower than that of Type 1, and its height varies from 50 to 80 cm. In the middle part of the body of the larger examples there are one or two horizontal lines marking the joint of the lower part to the upper half of the vessel. However, this joint is more evident on No. 11, which has an offset there (Fig. 16). Basket-handles, which are attached to the lowest part of the shoulder and rise up quite vertically, are high and u-shaped. The handles of some of the large vessels are quite high in order to use a pole to carry the vessel.

This type of basket-handle amphora is one of the widespread transport vessels. Their shape makes it possible to stack them in a ship quite easily, and as such reveals that

10 There is a more or less similar amphora in the local museum in Marmaris: it is larger than the samples that belong to Type 1 and its foot is narrower than our samples; this vessel was also found in the sea, see Şenol 2003, 3.

11 Karageorghis 1967 Tomb 2 pl. 13.15; 91.15.

12 This amphora was found during our underwater survey near Yılanlıada (Snake Island, Spurie) off the shores of Kelenderis, in a depth ca. 50 m, where no traces of a wreck was visible.

13 Zemer 1977, 31 pl. 8; see also Sagona 1982 fig. 4.3-5; Humbert 1991, 586-590 Types G-K figs. 7-11; Lehmann 1996 Form 421 c, d, e, f, g pls. 79-80; there are also some fragments of basket handle amphorae found in various excavation sites of Cilicia recently, see: Gates 1994, 196 fig. 8; Şenol & Kerem 2000, 87-88 no. 7 (Inv. No. 79-7-6) pl. 15; Şenol & Aşkın 2007, 274 No. 72 (Although the authors proposed that No. 70 and 71 in p. 273 are also fragments belong to basket handle amphorae, I think that they may belong to other forms of transport jars.

14 Nos. 10 and 13 represent an even more tapered version and might arguably represent a type of their own (Type 4).

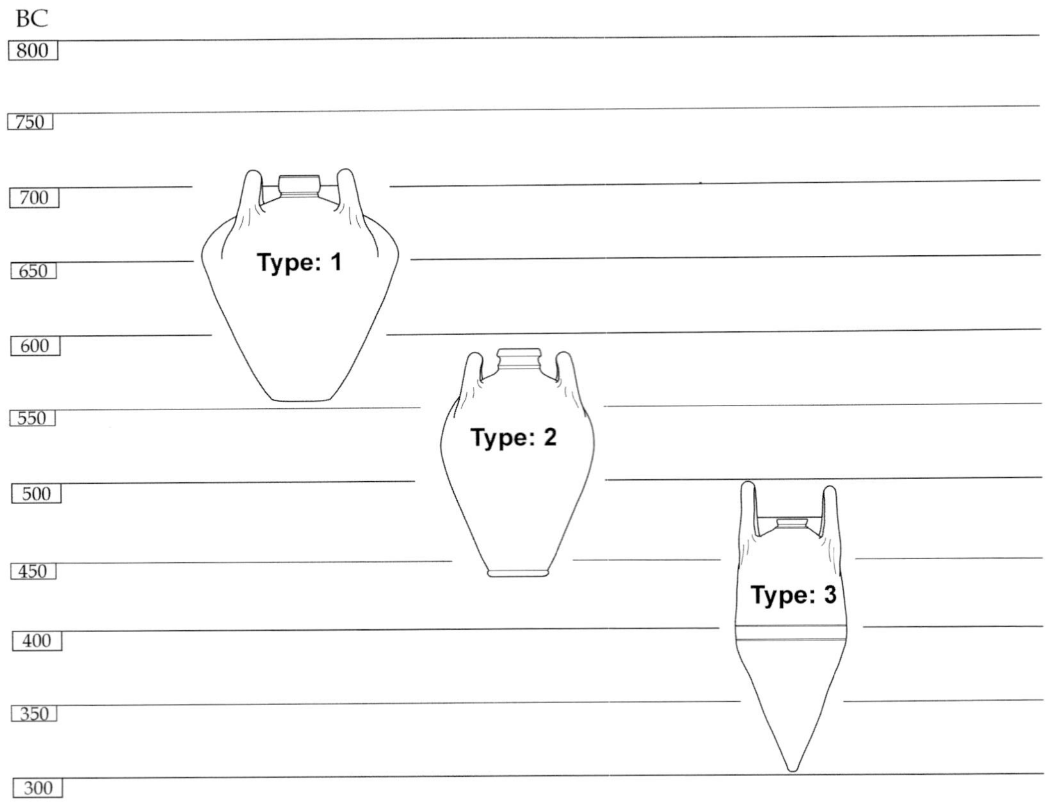

Table 1.

they were produced mainly for transportation purposes.

There are various sub-types of Type 3, and it is probable that the vessels with flaring rim and concave profiled neck were used for the transportation of liquids, especially wine and olive oil, while others, e.g. vessels with low mouth and without neck, were suitable for non-liquid foods.

Varia

No. 15 (Fig. 12) is a miniature amphora with pointed toe. This vessel was found in the same tomb as No. 14 in Kelenderis.

Its fabric is light red clay with small limestone and mica inclusions.

The amphora has a wide mouth with out-turned rim, which is joined to the shoulder without a neck; its oval body tapers gently and ends in a pointed toe; two low basket handles are attached on the lower part of the shoulder. There are traces of smoothing on the exterior, especially on the lower part down to the body.

Based on its size, especially on its wide mouth, it may be suggested that this vessel was used to keep (and also to transport) solid foods like butter or something similar.

The context of this small amphora, which, as previously mentioned, was found with No. 14, also makes it possible to date it to the late 5th and early 4th century BC.

CONCLUSION: THE EVIDENCE FROM KELENDERIS IN BROADER PERSPECTIVE

As previously noted, the earliest exsamples of the basket-handle amphora were used at the beginning of the 7th century BC,[15] and this type was still in use to the 3rd century BC (Table 1).[16] When compared with other contemporaneous forms of storage and transport vessels, it seems clear that a long period of time separated the emergence and decline of the basket-handle amphora, and we want to discuss briefly how the form of this type of vessel developed through time. Indeed, Kelenderis provides one of the rare instances of a site where the entire typological range of basket-handle amphorae is found.

Type 1 seems to be the oldest type of basket-handle

amphora found in Kelenderis and according to other chronological evidence this type must have been used in the 7th and 6th centuries BC.[17] Moreover, it may also be proposed that this is the first stage of the formal development (see Table above).

Although we have no samples from the habitation levels in Kelenderis, the amphorae discussed here under Type 2 may be considered as the second stage of development. Their bodies have lost the globular shape and have become oval. As noted above, the mouth form of No. 8 is quite close to that of Nos. 1 and 3 of Type 1, which may suggest that these types are more or less related. Although there is no direct chronological evidence, this type likely dates to the 6th and early 5th centuries BC.

The last stage of development of the shape is represented by the amphorae with pointed toe, which were discussed under Type 3 above. They were, according to the finds from Kelenderis, especially popular in the 5th and 4th centuries BC, and similar vessels found in other places also support this dating.[18]

There are various proposals concerning the provenance of basket-handle amphorae; among these Cyprus seems to be the foremost region as a production centre, since the whole series of forms from the oldest to the latest types were found there.[19] A recent addition to this proposal is that the basket-handle amphorae were produced at more than one place in the Eastern Mediterranean Region: both in Cyprus and also in Palestine.[20] Adding to this latter proposal, I suggest that it is more acceptable to attribute the basket-handle amphorae to various places in the Eastern Mediterranean basin instead of crediting them to only one production centre. From this point of view I want to propose that Kelenderis (or another port on the coast of Rough Cilicia) is another candidate for being a production centre of this type, in particular the flat-based Type 2. I hope this hypothesis will be supported by new evidence related to the production and distribution of this type in the future.

CATALOGUE

Note: Measurements are in cm; if not cited, the samples given below are in the depot of the Kelenderis excavation.

Type 1

No. 1 (Fig. 1) Inv. No. K.92 AG 001 (Silifke Museum, Inv. No. 2987). From the Lower City at Kelenderis,now displayed in the Local Museum in Silifke. H.: 61.5; diam. of mouth: 11; diam. of body: 52; diam. of base: 15; broken parts on the body mended and restored with plaster; cream, reddish cream clay with limestone inclusions; there are traces of smoothing on the surface.

No. 2 (Fig. 2) Inv. No. 13- 252. From the sea and displayed in the Amphora Museum in Taşucu. H.: 57.5 (from mouth to base): 66.5 (with handles); diam. of mouth: 10.5; diam. of body: 51.5; diam. of base: 14; mouth broken; thick limestone layer and organic materials on the surface; buff clay with limestone and sand inclusions.

No. 3 (Fig. 3) Inv. No. K.92 AG 002. From Kelenderis. H.: 11.7; diam. of mouth: 10; mouth and a part of the shoulder; interior of the vessel is light buff, exterior is dirty cream, limestone, mica and sand inclusions in the fabric.

No. 4 (Fig. 13) Inv. No.K.92 AK 020. From the Lower City at Kelenderis. Diam.: 3.7; just over half of one handle preserved; cream, reddish cream clay with limestone, mica and sand inclusions; 6 incised lines on the exterior, each of which are 1.5 to 2.5 cm long and ca. 1 or 2 mm wide.

No. 5 (Figs. 4, 14) Inv. No.K.92 AK 019. From the Lower City at Kelenderis. H.: 2.6; diam. 17; broken parts mended; base and a part of the body; light buff and greenish clay with quite large limestone and sand inclusions; very little mica; flat and quite thick wall with depressed underside.

15 For the development of the type see further Buhl 1983, 16-23 and for the attribution of some exsamples to Cyprus: Leidwanger 2005-2006 (2007).

16 For one of the final conclusions on the date of circulation of the basket handle amphora, see Lehmann 1996, 443-445 Form 421 pl. 79.

17 Cf. Humbert 1991, 580 fig. 1 b and 590.

18 Zemer 1977, 31 No. 24; Sagona 1982, 89-91 fig. 4.3-5; Humbert 1991, 586-590, fig. 7-11 (Type: F-K); Lehmann 1996, 443. A new tomb context discovered in 2011 in Kelenderis comprised of one basket-handle amphora with two unguentaria dated to the Early Hellenistic Period.

19 The neutron-activation analysis of the finds from Keisan has proven true the suggestion that the origin of the basket handle amphora is the eastern Cyprus, see Gunneweg & Perlman 1991, 591-599.

20 Cf. Gunneweg & Perlman 1991; Jacobsen 2002; Leidwanger 2005-2006 [2007]; Wolff 2011.

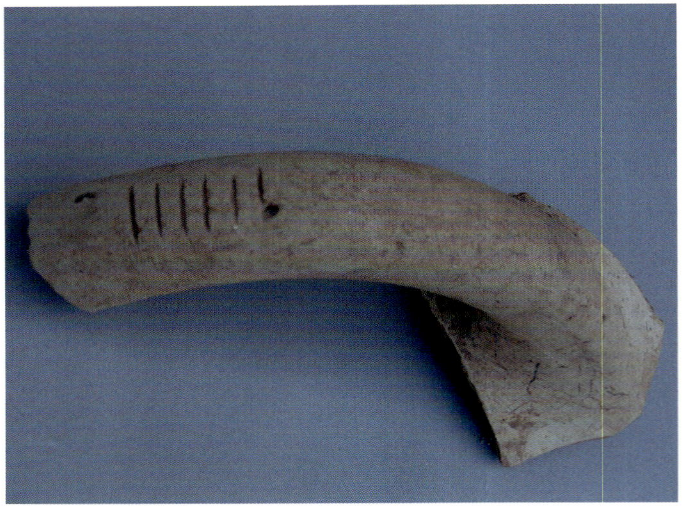

Fig. 13. An incised amphora handle of Type 1 found in the test trench in the Lower City; (No. 4); Photo: excavation archive.

Fig. 14. Base of an amphora Type 1 found in the test trench in the Lower City; (No. 5); Photo: excavation archive.

Type 2

No. 6 (Fig. 5) Inv. No. 9-251.From the sea; displayed in the Amphora Museum in Taşucu. H.: 68; diam. of mouth: 11.9; diam. of body: 45; diam. of base: 17.8; flakes on the surface; remains of organic materials on the surface; buff clay with limestone and sand inclusions.

No. 7 (Fig. 6) Inv. No. K.02 Y. Ada BL 013. Discovered during the underwater survey near Yılanlı Ada (Snake Island-Spurie) nearly 3 miles away from Kelenderis. H.: 66.5; diam. of body: 43; diam. of base: 15; light brown clay with limestone and sand inclusions; on the exterior and interior of the body are remains of organic materials.

No. 8 (Fig. 7) Inv. No. K.07 E 001. From the sea close to Kelenderis. H.: 27; diam. of mouth: 11.3; buff clay with big limestoneinclusions; exterior of the body is buff; on the surface are remains of organic materials.

Type 3

No. 9 (Fig. 8) Inv. No. 288. Probably from a looted tomb in Kelenderis and now displayed in the local Museum in Silifke. H.: 84.1, diam. of mouth: 11.7; diam of body: 42.8; diam. of base: 2.6; broken parts on the rim; thick limestone layer on the exterior of the vessel; buff clay with small limestone and sand inclusions.

No. 10 (Fig. 15) Inv. No. 5.1.63. From a looted tomb in Kelenderis and now displayed in the local Museum in Anamur. H.: 80 (without handles), diam. of mouth; 11.4; diam. of body 36; limestone inclusions on the surface; clay is light red.

No. 11 (Fig. 16) Inv. No. 11.1.65. Found in a looted tomb in Kelenderis and now displayed in the local Museum in Anamur. H.: 49.8; diam. of mouth: 13; diam. of body: 24; buff clay with limestone and mica inclusions.

No. 12 (Fig. 9) Inv. No.K.92 S BB 030. From the Lower City at Kelenderis. H.: 16.5; only pointed toe of the vessel survived; buff clay with small limestone and sand inclusions; traces of smoothing on the exterior; deep and horizontal grooves of wheel on the interior.

No. 13 (Fig. 10) Inv. No. 130-250. From sea and now displayed in Amphora Museum in Taşucu; H.: 50 (without handles); diam. of mouth: 12; diam of the body: max. 30; lower part of the body is missing; upper part of one of the handles is broken; shells and other organic materials on the interior and exterior.

No. 14 (Fig. 11) Inv. No.K.06 DN-A V BG 001. From a tomb in the East Necropolis of Kelenderis. H.: 5.3; diam.

Fig. 15. An amphora from a tomb from Kelenderis (No. 10); Anamur Museum. Photo: M. Dillon.

Fig. 16. An amphora from a tomb from Kelenderis (No. 11); Anamur Museum. Photo: M. Dillon.

of mouth: 11; diam. of body: ca. 30; a part from mouth, shoulder of the vessel was found; one of the loop handles is also found in its context which is not catalogued here; red clay with limestone and mica inclusions; clay is rough; thickened rim and convex profiled shoulder.

VARIA

No. 15 (Fig. 12) Inv. No. K.06 DN-A V BE 001. From the same tomb as No. 14; H.: 25.2; diam. of mouth: 8.2; diam. of body: 14.2; mended; buff, reddish buff clay and surface; quite big inclusions of limestone.

Cypriot Basket-handle Amphorae in Hellenistic Cyrenaica

BY KRISTIAN GÖRANSSON

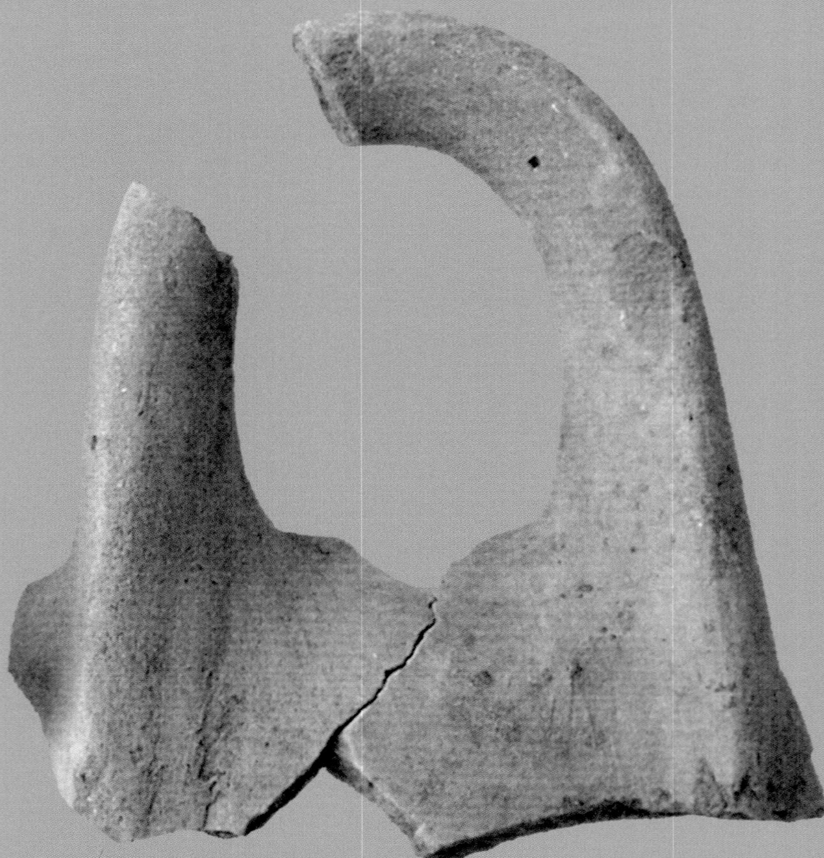

Cypriot Basket-handle Amphorae in Hellenistic Cyrenaica

BY KRISTIAN GÖRANSSON

Basket-handle or loop-handle amphorae appear to have evolved in Cyprus in the 7th century BC. The amphorae are characterised by their big handles arching high over the rim. In the early stages these amphorae had biconical bodies, but later bodies are more cylindrical and show longer toes.[1] Their heights vary from about 45 to 85 cm. The rim is vertical or rolled and the handles, which often are rounded in section, are arched above the rim. These amphorae are considerably larger than typical Greek transport amphorae, and they could contain some 65 to 80 litres. A filled amphora may have weighed around 100 kg. As a result, they must have been carried by two men with the help of a pole stuck through the handles, as is shown on a 6th century Cypro-Phoenician bronze bowl.[2] Basket-handle amphorae were common in the Eastern Mediterranean from the 7th century until well into the 4th century BC.

In 1960 Einar Gjerstad published a study of Cypriot pottery including basket-handle amphorae in which he traced the origin of these vessels to earlier Cypriot amphorae.[3] More recent scientific analyses support Gjerstad's belief. For example, neutron activation analysis of basket-handle amphorae found at Tell Keisan in Israel points to an origin in eastern Cyprus.[4] Gjerstad was not certain that all basket-handle amphorae were produced in Cyprus. He noted that although the majority of them were found in Cyprus, they were also known in Rhodes, Egypt and the Levant. He suggested that in the Levant there were probably non-Cypriot, local workshops producing such amphorae.[5] Still, the earliest types of basket-handle amphorae were exclusively made in Cyprus. Only in the Persian and Hellenistic periods were other centres of production established.[6]

Kristina Winther Jacobsen, in 2002, presented a distribution map of basket-handle amphorae.[7] Now, it is clear that several other sites can be added to the map, but Basket-handle amphorae are still predominantly found in Cyprus and in an area of the Eastern Mediterranean ranging from Rhodes and South Western Turkey, along the Syro-Palestinian coast and inland sites in Israel to the Nile Delta of Egypt. Thus the westernmost finds of basket-handle amphorae known so far are the finds from Egypt (for example Naukratis and Memphis) and Rhodes (Kameiros and Ialysos).

However, the 2004 and 2005 excavations of the Greek city of Euesperides (modern Benghazi) in Cyrenaica, Libya yielded an almost complete basket-handle amphora (Figs. 1 and 2).[8] The amphora was broken into numerous pieces and found in domestic contexts belonging to the ante-penultimate phase of the site, which can be dated to the first half of the 3rd century BC. The amphora has a small rolled rim and thick handles that arch above the rim. The excavations also yielded a lower handle terminus of another, similar basket-handle amphora (Fig. 3). These two vessels are, to the author's knowledge, the only examples of basket-handle amphorae found in Cyrenaica and probably the only ones known from any site west of Egypt or Rhodes. Morphologically, the closest parallels are perhaps two amphorae found in the excavations at Tell Sukas in Syria dating to the 5th or 4th century BC.[9] Another close parallel, of unknown – though clearly underwater – provenance is displayed in the Museum of Underwater Archaeology at Bodrum, Turkey. This complete basket-handle amphora is 86.5 cm high with a rim-diameter of 10.4 cm.[10] The Selfike Museum in Turkey holds another one of identical form in its collections. It is reported to come from the necropolis of Seleucia ad Calycadnum in Cilicia and is probably datable to the early 3rd century, i.e., shortly after the foundation of Seleucia by Seleucus I Nicator.

1 See Jacobsen 2002, fig. 2 for an overview of the morphology, and the more recent discussions by Leidwanger 2005-2006 [2007] and Wolff 2009 and 2011.
2 Markoe 1985, 57, 174-175.
3 Gjerstad 1960, 120, see also fig. 15.
4 Gunneweg & Perlman 1991.
5 Gjerstad 1946, 9 note 2.
6 Leidwanger 2005-2006 [2007], Wolff 2009; 2011.
7 Jacobsen 2002 fig. 3.
8 Göransson 2007, 170-173. For more information on the Euesperides excavations see also the preliminary reports published annually in *Libyan Studies* since 1999.
9 Buhl 1983 figs. VI, 65 and VI, 67.
10 Alpözen *et al.* 1995, 71. Inv. no. 4.1.95.

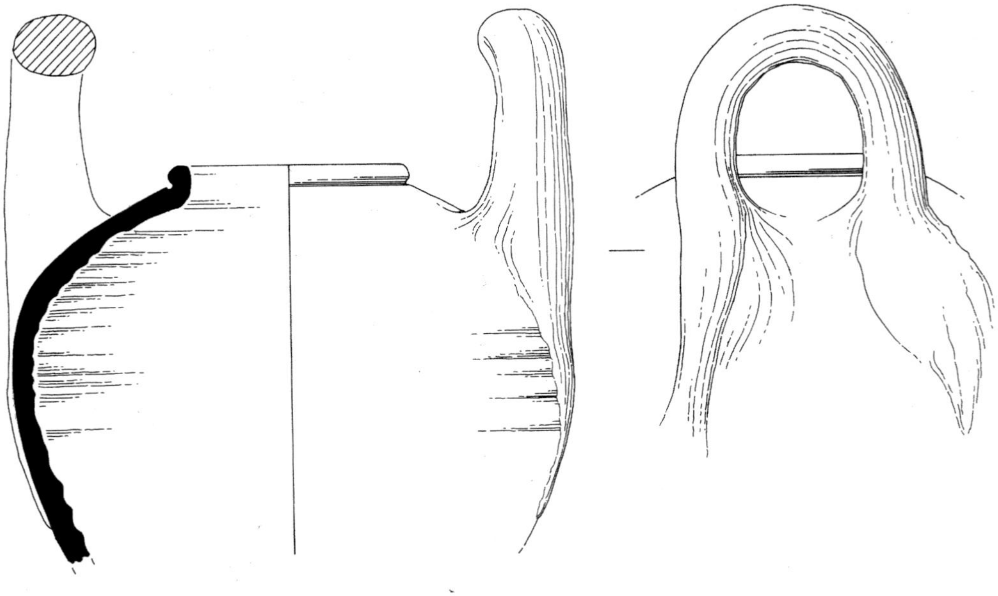

Fig. 1. Cypriot basket-handle amphora from Euesperides (Inv. No CP3000). Drawn by D.H. Hopkins.

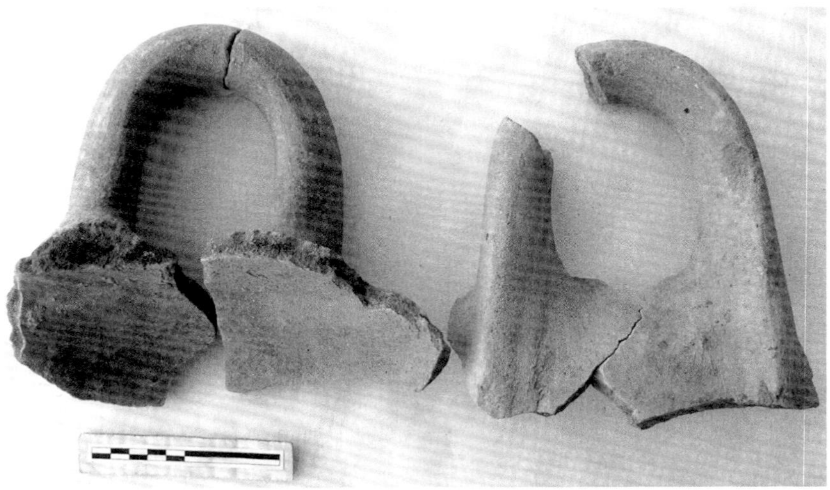

Fig. 2. Cypriot basket-handle amphora from Euesperides (Inv. No CP3000). Photo: K. Göransson.

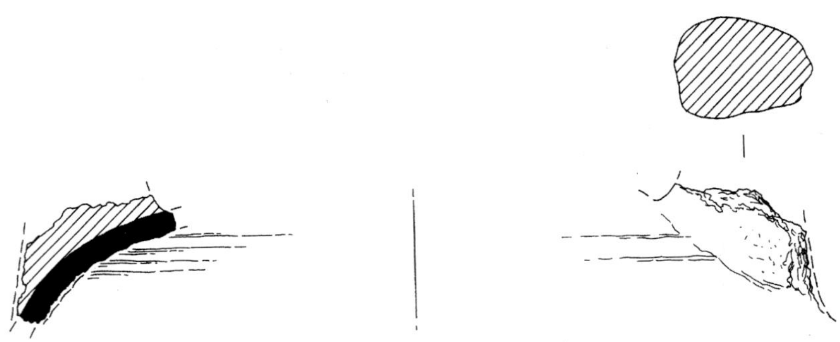

Fig. 3. Cypriot basket-handle amphora from Euesperides (Inv. No. CP4070). Drawn by D.H. Hopkins.

Due to the scarcity of basket-handle amphorae at Euesperides and the absence of evidence from other sites this far west it is difficult to assess the importance of these finds. It does, however, seem likely that the two amphorae at Euesperides reached the city via the shipping route along the coast from Egypt. With the exception of some decades of independence in the first half of the 3rd century (under Magas), Cyrenaica had been part of the Ptolemaic Kingdom since 322 BC.[11] Contacts with Egypt are thus likely to have been frequent until the revolt of Magas in 282 BC. Shortly after the reconciliation between Magas and Ptolemy II in 261 BC, Euesperides was abandoned and the city's inhabitants transferred to the newly founded city of Berenice a few kilometres away. Thus, any recovery of trade between Ptolemaic Egypt and Cyrenaica is likely to have passed Euesperides by. It is hoped that future investigations of other Cyrenaican cities will shed light on the extent of trade between Ptolemaic Egypt and Cyrenaica in the late 4th and early 3rd century BC.

FABRIC DESCRIPTION[13]

Colour	Reddish yellow to pink (7.5YR 8/4-6).
Hardness	Moderately hard, surfaces may be friable.
Fracture	Irregular, powdery.
Texture	Friable, otherwise fairly compact, fine-grained matrices.
Inclusions	Frequent to abundant, well-sorted, well-rounded rock and shell fragments showing varying degrees of weathering – probably beach sand temper – <2.0 mm in size. Quartzite fragments, well-rounded, probably part of the sand component, most are <0.5 mm in size. Rare biotite. Rare angular to sub-rounded quartz grains.
Voids	Most associated with inclusions, otherwise fine lenticular voids, c.<3.0 mm in length.
Surfaces	Surface slip of similar clay with fewer and smaller inclusions.

CATALOGUE

1. Euesperides Inv. No. CP3000

H. 30.0; D. 12.0. Rim, both handles and large part of body of Basket-handle amphora.
Date of context: First half of the 3rd century BC.
This amphora can be attributed to Humbert's type J, which has a rolled rim, no neck and handles that sometimes lean slightly towards the centre of the vessel.[12] The date suggested by Humbert (based on finds in the Levant) is the 5th century or earlier, but this would seem much too high for the contexts where the sherds were found, so it is likely that the amphora is residual.

2. Euesperides Inv. No. CP4070

L. 6.5. Lower handle terminus of Basket-handle amphora.
Date of context: 3rd century BC.

11 See Göransson 2007, 28-29 with further references for an overview of the political history of Cyrenaica in the Hellenistic period.

12 Humbert 1991, 587-588 fig. 10 and parallels on p. 587.

13 I am most grateful to Dr Keith Swift of the University of Oxford who made this fabric description.

Two Amphorae from the Swedish Cyprus Expedition in the National Museum of Denmark: Late Archaic through Late Classical Cypriot Trade

BY MARK L. LAWALL

Two Amphorae from the Swedish Cyprus Expedition in the National Museum of Denmark: Late Archaic through Late Classical Cypriot Trade

BY MARK L. LAWALL

Studies of Cypriot trade have tended to focus on the Bronze and Iron Ages and then, later, on the mid to late Roman period. While there have been scattered publications of amphorae from the Archaic and Classical periods and many publications of Hellenistic stamped amphora handles,[1] there has been little effort to define the broader patterns of commerce as has been attempted in earlier and late periods.[2] There have been efforts to consider Cypriot trade and other forms of Aegean contact in the Archaic and Classical period with a focus on either textual sources or fine ware imports,[3] but amphorae have never played a substantial role in these studies. In large part, this shortcoming is understandable in light of the unevenness of publication and the difficulties of access to sites in northern Cyprus. At this point, however, it seems productive to bring together the disparate evidence for the Archaic and Classical periods and to begin identifying emerging patterns in the current state of the evidence.

This paper begins with a reconsideration of two amphorae from Tomb 80 from the Swedish excavation of the Evrethades necropolis at Marion.[4] Marion Tomb 80 included at least two, chronologically distinct, groups of grave goods. The earlier assemblage included a late Archaic amphora likely from Caria (Fig. 1).[5] This earlier group also included a local basket-handled amphora already published by Kristina Winther Jacobsen; this class of amphora is not discussed in this paper's consideration of Aegean imports and local imitations but is covered by other papers in this volume.[6] The second nearly complete jar in the tomb group likely dates to the mid to third quarter of the 4th century (Fig. 2).[7] In this case, however, the amphora does not appear to be an import. Instead the jar appears to be a local Cypriot type emulating jars from the north Aegean.

With these two examples as the basis, the paper then surveys the current state of broader trends in amphora distributions in and around Cyprus for the late Archaic and Classical periods. This survey depends almost entirely on published material – a dataset that only allows for the most preliminary impressions. Even so, the regional distinctions that I shall draw within Cyprus and the changing situation of Cyprus in the broader world of Mediterranean commerce bring to mind very similar suggestions that others have built on very different sets of data.[8] In this sense, the hypotheses I shall be developing seem more promising than might otherwise be the case when one starts with only two objects and is dependent on the narrow record of published information (as I know well from two decades of research in the storerooms of the Aegean and Pontic worlds). It must be emphasized, however, that the published record for any region's amphora trade often misses the most interesting elements of distribution patterns, and the same is undoubtedly true of Cyprus.[9] So I shall close with some simple goals for future research that could confirm or reject the offered hypotheses. In other words, the apparent conclusions in this paper as to patterns of Cypriot trade are only to be taken as preliminary hypotheses, possibilities, based on an admittedly small set of data, which can only become conclusions once more data are brought to bear.

RECONSIDERING TWO AMPHORAE FROM TOMB 80, MARION

The Late Archaic Amphora[10]

The earlier of the two complete amphorae from Tomb 80 is missing only chips from the rim and spalled flakes from the body (Fig. 1). The rim has an everted, airfoil profile with a wide relief band just below the rim. A ridge and a groove mark the base of the neck. The single-shaft handles attach smoothly to the shoulders – there is no thumb impression as one sometimes finds at the base of a handle. There is a pre-firing mark incised on the shoulder, in the form of an upright loop. The wide ring toe has a bevelled lower edge; and the broad curve of the bottom of the vessel is visible within this ring base. The fabric is streaky brown and grey, smooth with much mica both silver and gold, some of it showing coarser grains. The fabric itself shows readily visible opaque, sometimes large, blackish chunks, and readily visible yellowish lime bits, along with rare small grayish glassy bits.[11]

Fig. 1. Collection of Classical and Near Eastern Antiquities, The National Museum of Denmark, i.n. 9707 (scale 1:5).

Fig. 2. Collection of Classical and Near Eastern Antiquities, The National Museum of Denmark, i.n. 9714 (scale 1:5).

1 Archaic and Classical amphorae mostly appear in publications of tomb assemblages, see *SCE* II for publication of the groups tomb by tomb; *SCE* IV.2 for brief (and now largely outdated) discussion of the amphora types. For studies of stamped handles from Cypriot sites, see, e.g., Hall 1885; Sztetyłło 1976; Nicolaou & Empereur 1986; Nicolaou 2005 (with references to her numerous reports 'Inscriptiones Cypriae Alphabeticae' in *RDAC* which often include stamped amphora handles); Meyza 2004; Calvet 1972; 1978; 1980; 1982; 1993; Barker 2004; and this volume; Çankardeş-Şenol & Şenol, this volume; Finkielsztejn this volume.

2 Exceptionally, see Lund 2006 and graphs and comments by period in Jacobsen 2006, 304-305; on Hellenistic trade and Cyprus, see Mehl 1995; Elaigne 2004; Yon 2007; Michaelides 1996.

3 Pouilloux 1975; 1976a; 1976b; 1989; Raptou 1999; Maier 1985; amphorae do figure somewhat more in Collombier 1987 (245-246) and Reyes 1994.

4 *SCE* II, 366-454, with Tomb 80 only briefly presented pp. 414-417, with fig. 178, 8-11.

5 *SCE* II, 416 no. 17 pl. 79.2 middle row.

6 *SCE* II, 416 no. 1; Jacobsen 2002, 169-170.

7 *SCE* II, 416 no. 5 pl. 79.2 lower row.

8 E.g., Bekker-Nielsen 2004 on road networks in different regions of Cyprus; Balandier 2000 and 2002 addressing the Cypriot topography in terms of defensive networks; but most importantly Lund 2006 on the basis of various classes of pottery, including but admirably not limited to amphorae, in the Hellenistic and early Roman periods; see also Dobosz this volume.

9 Stella Demesticha and Anthi Kaldeli emphasized this point in the discussion following this paper's delivery in Athens.

10 See *supra* note 5. *SCE* IV.2, appendix V, nr. 33 for the pre-firing mark on the shoulder. The jar is listed in Nys & Åström 2004, 10.

11 Height 55.3, Rim diameter 13.6, Toe diameter 7.6; Munsell value for the fabric 10YR 6/6.

The overall form is generally familiar thanks to early studies by Iraida Zeest, Iozef Brašinskij, and Virginia Grace of Samian amphorae in the 1960s and 1970s.[12] Starting in the early 1980s Pierre Dupont distinguished an often thicker-rimmed Samian type from the thinner echinoid-rimmed Milesian type.[13] Milesian and now Ephesian regional production have been largely supported;[14] the Samian identification has been consistently difficult to prove with so much certainty.[15] Further studies of the distribution of shapes across the region and coordinating variation in form with visible variation in fabric permit the suggestion that production in northern Ionia used a thick rounded rim, often with a continuous curve from the neck to the shoulder, and an elaborately modelled ring base;[16] production on and near Samos involved a thick rounded rim but now with a cuff at the base of the neck and simpler ring toe;[17] and southern Ionian areas preferred the echinoid or everted airfoil rim, also with some form of articulation at the base of the neck, and sometimes a fairly elaborate toe.[18]

The pre-firing inscription on the shoulder at first glance could complicate this argued southeastern Aegean provenance. The letter-form is not common at all in the Aegean, but is attested as a Cyprosyllabic Rho and was identified as such in the initial publication.[19] If this reading is correct, the jar must have been produced on Cyprus. The fabric, however, does not encourage this conclusion. Fabric, shape and the letter-form, however, would all fit well with a Carian provenance. The letter appears in multiple examples as the Carian letter transliterated as T.[20] Such pre-firing letters on amphorae from this region (especially those attributed to Samos) have been gathered by Alan Johnston,[21] so such a practice is well-established in southern Asia Minor in the Archaic period.

Two other tombs from Marion, tombs 84 and 71, contain similar amphorae. The example from Tomb 84, with its wider ring base and more outswung handles may be the earliest of the three. The tomb 71 example, with a more egg-shaped body and upright handle stance (also seen in the Tomb 80 example) may be roughly contemporary with Tomb 80 though of a different production centre. The published chronology for all three tombs is late Cypro-Archaic II, but some refinement to this date can be derived from comparanda at Aegean, Levantine and Pontic sites.

A late 6th-century date for the Marion tomb 80 jar may be concluded from the general trajectories of development in this southeastern Aegean class. The cylindrical neck with relatively heavier handles set in the upper half of the neck and attaching with a fairly upright profile at the shoulder are all characteristics that are developed well beyond the late 8th- through 7th-century examples from Methone, Meẓad Ḥashavyahu and Ashkelon, and the thin, widely arched handles seen in the Pabuç Burnu shipwreck of the first half of the 6th century.[22] Early sites of Greek trade and settlement in the Pontic region begin to get closer to the form of the Tomb 80 jar. Berezan Well 5, from the mid 6th century BC, includes Ionian jars with more deeply hollowed toe and handles still thin and outswung.[23] Profiles more closely resembling that seen with the Marion amphora are published from Berezan period I, dated to the mid to third quarter of the 6th-century.[24] The Tomb 80 jar closely resembles the profile of a Milesian amphora that Bîrzescu places as latest in the 6th century sequence from Histria.[25] Likewise, jars published from independently datable late 6th- or earliest 5th-century contexts at Aegina, the Athenian Agora, Miletos, and Klazomenai provide close parallels for the Marion jar.[26]

The Late Classical 'Aegeanizing' Amphora[27]

The second nearly complete amphora from Tomb 80 preserves half of the rim, both handles and a large part of neck; shoulder, body and toe are complete. (Fig. 2) The outflaring sharp rim has a groove separating the rim from the neck. The handles are fairly round in section with thumbprints at their lower attachments. The conical body ends with small, short stem toe, whose profile has a thickly rounded outer edge and concave to convex profile around a shallow hollow in the base. The fairly pale, heavily slipped surface shows very slight traces of mica. The core shows a dense packing of readily visible medium sized blackish and red brown rounded bits.[29]

The general form is readily identifiable with the north Aegean of the latter half of the 5th century and much of the 4th. The best known Aegean form is that of the often-stamped amphorae of Thasos, but Mende, Akanthos, Samothrace, and Ainos, as well as likely other sites as yet unidentified produced jars sharing the sharp wedge-like rim, conical body and stem toe emulated by these Cypriot jars.[30] Mende, with its frequent use of a narrow stripe painted around the lower part of the body or less often around the base of the neck, is the most likely prototype for many Cypriot jars of the sort seen in Tomb 80 (though that one lacks the painted band).[31]

And yet, despite these similarities, especially in the idiosyncratic decoration seen in the Mendean amphorae, the Cypriot versions differ from the Aegean models. The profile of the toe is much more smoothly rounded in its contours; the upper part of the Cypriot necks are often marked by a series of parallel, horizontal grooves – generally more so than appear on the Aegean versions; and the rim is less distinctly articulated than is the case for the Aegean prototypes.

The precise date of the introduction of this 'northern Aegean' Cypriot type is not known, but it can be narrowed down. A tomb group from Tremithousa near Paphos provides an early example of such Cypriot imitations.[32] Five of the six amphorae published from this tomb group appear to be imported northern Aegean amphorae. These are all datable to the third quarter of the 5th century with reference to examples from datable deposits in the Aegean. The sixth jar in the group, a fairly rotund jar, in the lower right corner of the published group photograph, shows an unusual thickened ridge under the rim and a thick-edged flaring toe. Such treatment of the rim and toe contrasts with northern amphorae as is clear from a comparison with roughly contemporary, late 5th century jars found on Thasos.[33] A very similar jar is published from Vouni, tomb 6, though unfortunately this tomb group does not contain other narrowly datable amphorae. An unpublished tomb group from Marion studied by Virginia Grace included a similarly early Cypriot version of the northern Greek form along with Chian amphorae representing two nearly contemporary types datable to the third quarter of the 5th century.[34] A very similar form of amphora, in clearly Cypriot fabric was found in well deposit R13:4 in the Athenian Agora, also datable to the third quarter of the 5th century.[35] Assuming that the Cypriot imitations with

12 Зеест 1960, type 3; Брашинский 1967; Grace 1971.
13 Dupont 1982; and this distinction has been explored in more detail in Dupont 1998, 164-186; 1999; 2000, 57-62; 2007. Other typological overviews of this class are provided by Абрамов 1993; Монахов 2003, 25-42; Sezgin 2009.
14 Kerschner & Mommsen 2005 on Ephesian production; alongside Dupont's research (see previous note), fabric studies have also been carried out by Seifert 2000 and 2004; Johnston & Domingo 1997, esp. 64-65; Domingo & Johnston 2003, 34-35.
15 Whitbread 1995, 122-133; Johnston & Domingo 1997, 62-68.
16 The form is often found at Klazomenai, see Ersoy 1993; 2004; Sezgin 2009, 325-348; Carlson 2004; Carlson & Lawall 2007; and Dupont 2010.
17 For Samos and the vicinity, see Dupont 1998; Grace 1971; Docter 2000 fig. 8; Sezgin 2009, 287-310.
18 For the area of Miletos, see similar forms published from Didyma, see Schattner 1998; for Miletos itself Voigtländer 1982; Bîrzescu 2009; Sezgin 2009, 227-286.
19 SCE II, Appendix V no. 33.
20 See Adiego Lajara 2007, 82-83 nos. E.Ab 6 and E.Ab 7, 86 no. E.Ab 18 and 87 no. E.Ab19. I thank Alan Johnston for advice on pursuing possible Carian letter forms.
21 Johnston 2006, 26-27 and Table 2; further examples are gathered by Μπέσιος *et al.* 2012; Waldbaum 2011 nos. 535 and 536.
22 Methone: Μπέσιος *et al.* 2012 nos. 16 and 18; Meẓad Ḥashavyahu: Naveh 1962; Ashkelon: Waldbaum 2011 nos. 496, 504, and 533; Pabuç Burnu: Greene *et al.* 2008.
23 Монахов 1999 fig. 4.1.
24 Чистов 2012, 20 pl. 1.
25 Bîrzescu 2012, 142 no. 1274 fig. 42 pl. 60.
26 Aegina: Johnston 1990 no. 107; Athenian Agora: Roberts 1986 nos. 412 and 413 for the general form of the body, toe and handle stance though different in the rim and treatment of the base of the neck; Lawall 1995, 184 (type S/3); Miletos: Voigtländer 1982 fig. 28 nos. 172-174, 181; Klazomenai: Ersoy 1993 pls. 195, 232, 237.
27 *SCE* II, 416 pl. 79.2 lower row.
28 Height 57.2 cm. Rim diameter 11.7 cm. Toe diameter 5.7 cm.
29 Munsell colour of surface ranges between 10YR7/6 and 7.5YR7/6.
30 Studies of northern Aegean production in the Classical period, see Lawall 1995 and 1997; more recently see Αναγνωστοπούλου-Χατζηπολυχρόνη 2004 and Garlan 2004 on production at Mende; Τρακοσοπούλου-Σαλακίδου 2004 on Akanthos; Καραδήμα-Μάτσας 1994 on Samothrace; Karadema 2004 on Ainos; and Lawall 2002[2003] on material from the Troad. In addition, Garlan 1999 (on Thasos); 1997 (Ouranopolis) and 2006 (on Akanthos); for Torone amphorae, see Paspalas 1990 and Peirce 2001.
31 For Mendean amphorae with such painted decoration, see most clearly in the illustrations for Papadopoulos & Paspalas 1999 figs. 2-4; examples found at Torone (Paspalas 1990 fig. 8; Peirce 2001 fig. 102 with incised line around the lower body) may represent local production so the painting may not be limited to Mende. Cypriot examples with similar linear decoration, sometimes the Cypriot versions use an incised line instead of a painted line, but the decorative result is the same, see for examples *SCE* II Tomb 15 pl. 40.6; Tomb 43 pl. 54; Tomb 72 pl. 76.
32 Raptou 2001.
33 Grandjean 1992; and for other late 5th-century, northern Aegean jars of similar date, see Lawall 1995, Chapter 6; Монахов 1999, Chapter 3.
34 From the Virginia Grace archives in the American School of Classical Studies: A manuscript on this tomb group is dated October 24 1955; a follow-up note of April 2 1975 indicates that the manuscript was never published. The Chian types in this tomb include both the highest bulging neck type (similar to SCE II Vouni Tomb 3 pl. 101) and the earliest of the straight neck types (on this sequence of Chian amphorae, see Lawall 1998).
35 P11388 (Unpublished), I thank Paul Reynolds for first suggesting to me the possibility that this amphora was Cypriot.

their fairly rounded body and short, flaring stem toe, are somewhat later than the North Aegean prototypes, the Cypriot sequence should start no earlier than the third quarter of the 5th century.

The most extensive, published, sequence of amphorae of this 'northern Aegean' Cypriot class is found in the Marion and Vouni tombs. Any effort to place the published examples in chronological order, however, is hampered by the multiple periods of use of many of the tombs. For example, Tomb 67 at Marion includes a possible imitation of a Chian amphora, whose shape places it near or before 450 BC along with two examples of stem toe jars, also Cypriot, of more conical forms than those seen in the earliest stages of the 'north Aegean' style amphorae.[36] Here, then, there could be a half-century spread or longer between the various amphorae present. Marion Tomb 34, on the other hand, provides a seemingly much narrower range of dates in the amphorae and provides a very useful later stage in the development of the 'north Aegean' style amphorae. The tomb includes two imported Mendean or Mendean-related amphorae, both of which are well-paralleled in Pontic tumuli of ca. 360-330 BC.[37] The Tomb 34 Cypriot jar has a fairly baggy lower section of the body; a very plain, but tall, rim; and an elaborately articulated toe. Marion tomb 55 also includes a late 4th century northern Aegean imported jar,[38] perhaps datable closer to 320 BC given its very narrow form. The Cypriot amphorae in this group show a range of body forms from conical to more rounded as in Tomb 34. From these two cases, Cypriot jars with a baggier form in the lower half of the body appear later than those with a tauter, conical form. A tentative sequence based on amphora form can be proposed between the earliest and this later datable point:

1. Short neck, rotund body, short stem toe: late 5th century BC – Vouni tomb 6, Vouni tomb 15, Tremithousa material.

2. Taller neck, low rim, conical lower half of body, plainer version of modeled stem toe: end of 5th through mid 4th century BC – (in possible chronological order) – Marion tombs 18, 67 (top row farthest to the left), 57, 43, 58 (top row, two jars on the right side).

3. Higher rim, more elaborated toe, still fairly conical lower body: mid 4th century BC – Marion tombs 80, 45, 40, with the following three as leading into the next stage: Marion tombs 15, 91, 44, 72.

4. High rim, baggy lower body, sharply articulated base of toe: second half 4th century – Marion tombs 31, 34.

PRELIMINARY COMMENTS ON AEGEAN AND 'AEGEANIZING' AMPHORAE IN CYPRUS, CA. 500-300 BC

These two amphorae from different periods of use of Tomb 80 exemplify two aspects of the amphora record of Cyprus: amphorae imported from the Aegean and locally produced amphorae emulating those imports. A third aspect of the Cypriot amphora record points eastward: the amphorae in the Levantine tradition, again whether imported or locally produced. Zoroğlou, Göransson, Çankardeş-Şenol and Şenol, and Greene, Leidwanger and Özdaş discuss jars in this Levantine tradition in this volume and they are gaining attention elsewhere, too.[39] The discussion here, therefore, will focus on Aegean and 'Aegeanizing' amphorae and the trends they might indicate in the economy of late Archaic and Classical Cyprus.

The late 6th century BC

The earlier of the two amphorae discussed here typifies the nature of Aegean imports in the tomb groups from Marion datable to the second half of the 6th century: they show very little diversity and nearly all of those that can be recognized in the published photographs came from the southeastern Aegean region.[40]

A few published, Late Archaic Aegeanizing amphorae from the inland region of Nicosia, from Deneia and Ayioi Omologites, raise a tantalizing possibility – if in fact they are not imports – that inland Cypriot producers in the late 6th century were already producing amphorae on the most readily available model: amphorae of the southern Aegean. Details of the toes and rims are quite different but the basic idea recalls the Ionian imports seen at Marion.[41] Further south, quite near Kition but inland, Panayia Ematousa also shows primarily Ionian and, rare, Chian imports in its Archaic phases.[42]

Publications from sites on the southern and eastern coasts of Cyprus show more diversity in the range of imports. At Kition to the south, late 6th-century imports include Chian, Attic, rare Corinthian Type A, rare Klazomenian, possible northern Aegean, and an apparent dominance of various southern Aegean forms, some of which Alan Johnston was hesitant to attribute directly to the Aegean producers themselves on account of oddities in form.[43] At Salamis on the east coast, from the tombs and their vicinity there is great diversity of types: Attic (though the published examples are mostly of the late 7th-century SOS type), white-slipped Chian, mid to late 6th-century Lesbian, possibly 6th-century Corinthian (Type A), and late 6th-century Klazomenian, in addition to a few Ionian examples.[44] The published pieces from the Archaic settlement show a much higher proportion of Ionian types.[45] At both of these sites, this range of imported amphora types appears in both burial groups and from settlement excavations.

From these two contrasting patterns, at Marion and vicinity on the one hand and Salamis and Kition on the other, two variables emerge as potentially significant. First, the two regions differ in terms of the diversity of imported types. While the northwestern part of the island seems to be drawing on only a narrow range of Aegean amphora-borne products, and while the inland regions accessible from the northwest then chose those forms for emulation; by contrast, the eastern and southern parts of the island drew on a wider range of sources. Obviously, as more material is studied from the northwestern part of the island, greater diversity may begin to emerge.

Even so, the currently available data raise two hypotheses. First, the consistency of southeastern Aegean sources for the Marion-area jars, their presence in elite tombs, and their emulation in local, inland production (if that is indeed the situation nearer Nicosia) are all features that might be expected in a situation of deliberately organized shipping between elite households. Second, northwestern Cyprus may have had such close and frequent contact with the southeastern corner of the Aegean that the imports from this region and the local Cypriot versions should all be considered part of one large regional zone of circulation and amphora style. These are neither mutually exclusive nor necessarily connected hypotheses, so they should be considered in turn.

As for aristocratic links, with the admittedly scanty record limited to tomb material it is not possible to assert an *exclusive* aristocratic control of these imported goods. Even so, the limited range of types found in these tombs (to keep the argument based on positive evidence) indicates the sort of selectivity and deliberate arrangement that might be expected in a closely managed economy. The appearance of locally produced jars of similar form at sites inland from the northwest coast indicates the presence of some degree of overland movement to allow for those sites to be familiar with the imports now published from the coast. In other words, the published, inland emulations are taken here as proxy evidence for unpublished (perhaps undiscovered) imported prototypes. Such overland movement is often considered to have been of minimal scale (e.g., Bekker-Nielsen, this volume), but the points of similarity noted here between the northwestern sites and the area of Nicosia would bear further exploration.

The second hypothesis, that the southeastern Aegean and western Cyprus simply represent a broad region of shared amphora styles and 'localized' circulation of goods, could hold true even if the current pattern suggesting aristocratic links proves false. If the tomb finds and their apparent selectivity are eventually shown to be simply the most archaeologically visible aspect of a broad distribution of southeastern Aegean jars and their locally produced counterparts, then the general dominance of that form echoes the amphora record in the southeastern corner of the Aegean (southern Ionia into Caria). Sea travel between western Cyprus, the southern tip of Lycia, and Pamphylia

---

36 Virginia Grace's notes from December 18 1951 indicate that all three jars from tomb 67 are imitations.
37 *SCE* II pl. 48; and see Монахов 1999 pls. 160, 161, 167, 168, 176, 179, 180, 181.
38 *SCE* II Tomb 55.30 pl. 62.
39 E.g., Marangou & Marchand 2009; Leidwanger 2005-2006 (2007); Jacobsen 2002.
40 For other such late Archaic southeastern Aegean imports from the Marion necropolis, see *SCE* II Tombs 71, 83, 84, and 94.
41 Deneia, see Γεωργίου 2005 nos. 27, 28, 31 pls. 3-4; Ayioi Omologites tombs include a tall, bobbin shaped Chian amphora (Tomb 34 no. 1) and a local(?) jar with a heavy rounded rim (Tomb 29 no. 9 pl. 45, in Hadjicosti 1993).
42 Jacobsen 2006, A18 and A19.
43 Johnston 1981. At Kition, too, there are 5th-century stamped fragments from a similar range of sources (a Chian sphinx stamp and a southern Ionian/Carian region stamp with the monogram AΦY, noted in the Virginia Grace archives, but not published so far as I know).
44 Karageorghis 1970, Tombs 52, 84.13 and 16 (both Attic), 33.22 (Clazomenian), 6.10, 10.15 and 10.27 (Attic), 29.3 (Lesbos region), pl. 198.55 (Attic?), pl. 202.266 (Corinthian type A); Karageorghis 1967, Tomb 19.5 (Milesian).
45 Calvet & Yon 1977 pls. 10-12.

(generally in a counter clockwise direction) is well attested in later sources. The Lycian end of the route is then linked in to travel northwestwards to Rhodes and into the Aegean. The gap in the amphora evidence for such a stylistic and commercial zone is the Lycian and Pamphylian coasts in the Archaic period. Admittedly, this would seem to be a very wide 'local zone' but the dominance of one general amphora form would be read in this fashion quite readily for the Aegean basin itself.

That this 'southeastern Aegean-western Cyprus zone' – whether a function of ease and frequency of travel or more complex aristocratic ties – was limited to western Cyprus is indicated by the much more diverse imports noted at Kition and Salamis. The amphora records at Kition and Salamis appear to have resulted from different shippers working a different zone of circulation.

Some indication of the parameters of this other zone of circulation may be seen in a comparison with amphora finds elsewhere in the Levant. The wider diversity of imported types at Salamis and Kition shares much with the general pattern of imports seen along the Levantine coast in the late 6th and earliest decades of the 5th century. For example, at Tel Megadim on the Carmel coast, as Sam Wolff reported at a recent conference of the American Schools of Oriental Research, the most common late Archaic types found are Chian, Milesian area, and Klazomenian, but there are also northern Ionian, northern Aegean, Corinthian A, and even Adriatic-Ionian sea (Corinthian Type B) amphorae.[46] Other sites provide a lesser range in published material, but the especially photogenic Chian late Archaic amphorae and at times some other Ionian amphorae are known from Tel Qiri, Yoqne'am, Tel Michal, Tel Keisan, Tel Dor, Ashkelon, Tel Ashdod and elsewhere.[47] Sites in Egypt, particularly in the Delta region, but also much further south, present a similar mix of southern and northern Ionian types.[48]

The material in Egypt could have been supplied by direct southeasterly routes from the Aegean.[49] Some of this material could have moved northwards along the Levantine coast as those ships worked their way back to the Aegean, cabotage fashion, using prevailing currents and coastal winds in the region.[50] The seemingly significant imports along the south coast of Cyprus and the southern Levantine coasts (from Ashkelon and northwards) are easiest to imagine using a well-attested routes direct from Rhodes to the region of Kourion and from southern Cypriot sites southeastwards to the Levant. Such routes follow the prevailing summer winds and are not attested in the opposite direction.[51] The attested line from Rhodes towards the Kourion area – and not to the Marion area[52] – would allow for the two separate zones of shipping seemingly indicated by the amphora records.

Late Classical Cypriot Imports: Marion, the rest of Cyprus and the Levant

Moving to the Classical evidence for Cypriot production and imports, the earlier division between northwest and southeast is far less noticeable.

The dominance of north Aegean style local amphorae seen at Marion is also seen at Ktima near Paphos and at Salamis on the opposite end of the island.[53] Two examples are published from the Kaloriziki necropolis.[54] At Salamis, it seems from the published material, the amphorae from the Classical tombs are more often actual imports from the north Aegean while the amphorae from the settlement areas are more likely local imitations. In the interior, near Nicosia, the earlier amphorae loosely imitating Ionian amphorae continue to appear.[55] At Kition, some northern Aegean forms, even seemingly true imports, appear; however, there are also various 4th-century southeastern Aegean imports, and a somewhat different form of local production with a narrow folded down rim.[56] There are Aegean forms with similar rims, but without knowing – at least I do not know – the appearance of the body and toe for the Kitian jars, it is not easy to identify a specific Aegean prototype. At any rate, in the 4th century, Kition shows an exceptional diversity of Aegean imports though still including the new, significant appearance of northern Aegean amphorae. The north and western coastal areas as well as Salamis in the east are all dominated by northern imports and Cypriot imitations thereof.

With the Classical period for Cyprus the possibility arises of comparing the land assemblages with those found in nearby shipwrecks. At this point, however, only one wreck is well-documented and datable to the 4th century: the Mazotos wreck.[57] This site, just off the south coast, not far from Kition, included primarily Chian amphorae along with two examples from the southeastern Aegean mushroom rim class, and one northern import, perhaps from Mende. Stella Demesticha dates the cargo to the third quarter of the 4th century, a date supported primarily by the Chian amphorae and one of the mushroom rim forms; however the Mendean jar does appear somewhat earlier (unsurprising for an isolated piece from a wreck). The significance of this wreck in light of the patterns just noted for land sites is the appearance of a mixture of Ionian amphorae as opposed to the northern dominance seen elsewhere on Cyprus. From a methodological standpoint, wreck sites are single samples; land sites represent aggregated patterns over many decades and centuries of use, dispersal, and discard. Even so, such concurrences between the maritime and terrestrial records deserve attention.

A strong northern Aegean presence is seen elsewhere in the Levant. At Tell el-Herr in the western Sinai, there is a mix of northern Aegean, Chian and Samian material in the published finds with the dates starting ca. 440/430 and continuing into the 4th century.[58] Saqqara shows mostly still southern Aegean material – though little has been published.[59] The Balamun survey finds include Chian, north Aegean and southeastern Aegean mushroom rim amphorae.[60] Elephantine, too, has little published from this period, but there is a mix of Chian and northern Aegean fragments despite the great distance of the site from the Mediterranean coast.[61] Chian and northern Aegean fragments are also published from Mendes.[62] From modern Israel, Apollonia-Arsuf shows late 5th-4th century northern Aegean amphorae alongside both rounded rim and mushroom rim amphorae of the southeastern Aegean. Fragments of the latter class are also published from Gilʿam, Lachish and Shiqmona.[63] Gérald Finkielsztejn has kindly reported numerous examples of northern Aegean imports as well as a few 4th-century Chian fragments found in excavations at Akko.[64] Tel Michal includes some fairly early examples, perhaps even earlier than 450 BC, but also with northern and Chian amphorae. Tel Dor shows an immense range of 5th- and 4th-century Aegean imports (and some historians have used this fact to argue for unusually close ties between Athens and Dor).[65] Further up the Levantine coast and across the Cilician coast the published record is especially scanty. At the workshop in Athens, Levent Zoroğlu reported on some tomb groups from Kelenderis with Cypriot or locally produced Cilician amphorae of the northern Greek form, and this form is also seen at the Karaçalli necropolis near Antalya and at Nagidos.[66] The Anamur museum's amphora collection, numbering roughly 140 pieces, many of which are finds from underwater sites, includes two Chian amphorae

---

46 Wolff pers. comm. Early Archaic material is also well-known from sites in the Sinai and the Nile Delta, e.g., Migdol (Oren 1984); Meẓad Ḥashavyahu (Naveh 1962; Fantalkin 2001).

47 Tel Qiri: two Chian fragments (Ben-Tor & Portugali 1987 nos. 2 and 9 fig. 5) and four Samian area fragments (nos. 1, 3, 6, 8 fig. 5); Lachish: one Chian fragment (Tufnell 1953 no. 508 pl. 96); Yoqne'am: one Chian rim (Ben-Tor et al. 1983 fig. 9.14), Tel Michal (Singer-Avitz 1989 no. 13 fig. 9.1, and no. 7 fig. 9.15; and see Conrad 1989); Tel Dor: Stern (ed.) 1995 no. 27 fig. 2.16 Miletos area no. 10 fig. 2.20 early-mid 5th-century Samos or northern Ionia, nos. 48-49 fig. 2.26a Ionian, no. 1 fig. 3.13 Chian late 6th century BC, and others on the same figure could be from the Samos/Miletos region; Ashkelon: S. Wolff (2002 visit) showed me drawings of Chian, Clazomenian, and possible northern Greek fragments of the late 6th c. (earlier material, with a similarly diverse range of sources but still with an Ionian focus, see Waldbaum 2011); Ashdod: Dothan 1971, Chian; and for the early 5th century two Samian fragments from Atlit tombs 35 and 857 (Johns 1933 pl. 32), and another Samian jar top from Tell Abu Hawan (Hamilton 1934 no. 11 pl. 23).

48 Naukratis: e.g., Petrie 1886 pl. 16 (and for the best illustrations, see www.petriecat.museums.ucl.ac.uk); Johnston 2006 Table 1 provides a handy list of inscribed Archaic amphorae from Egypt; and Gantès 2007 updates the publication of amphora fragments from the more recent excavations by W.D.E. Coulson and A. Leonard; Tell el-Maskhuta: Holladay 1982 pl. 26 with Chian and Clazomenian fragments; Buto: Bourriau & French 2007 fig. 1 (Chian, Klazomenian, Ionian); Cairo: Gascoigne 2007 fig. 1.3 (Klazomenian misidentified as Chian); Elephantine: Aston 2007, 438-441 fig. 14.

49 Arnaud 2005, 213-215.

50 Arnaud 2005, 221-222.

51 Arnaud 2005, 219, 221.

52 Stewart & Martin 2005 fig. 6 suggest a route eastward from the Aegean along the Lycian and Pamphylian coast that then turns south to western Cyprus before turning along the southern coast of Cyprus; cf. Arnaud 2005, 219-221 describing circulation in the Lycian-Pamphylian-Cyprus region as counter-clockwise.

53 Ktima, see Deshayes 1963; Salamis, see Kargeorghis 1973 pls. 168, 169, 199, 287.

54 Benson 1973 K903 and 904 pl. 53.

55 Flourentzos 1986 (Ayioi Omologites).

56 Salles 1993b fig. 233.

57 Demesticha 2009; 2011.

58 Gratien & Soulié 1988 figs. 15-18; Defernez 1997 figs. 6-7; Gratien 1997 figs. 2a and 2b.

59 French & Ghaly 1991 nos. 1-4 and 6 (no. 5 is a Hellenistic Koan toe).

60 Spencer 1996, pl. 79 nos. 12 and 17, pl. 82, nos. 2-5, pl. 83, no. 4.

61 Aston 2007.

62 Hummel & Shubert 1994 (nos. 5-7 fig. 1) and p. 6 mentions Samian imports as well.

63 Gilʿam: Stern 1970 nos. 3-5 pl. 15; Lachish: Tufnell 1953 no. 504 pl. 96; Shiqmona: Elgavish 1968 nos. 147-149 pl. 61 and nos. 31 and 32 pl. 35, though the latter could be a Greco-Italic amphora of the late 4th or early 3rd century.

64 Finkielsztejn pers. comm.

65 Stewart & Martin 2005; Stern ed. 1995 figs. 2.35, 3.13; Stern 1995 fig. 5.12, a southeastern Aegean mushroom rim jar of the very late 4th or even early 3rd century BC (published as 5th century).

of the 4th century, one Thasian jar, one other possibly northern amphora, and five Cypriot or Cilician amphorae in the northern Aegean style.[67]

So the pattern on Cyprus, with the exception so far of Kition and its vicinity (including the Mazotos wreck offshore), is the dominance by imports from the north Aegean, and at roughly the same time the imitation of such jars over much of island. The interior seems to still make a more Ionian form. The late Classical pattern in the Eastern Mediterranean shows a continuing mix of imports from the Aegean moving towards Egypt, some presumably circulating east and northwards around the region, and other Aegean imports coming past Cyprus to the Levantine coast. While this latter circulation zone appears to have run along the south coast of Cyprus at least as far eastward as Salamis in the Archaic period, in the late Classical period it seems more focused on the south-central coast of the island (Kition region). The rest of Cyprus and the Cilician coast now seems quite insulated from this zone and instead has some manner of more intensive connection with shipping from the north Aegean. Related to this increase in northern Aegean jars and their imitations in Cyprus may be the fact that north Aegean jars are also much more common in the southeastern Aegean in the late 5th and 4th centuries than had been the case earlier.[68]

REJECTING THE HYPOTHESES

As indicated throughout this paper, the suggested patterns in the amphora record described here and their tentative explanations never move beyond the state of preliminary hypotheses based on admittedly sparse evidence. Therefore, it seems fitting to close with a consideration of how these hypotheses of patterns might be refuted. Publications of more amphora assemblages beyond grave groups would be most useful. If diagnostic fragments from multiple, late Archaic sites, from defined groups of strata, can be documented even in terms of fairly general quantities of the contributions of the different Aegean exporters, then we would be on much firmer ground in making comparisons across the island. For the late 5th-4th century pattern of strong northern presence, we are on safer ground since the argument depends on more positive evidence – the many northern Aegean amphorae and their many imitations. Further exploration of 4th-century amphora production at Kition and in the interior – both areas where the northern ideas do not seem to have taken hold – would clarify the extent of this late Classical phenomenon.

Thus far, only one time period and region in the eastern Mediterranean (in the pre-Roman period) has been the subject of increasingly detailed publications of amphora assemblages and that is Hellenistic Israel thanks in large part to our colleague Gerald Finkielsztejn. I hope that this very preliminary view of Archaic and Classical Cyprus will encourage those eager to refute this paper to start sorting through boxes and boxes of dusty Archaic and Classical sherds!

66 For Karaçalli, see Çokay-Kepçe 2006, 145; for Nagidos, see Şenol & Aşkin 2007.
67 Nicholas Rauh, pers. comm. Nov. 2007.
68 Lawall 2006.

ACKNOWLEDGEMENTS

I would like to extend my particular thanks to Bodil Bundgaard Rasmussen for inviting me to study the two amphorae now in the National Museum of Denmark that are the focus of this paper. I am also grateful to Gérald Finkielsztejn, Donald Ariel and Sam Wolff for encouraging and facilitating a visit to Israel in 2002 during which time I had the opportunity to see finds from various Israeli sites mentioned here.

Preliminary Remarks on Cypriot Amphorae and Stamps from Alexandria

BY GONCA CANKARDEŞ-ŞENOL & AHMET KAAN ŞENOL

Preliminary remarks on Cypriot Amphorae and Stamps from Alexandria

BY GONCA CANKARDEŞ-ŞENOL & AHMET KAAN ŞENOL

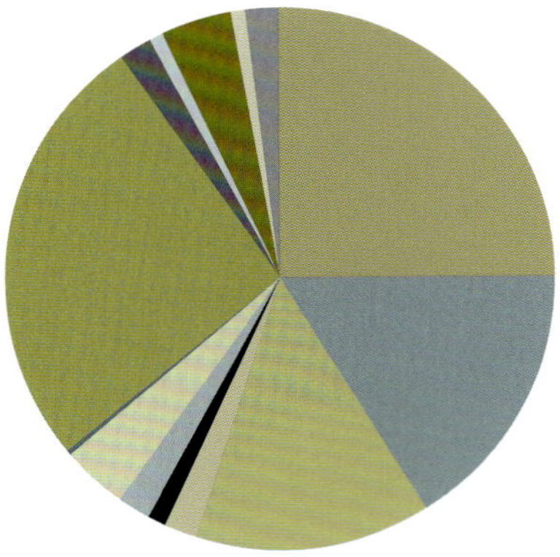

Diagram 1. Dispertion of amphora types found in the rescue excavations in Alexandria dated to the Hellenistic Period.

Cyprus, being a major producer of wine and oil in the Mediterranean basin,[1] exported its production to various centres in Egypt. Cypriot goods carried in basket-handled amphorae from 8th century BC until the middle of the Hellenistic Period have been recovered by archaeological excavations throughout Egypt. Tebtynis, Bouto, Naucratis, Tell el-Maskhuta, Tanis, Karnak, Elephantine, Mendes, Migdol and Tell el-Herr have all provided numerous examples of well-known basket-handle Cypriot amphorae.[2] And salvage excavations carried out in Alexandria have produced new evidence for the scale of importation of basket-handle amphorae during the Hellenistic Period from Cyprus and the Levant. However, the Alexandrian examples of this form are divided into three major categories: Levantine production, Cypriot production and Egyptian imitations.[3] The distinctive appearance of Egyptian clay permits us to distinguish Egyptian production of basket-handle amphorae from the middle of the 4th century BC to the middle of the 3rd century BC.[4] The earliest production of basket-handle amphorae is confidently determined as Cypriot,[5] but it remains difficult to separate these groups accurately since both the Levantine group and some Cypriot types have fabrics of similar appearance, and their production centres, typological sequences, and fabrics are poorly understood.[6] As a result, the later series of basket-handle amphorae have been attributed to Levantine centres, though some later Cypriot forms have been discovered on the Island.[7] Another important reason for this confusion may be an increase of the production scale in the island during the Hellenistic Period. Such an increase, perhaps due to the rise of global commerce, might account for a diversification of fabrics[8] and radical changes in form[9] with different amphora forms appearing as 'Kouriaka'.

Stamps began to be used on basket-handle amphorae after the second half of the 5th century BC as proven by a well-stratified example from Amathous.[10] Stamps applied on the Cypriot amphorae of this shape are not attested in the contexts in Alexandria, although its late version is present in modest quantities.[11]

During the Ptolemaic Period, commercial ties continued between Cyprus and Egypt. The interest of the Ptolemies in the island depended not only on military requirements but also on the rich natural sources of the island. Exportation of Cypriot wine to Egypt – as attested by archaeological excavations in Alexandria, sites in Fayoum and Taposiris Magna – has been confirmed by documents in the Zenon Archive.[12]

Amphorae furnish the most significant clues regarding the arrival of Cypriot products to Alexandria. The excavations made by the Centre d'Études Alexandrines (CEAlex) in various parts and quarters of the city have led to the discovery of numerous fragments belonging to Cypriot amphorae in the Hellenistic Period (Diagram 1).

Cypriot amphorae reached Alexandria in proportions similar to Adriatic Italian amphorae (Lamboglia type 2), trailing well behind the three principal Aegean amphora types: Rhodes, Cnidus and Cos.[13] Cypriot amphora stamps comprise 10% of the total stamped handles found in Alexandria dating to the late 4th and 3rd centuries BC.[14] Knowing that not all the Cypriot amphorae were stamped, this is a significant result confirming the substantial Cypriot wine consumption in Hellenistic Alexandria.

The Cypriot amphora forms and stamps found in Alexandria present a variety of types used in the repertory of Cypriot amphora producers. Stamps were not applied on all of the amphorae produced on the island, but some

Location of CEAlex excavations, superimposed on El-Falaki Map (1866), modified for Heptastadion (Hesse 2002).
© CEAlex, C. Shaalan, september 2010.

Map. Excavation Sites of CEAlex in Alexandria.

producers did use stamps between the 4th and 2nd centuries BC.[15] Amphora production on the island mainly occurred at Kourion, Kition, Paphos and probably at Salamis.[16]

---

1 Şenol 2004, 10-14; Şenol 2009, 104.
2 Tebtynis: Marangou & Marchand 2007, 252; Tell el-Herr: Defernez 2001, 352-439; Gratien 1996, 74 fig. 8; Gratien 1997, 71 no. 5-70 fig. 1; Defernez 2007a, 566-569, 613 nos. 24-28 fig. 8; Defernez 2007b, 36; Naucratis: Gantès 2007, 148-149; Mendes: Hummel & Shubert 1994, 7 fig. 1; Tell el-Maskhuta: Holladay 1982, 129 pl. 26; Karnak: Masson 2007, 366 fig. 1.2; Masson 2011, 269-310; Elephantine: Aston 2007, 436 no. 2290 fig. 12; Migdol: Oren 1984, 18 fig. 11, 24 fig. 29; Bouto: Bourriau & French 2007,120.
3 Defernez & Marchand 2006, 79 fig. 7.
4 Marangou & Marchand 2007, 253 figs. 72-75; Defernez 2007a, 567.
5 Courtois 1980, 358.
6 Jacobsen 1998, 351; Leidwanger 2005-2006 [2007], 28. Although the Phoenician fabric of the earlier production was grouped by Master, the production zones were not pointed out precisely, see Master 2003, 52-56. In four different clay groups of basket handle amphorae, three are identified as Levantine while only one group is Cypriot in Berythus, see Aubert 2004, 39.
7 Jacobsen 2002, 178 figs. 4-5.
8 Defernez 2007b, 36 fig. 23.6.
9 Marangou & Marchand 2009, 244.
10 Marangou & Marchand 2009, 244.
11 For an example to one of the earliest stamps on a basket handle amphora dated to second half of the 5th century BC, see Marangou & Marchand 2009, 243, and 245 fig. 23.2. A1. For Hellenistic basket handle amphorae with stamps impressed on the lower part of handles, see Calvet 1972, 54-55 nos. 109-110; Grace 1950, 146 nos. 89-93.
12 Michaelides 1996, 140-142.
13 Şenol 2007, 61-63.
14 Cankardeş-Şenol forthcoming Diagram 3.
15 Calvet 1986, 505-514.
16 Although some stamps with an ethnic indicating the production at Paphos and Kition have been found, no amphora production workshops have been discovered at none of these sites on the island until now. See, Grace 1979, 178-188; Calvet 1972, 52-55 and some examples classified under the unidentified stamps between the pages 57 and 70; Calvet 1982, 41-45; Calvet 1986, 505-514; Calvet 1993, 70-73.

Fig. 1a. CyA1.

Fig. 2a. CyA2.

Fig. 1b. CyA1.

Fig. 2b. CyA2.

The Cypriot amphorae mentioned in this paper come from eight different excavation sites located in different parts of Alexandria. The Cricket Playground (CRI), the garden of the former British Consulate in Alexandria (CON), and the Diana Theatre (DI) sites are close to the quarter of ancient Alexandria where royal buildings (palaces) once stood, all of them west of the Cape of Lochias. The Billards Palace (BI) and the former Garage Lux (L) sites are situated in the centre of the modern city and close to the well-known *Caesareum*. The property of the Greek Orthodox Patriarchate, near Fouad Street (F) is located on the property of the city centre of Alexandria and not far from the Canopic Road. The Alabaster Tomb (Terra Santa) (TAL) is situated in the south-east of the Royal quarter of the city and at a distance from the city centre. The excavations here were conducted in the modern Latin cemeteries. These stand very close to the Alabaster Tomb, which was itself allegedly a part of Alexander the Great's Tomb. The Gabbari site (GAB) is the Necropolis located in the west part of Alexandria – outside the Ptolemaic city walls (Map 1).

FABRIC GROUPS

The Cypriot amphorae found in Alexandria have been divided into four main fabric groups.

Fabric 1

The colour of the paste varies in reddish tones (5YR 7/6 reddish yellow – 10 R 6/6 light red – 2.5 YR 4/8 red). The paste contains numerous limestone and other inclusions and has the porous texture that is a characteristic of the Kourion fabric.[17] The amphorae classified in this group have stamps bearing abbreviated names (Group A, CyAS2), symbols accompanying monograms or Cypriot syllabary signs (Group C, CyAS13-19-Kourion group), and Cypriot syllabary signs (Group D, CyAS20 and CyAS25).

The Cypriot amphorae belonging to the Kourion group found in Alexandria are classified as three main types.

CyA1. Inv. No.: CON.96.10357.3.6 (Fig. 1.a-b)
Band-formed rim with a slight ridge on the lower part

Rim diameter: 10.5 cm; colour of the clay: 10 R 6/6 light red; colour of the surface: 10 R 7/6 light red; inclusions: chamotte, limestone, shells, reddish stones.

Similar stamped examples of this well-known form have been found in Kition.[18]

CyA2. Inv. No.: CON.96.10094.3.9 (Fig. 2.a-b)
Triangular rim slightly inverted inside.

Rim diameter: 14.5 cm; colour of the clay: 5 YR 6/6 reddish yellow; colour of the surface: 5 YR 7/4 pink; inclusions: limestone, sand, shells, reddish stones

A close parallel to this form with the same fabric and with a stamp impression on the handle has been found in Kition.[19] Another similar form found in Tebtynis.[20]

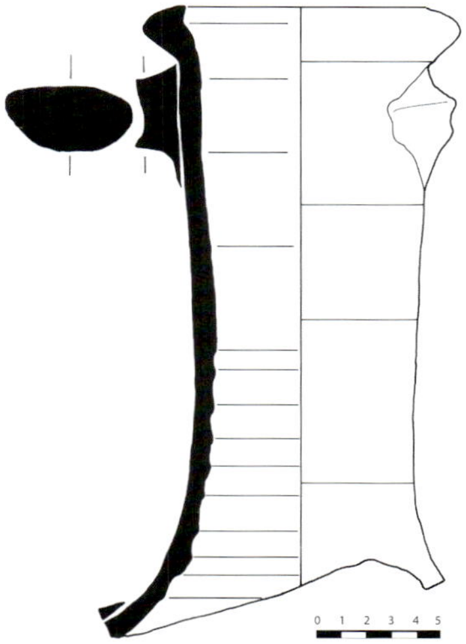

Fig. 3. CyA3.

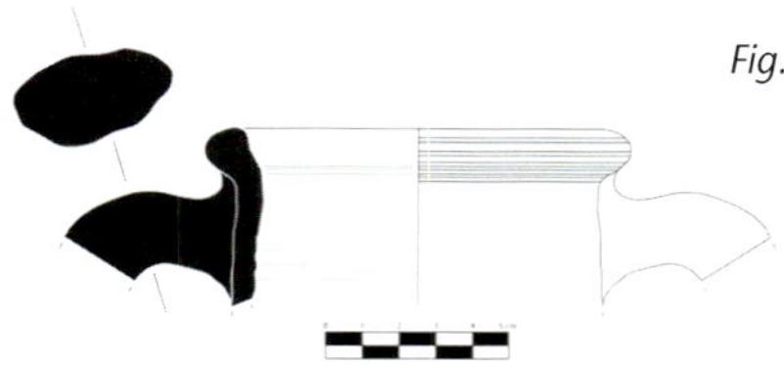

Fig. 4a. CyA4.

Fig. 4b. CyA4.

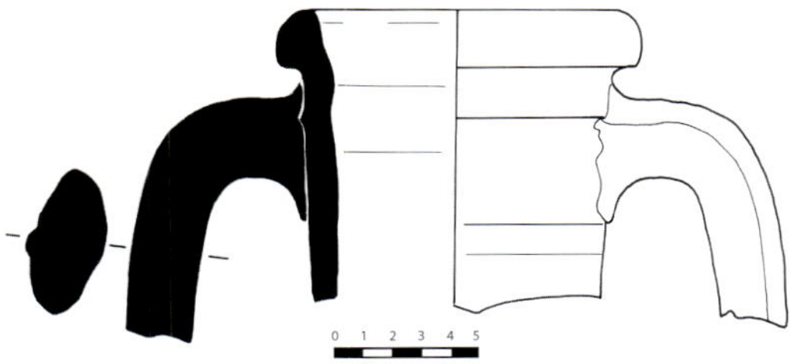

Fig. 5. CyA5.

CyA3. Inv. No: TAL.40053.12.23 (Fig. 3)
Triangular rim with a distinctive ridge inside the rim; tall, narrow neck and traces of oval sectioned handles. Smears of reddish paint under the rim and traces of actual letters on the neck.

Rim diameter: 9.6 cm; colour of the clay: 10 R 6/6 light red-5 YR 6/3 light reddish brown; colour of the surface: 5 YR 8/2 pinkish white; inclusions: Lots of big pieces of limestone and sand.

A similar amphora with a rectangular stamp impression on the top of the handle has been found in Maresha excavations.[21]

CyA4. Inv. No.: CON.97.11368.1 (Fig. 4.a-b)
Out-curved rim with a cylindrical neck. Upper connections of the handles are conserved.

Rim diameter: 8.4 cm; colour of the clay: 7.5 YR 5/6 red; colour of the surface: 7.5 YR 6/6 light red; inclusions: Lots of limestone, sand, shells and chamotte.

CyA5. Inv. No.: CRI.96.4192.2.3 (Fig. 5)
Out-curved rim, a cylindrical and a tall neck with a ridge between the upper connection of the oval sectioned heavy handles.

Rim diameter: 10.7 cm; colour of the Clay: 10 R 6/6 light red; colour of the surface: 10 YR 8/3 very pale brown; inclusions: Quartz, sand, limestone.

A complete Kourion group amphora which was found with other basket-handle amphorae in Askhelon, dated to the late Persian/early Hellenistic periods, has a similar form.[22] Close complete examples were found in Salamis dating to the 3rd century BC.[23]

17 See the thin section photo of Kourion amphora body sherd, Meyza 2004, 274 fig. 4:1.
18 Calvet 1982, 43 fig. 21.120; Calvet 1993, 70.95, 72.102.
19 Calvet 1993, 73 fig. 72.105.
20 Ballet *et al.* 2012, 168 no. 725.
21 Ariel & Finkielsztejn 2003, 143, CY1 930/84.70.764.
22 Barako 2008, 454 no. 24.
23 Diederichs 1980, 25 figs. 43-44.

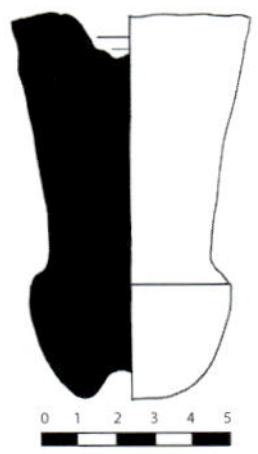

Fig. 6. CyA6.

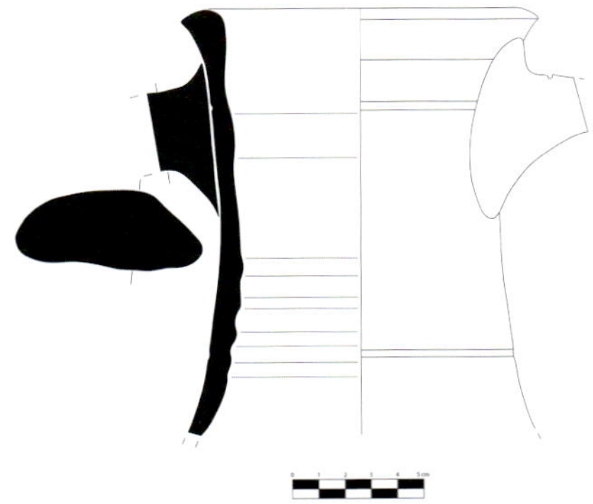

Fig. 7a. CyA7.

Fig. 7b. CyA7.

CyA6. Inv. No.: FOU.00.10028.106.80 (Fig. 6)
Slightly hollowed solid foot.

Diameter of base: 3.2 cm; colour of the clay: 5 YR 5/6 yellowish red; colour of the surface: 5 YR 8/2 pinkish white; inclusions: Quartz, white sand, chamotte.

Similar hollowed toes have been found in Paphos dated to the late 4th to 3rd centuries BC.[24] A smaller version of this toe found in Akko was dated broadly to the 4th to 2nd centuries BC,[25] but the context dates of the excavations in Alexandria indicate that this form of toe did not continue in production after the mid-3rd century BC.

Fabric 2
The clay colour varies from pinkish/whitish to pale yellow. It contains numerous inclusions as limestone, sand and chamotte. Amphorae of this fabric group have stamps with monograms or abbreviated names (Group A, CyAS1, CyAS3-8), complex monograms (Group B, CyAS9), Cypriot syllabary signs (Group D, CyAS21-23) and anepigraphic stamps (Group E, CyAS26-27). Group D may be better considered as a sub-group of Fabric 2 since the stamped fragments present somewhat different characteristics having more homogeneous pale clay. Amphorae of Fabric 2 are more numerous than other Cypriot amphorae in the rescue excavations in Alexandria.

CyA7. Inv. No.: CON.96.10094.6.1 (Fig. 7.a-b)
Slightly triangular rim, broad neck with a tiny groove between the upper handle connections are the main characteristics of this form. The ovoid formed body is tapering with a solid conical toe.

Rim diameter: 13.5 cm; colour of the clay: 5 YR 7/6 reddish yellow; colour of the surface: 10 R 8/3 very pale yellow; inclusions: Quartz, sand, few limestone, very little chamotte.

CyA8. Inv. No.: CRI.96.4081.1 (Fig. 8.a-b)
Out-curved triangular rim, cylindrical neck and oval sectioned heavy handles. It bears a rubbed out rectangular stamp on the top of its handle. One handle is missing.

Rim diameter: 7.2 cm; colour of the clay: 10 YR 8/4 very pale brown, colour of the surface: colour coated; inclusions: Quartz, sand, chamotte.

For the stamp see CyAS1. Similar Cypriot amphorae were found in Nagidos excavations dating to the second quarter of the 3rd century BC.[26]

CyA9. Inv. No.: LUX.02.31315.5.1 (Fig. 9.a-b)
Out-curved triangular rim with a handle attachment. It bears a stamp on the handle.

Rim diameter: 12 cm; colour of the clay: 2.5 YR 6/3 light red; colour of the surface: 5 YR 8/3 pink; inclusions: Quartz, sand, chamotte.

For the stamp, see below CyAS7.

CyA10. Inv. No.: TAL.03.40034.65 (Fig. 10.a-b)
Out-curved rim with oval sectioned handle. It bears a stamp on the top of the handle.

Rim diameter: 10 cm; colour of the clay: 5 YR 6/6

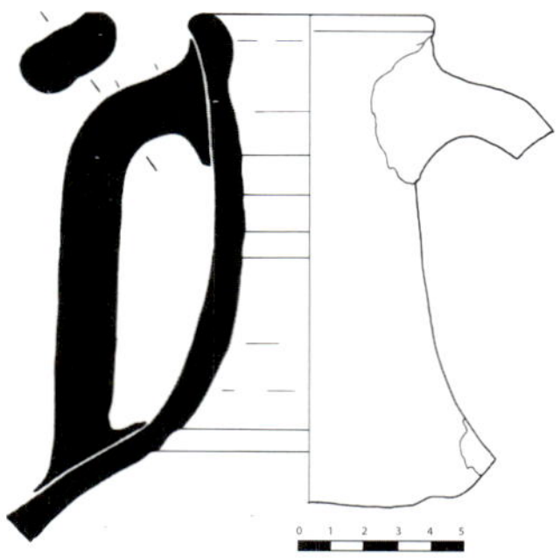

Fig. 8a. CyA8.

Fig. 8b. CyA8.

reddish yellow; colour of the surface: 7.5 YR 8/4 pink; inclusions: Quartz, sand, a few particles of limestone, chamotte.

For the stamp, see below CyAS23.

CyA11. Inv. No.: CON.96.10118.5.4 (Fig. 11.a-b)
Slightly outcurved rim with an oval sectioned handle.

Rim diameter: 13 cm; colour of the clay: 7.5 YR 8/4 pink; colour of the surface: 5 YR 8/4 pink; colour of the core: 2.5 YR 6/6 light red; inclusions: Quartz, sand, calcareous, chamotte.

A similar amphora found in Tebtynis has been dated to the late 4th to early 3rd centuries BC.[27] Another example of this form with a circular stamp on the handle has been found in Kition.[28]

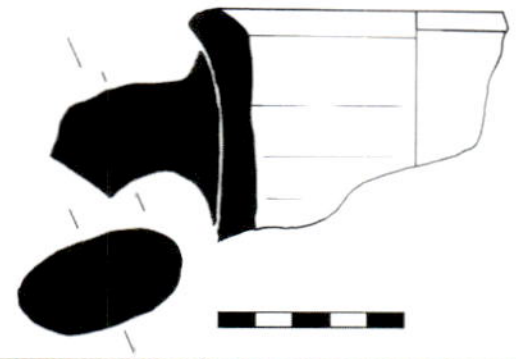

Fig. 9a. CyA9.

Fig. 9b. CyA9.

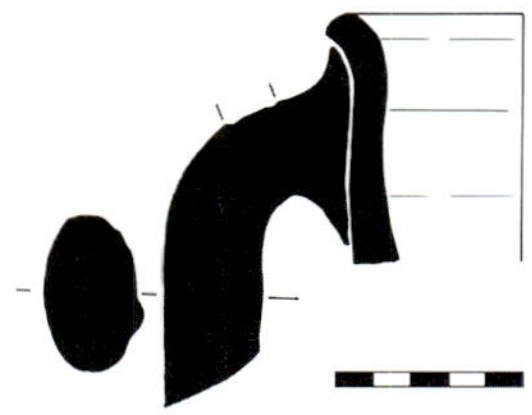

Fig. 10a. CyA10.

Fig. 10b. CyA10.

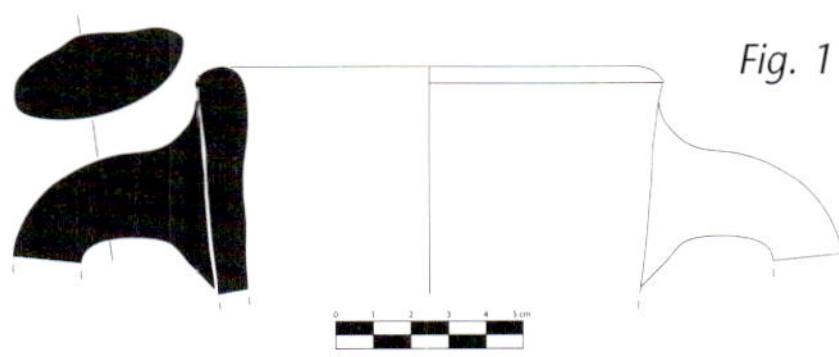

Fig. 11a. CyA11.

Fig. 11b. CyA11.

24 Lund 1993a, 119 nos. C352-353; Calvet 1986, 513; Grace 1979, 178.
25 Ariel 2005, 190 fig. 1:7.
26 Şenol & Aşkın 2007, 275 nos. 75-77.
27 Marangou & Marchand 2007, 250 fig. 44.
28 Calvet 1982, 45 no. 126 fig. 23.

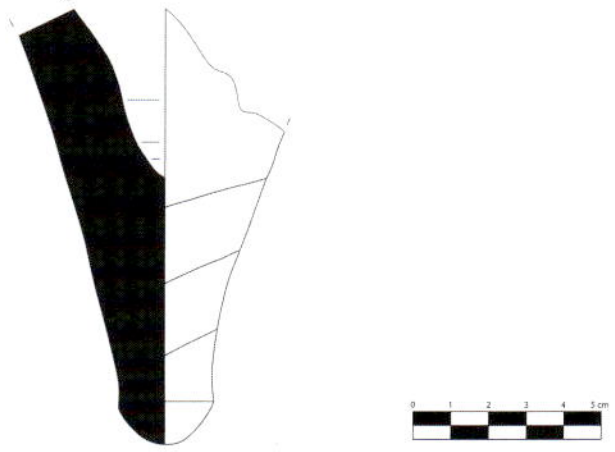

Fig. 12a. CyA12.

Fig. 12b. CyA12.

CyA12. Inv. No.: CON.96.10173.2.1 (Fig. 12.a-b)
Solid conical spike.

Diameter of base: 2.1 cm; colour of the clay: 5 YR 7/4 pink; colour of the surface: 5 YR 8/4 pink; inclusions: Quartz, sand, chamotte.

Fabric 3

This fabric contains quartz, sand, shells and some limestone with porous texture as the characteristic of other Cypriot clay compositions. Its colour varies from reddish to reddish yellow due to the firing process. Some handles of this amphora group have complex monogram stamps (Group B, CyAS10-12).

CyA13. Inv. No.: CON.96.10211.9.2 (Fig. 13.a-b)
Only the out-curved rim is preserved.

Rim diameter: 10.5 cm; colour of the clay: 10 R 6/6 light red; colour of the surface: 10 YR 8/3 very pale brown; inclusions: Quartz, sand, chamotte.

A cylindrical narrow neck with heavy handles and an ovoid body tapering to a hollow toe are the main characteristics of this group.[29]

CyA14. Inv. No.: CON.96.10173.1.4 (Fig. 14.a-b)
Hollow foot.
Diameter of foot: 3.2 cm; colour of the clay: 10 R 5/6 red; colour of the surface: 10 R 6/4 pale red; inclusions: Quartz, sand, shells, chamotte.

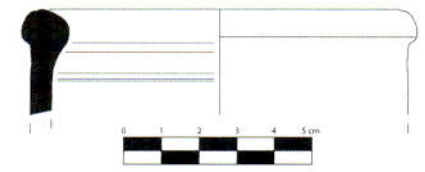

Fig. 13a. CyA13.

Fig. 13b. CyA13.

Similar toes of Cypriot amphorae found in Naucratis are dated to the late 4th century BC.[30]

Fabric 4

The clay is reddish and the fabric has rare limestone specks with some chamotte and grit. Its texture is soapy and lacks the porosity familiar from Fabric 1 and Fabric 3. This fabric is only represented with one stamped handle in Alexandria, CyAS24 bearing a syllabary sign in Group D.

Groups of Cypriot Stamps in Alexandria

Alongside classification of the jars by fabric, Cypriot stamps from the rescue excavations have been sorted into five groups on the basis of characteristics of the inscriptions and images:

Group A. Stamps with simple monograms or abbreviated names (CyAS1-8, stamps having two letters or abbreviation with three or more letters).

Group B. Stamps with complex monograms, i.e., three or more interconnected letters, which do not permit restoration of a name or beginning of a name (CyAS9-12).

Group C. Stamps with symbols alongside monograms, simple or complex, or Cypriot syllabary signs (CyAS13-19).

Group D. Stamps with only Cypriot syllabary signs (CyAS20-25).

Group E. Anepigraphic stamps (CyAS26-27, one of which may be identified as a gem stamp, cf. CyAS27).

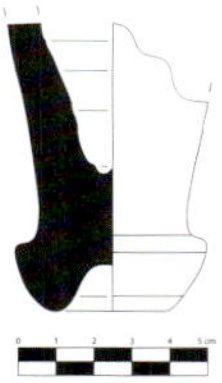

Fig. 14a. CyA14.

Fig. 14b. CyA14.

Fig. 15a. CyAS1. Not to scale.

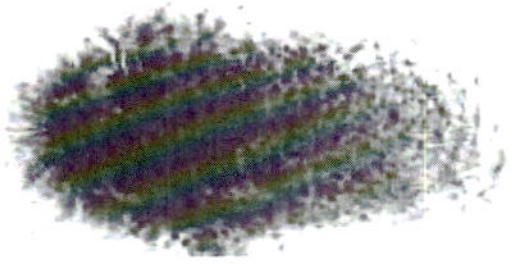

Fig. 15b. CyAS1.

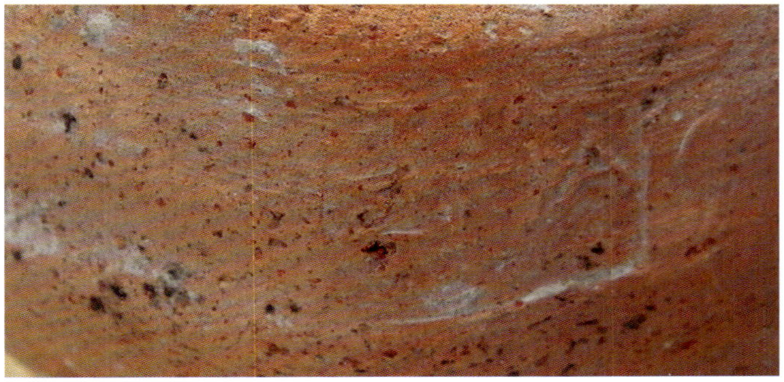

Fig. 16a. CyAS2. Not to scale.

Fig. 16b. CyAS2.

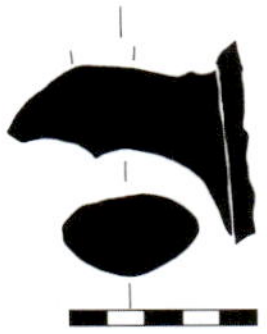

Fig. 16c. CyAS2.

Fig. 16d. CyAS2.

Group A. Stamps with simple monograms or abbreviated names:

CyAS1. Inv. Alex. CRI 955 (CRI.96.4081.1) (=CyA8) (Fig. 15.a-b)
Oval stamp ? x 0.9 cm.[31]

XP[..]

The stamp bears an abbreviated name Χρ[..]. The third letter is tentatively suggested to be Ω. A similar amphora at Nagidos bears a circular stamp with two monograms or an abbreviated name ΣΑ(, probably indicating the ethnic *Salamis* (?). The stratum at Nagidos where this stamp has been attested contains a coin dated to the period of Ptolemaios II, c. 285-246 BC.[32] Another stamp with the same abbreviation has been found at Salamis in a context dated to the end of the 4th century BC.[33]

CyAS2. Inv. Alex. F 144 (Fou.03.10813.4) (Fig. 16.a-d)
Rectangular, 1.8 x 1.6 cm. Fabric 1: 5 YR 7/6 reddish yellow,

29 Zemer 1977 no. 24 pl. 8; Calvet 1986, 506 fig. 1a; Meyza 2004, 276 fig. 8.
30 Gantès 2007, 149 fig. 2.2-5.
31 The rubbings of stamps are in their actual sizes.
32 Cankardeş-Şenol & Alkaç 2007, 325 no. 52.
33 Calvet 1972, 59 no. 119.

Fig. 17a. CyAS3. Not to scale.

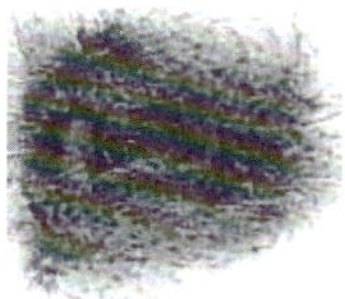

Fig. 17b. CyAS3.

Fig. 17c. CyAS3.

Fig. 18a. CyAS4. Not to scale.

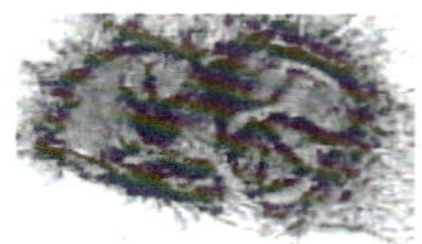

Fig. 18b. CyAS4.

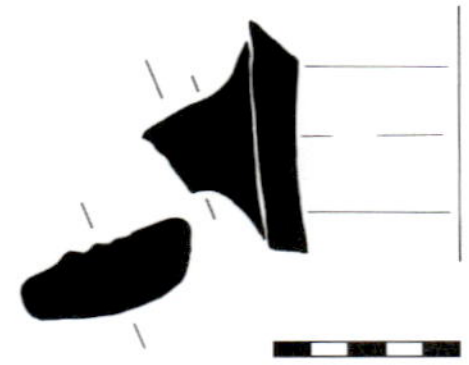

Fig. 18c. CyAS4.

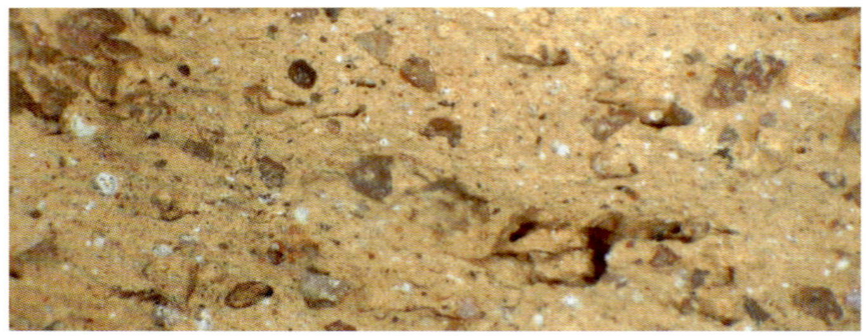

Fig. 18d. CyAS4.

surface: 5 YR 7/6 reddish yellow.

Τιμο-

στρα(

The stamp bears the name Τιμόστρατος in abbreviated form. It is one of the rare types of Cypriot stamp that permit restoration of the complete name. A name beginning with Τιμ- (retrograde) attested on a stamp from the Benaki Collection, may refer to the name Τιμόστρατος.[34] The same stratum at Fouad site included a Knidian anepigraphic prow stamp (F 145) dated to late 4th to early 3rd centuries BC.[35]

Cf. the Rhodian eponym Τιμόστρατος who is dated to Period Ib (c. 270 to c. 247 BC).[36]

CyAS3. Inv. Alex. F 149 (Fou.03.10829.10) (Fig. 17.a-c) Circular, R: 1.4 cm. Fabric 2: 5 YR 6/6 reddish yellow, surface: 10 YR 8/4 very pale brown.

ΔΩ(retr.

Inscriptions attest the names Δωρόθεος at Kition[37] and Δωσίθεος at Paphos.[38]

CyAS4. Inv. Alex. F 155 (Fou.03.10836.5) (Fig. 18.a-d) Circular (?). Clay: 7.5 YR 7/6 reddish yellow, surface: 10 YR 8/4 very pale brown. Reddish paint on the handle (7.5 YR 7/6 reddish yellow).

Pomegranate ΟΔ(or ΔΟ(

It is probable that two stamps are impressed side by side on the handle, one of which contains a simple monogram of two letters (Δ in an O) and the other has a pomegranate symbol. The two letters refer to a name beginning with ΔΟ([39] or ΟΔ(.[40] The pomegranate symbol is frequently attested on Cypriot productions, and a similar

Fig. 19a. CyAS5. Not to scale.

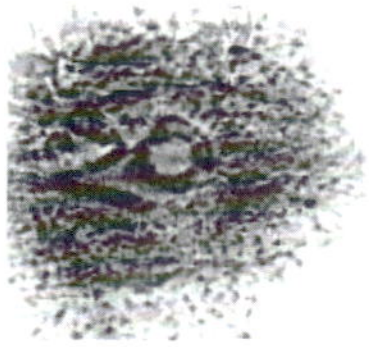

Fig. 19b. CyAS5.

Fig. 19c. CyAS5.

pomegranate stamp accompanying a stamp containing two letters (K and Y in retrograde) or Cypriot syllabary signs (?),[41] has been recovered during the excavations at Nagidos in Cilicia.[42] Another similar combination with KY(abbreviation and pomegranate symbol is preserved in the Benaki Collection at the Greco-Roman Museum in Alexandria.[43] An anepigraphic stamp with the same symbol has been published among the material from Samaria.[44] At the Fouad site, the stratum where this Cypriot double stamp was found also contained a Thasian stamp naming Κρατιστῶναξ (F 154) dated to c. 325-310 BC (according to the Thasian stamp chronology by Debidour) or c. 308-298 BC (by Tzochev).[45]

CyAS5. Inv. Alex. F 193 (Fou.03.11007.18). (Fig. 19.a-c) Circular (?). Clay: 7.5 YR 8/6 reddish yellow, surface: 2.5 YR 6/8 light red.

ΣO(or MO(

The stamp either contains a simple monogram (M/Σ and O) or an abbreviation (if one assumes the two letters are not intended to overlap one another's space to create one symbol from two letters) ΣO(, MO(or OM(of a Greek name as Ὁμίλος, Ὁμόνοια, Ὁμφοκλέης, Σόλων, Σουφρονιεύς, Μοκάπολις, Μόλης, Μόρανδρος, Μοσχίων or Μόψος).[46] This stamp can be compared with those bearing the lotus symbol above and complex monogram with letters M, A and O below, CyAS17-18. But CyAS5 seems to be a complete and well-preserved stamp containing only two letters. Moreover, the clay colour and characteristics are completely different from CyAS17 and 18 below.

CyAS6. Inv. Alex. L208 (Lux. 02.40313.50) (Fig. 20.a-c) Circular, D. 1.3 cm. Clay: 2.5 YR 8/2 white, surface: 2.5 YR 8/2 white.[47]

ON(retr. or NO(

The stamp may abbreviate a name beginning with either ON or NO, such as, with regard to names on Cypriot inscriptions: Νουμήνιος, Νουτίων or Ὀνασαγόρας,

34 Grace 1979, 187 no. 18 (Alex. ABC 0763.01). For this name appearing with syllabary signs (ti-mo-sa) on an amphora stamp from Ras el-Bassit (Posidéion), see Calvet & Masson 1988, 24; Masson 1986, 38.
35 Cankardes-Şenol forthcoming no. 32.
36 www.amphoralex.org.
37 Fraser & Matthews 1987, 145 (3rd century BC). The same name also occurs at Kourion in the 3rd century AD (see *ibidem*, 145).
38 Fraser & Matthews 1987, 146 (225 BC).
39 I.e. Δόξανδρος (Fraser & Matthews 1987, 142).
40 A published name beginning with Oδ(from Cyprus is not known but for rare names from elsewhere, see Fraser & Matthews 1987, 347.
41 Related to the ethnic of Cyprus or the names beginning with Ku- from Cyprus (i.e. Κυπράγορας, Κύπρης, Κύριος, Κυπρόδαμος, Κυπροθάλης, Κυπρόθεμις, etc., see Fraser & Matthews 1987, 279).
42 Cankardeş-Şenol & Alkaç 2007, 326 no. 53.
43 Alex. ABC 0912.39.
44 Reisner *et al.* 1924, 310 no. 4 and 316 no. 13.
45 The stamped amphora handles from the Fouad site have been studied and classified by the author. See also Canoğlu 2011, 89 no. 19. For the chronology of Thasian stamps see Debidour 1986, 331; Tzochev 2009, 65.
46 Fraser & Matthews 1987, 319-320, 349 and 409-410.
47 Published in Cankardeş-Şenol 2006, 131 fig. 200.

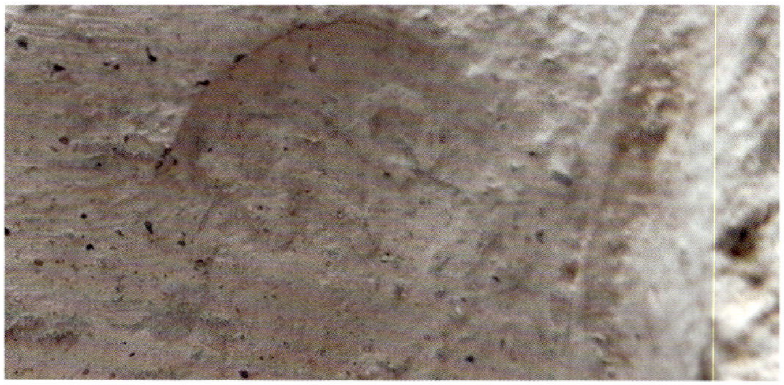

Fig. 20a. CyAS6. Not to scale.

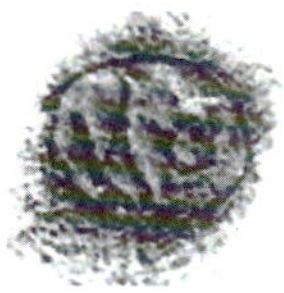

Fig. 20b. CyAS6.

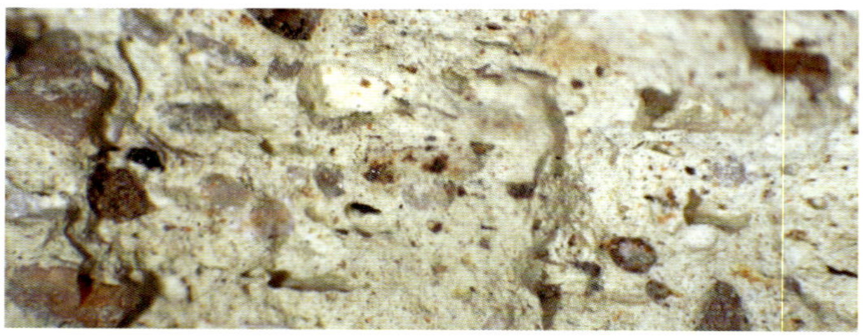

Fig. 20c. CyAS6.

Fig. 21a. CyAS7. Not to scale.

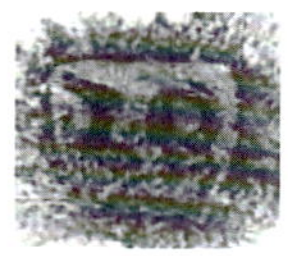

Fig. 21b. CyAS7.

Ὀνάσανδρος, Ὀνάσας, etc.[48] The abbreviation ON(occurs on oval stamps among the finds at Kourion.[49] Monogram stamps reading ONA(are also attested at Kourion.[50]

CyAS7 (=CyA9). Inv. Alex. L 280 (Lux. 02.31315.5.1) (Fig. 21.a-b)
Rectangular stamp, 1.3 x 1.0 cm.

ΟΣ(*retr.*(?)

The names beginning with ΟΣ(are very rare in Greek,[51] so the abbreviation more likely reads ΣΟ(with retrograde sigma. For names starting ΣΟ(, see CyAS5 above.

CyAS8. Inv. Alex. TAL 134 (TAL 03.50029.11) (Fig. 22.a-c)
Circular stamp, D: 2.0 cm. Fabric 2: 2.5 Y 8/2 white, surface: 2.5 Y 8/2 white.

[.....]θ(or Θ[......]

Only the letter theta is legible, the preserved part of the second letter is difficult to restore. It can be the beginning of the name written in retrograde or an abbreviation ending in theta. There are many possibilities for names beginning with the letter theta.[52]

Group B. Stamps with complex monograms:

CyAS9. Inv. Alex. CON 308 (CON.96.10061.03) (Fig. 23.a-c)
Circular stamp, D. 1.7 cm. Fabric 2: 10 YR 6/4 light yellowish brown, surface: 2.5 YR 8/2 white.[53]

Π Α Τ Ο (?)

The stamp bears a complex monogram containing the letters pi, alpha and tau (?). The circular frame might be read as a further letter, omicron. Three more similar stamps with an addition of rho attached to the right leg of the pi are preserved in the Greco-Roman Museum in Alexandria.[54] A similar example having a letter rho comes from Kition.[55] All of these stamps could belong to the same production site/workshop, and the monogram may have been the emblem of the same workshop used by the potter during his activity. The potter, or someone detailed to this work, possibly impressed a second seal because the first one was overused.

A probably identical stamp was found at Salamis in a context dated to the late 4th to early 3rd century BC.[56] This

Fig. 22a. CyAS8. Not to scale.

Fig. 23a. CyAS9. Not to scale.

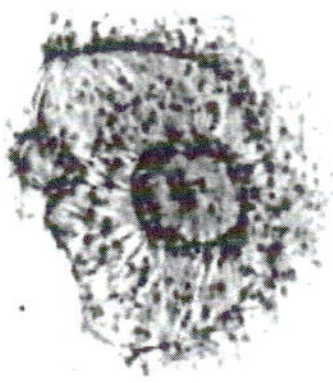

Fig. 22b. CyAS8.

Fig. 23b. CyAS9.

Fig. 22c. CyAS8.

Fig. 23c. CyAS9.

dating is also confirmed by the context in the Consulate site. A Rhodian eponym stamp naming Τιμο(, [Matrix: RE-TIMO(-001) dated to Period Ia (c. 304-c. 271 BC)] was found in the same stratum as CyAS9.

CyAS10. Inv. Alex. CON 314 (CON.96.10283.06) (Fig. 24.a-c)

Circular stamp, D. 2.4 cm. Fabric 3: 10 R 5/6 red.[57]

A, E, K, Δ, A, Π?

The stamp bears a complex monogram containing at least five or six letters in a circular frame (if not an omicron). Two identical stamps, one of which is better preserved and allows restoration of the letters on the upper part of CyAS10, are held in the Benaki Collection in Alexandria.[58] Another complex monogram with different letters in the Benaki Collection was published by V. Grace.[59]

48 For these names and other numerous possible names beginning with ON(in Cyprus see, Fraser & Matthews 1987, 340, 349-351.

49 Alex. ABC 0763.37. See also Grace 1979, 187 no. 14 (ON( ) and no. 16 (ONA(retr., from Kourion, the sanctuary of Apollo, was found with a parallel stamp for no. 14). This can be an indication of the abbreviation ON(beginning with ONA-; Calvet 1982, 42 no. 116 (from Kition).

50 Meyza 2004, 278-279 and note 21 fig. 20.

51 Cf. Masson 1983, 197 (Ὄσιρις, on a syllabic text).

52 Cf. Fraser & Matthews 1987, 208-229. See also Masson 1982, 411 (Θοάντα, on a syllabic text).

53 Cankardeş-Şenol 2000, 371 no. 175.

54 Alex MGR P.10881; Alex MGR P. 10952

55 Calvet 1993, 77 no. 118 (restored as Πατρ(, or Πρατ( ).

56 Calvet 1972, 3 and 61 no. 123.

57 Cankardeş-Şenol 2000, 372 no. 176.

58 Grace 1979, 187 no. 24 fig. 24 pl. XXIX, for the better preserved example; another one is ABC 0763.41, which was also mentioned by Grace under no. 24.

59 Grace 1979, 187 no. 25 pl. XXIX (Alex. ABC 0763.32 and 33 – not published).

Fig. 24.a CyAS10. Not to scale.

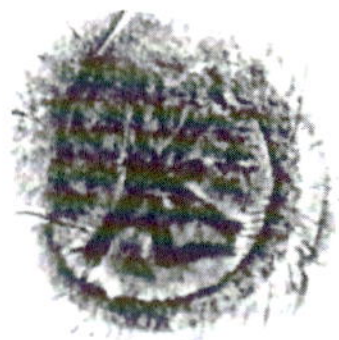

Fig. 24.b CyAS10.

Fig. 24.c CyAS10.

Fig. 25a. CyAS11. Not to scale.

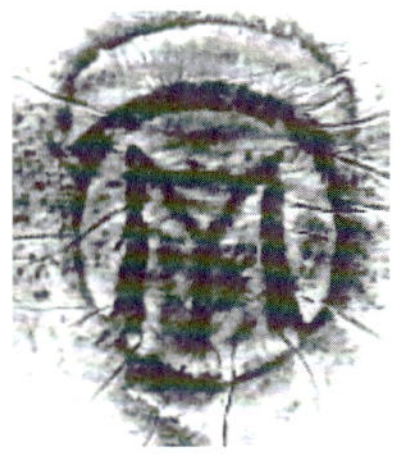

Fig. 25b. CyAS11.

Fig. 25c. CyAS11.

CyAS11. Inv. Alex. GAB 750 (GAB.97.20008.3.1) (Fig. 25.a-c)
Circular stamp, D. 3.0 cm. Fabric 3: 2.5 YR 5/6 reddish yellow, surface: 5 YR 8/2 pinkish white.[60]

ΠΑΡ(?

As with CyAS10, this complex monogram either rests within a circular frame or is accompanied by an omicron. Among the finds from Salamis an identical stamp (classified as unidentified) was found in context where a Rhodian fabricant stamp naming Imas was also found.[61] The fabricant is dated to Period IV (c. 160-c. 146 BC). A similar stamp from Kition Bamboula is restored as ΠΥΡ(or ΜΥΡ(by Calvet.[62]

CyAS12. Inv. Alex. TAL 085 (TAL.03.40034.367ISO143) (Fig. 26.a-c)
Circular stamp, D: c.1.8 cm. Fabric 3: 5 YR 6/6 reddish yellow, surface: 7.5 YR 6/6 reddish yellow.[63]

Ρ, Α, Κ, Π ?

A complex monogram stamp again either enclosed in a circle or accompanied by an omicron. The restoration of the letters on this stamp is based on an identical, better preserved stamp published by Grace.[64] Two stamps identical to CyAS12 are held in the Benaki Collection.[65] Given the presence of similar letters, CyAS12 may form a group with CyAS9 and CyAS11. CYAS10 may be excluded as it exhibits different and more numerous letters.

Fig. 26a. CyAS12. Not to scale

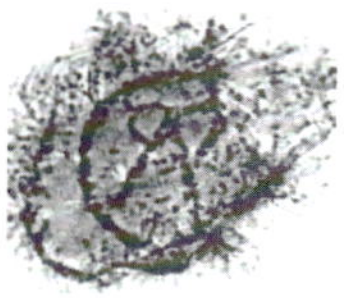

Fig. 26b. CyAS12.

Fig. 27a. CyAS13. Not to scale

Fig. 27b. CyAS13.

Fig. 26c. CyAS12.

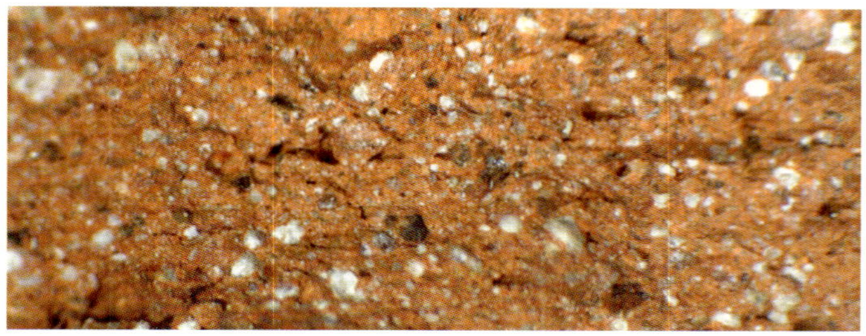

Fig. 27c. CyAS13.

Group C. Stamps with symbols and monograms or Cypriot syllabary signs[66]**:**

CyAS13. Inv. Alex. CON 344 (CON.97.10542.01) (Fig. 27.a-c) Oval stamp, 2.8 x 0.9 cm. Fabric 1: 10R 5/6 red. Cankardeş-Şenol 2000, 372, no. 177.

kantharos

monogram or syllabary sign ?

Comparable both with a stamp classified as Kouriote in the Benaki Collection[67] and with CyAS14, below. The kantharos symbol on CyAS13 has a longer and slimmer base and body than those that appear in these other two examples. A stamp from Salamis is also similar, but unfortunately the monogram or the syllabary sign under the symbol is not legible.[68] An example from Kition is probably closer to CyAS13.[69]

60 Cankardeş-Şenol 2001, 401 no. 8.
61 Calvet 1972, 31 no. 56 and 62 no. 125.
62 Calvet 1982, 51 no. 134.
63 Cankardeş-Şenol 2006, 133 fig. 204.
64 Grace 1979, 187 no. 25 pl. XXIX.
65 Alex. ABC 0763.32 and 0763.33.
66 Or "Composite Type Stamps" as named by Grace (see Grace 1979, 182). I prefer to use a more detailed label to explain what the group contains, especially when it is necessary to indicate that the symbol is accompanied by a Greek monogram or a Cypriot syllabary sign. For Cypriot syllabary signs, see Masson 1983, 58, 59, 62, 63 and 67 figs. 1-6; Masson 1995, 66.
67 Grace 1979, 182-183 and 187 no. 27 (Alex. ABC 0763.40); cf. no. 33.
68 Calvet 1972, 67 no. 141.
69 Cf. Calvet 1982, 42 no. 117.

Fig. 28b. CyAS14.

Fig. 28a. CyAS14. Not to scale.

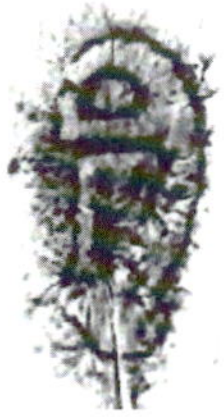

Fig. 29b. CyAS15.

Fig. 29a. CyAS15. Not to scale.

Fig. 28c. CyAS14.

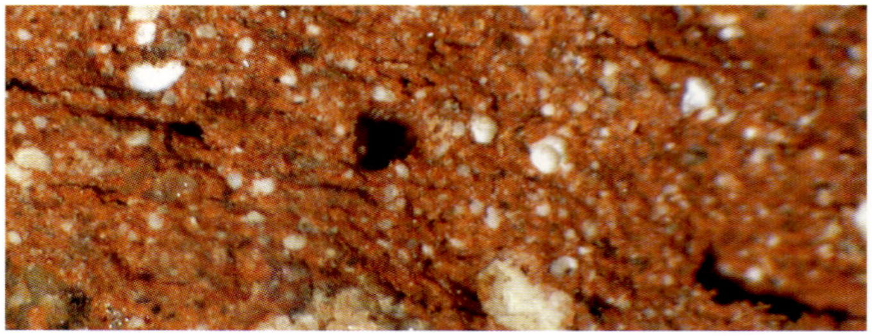

Fig. 29c. CyAS15.

CyAS14. Inv. Alex. TAL 066 (TAL.03.40034.145) (Fig. 28.a-c)
Oval, 2.3 x 1.1 cm. Fabric 1: 2.5 YR 5/8 red, surface: 2.5 YR 6/6 light red.[70]

kantharos
syllabary sign (ta- ?)
See discussion, CyAS13.

CyAS15. Inv. Alex. CRI 604 (CRI.97.6184) (Fig. 29.a-c)
Oval, 2.4 x 0.9 cm. Fabric 1: 2.5 YR 4/8 red, surface: 7.5 YR 7/4 pink.[71]

Syllabary sign (ya- ? or an omicron)
device (herm ?) and syllabary sign ?

The oval formed stamp has a syllabary sign ya- or an omicron above. An horizontal short line beneath the omicron-like sign and a vertical line attaching to each other on the left may be suggested as forming the letter gamma or more probably the letter pi, particularly given the existence of a very short vertical line that appears to furnish the right bar of the letter pi. Below all, there is a symbol which may interpreted as a herm(?) or a column (?) as seen on a stamp from the Benaki Collection.[72] To the left of the vertical line, just below the horizontal line, an unidentified symbol or a syllabary sign representing pe- is visible. It is also possible that the omicron-like sign is below and the horizontal and vertical lines are above it.

CyAS16. Inv. Alex. CRI 1295 (CRI.94.3.1011.3.1) (Fig. 30.a-c)
Rectangular, 2.5 x 1.4 cm. Fabric 1: 2.5 YR 4/8 red, surface: 2.5 YR 6/6 light red.

symbol

Fig. 30a. CyAS16. Not to scale.

Fig. 30b. CyAS16.

Fig. 31a. CyAS17. Not to scale.

Fig. 31b. CyAS17.

Fig. 30c. CyAS16.

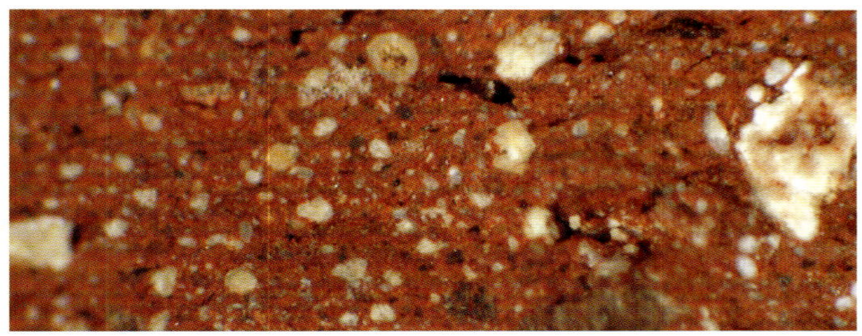

Fig. 31c. CyAS17.

monogram(?)

The letters constituting the monogram are not well preserved. The form of the stamp is more angular with curved corners on the lower part, whereas, the upper part seems more oval. An identical example has been attested among the finds from Kition-Bamboula with a preserved rounded-form rim fragment.[73]

CyAS17. Inv. Alex. F 128 (Fou.03.10894.14) (Fig. 31.a-c) Oval, 2.4 x 1.0 cm. Fabric 1: 2.5 YR 4/8 red, surface: 2.5 YR 6/4 light reddish brown.

lotus
M A
O

A similar monogram appears on CyAS18 below. Alpha is inverted and its horizontal bar is placed between the diagonal bars of mu; the omicron is attached just below the inverted alpha. Identical stamps are known from the Benaki collection,[74] Cyprus Museum,[75] Kourion,[76] and Salamis.[77]

70 Cankardeş-Şenol 2006, 133 fig. 203.
71 Cankardeş-Şenol 2000, 499 no. 162; Cankardeş-Şenol 2006, 133 fig. 202; Cankardeş-Şenol 2007 fig. 23.
72 Grace 1979, 187 no. 31. For a *herm* symbol see *ibid*. no. 29.
73 Calvet 1986, 510-511 fig. 4.8; Calvet 1993, 70 no. 95.
74 Grace 1979, 187 no. 28 pl. XXIX (Alex. M ABC 35).
75 Myres & Ohnefalsch-Richter 1899, 98 nos. 2342-2344.
76 Meyza 2004, 277 fig. 14.
77 Calvet 1993, 71 no. 98 (=Calvet 1986, 510-511 fig. 4.3) dated to the end of the 4th century BC.

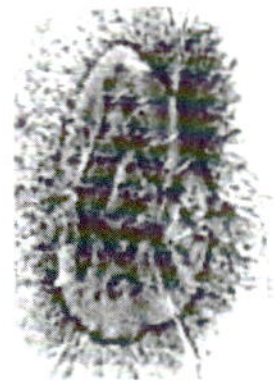

Fig. 32.b CyAS18.

Fig. 32.a CyAS18. Not to scale.

Fig. 33.b CyAS19.

Fig. 33.a CyAS19. Not to scale.

Fig. 32.c CyAS18.

Fig. 33.c CyAS19.

CyAS18. Inv. Alex. TAL 112 (TAL 03.50033.137) (Fig. 32.a-c) Oval, 2.0 x 1.1 cm. Fabric 1: 10 R 4/6 red, surface: 5 YR 7/2 pinkish gray.[78]

lotus
M A
O

This stamp is close to CyAS17 (and the parallels cited there), but the lotus on this stamp has two petals while those on the other two stamps have three.[79] CyAS18 is surely from the same workshop as CyAS17, but the matrices are different. Another Cypriot stamp with syllabary signs (CyAS24) was found in the same context. The other stamps from this context bear the names of Rhodian fabricants Θη(and Ευπο(dated to the late 4th to the early 3rd centuries BC and the Rhodian eponyms, Σωσίδαμος and Ἀπατούριος dated to the late 4th century BC.[80]

CyAS19. Inv. Alex. TAL 164 (TAL 03.40034.526) (Fig. 33.a-c) Rectangular, 1.7 x 1.2 cm. Fabric 1: 2.5 YR 4/8 red, surface: 10 R 5/6 red.

IΔ
symbol (a mask?)

The monogram may also indicate an abbreviation of a name beginning with Δι- or Ιδ-.[81] The symbol below is rubbed out on our example. A similar stamp is found at Maresha.[82] The delta is clearly preserved in the photograph, whereas, the drawing includes an iota to the left of delta. For the symbol, Ariel and Finkielsztejn suggest a mask viewed frontally. The fragment from Maresha preserves the upper part of the amphora with one stamped handle, rim and neck; this form resembles the amphora type attributed to Kition.[83] A similar type of amphora fragment with a stamp bearing AN(has been attested in the excavations at Kourion.[84]

Fig. 34a. CyAS20. Not to scale.

Fig. 35a. CyAS21. Not to scale.

Fig. 34b. CyAS20.

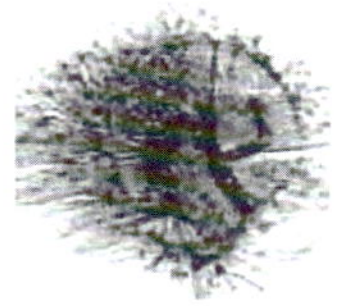
Fig. 35b. CyAS21.

Fig. 35c. CyAS21.

Fig. 34c. CyAS20.

Fig. 35d. CyAS21.

Group D. Stamps with Cypriot syllabary signs:

CyAS20. Inv. Alex. GAB 866 (GAB.98.5000.9) (Fig. 34.a-c)
Circular, R. 1.4 cm. Fabric 1: 2.5 YR 4/6 red.[85]

Two Cypriot syllabary signs

The signs are suggested to refer to ta- and pe- in the Cypriot syllabary.[86]

CyAS21. Inv. Alex. F 011 (Fou.00.10028.37) (Fig. 35.a-d)
Circular, R. 1.5 cm. Fabric 2: 7.5 YR 7/4 pink.[87]

Syllabary signs or Phoenician letters

Probably the same signs or letters also appear on CyAS23. The sign/letter on the right side can be read as retrograde (?) sa- in Cypriot syllabary signs or as retrograde nun in Phoenician alphabet. The sign/letter on the left side is partially preserved and does not allow for a restoration.

---

78 Cankardeş-Şenol 2006, 133 fig. 201.
79 Grace 1979, 187 no. 28.
80 The stamps bearing the names of the producers from the site have been studied and dated by G. Cankardeş-Şenol with regard to the profiles of the handles. For the dates of the eponyms see, Finkielsztejn 2001a, 55.
81 For the names beginning with Δι- appearing on Cyprus see Fraser & Matthews 1987, 130-142. Names beginning with Ιδ- are not attested on Cypriot inscriptions, but the ethnic of Idalion in abbreviated form can be another suggestion for letters Ιδ(.
82 Ariel & Finkelsztejn 2003, 143, Cy 1.
83 See also Calvet 1993, 72 no. 101; Meyza 2004, 275 fig. 5-6.
84 Oliver 1983, 279-280 no. 10 fig. 6.9.
85 Cankardeş-Şenol 2001, 405 no. 17.
86 Masson 1983, 67 fig. 6.
87 Cankardeş-Şenol 2006, 133 fig. 205.

Fig. 36a. CyAS22. Not to scale.

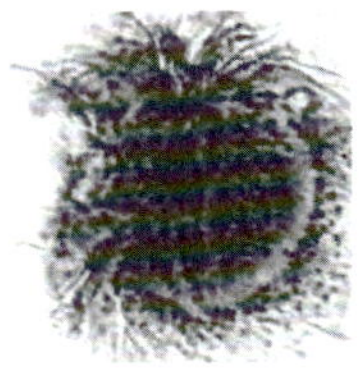

Fig. 36b. CyAS22.

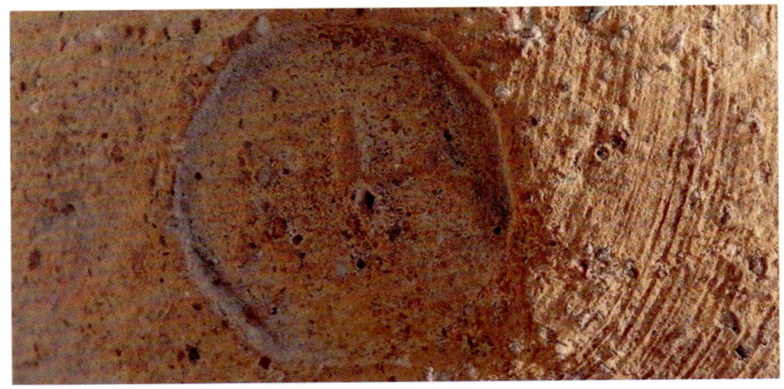

Fig. 37a. CyAS23 (=CyA10). Not to scale.

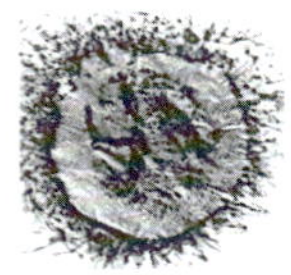

Fig. 37b. CyAS23 (=CyA10).

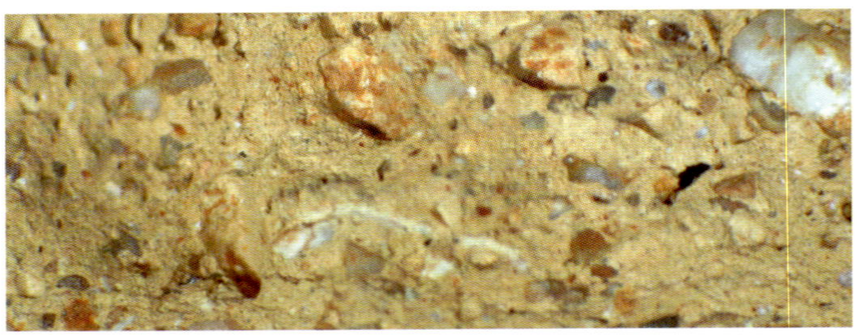

Fig. 36c. CyAS22.

Fig. 37c. CyAS23 (=CyA10).

CyAS21 was found in a stratum with Rhodian stamps datable to the late 4th to early 3rd centuries BC.

CyAS22. Inv. Alex. CON 1349 (CON. 96.10282.3) (Fig. 36.a-c)
Circular, R. 1.7 cm. Fabric 2: 5 YR 7/6 reddish yellow, surface colour: 5 YR 7/6 reddish yellow.

Syllabary sign (?) or a symbol (?)

The letters (syllabary sign ?) or the symbol on the stamp are not identified. The same stratum, where CyAS22 was found, also included an unrestorable Rhodian eponym stamp dated to the late 3rd to the early 2nd centuries BC.

CyAS23 (=CyA10). Inv. Alex. TAL 039 (TAL.03.40034.65) (Fig. 37.a-c)
Circular, R. 1.5 cm. Fabric 2: 5 YR 6/6 reddish yellow, slip: 7.5 YR 8/4 pink.[88]

Syllabary signs

The stamp bears two syllabary signs or two letters from the Phoenician alphabet. The letter on the left side may refer to the syllabary sign –sa or Hebrew nun, while the sign/letter on the right side is not identified (cf. CyAS21). From Kition-Bamboula, a rectangular stamped handle displaying Phoenician letters, with the first one resembling the character on the left, has been classified under "Phoenician stamps" belonging to an amphora produced in the Levant. The letters are identified as a mem and kaph.[89]

CyAS24. Inv. Alex. TAL 144 (TAL03.50033.296) (Fig. 38.a-c)
Oval, 1.3 x 1.1 cm. Fabric 4: 2.5 YR 5/6 red, surface: 2.5 YR 5/6 red.

Syllabary sign(s)

Fig. 38a. CyAS24. Not to scale.

Fig. 38b. CyAS24.

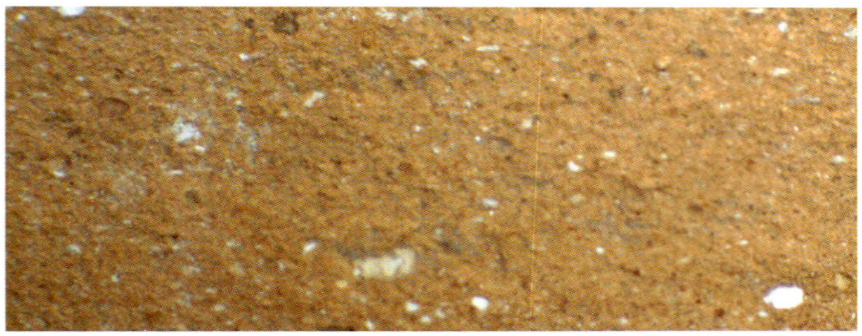

Fig. 38c. CyAS24.

Fig. 39a. CyAS25. Not to scale.

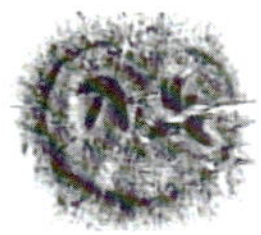

Fig. 39b. CyAS25.

Fig. 39c. CyAS25.

The stamp seems to bear syllabary signs. The upper part of the stamp is rubbed while below the sign ta- is identified. On the left of the sign, a small circular form can be suggested as ya-.[90] CyAS18 is from the same stratum.

CyAS25. Inv. Alex. TAL 159 (TAL 04.60013.80) (Fig. 39.a-c)
Circular, R: 1.3 cm. Fabric 1: 2.5 YR 5/6 red, surface: 2.5 YR 5/8 red.[91]

Syllabary signs

The stamp has two syllabary signs identified as ke- on the right and ti- on the left (reading retrograde), thus, refering to the ethnic of Kition. Stamps bearing the same signs have been already distinguished by Masson.[92] This stamp from Alexandria presents a new die bearing the ethnic of the production center, Kition.

88 Cankardeş-Şenol 2006, 133 fig. 206.
89 Calvet 1982, 47-48 no. 129 fig. 25.
90 For a stamp with the same signs from Kourion, see Meyza 2004, 280 fig. 35.
91 Cankardeş-Şenol 2006, 133 fig. 207.
92 Masson 1983, 23-25 figs. 1-2.

Fig. 40b. CyAS26.

Fig. 41b. CyAS27.

Fig. 40a. CyAS26. Not to scale.

Fig. 41a. CyAS27. Not to scale.

Fig. 40c. CyAS26.

Fig. 41c. CyAS27.

Group E. Anepigraphic stamps:

CyAS26. Inv. Alex. DI 422 (DI.97.4262.02) (Fig. 40.a-c) Oval, 1.4 x 0.9 cm. Fabric 2: 7.5 YR 7/4 pink. Reddish paint on the handle (5 YR 6/8 reddish yellow).[93]

caduceus

An oval formed anepigraphic stamp with a caduceus symbol. Some unclassified stamps with a caduceus symbol from Salamis have been found in contexts datable to the late 4th to early 3rd centuries BC.[94] Anepigraphic stamps with varied devices are known on amphoras produced at Kourion[95] but the clay colour of CyAS26 is different from that group.

CyAS27. Inv. Alex. TAL 076 (TAL.03.20173.27.4) (Fig. 41.a-c) Oval, broken below x 1.3 cm. Fabric 2: 7.5 YR 5/6 strong brown, surface: 7.5 YR 6/4 light brown.

a man (sitting ?)

monogram?

The stamp bears a male figure given in profile, facing right and seated. His right hand seems to be lifted up and probably holds something. The lower part of the stamp is broken. Although it is classified as an anepigraphic stamp in our catalogue, it may bear a monogram below the image. Perhaps a parallel stamp with a person sitting above a monogram has been recorded among the finds from Kition in a context of the late 4th century BC.[96]

ABBREVIATIONS

The following abbreviations are used in this paper:

ABC:	Alexandria Benaki Collection
BI:	Excavation site in Billards Palace
CEAlex:	Centre d'Etudes Alexandrines
CON:	Excavation site in the garden of the former British Consulate in Alexandria
CRI:	Excavation site in the Cricket Playground
CyA:	Cypriot Amphora
CyAS:	Cypriot Amphora Stamp
DI:	Excavation site in the Diana Theatre
F:	Excavation site in the property of Greek Orthodox Patriarchate, near the Fouad Street
GAB:	Excavations in the Necropolis of Gabbari
L:	Excavation site in the former Garage Lux (the Caesareum site)
M ABC:	Miscellaneous group in the Alexandria Benaki Collection
TAL:	Excavation site in the Alabaster Tomb (Cemetery of Terra Santa)

93 Referred to in Cankardeş-Şenol 2000, 258 no. 211.
94 Calvet 1972, 65-66 nos. 138-139; and pages 2 and 4 for the dates of contexts.
95 Cf. Grace 1979, 187 nos. 31-33.
96 Cf. Calvet 1986, 511 no. 3.

Cypriot Amphora Stamps of the Hellenistic Period Found in Israel

BY GÉRALD FINKIELSZTEJN

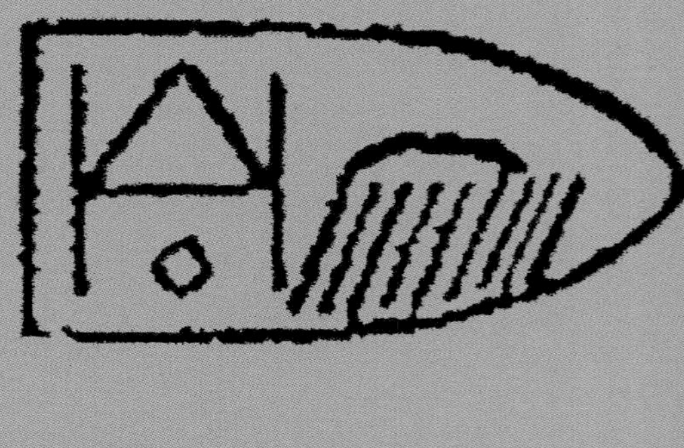

Cypriot Amphora Stamps of the Hellenistic Period Found in Israel

BY GÉRALD FINKIELSZTEJN

A substantial number of certainly or probably Cypriot stamped amphora handles have been found in excavations in Israel, and those known to the author are preliminarily presented here. All seem to be dated to the Hellenistic period, rather early, i.e. 3rd century BC. Since they were found in a land where they were imported, the primary ambition of this article is to present the finds, with some questions asked rather than solved. This is due to the fact that, except for those identified as Kouriote, other productions are less well known, although some physical aspects of the handles do share common features with those from Kourion. Indeed, the profile and size of the handles and the rims, as well as the relation between these parts on the fragments found on the Kouriote ones are the leading elements used here to tentatively identify these fragments as Cypriot. The differences lay primarily in the aspects of the fabrics and in the style of the stamps. I hope that the present catalogue will contribute to the better knowledge of the Cypriot productions. The presentation, however, is partly impaired by the absence of some necessary data, due to practical limitations. A comprehensive description of stamped fragments, especially of series not so well known, should include drawings of the profiles of the rims and handles still attached together as well as some thin sections of the various fabrics. The collection of the data was made in the course of two decades, in various conditions. The fragments will eventually be fully published in the catalogues of the excavation reports of the various sites where they were found. However, as of today, the technical processing of most of them has not yet been undertaken. Therefore, the profiles and fabrics shall be simply described here in words.[1]

CATALOGUE

Seventy-six stamped pieces (including one complete amphora) and one unstamped amphora (**43**) are presented, in the following order: 1 Paphian (no. **1**), 15 Kouriote (nos. **2-16**), 24 probably or maybe Kouriote (nos. **17-40**), 38 certainly or probably Cypriot, including 28 in Greek script, with or without devices (nos. **41-66**), and others with script of uncertain identity (nos. **54**, **57-58**, rather in Phoenician(?) **63-66**, seven in Phoenician script (nos. **67-73**), two with only a device (nos. **74-75**) and one of unclear reading (no. **76**).

The first column provides the catalogue number and the find place when known; illustrations are in the second column; the reading of the stamp, the description of the fabric (when recorded), the type of rim (when recorded) and other physical parameters are listed in the third column; the references for publication of the object (if any) or for parallels are given in the fourth column.[2]

Scales: The illustrations of the stamps are normally at approximately 1:1; however, when they are not, the catalogue number is preceded with one of the two following signs: * = close to scale 1:1, and ° = not at scale 1:1.

FABRICS

Only the visual macroscopic aspect of the fabrics is described. Petrographical analysis was not available. The codes for the description of the fabrics are as follows: [ ] = fabric; [( )] = core; not in any brackets = surface; <u>underlined</u> = cover; Bg = beige; Bn = brown; bt = bright; dk = dark; Gn = green; Gy = grey; incl. = inclusions; lt = light; mic = shining particles ("mica"); NR = not recorded; Pk = pink; Rd = red; v = very; Wh = white; Ye = yellow; +, ++, +++ = "few", "some", "lots of" inclusions, with added (+) for intermediates. When two color codes are attached, the first one is to be understood "-ish" (e.g. PkBg = pinkish beige).

RIM TYPES

The rim types are based on the order of presentation established by Henryk Meyza,[3] hence the letter "M" preceding the type number: Type M1 triangular more or less hollow rim;[4] Type M2 out-turned rim, the fold being more (Type M2a) or less (Type M2b) close to the neck;[5] Type M3 thickened rounded rim;[6] Type M4 double profiled rim.[7] Although these profiles correspond to Kouriote amphorae, not all the examples presented here are necessarily to be attributed to that production, but, most probably, to other Cypriot productions.

No.	Illustration	Reading and Fabric	References
PAPHOS			
°**1.** Paphos Tel Gezer		Παφί(ων?) Fabric: NR	Macalister 1912, fig. 467.19. See Grace 1979, pl. XXVIII.4-5, with double axe between the two syllables; fabric: [ltYeBn(Pk)] incl. ltYeBn. Attribution to Pamphylia in Brixhe 2012, 173-174 nos. 351-352.
KOURION			
2. Kourion Akko, Municipal Museum		AP(Tripod A NA(retrograde monogram Fabric: NR	See Grace 1979, 186, pl. XXVIII.8 (different die). Greek version of **3**. See no. **4**.
3. Kourion Akko Citadel		AP(Tripod ΠΑ *na* (syllabary sign) Fabric: NR	Finkielsztejn 2000, 211, pl. 110.a. Syllabic version of **2**. See no. **4**.
4. Kourion Tel Akko		AP(Tripod A Double axe Fabric: [Rd] incl.+(+) Rd ltBn	Grace 1979, pl. XXVIII.3: probably same die. See nos. **2** and **3**.
5. Kourion Tel Akko	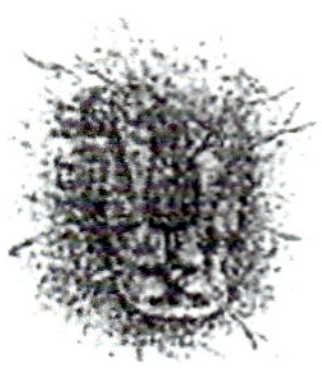	Cantharos or Lotus on letter/monogram? Fabric: [dkRd] incl.+++ dkRd	See Grace 1979, pl. XXIX.28; Meyza 2004, 277, fig. 14: lotus with monogram.

1 On the Cypriot amphorae, see Calvet 1986 and Meyza 2004. The unpublished stamps from Tel Akko a presented here courtesy of Michal Artzy.

2 VGC = Virginia Grace's Cards in the American Classical School at Athens.

3 Meyza 2004, 275-276.

4 Meyza 2004, figs. 5-6; Calvet 1972, 53, fig. 116 no. 107; 1993, 73 no. 105 fig. 72.

5 Type M2a: Meyza 2004, fig. 7; Grace 1979 pl. 28.1-2, 9a; Calvet 1982, 43 no. 120 fig. 21; Type M2b: Grace 1979, pl. 29.23a; Calvet 1993, 71-72 nos. 96, 102.

6 Meyza 2004 fig. 8; Calvet 1993, 70, no. 95.

7 Meyza 2004 fig. 9.

No.	Illustration	Reading and Fabric	References
6. Kourion Tel Jaffa		Herm to right between letters Φ (or torch?) and I (or a device?) Fabric: [RdYe] incl.+++ ltBn	Fabric close to nos. **16** and **11**. Same layout but not same die as Meyza 2004, 282, fig. 49.
***7.** Kourion Samaria		Rhodian rose NA((monogram) Fabric: NR incl.+++	Finkielsztejn 1990, no. 449. See Grace 1979, 182, pl. XXIX.26-29; Sztetyłło 1976, 92, no. 347: association rose and monogram.
8. Kourion Tel Akko	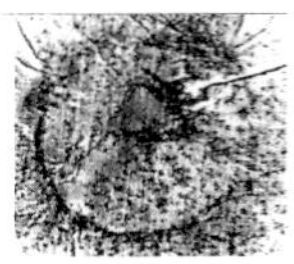	A Fabric: [RdBn] incl.+(+) dkRd	Meyza 2004, 279, fig. 29: same die; See Calvet 1993, 72, nos 103-104: different dies;
°9. Kourion Samaria		Monogram ΔΗΜΟ(Device Fabric: NR	Reisner et al. 1924, 316, D 12. VGC: already noted and classified as Kouriote; Calvet 1972, 53, no. 102: same die; Meyza 2004, 277, fig. 15 = p. 280, fig. 30: different die or better impressed (?).
***10.** Kourion Tel Akko	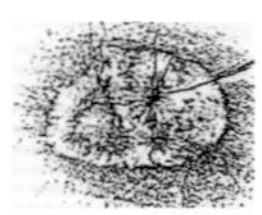	ΔΙ(or ΙΔ(retrograde Fabric: [RdBn] incl.+++ Rd	VGC: very close script, different die, classified as Kouriote.
11. Kourion Tel Jaffa		Syllabary: *a* Fabric: [Bn (YeBn)] incl. +++ vltBn Most probably burnt	Fabric close to nos. **6** and **16**.
°12. Kourion Akko Citadel		Syllabary: *na* Fabric: NR	See Grace 1979, pl. XXVIII.9b; Calvet 1982, 43, no. 119; Meyza 2004, fig. 39. See nos. **13-16**.

No.	Illustration	Reading and Fabric	References
°**13.** Kourion Akko Citadel		Syllabary: *na* Fabric: NR	See nos. **12, 14-16.**
14. Kourion Tel Akko	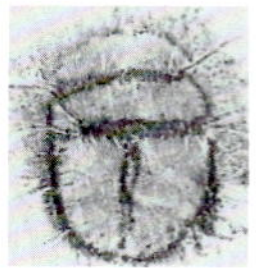	Syllabary: *na* Fabric: [RdBn] incl.++ Rd Red paint on top	See nos. **12-13, 15-16.**
15. Kourion Tel Akko		Syllabary: *na* Fabric: [ltRdBn] incl.++(+) ltRdBn	See nos. **12-14, 16.**
16. Kourion Tel Jaffa		Syllabary: *na* Fabric: [ltRdBn] incl.++(+) [ltBn] ltRdYe	See nos. **12-15**. Fabric close to nos. **6** and **11**.
KOURION?			
17. Kourion? Tel Akko	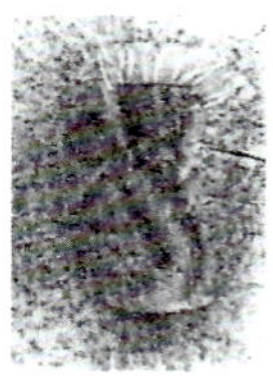	Pelet (?) A cornucopia Fabric: [dkRd] incl.+++ ltRdBn	Maybe Kourion by style of stamp, i.e. association of letter and device next to the other, similar to that in Grace 1979, 187, pl. XXIX.29.
18. Kourion? Tel Akko	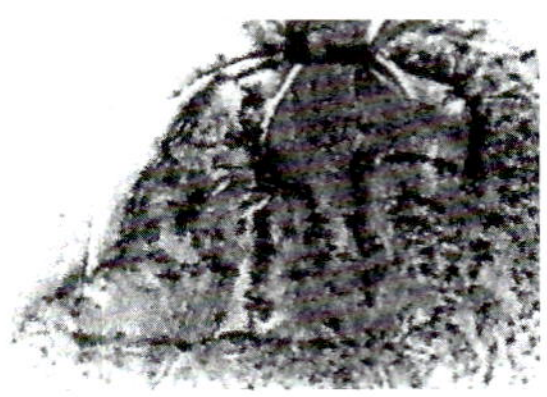	] . ΦΓο(Fabric: [ltBn] incl.++(+) Bg Rim Type M2b Relatively broad handle.	See Calvet 1972, 58, no. 116: to be read rather ΦΓ̣/Π̣[, but not sure it is same die ; 1978, pl. LVI.64: could be also retrograde; see Grace 1979, 187, pl. XXIX.12; Meyza 2004, 279, fig. 25 (letters Γο with same layout); however, for the two latter ex., Γο could be the syllabary sign for *ra*.

No.	Illustration	Reading and Fabric	References
19. Kourion? Tel Akko		A Fabric: [btRd] incl.++ btRd Rim Type M2b	This kind of fine letter on a rough fabric may be Kouriote: Calvet 1993, 72, nos. 103-104; Meyza 2004, 279, figs. 28-29.
20. Kourion? Tel Akko	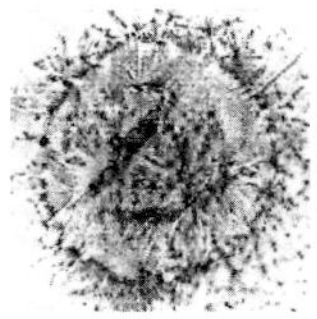	A in circle Fabric: NR	This kind of fine letter on a rough fabric may be Kouriote: Calvet 1993, 72, nos. 103-104; Meyza 2004, 279, figs. 28-29.
21. Kourion? Tel Akko	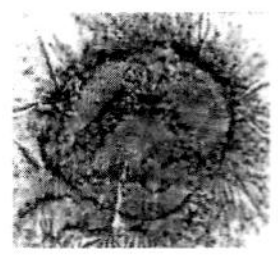	Δ Fabric: [Gy] incl.+++ Gn	This kind of letter on a rough fabric may be Kouriote: Meyza 2004, 281, fig. 43.
22. Kourion? Tel Akko	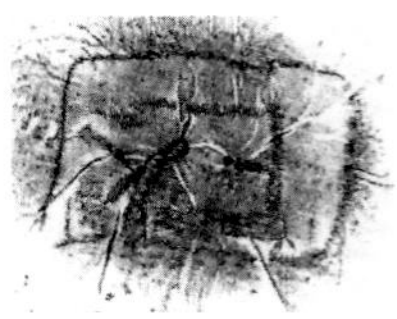	EY(retrograde Fabric: [ltRd] incl.++ Rd/ RdBn Rim Type M1	See Grace 1979, 187, pl. XXIX.13 (non retrograde, circular die); see no. **23**.
°**23.** Kourion? Samaria	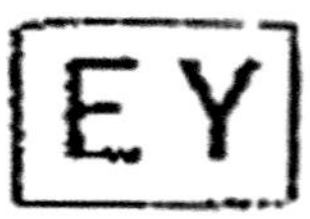	EY(Fabric: NR	Reisner et al. 1924, 316, D 16. See no. **22**.
24. Kourion? Tel Akko		ΔI(retrograde or IΔ(Fabric: [ltRd(Bn)] incl.+++ ltBn	This kind of letter on a rough fabric may be Kouriote: Meyza 2004, 281, fig. 43.
25. Kourion? Tel Akko	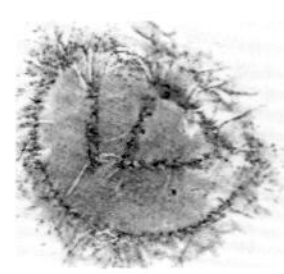	ΔI(retrograde or IΔ Fabric: [Wh] incl.+++ Wh	See Calvet 1972, 67, no. 142 (with a grape cluster to left); VGC: very close die, classified as Kouriote.
26. Kourion? Tel Akko		X or cross Fabric: [dkRd] incl.++(+) dkRd	This kind of fine letter on a rough fabric may be Kouriote: Calvet 1993, 72, nos. 103-104; Meyza 2004, 279, figs. 28-29.

No.	Illustration	Reading and Fabric	References
27. Kourion? Tel Akko	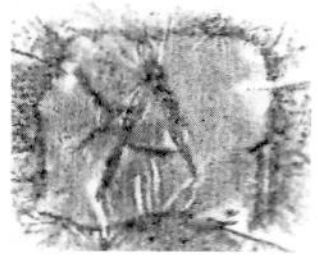	AK(retrograde monogram Fabric: [Rd] incl.+ ltBn	VGC: AY, close style, classified as Kouriote.
***28.** Kourion? Akko Citadel		AY(monogram Fabric: NR	Die different from nos. **29-30**. This kind of fine letter on a rough fabric may be Kouriote: Calvet 1993, 72, nos. 103-104; Meyza 2004, 279, figs. 28-29.
29. Kourion? Tel Akko		AY(monogram Fabric: NR Relatively broad handle	Die different from nos. **28** and **30**.
°**30.** Kourion? Samaria		AY(monogram Fabric: NR	Reisner et al. 1924, 316, D 11. Die different from nos. **28** and **29**.
31. Kourion? Tel Akko		M Fabric: [ltRd] mic+++ ltRd	See Meyza 2004, 274, fig. 3, 277, fig. 14: include same monogram.
***32.** Kourion? Tel Akko		MA(monogram Fabric: [PkBg] incl.+ ltBg	See Calvet 1993, 71, no. 97, fig. 64; Meyza 2004, 277, fig. 13: includes same monogram; VGC: same monogram with flower similar to no. **39**, classified as Kouriote.
33. Kourion? Tel Akko	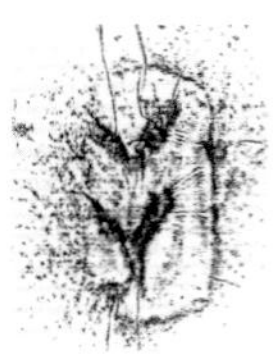	Close to or actual syllabary signs. Fabric: [Rd] incl.++(+) lGn	Same die as no. **34**. Ariel 2007, 259-260.

No.	Illustration	Reading and Fabric	References
34. Kourion?	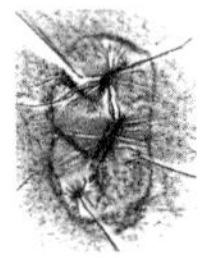	Close to or actual syllabary signs. Fabric: NR	Rockefeller Museum, Jerusalem (PAM P 3564) Same die as no. **33**.
35a. Kourion? Tel Jaffa	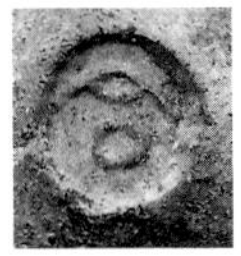	Syllabary: *ya lu* (?) Fabric: [ltBn] incl.+++ ltBn	Finkielsztejn forthcoming a.
35b. Kourion? Tel Jaffa		Rim Type M2b Toe incorrectly restored.	
36. Kourion? Tel Akko	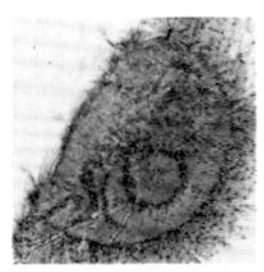	Unclear script (syllabary?) Fabric: [ltBn] incl.+++ ltBn Rim Type M2b	See Calvet 1972, 59, no. 117, Meyza 2004, 280, fig. 33: similar signs.
37. Kourion? Tel Akko		Caduceus Fabric: [RdBn] incl.+++ RdBn	See Calvet 1972, 65-6, nos. 138-9. Fabric may be Kouriote.
38. Kourion? Tel Akko	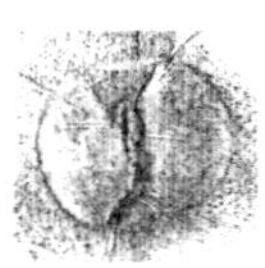	Cornucopia Fabric: [dkRd] incl.++ Bn Wh Red paint on top	Maybe Kourion by style of stamp, similar to that in Grace 1979, 187, pl. XXIX.30 (dolphin).

No.	Illustration	Reading and Fabric	References
°**39.** Kourion? Samaria		Flower? Sketchy Rhodian rose? Fabric: NR	Reisner *et al.* 1924, 316, D 14. See Grace 1979, pl. XXIX.28; Meyza 2004, 277, fig. 14 (lotus with monogram), 283, fig. 56: maybe same die. See no. **32**.
40. Kourion? Tel Akko	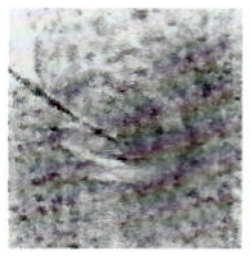	Incuse circle Fabric: [dkRd/ltBn] dkBn	See Calvet 1972, 69, fig. 160, no. 148, Meyza 2004, fig. 59: similar technique.
CYPRUS			
41. Tel Jaffa		Unstamped Fabric: [dkRd] dkRd Rim Type M1	

No.	Illustration	Reading and Fabric	References
***42a.** Maresha		Δ Mask Rim Type M1	Ariel & Finkielsztejn 2003, no. Cy 1.
42b. Maresha	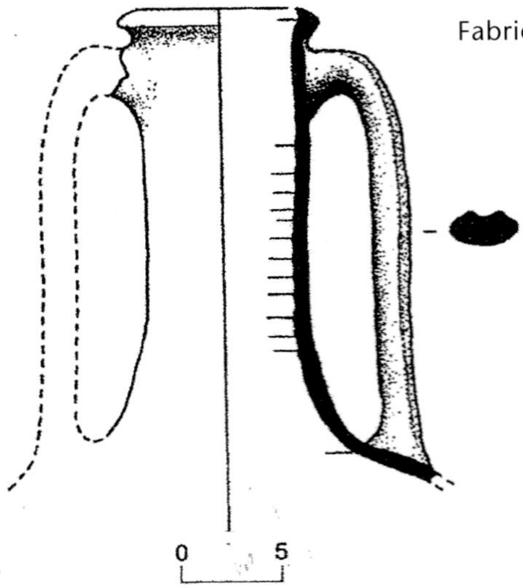	Fabric: see publication	
43. Tel Akko	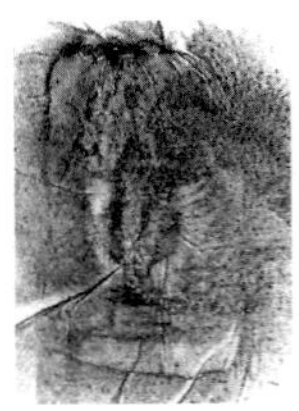	- - - ṂẠỌ[Vase Fabric: [ltRdBn] mic++(+) ltBn	
***44.** Tel Jaffa		OΓ or pellet Γ Fabric: [PkBg] incl+ Bg	Fabric close to no. **71**.
45. Tel Akko	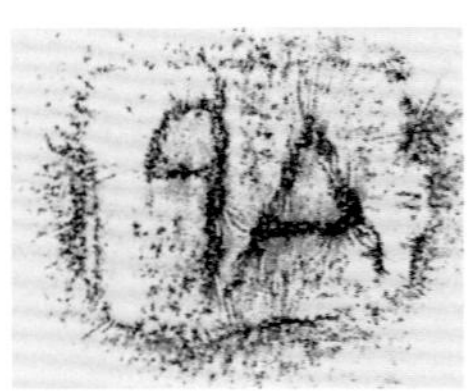	AP(retrograde Fabric: [Rd] incl.++ mic+++ Rd	This abbreviation is common on Kouriote stamps of the "Tripod" serie, but also alone: Calvet 1993, 72, fig. 69, no. 102 (rather than ΔA).

No.	Illustration	Reading and Fabric	References
***46.** Tel Jaffa		ΔZ or Δ or N N Δ Fabric: [ltBn(ltRdYe)] incl.+++ ltBn	Finkielsztejn forthcoming a.
47. Tel Akko	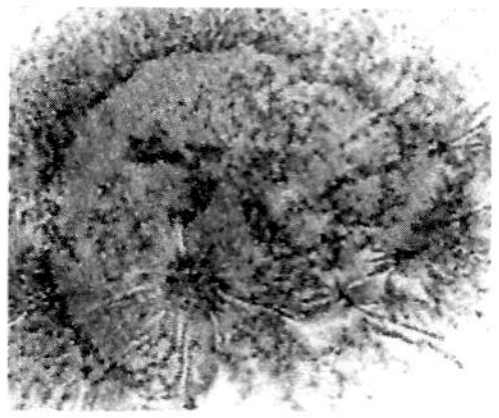	Ọ -? K Dot Fabric: [ltYeRd] incl.++(+) ltBn	
***48.** Tel Jaffa		Δ.Δ. or N.Δ.Δ. or Z.Δ.Δ. monogram? Fabric: [RdYe] incl.+ mic++ vltBn	Calvet 1993, 76, no. 114, fig. 81, with profile of handle and rim (Type M3): same die; 1972, 63, no. 129, similar style, but monogram AΔ clear there. None identified as Cypriot.
°**49.** Samaria		TE and ΔΔ or ΓΔ monograms? Fabric: NR	Reisner *et al.* 1924, 316, D 17.
50. Tel Akko	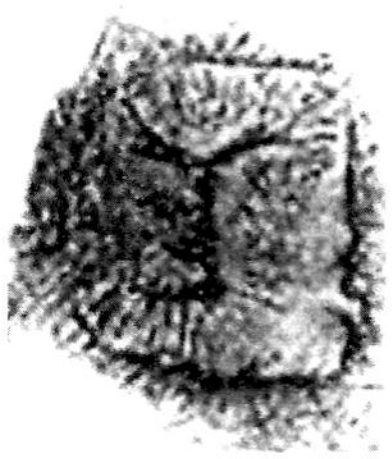	Monogram: EY(retrograde, rather than EΛ(non retrograde Fabric: [Rd/dkRd] incl.+ mic+++ Rd/dkRd Rim Type 2b	
***51.** Tel Jaffa		MAPOY? monogram Fabric: [Rd] incl.++ RdYe Bg	Published examples from Cyprus and Alexandria: Calvet 1972, 62, no. 125 (with beige cover); 1982, 51, no. 134: same monogram, close or identical die. Πανάγου 2010, 342 with note 890 fig. 5 pl. 43 (with references and refutation of the attribution to Poros). See no. **52**.

No.	Illustration	Reading and Fabric	References
***52.** Tel Jaffa		ΜΑΡΟΥ? monogram Fabric: [ltYeRd (ltBn)] incl.+ ltYeRd	See no. **51**.
53. Tel Akko		Μ Κ̣ ? Fabric: [ltRd] incl.+ mic+ ltBn	See Calvet 1982, 44, no. 122: seems different die (different reading, but not clear on picture).
54. Tel Akko		Device? Monogram? Fabric: [ltBn(Bn)] incl.++ ltBn ltBg	See Calvet 1972, 65, no. 135: close but not necessarily identical device.
55. Tel Akko	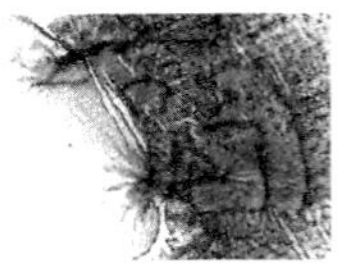	]Ο̣ Σ]ΔΙ Fabric: [dkRd] dkBn Rim Type M1	
***56.** Tel Jaffa		]ΑΠ . [Fabric: [ltRdYe] incl.+ ltBg	Finkielsztejn forthcoming a.
***57.** Tel Akko	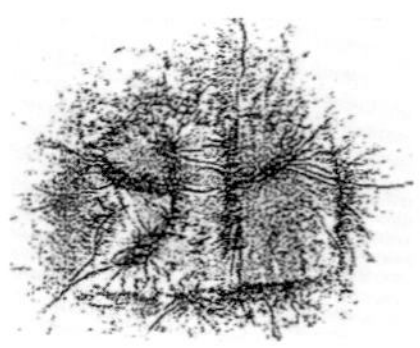	Unclear script: Greek ΕΡ(, with *epsilon* retrograde or Phoenician *resh/dalet beth*? Fabric: [PkBg] incl.+++ ltBg Rim Type M2b	See Meyza 2004, 279, fig. 24, ΕΡ(; Calvet 1982, 47-48, no. 129, letter to left = our letter to left; profile of handle could be "Cypriot". Light fabric is associated with Cypriot Phoenician stamps. Both letters similar to no. **58**. VGC: right letter on no. **67** and left letter here associated on a stamp from Alexandria.

No.	Illustration	Reading and Fabric	References
***58.** Tel Akko	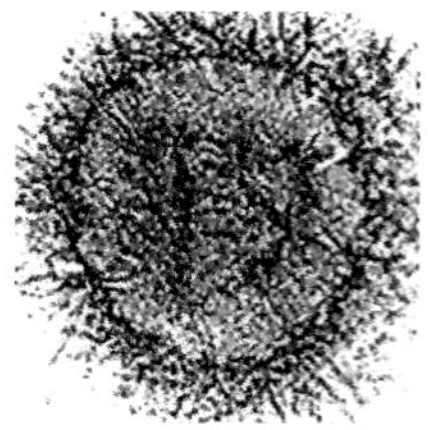	Unclear script: Greek retrograde EP(or Phoenician *beth resh/dalet?* Fabric: [PkBg] incl.+++ ltBg	See Meyza 2004, 279, fig. 24, EP(; Calvet 1982, no. 129, letter to left = our letter to right; profile of handle could be "Cypriot". Light fabric is associated with Cypriot Phoenician stamps. Both letters similar to no. **57**.
59. Tel Akko	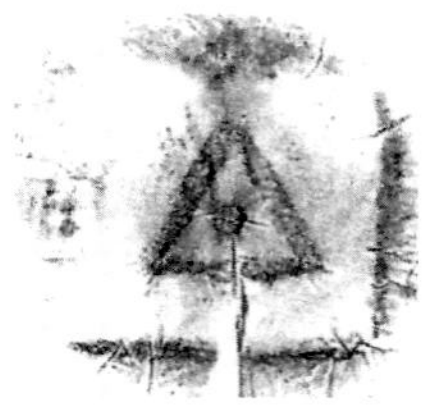	Δ with dot inside Fabric: [dkRd] incl.+(+) mic+++ Rd Rim Type M3	Die different from no. **60**.
60. Tel Akko		Δ with dot inside Fabric: [btRd] incl.+(+) mic+++ ltBn Rim Type M2b	Die different from no. **59**.
61. Tel Akko	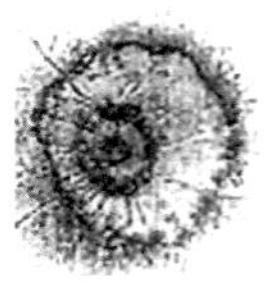	O with dot inside Fabric: [Rd] incl.++ mic+ RdBn	
***62.** Tel Akko	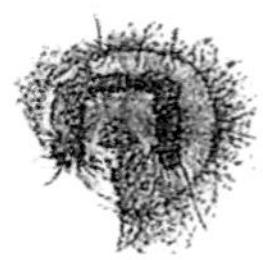	Π with dot inside Fabric: Bg(PkBg)] incl.+++ Bg	Similarities with Calvet 1972, 64, fig. 143, no. 132 (square stamp).
63. Tel Akko		Unclear (Greek?) monogram Fabric: [Pk] incl.+++ vltPk Complete neck with one and a half handles Rim Type: NR	

No.	Illustration	Reading and Fabric	References
64. Tel Akko	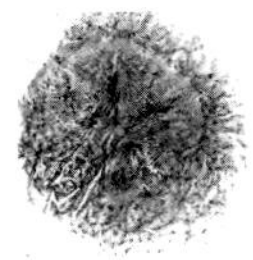	Unclear (Greek?) monogram. Fabric: [Pk] incl.+++ Pk	
65. Tel Akko	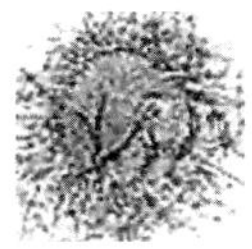	NK(retrograde monogram or Phoenician? [Wh] incl.+++ Wh Rim Type M2b	See Calvet 1972, no. 128: monogram N/ΛK. Light fabric as is the case for vessels stamped in Phoenician.
***66.** Tel Akko	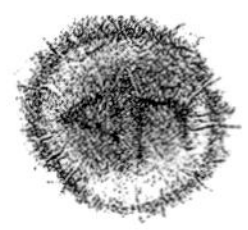	Unclear script: Phoenician *het dalet/resh*, rather than Greek ΔΠ? Fabric: [Wh(PkBg)] incl.+++ Wh Rim Type M2b	See Calvet 1982, 47-48, no. 129, letter to right = our letter to right; profile of handle could be Cypriot. Light fabric as is the case for vessels stamped in Phoenician.
°67. Tel Gezer		Phoenician *het tav* Fabric: NR	Macalister 1912, fig 467.26. See Calvet 1982, 47-48, no. 129, letter to right = our letter to right; profile of handle could be Cypriot. VGC: letter to right here and letter to left on no. **57** associated on a stamp from Alexandria.
°68. Akko, Municipal Museum	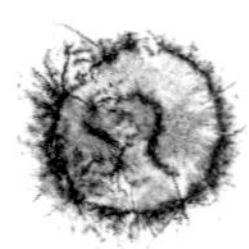	Phoenician *nun lamed* retrograde or symbol? Fabric: NR	See no. **72a**: sign to right (retrograde) similar sign on right here (non retrograde). See no. **73**, here: letter to left here same as second from right there.

No.	Illustration	Reading and Fabric	References
***69.** Tel Jaffa		Phoenician *resh nun*, rather than Greek Γ (retrograde) Z (non retrograde) Fabric: [ltPkBg] incl.+++ YeWh Rim Type M3	Same production as no. **70**.
***70.** Tel Jaffa		Phoenician *resh resh* retrograde Fabric: [ltPkBg] incl.+++ ltBg Rim Type M3	Same production as no. **69**. VGC: Benaki Collection, similar two signs, oriented from right to left (i.e. non retrograde if Phoenician) in a square die, with similar profile and fabric. Double letters on amphora stamps are common on Punic stamps.
***71.** Tel Jaffa		Phoenician] *tav*. [Fabric: [ltPkBg] incl.++(+) ltBn	Fabric close to no. **44**. See no. **72a**: letter to left (retrograde) similar to central letter here (non retrograde).

No.	Illustration	Reading and Fabric	References
°**72a**. Cesarea, Hippodrome		Phoenician tav Dot nun retrograde (suggested reading: J. Naveh)	Finkielsztejn forthcoming b See nos. **68** and **71**.
72b. Cesarea, Hippodrome		Rim Type M2b Fabric: [ltBn] incl.++ ltBn	
***73**. Tel Akko		Phoenician *vav lamed* Dot *nun vav*? Fabric: NR Rim Type M3	See no. **68**: letter to left same as second from right here.
°**74**. Tel Akko	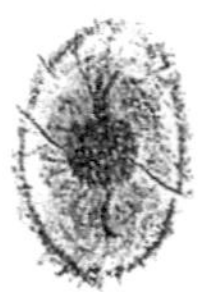	Pomegranate Fabric: [Wh] incl+++ Wh	
75. Samaria	**13. Pomegranate in a circle**	Pomegranate Fabric: NR	Reisner *et al.* 1924, 316, D 13. Same device on no. **74**.
76. Tel Akko		Unclear device (or letters?) Fabric: [ltBn(Bn)] mic+++ ltBn	

Rhodian Amphorae from Cyprus: A Summary of the Evidence and the Issues

BY CRAIG D. BARKER

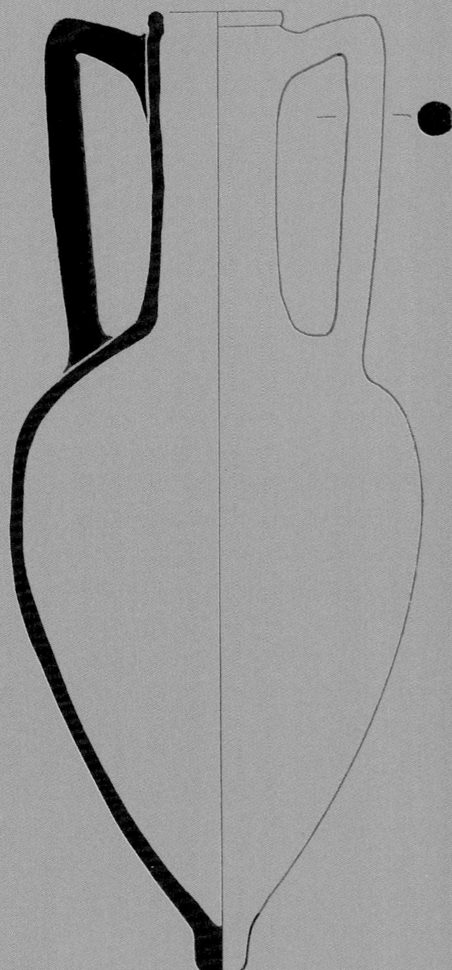

Rhodian Amphorae from Cyprus: A Summary of the Evidence and the Issues

BY CRAIG D. BARKER

INTRODUCTION

This paper is an attempt to present an overview of the evidence of importation of Rhodian amphorae into Cyprus during the Hellenistic era, and of the history of the publication of that material. It is also a chance to examine some of the major issues and problems in Rhodian amphorae research in Cyprus and to question where those of us interested in issues of amphora studies and Hellenistic trade can go from here. This paper shall focus in particular on Paphos and the western areas of the island, not only because it is the area in which I have conducted my own studies, but also because of the important role played by the harbour of Nea Paphos in the period of the Ptolemaic reign; indeed John Lund has described Paphos as the "linchpin" in Hellenistic trade relations between Rhodes and Alexandria,[1] and the evidence of amphorae importation goes some way towards confirming this argument. It is important to remember, however, that many of these issues are also relevant to Rhodian amphorae studies elsewhere on Cyprus and indeed across the eastern Mediterranean as a whole.

THE EVIDENCE OF RHODIAN AND OTHER IMPORTED STAMPED AMPHORAE MATERIAL FROM ARCHAEOLOGICAL CONTEXTS IN CYPRUS

In any investigation of the importation of Rhodian amphorae to Cyprus, the quantity of material found on the island must be emphasised. Nearly two decades ago Demetrios Michaelides, in a landmark paper at the second colloquium for the study of Hellenistic ceramics (held appropriately in Rhodes), revealed the wealth of Rhodian amphora evidence from Cyprus.[2]

He wrote that more intact Rhodian amphorae have been found on Cyprus than anywhere else in the Mediterranean outside of Rhodes itself,[3] the direct result of a seemingly unique Hellenistic burial custom to western Cyprus, first noted as the result of salvage excavations he conducted in the 1980s in the eastern necropolis of Nea Paphos.[4] Further excavation, especially rescue excavations of additional tombs around Paphos (in the northern and eastern necropoles of the city) and across the wider western region of the island, in the intervening two decades as the tourist trade has boomed, has uncovered even more evidence of this custom of burials of two amphorae in simple shaft-graves (or *mnema*-graves). Similarly systematic scientific excavations at the 'Tombs of the Kings' necropolis between 1977 and 1990 also revealed traces of this practice.[5] This custom displayed a practice of interring two amphorae, almost always Rhodian, upright at the feet of the burial or either side of the head.[6] The custom demonstrated not only the dominance of Hellenistic trade routes between Rhodes and Alexandria using Paphos harbour as a major trading point along the way, but in principle the practice provided an archaeological *terminus post quem* for the burial with four datable stamped handles in each grave context with Rhodian amphorae. Despite many of the graves being damaged or de-contextualised (often with the tops of the amphorae being damaged by ploughing because they were sticking above the top of the shaft-graves), enough intact amphorae survived for Michaelides to claim a higher preservation rate of Rhodian vessels than anywhere other than Rhodes itself. In 1990 he wrote of 130 intact amphorae in the Paphos Museum alone[7] – that number has dramatically increased subsequently as the result of rescue excavations across the western coast of the island.

Along side the Paphian tomb material, Hellenistic amphora material was well known from a number of other sites, and in terms of large-scale publication of stamped Hellenistic amphora evidence from Cyprus we see several landmark publications representing excavations from across the island.

A summary of published stamped amphora handles from Cyprus provides an interesting overview of the context of the finds, even in the form of a far from comprehensive list. The finds of stamped Rhodian and other stamped Hellenistic amphorae material across Cyprus include:[8]

Paphos

Domestic: The publication of stamped amphora handles recovered by the Cypriot excavations of the House of Dionysos at Paphos[9], and subsequent Polish mission excavations of nearby domestic quarters.[10]

Public buildings: Stamped amphora handles recovered

from the area of the Odeion, the Gymnasium and Asklepieion were published by Ino Nicolaou;[11] a limited number have been published by the Italian mission working in the so-called "Garrison's Camp" area of Kato Paphos;[12] and a limited number of handles recovered at the site of the Hellenistic-Roman theatre of Paphos will be published by the Australian mission in the near future.[13]

Maritime: Over 300 stamped handles were recovered during harbour dredging in 1964;[14] they were eventually published by Ino Nicholaou.[15]

Funeral: Stamped handles of amphora and intact vessels have been excavated from a large number of graves and tombs in the Paphos region. As well as those recovered by Michaelides in the eastern necropolis mentioned earlier, the largest corpus is the one resulting from the excavation of the so-called "Tombs of the Kings" between 1977 and 1990 by Sophocles Hadjisavvas.[16] These will be published in the near future.

In addition there have been publications of individual stamped handles or intact vessels from a number of tombs around various locations in the Paphos area.[17]

Private collections: A number of handles (over 270) from the George Eliades private collection were published by Zofia Sztetyłło in the 1970s.[18]

Kition

There have been two catalogue publications of stamped amphora handles recovered by the French mission.[19]

Salamis

There have been two catalogue publications of stamped amphora handles recovered by the French mission in excavations prior to the invasion.[20]

Polis

Eleven intact amphorae excavated from Tomb ΜΠ 3339 by Eftychia Zachariou in 1997 were published by Ino Nicolaou in 2005.[21]

Kyrenia Shipwreck

Mark Lawall is in the process of publishing the early Rhodian and other imported amphorae found in the Kyrenia shipwreck site in the early 1970s.[22]

Cesnola Material

A number of unprovenanced intact Rhodian amphorae recovered from the 19th century diggings of American consul Luigi Palma di Cesnola were reported in a number of publications from the 19th century. A number of these jars eventually ended up in the John Ringling Museum in Sarasota, Florida, while a large number of stamped Rhodian amphora handles formed part of the Cesnola collection of the Metropolitan Museum of Art in New York.[23]

---

1 Lund 1999a, 201.
2 Μιχαηλίδες 1990a.
3 Μιχαηλίδες 1990a, 187.
4 See for example, Michaelides' work in the eastern necropolis in publication such as Michaelides 1984, Michaelides & Sznycer 1985; and Michaelides & Mlynarczyk 1988; Μιχαηλίδες 1990. Further confirmation of the quantity of Rhodian amphora found in Hellenistic tombs around Paphos comes from *pers comm.* with D. Michaelides and E. Raptou, who have both excavated many tombs for the Department of Archaeology during rescue excavations.
5 Cf. Hadjisavvas 1985a and 1985b. The first observation of the doubling of Rhodian amphorae in Paphian tombs was made at this site: Hadjisavvas 1980b. I wish to express gratitude to Dr Sophocles Hadjisavvas for permission to study the stamped amphora handles from the 'Tombs of the Kings' site for his final excavation report.
6 See Barker 2004 for further discussion on this practice.
7 Μιχαηλίδες 1990a, 187-188.
8 See also Nicolaou 2005, 1-2.
9 Nicolaou 2005, 17-263.
10 Sztetyłło 1976; *eadem* 1984 and 1991.
11 Nicolaou 2005, 359-382.
12 Stamped handles have been published in, amongst others, the following reports: Giudice *et al.* 1993; 1994; 1996.
13 C. Barker forthcoming.
14 Nicolaou 1966, 601 footnote 94.
15 Nicolaou 1966, 267-357.
16 I wish to express my gratitude to Dr Hadjisavvas for his support of the Australian mission assisting him in the recording of the finds from the Hellenistic necropolis, and for his permission to mention the Rhodian material he excavated there. For more on the site, see the two publications mentioned *supra* in footnote 5; also Dr Hadjisavvas' annual updates of the excavations published in the *RDAC* and *BCH*.
17 These include: amphorae from Ktima Paphos (Markides 1916, 13-14; Deshayes 1963, 301-302); seven amphorae from chamber tomb ΜΠ 2423 Vasiliko, Paphos (Hadjisavvas 1980a); amphorae from excavations at Polis (Munro 1891 and Munro & Tubbs 1891; and amphorae from Department of Antiquities excavations at Pegeia: Barker 2002a.
18 Sztetyłło 1976.
19 Calvet 1982; 1993.
20 Calvet 1972; 1978.
21 Nicolaou 2005, 383-392.
22 Lawall 2011.
23 Hall 1885; Myres 1914; Grace 1948, 144-147.

Individual or Small Scale Finds

Individual stamped handles from isolated finds have been published almost continuously for a number decades by Ino Nicolaou in the "Inscriptiones Cypriae Alphabeticae" series published annually in the *Report of the Department of Antiquities, Cyprus*.[24] An additional fifteen mostly unprovenanced intact Rhodian amphorae held in the Cyprus Museum at Nicholson were published in the mid-1980s.[25]

WHAT DOES THIS EVIDENCE TELL US?

What is important about all of this Cypriot evidence is that we see Rhodian amphorae being located and published from a variety of sources (including both stratified and unstratified): funerary, domestic, public structures, marine finds, isolated finds, surface finds, and private collections where handles were kept for intrinsic or epigraphic value. It is indicative of the broader use of amphorae for a wide range of purposes in Hellenistic daily life.

In Cyprus, however, like elsewhere, publication was almost exclusively focused on stamped material – either the stamps on individual handle finds, or of intact amphorae, and of periodically upper parts of vessels with both handles surviving or at least preserved in a state where they could be restored. The large volume of surviving material was a bonus, as it meant that there was an opportunity to confirm eponym and fabricant stamped combinations, or to identify previously unknown links, which could assist with the tightening of the chronological framework. [26]

Ino Nicolaou's publication of Rhodian eponym-fabricant combinations from Cyprus in 2005[27] (many of them previously unknown) offers an excellent example of the value of furnishing such information, both to assist with chronological refinement and to show linkages of stamps. She lists 111 previously published links (or name combinations), 39 previously unpublished from museum collections, as well as 11 from tombs in Polis, 8 from Paphos harbour, and 8 from the House of Dionysos (177 combinations in total). It is the largest published corpus of linkages between eponyms and fabricants, and again indicative of the overall scale of material from Cyprus.

QUANTITIES OF STAMPED AMPHORA HANDLE FINDS IN CYPRUS

While the corpus numbers for the island are not on the same scale as the Alexandrian Museum figures,[28] all of the material that has been published clearly demonstrates the sizeable numbers of stamped amphorae excavated in Cyprus, and implies the scale of the trade.

Paphos: House of Dionysos (784 stamped handles)[29]
Paphos: Polish mission excavations at *Maloutena* (388 stamped handles)[30]
Paphos: harbour dredging (386 stamped handles)[31]
Paphos: The 'Tombs of the Kings' (734 stamped handles, as yet unpublished)[32]
Paphos: Odeion, Gymnasium & Asklepieion excavations (111 stamped handles)[33]
Paphos: George Eliades private collection (274 stamped handles)[34]
Salamis: French mission (222 stamped handles)[35]
Kition: Kition-*Bamboula* (200 stamped handles)[36]
Polis: Tomb ΜΠ 3339 (11 whole Rhodian amphorae)[37]
Cesnola Collection: various unknown sources (at least 31 whole amphorae and over 125 stamped handles)

As mentioned earlier, there are many smaller-scale publications and individual finds of material to be added to this corpus; for example the Rhodian amphorae finds from burials at Kourion[38] and at Episkopi.[39]

So overall, the wealth of stamped Hellenistic amphora material from the island is staggering and truly indicative of Cyprus' position in the eastern Mediterranean and of the role it played in large-scale trade.

PROBLEMS AND ISSUES

So let's look at some of the problems one is faced with when examining the evidence from Cyprus.

Firstly, unpublished material. The ever-present issue of unpublished excavated material hampers the holistic study of the Hellenistic importation of amphorae to Cyprus. Of course, this is not a problem specific to Cyprus, nor to amphora studies, but it remains a major issue in terms of attempting to synthesize the material.[40] Despite the large scale of the material that has been published already or is in preparation, a great deal of Cypriot amphora material has never seen the light of day. Much of it has been found in Nea Paphos itself, and more widely across the western regions of the islands in rescue digs by the Department of Antiquities of Cyprus, in the same manner as the eastern necropolis excavations that alerted Michaelides to the duplication practice in the first place back in the 1980s. Endemic of a broader problem in classical archaeology and well beyond this discussion, it is worth emphasising that large-scale synthesis of amphora material from Cyprus will be difficult unless even more material becomes accessible and fully published.

Secondly, there is an over-reliance on stamped amphorae material over unstamped material. Again a problem which is not Cypro-specific, but there remains a clear need to publish unstamped evidence, as well as the stamped material to give a truer indication of Hellenistic trade patterns on the island. This is particularly important in cemetery contexts as it gives a greater indication of the total number of vessels interred, and in the case of disturbed contexts of the total number of burials. Most importantly of course, it allows for quantitative analysis of the proportions of stamped to unstamped material. Without a clearer indication of the total number vessels, it is not possible to create truly accurate models of the volume of trade. Increasingly, those focusing on amphora studies are beginning to turn their attentions to this problem,[41] and one hopes future decades will see this problem rectified.

NOTICEABLE TRENDS IN HELLENISTIC AMPHORAE IN CYPRUS

Rhodian Dominance Amongst the Material Found

Like other eastern Mediterranean centres, there is a noticeable predominance of Rhodian material over other production centres, including seemingly Cypriot amphorae themselves. Given the previously noted caveat about the focus on the publication of stamped material, it is conceivable that our data simply records a predominance of Rhodian stamped material and renders a false impression regarding the overall pattern of amphorae importation and trade. Again this is a trend which is not specific to Cyprus, for the same pattern is visible across the broader eastern Mediterranean region. However, it is a pattern that needs to be treated with caution as it may truly reflect merely the predominance in the importation of stamped amphorae, rather than total amphorae trade.

Certainly the stamped amphora handles give us clear indication of the clear dominance of Rhodian over other production centres: and although we see importation from a wide variety of sources including Chios, Kos, and Knidos, it is proportionally minute compared to Rhodian material in publish corpuses of stamped amphora handles. This is revealed by the following examples.

Rhodian stamped amphora handles make up 97% of stamped amphora evidence from the 'Tombs of the Kings' necropolis (Fig. 1).[42]

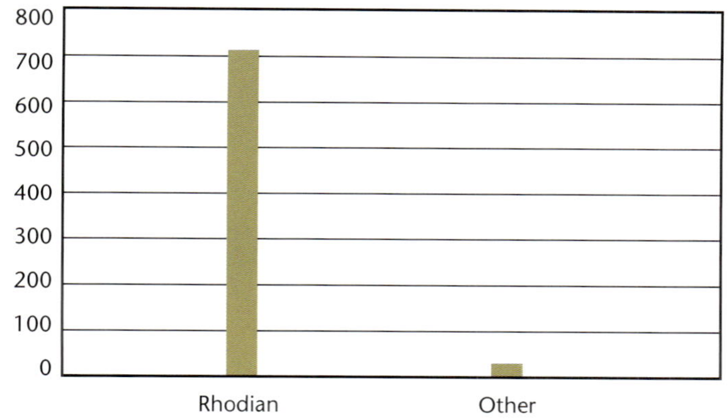

Fig. 1. Stamped Amphora Handles from the 'Tombs of the Kings', Nea Paphos (Barker 2004 and unpublished Ph.D. 2004).

24 Nicolaou has been publishing the series in the *Report of the Department of Antiquities,* Cyprus since 1961: most issues contain some stamped amphora handles.
25 Nicolaou & Empereur 1986. A list of names on some stamps held in the collection of the Cyprus Museum was published in Myres & Ohnefalsch-Richter 1899, 95-98.
26 See for example Barker 2002b. More significantly, Ino Nicolaou (2005) demonstrates time and time again the ability to link the names of eponyms and fabricants when the context was secure.
27 Nicolaou 2005.
28 Fraser 1972, 165.
29 Nicolaou 2005, 19-242.
30 Sztetyłło 1991.
31 Nicolaou 2005, 267-350.
32 Barker 2004.
33 Nicolaou 2005, 359-381.
34 Sztetyłło 1976, 7.
35 Calvet 1972; 1978, 222-234.
36 Calvet 1982; 1993.
37 Nicolaou 2005, 383-390.
38 McFadden 1946.
39 Oliver 1983.
40 At least the Department of Antiquities of Cyprus is aware of this problems and ways of tackling it: cf. Hadjisavvas & Karageorghis (eds.) 2000.
41 Lawall 2005.
42 Full results from the 'Tombs of the Kings' are to be published in the future, I thank Dr Hadjisavvas for permission to present preliminary results here.

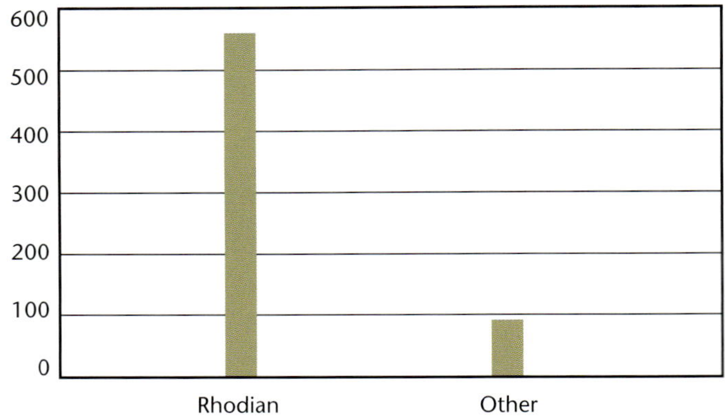

Fig. 2. Imported Stamped Amphora Handles from the Polish excavations at Maloutena Nea Paphos (Sztetyłło 1976 and 1991).

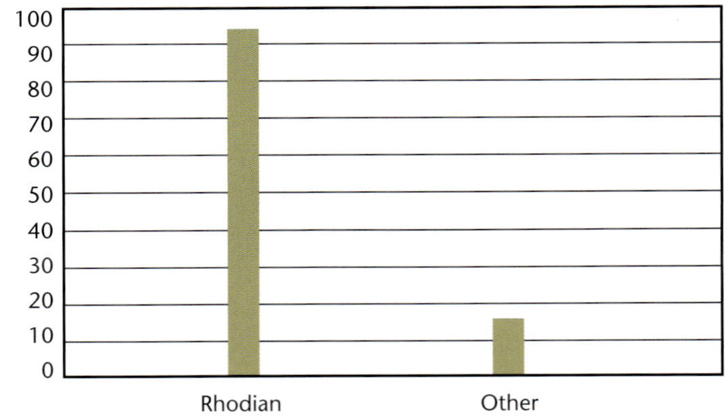

Fig. 4. Imported Stamped Amphora Handles from Department of Antiquities Excavations at the Odeion, Nea Paphos (Nicolaou 2005).

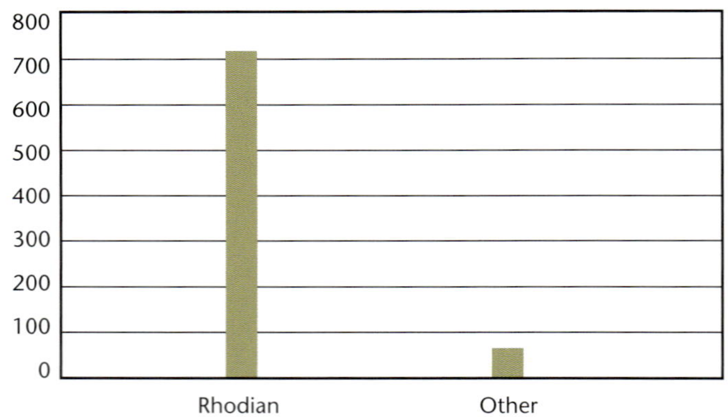

Fig. 3. Imported Stamped Amphora Handles from Department of Antiquities Excavations at the House of Dionysos, Nea Paphos (Nicolaou 2005).

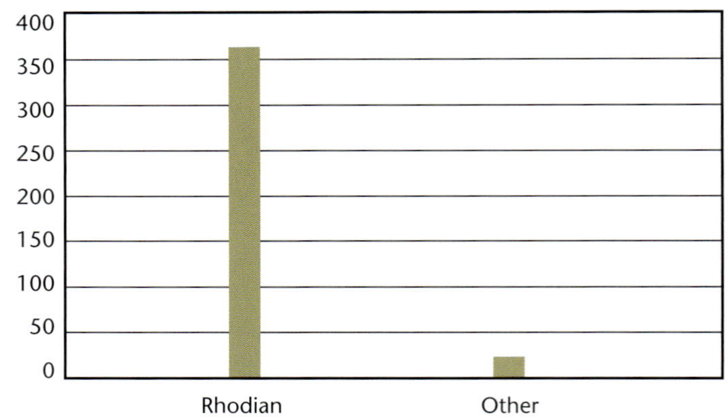

Fig. 5. Imported Stamped Amphora dredged from Paphos Harbour (Nicolaou 2005).

86% of the amphora handles excavated by the Polish team at the *Maloutena* area of Nea Paphos was Rhodian in origin (Fig. 2),[43] and an even higher percentage of the material published by Ino Nicolaou[44] was from Rhodes: 92% of the stamped handles recovered by the Department of Antiquities excavations of the House of Dionysos (Fig. 3), 94% of the amphora stamped recovered from the Paphos harbour dredging project (Fig. 5), and 86% from the Paphos Odeion area (Fig. 4).

While the published figures are not as high in the eastern parts of the island as they are at Paphos, there is nevertheless a decidedly higher proportion of Rhodian material here as well: 66% of the published Kition material was imported from Rhodes (Fig. 7),[45] and 57% of the Salamis material (Fig. 6).[46]

A similar pattern of course is discernable throughout the eastern Mediterranean: from excavations at Jerusalem[47] (94% of the stamped amphorae were Rhodian), at Tel Anafa[48] (96% of the amphora material was from Rhodes), at Dor[49] (74% of recovered material was Rhodian), at Tel Beersheba[50] (80% of the stamped material is from Rhodes), at the Polish excavations of Kom el-Dikka in Alexandria[51] (78% of the recovered stamped amphora handles), from the collection of the Alexandria Museum[52] (over 88%), and from Tarsus in Turkey[53] (82% of the excavated stamped handles).

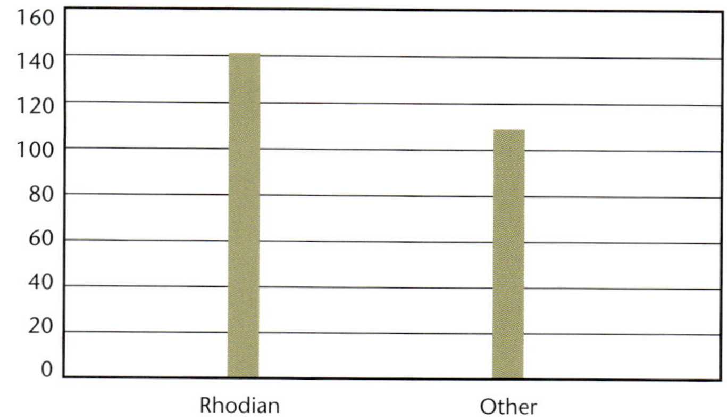

Fig. 6. Stamped Amphora Handles from French excavations at Salamis (Calvet 1972 and 1978).

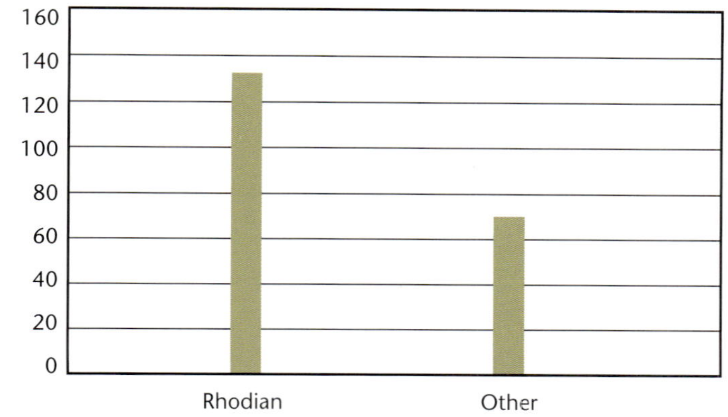

Fig. 7. Stamped Amphora Handles from French excavations at Kition (Calvet 1982 and 1993).

Any future inclusion of unstamped material alongside the stamped material will give us more quantitative data with which to analyse whether this Rhodian dominance of the Hellenistic wine trade was genuine, or rather reflected only by the percentage of vessels that were actually stamped. In other words, our conclusions may mistakenly be driven by the dominant publication of stamped Rhodian vessels. Other production centres conceivably put more vessels into circulation which, nonetheless, have gone unrecorded or inaccurately recorded precisely because of the absence of stamps.

If the figures from the stamped evidence accurately reflect overall patterns of trade, then what are the greater implications for the role of Cyprus in Aegean-Egyptian Hellenistic trade networks? This issue has been examined by a number of people; as mentioned earlier, the harbour of Nea Paphos has been described as the "linchpin" in Hellenistic trade relations between Rhodes and Alexandria.[54] Prevailing wind patterns and counter-clockwise currents circling Cyprus meant that Paphos' harbour played a more significant role in west to east and north to south routes.[55] It seems as though Rhodian amphorae bearing wine to be traded for Egyptian grain were often being unloaded along the way in Cypriot ports, which thus served as secondary markets. The directionality of trade may also explain why there are proportionally more Rhodian amphorae finds in the west than at Salamis or Kition – the concentration of Rhodian trade on the west coast becomes diluted as one goes further east on the island.

Further study here is required, with the potential outcome of giving us a greater understanding of the role of an emporium such as Paphos within the larger framework of Aegean to Alexandria trade, not to mention, the benefits to be reaped from evidence of trading patterns within Hellenistic Cyprus from west to east.

Issues of Amphorae Chronology

As Ino Nicolaou has stated, "there is steady import of wine from Rhodes to Cyprus throughout the period of Ptolemaic rule".[56] There is clear evidence of this from multiple sites around the island, that the volume of trade of Rhodian vessels is high from the 3rd century BC onwards, the Kyrenia wreck being among the earliest evidence. Peaks of

43 Sztetyłło 1991.
44 Nicolaou 2005.
45 Calvet 1982; 1993, 61-80.
46 Calvet 1972; 1978, 222-234.
47 Ariel 1990.
48 Ariel & Finkielsztejn 1994, 183-240.
49 Rosenthal-Heginbottom 1995, 183-204.
50 Coulson *et al.* 1997.
51 Sztetyłło 1975; 1978; 1990; 1992a; 1992b.
52 Fraser 1972, 165.
53 Grace 1950.
54 Lund 1999, 201.
55 See for example Hohlfelder & Leonard 1994, 45 and Murray 1995.
56 See Nicolaou 2005, 1-14 for an introduction and summary of many issues in Rhodian amphorae chronologies in Cyprus.

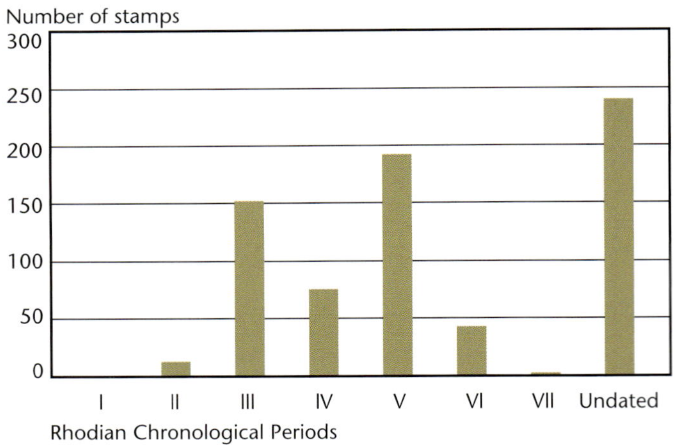

Fig. 8. The chronology of the unpublished Paphos Rhodian stamps from the Department of Antiquities excavations at the 'Tombs of the Kings', Nea Paphos, calculated using Finkielsztejn's revised chronology.

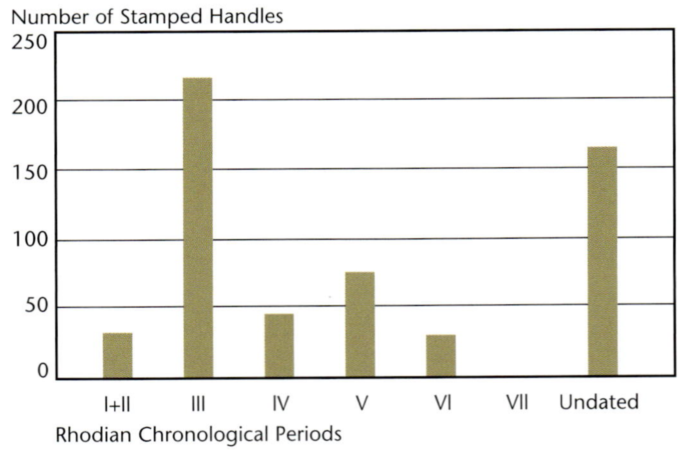

Fig. 10. The chronology of the published Paphos Rhodian stamps from the Polish excavations at Maloutena *Nea Paphos (Sztetyłło 1976 and 1990). The dating of these stamps was published using the old high Grace/ Empereur high chronology.*

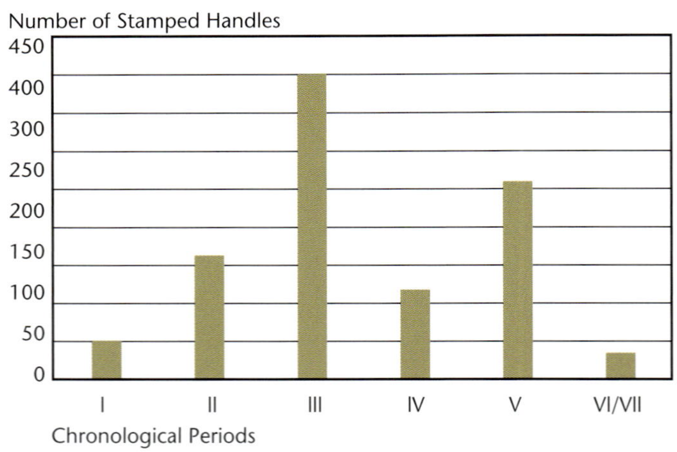

Fig. 9. The chronology of the published Paphos Rhodian stamps from the Department of Antiquities excavations in various sites across Nea Paphos (Nicolaou 2005), calculated using Finkielsztejn's revised chronology.

trading activity are visible in the first decades of the 2nd century BC, and again in the later decades of that century. What is required, however, is an overall standardisation of the calculation of the chronological results of the stamped material, especially in line with the refinement of the chronology in recent years as the result of Gerald Finkielstejn's revised lower chronology.[57]

What is needed is a re-examination of the earlier publications of the corpuses of stamped amphora handles from Paphos, Kition and Salamis, so that these may be re-aligned and the results recalibrated with Finkielsztejn's lower chronology, alongside a greater understanding of the linkages that existed between eponym and fabricant names.

Because of the wealth of Cypriot material, re-examinations such as this would allow for more nuanced research into chronological patterns. Patterns generated in basic chronological charts, yet to be recalibrated for the Finkielstzejn chronological revisions, render intriguing results that could obviously benefit from more detailed and nuanced investigation. Up until now, like most other charted areas of the eastern Mediterranean, the Rhodian stamps from Cyprus have demonstrated a peak in Virginia Grace's chronological Period III (see Figs. 10-12).[58] Even with chronological refinements, this heightened 2nd century BC activity should still mark its presence – as can be seen in Nicolaou's publication of the material dredged from Paphos harbour in the 1960s, and of her husband's excavations at the House of Dionysos, and the Odeion/ Gynmasium area of Paphos using the lower chronology – where peak counts are visible in Period III and Period V (Fig 9).[59]

One of the interesting assemblages at this point are the stamped handles from the 'Tombs of the Kings' necropolis. The unpublished material suggests a peak in Rhodian imports during the later decades of the century rather than during Period III (Fig. 8).[60] The fact that this evidence does not fit the prevailing pattern is not necessarily a problem.

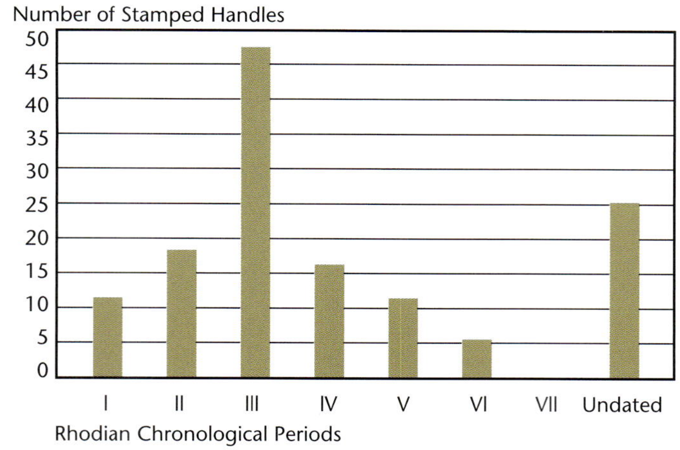

Fig. 11. The chronology of the published Kition Rhodian stamps (Calvet 1982 and 1993). The dating of these stamps was published using the old high Grace/Empereur high chronology.

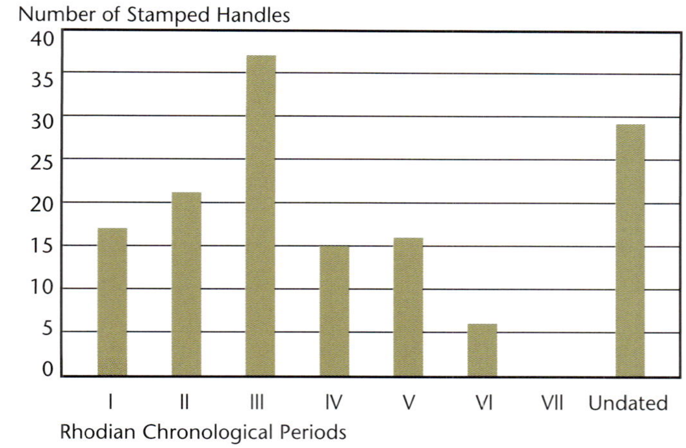

Fig. 12. The chronology of the published Salamis Rhodian stamps (Calvet 1972 and 1978). The dating of these stamps was published using the old high Grace/Empereur high chronology.

As is demonstrated by the finds recorded at the House of Dionysos and in other buildings in that zone of the ancient city, as well as by those in the harbour, the peak period of exportation from Rhodes to Cyprus (on route to Alexandria) may very well have been the first decades of the second century BC (during Period III). Conceivably, the pattern from the 'Tombs of the Kings' merely reflects the fact that the peak period of burial activity at this particular necropolis occurred half a century later (during Period V). A shifting pattern of burials possibly occurred at Paphos as the space for graves closest to the city was used, forcing inhabitants to develop newer cemeteries progressively further away from the city. According to this hypothesis, we would expect to see peak burial activities of Period III in the northern and eastern necopolies of the city, with peak activities of the later Rhodian production periods occurring further out in the areas around the 'Tombs of the Kings' graves. Such a hypothesis can only be proven through the publication of materials from additional tomb excavations along the perimeter of the Hellenistic capital of Cyprus. Whether true or not, the example of the finds from the 'Tombs of the Kings' does demonstrate one of the potential areas where a greater understanding of the chronology of the stamped imported amphorae in Cyprus can lead us in future.

There is also the more localised ability of the stamped amphorae material to provide *terminus post quem* for deposition of grave goods. While many of the graves at the 'Tombs of the Kings' necropolis were disturbed by looting and quarrying during antiquity, the surviving intact graves excavated by Dr Hadjisavvas' team at the 'Tombs of the Kings' demonstrate the massive potential for understanding the history of the use of the necropolis.[61]

This chronological concept has application across a wider scale, and the use of the stamped material to help date stratified deposits must be improved, especially insofar as in funerary contexts from Paphos and from the surrounding areas near Paphos are concerned. It may also help with the interpretation of transformations in a given site; for example, from the 'Tombs of the Kings' we see an

57 There is considerable recent publication on the discussion about the revision of Virginia Grace's chronological assignation of eponym names, especially by Gerald Finkielsztejn and Mark Lawall. The debate falls outside of the scope of this paper, although any refinement of chronological determination has considerable value for Cypriot Rhodian amphora studies. See for example: Finkielsztejn 2001a; 2004; and Lawall 2002.

58 See, for example, chronological ranges of stamped Rhodian amphorae published by Sztetyłło and Calvet.

59 Nicolaou 2005, 8, fig. 3.

60 The larger number of undated material in this chart includes broken and unreadable stamps, which are often excluded from other published tallies.

61 Barker 2004.

interesting phenomenon. It has often be suggested that the architectural design of the peristyle-tombs, with their Alexandrian styles, points specifically to their use with the burials of the Ptolemaic elite. This assumes that the poorer, local populations used more standard shaft-graves and traditional chamber tombs. However, the use of Rhodian amphorae in all types of tomb design, with tomb use (as dated by the amphora stamps) extending over a wide time period, helps to confirm Hadjisavvas' interpretation that these were family burials,[62] and as such that they were used over a number of generations.

The Nature of Secondary Use of Amphorae

On this issue, greater levels of research are required, especially into the spread of the amphorae burial custom we have discussed in passing. Michaelides first suggested the practice from the eastern necropolis of Paphos; however, the evidence for the 'Tombs of the Kings' and from other burials, such as the 11 amphorae found in duplicates at Polis by Eutychia Zachariou, demonstrates that the practice was widespread throughout the western region of the island.

Michaelides speculated that the custom had its roots much earlier than the Hellenistic period, and that it probably began in the late Cypriot Classical period, where locally produced amphorae were used and occasionally imported vessels such as a Thasian vessel in Tomb ΜΠ 3021 or a proto-Rhodian vessel in tomb ΜΠ 2691.[63] The custom of using two standing Rhodian amphorae seems to have begun in the mid-3rd century BC and continues until the Roman domination of the island. Why Rhodian vessels were preferred over amphorae from other production centres, we don't know. It can be presumed, due to the shifting exchange patterns that occurred during the Ptolemaic occupation of the island, the dominance of Rhodian amphorae in the Cypriot marketplace caused them to achieve symbolic status for the new-found wealth enjoyed by the inhabitants of Nea Paphos as a direct result of their participation in international trade.

The examination of the 'Tombs of the Kings' material is important because it reminds us of our need and very real capacity to move amphora studies beyond issues of trade and manufacture, and to look at the wider uses of amphorae within a society, including secondary and tertiary uses.

THE NEED FOR CHRONOLOGICAL SYNTHESIS

Finally we come to the need for an overall chronological synthesis of Rhodian and other Hellenistic stamped material on the island, and the need for greater publication of material, including, and especially, unstamped evidence that furnishes us with a clearer indication of patterns of trade and of chronological usage. Although the stamped handles of imported Hellenistic amphorae found in the 'Tombs of the Kings' demonstrate the capacity to render extremely nuanced interpretations from a quantitative perspective, the fact remains that we need to have as much of that data available as possible in order to formulate these interpretations in the first place. A greater understanding of what is found on the island, and what is not, will significantly help with our future interpretations.

CONCLUSIONS

Cyprus holds a wealth of amphorae material imported from Rhodes and other production centres, both stamped and unstamped, both published and yet to be published. We are lucky because of that abundant wealth of material from island, as Michaelides first alerted us in 1990, and the good catalogues of material already published, especially Ino Nicolaou's summary of eponym-fabricant combinations. There is significant quantitative data from the island for discussion on the nature of the volume and chronology of Hellenistic trade, and a chance to question the role of amphorae in other aspects of Cypriot society, including for example, their use in Paphian burial customs. It is our challenge now to do something with this wealth of material. We have as yet barely begun to scratch the surface.

---

62 See Hadjisavvas 1985a, 262.
63 Μιχαηλίδες 1990a.

Cyprus and Rhodes: Trade Links During the Hellenistic Period in the Light of Transport Amphora Finds

BY AGATA DOBOSZ

Cyprus and Rhodes: Trade Links During the Hellenistic Period in the Light of Transport Amphora Finds

BY AGATA DOBOSZ

The important economic role that Cyprus played during the Hellenistic period, and generally in Antiquity, due to its profitable location on the crossroads of the ancient trade routes, has frequently been underlined.[1] Hellenistic transport amphorae originating in non-Cypriot production centres, as well as local transport amphorae excavated in many places on the island itself and also outside it, constitute the best evidence for Cyprus' trade links. The predominance of Rhodian stamped amphora handles over those originating in other places is very clear on all of the archaeological sites in Cyprus where Hellenistic material has been excavated,[2] proving that Rhodes was a very important trade partner of Cyprus in that period.

The question of trade between Rhodes and Cyprus during the Hellenistic period, using transport amphorae as evidence of it, has already been examined in more or less detail.[3] The present article aims to look once more at the chronological distribution of Rhodian amphorae on the island in the light of Gérald Finkielsztejn's lower chronology,[4] and also to understand the position of different regions/towns as trade partners of Rhodes and centres of trans-shipment of Rhodian products at that time. Some recently published studies concerning transport amphorae and their stamped handles found in Cyprus, for example by Craig Barker (2002b and 2004), Ino Nicolaou (2005), Antigone Marangou (2009), Zofia Sztetyłło (2010) and Mark Lawall (2011), have allowed us to study much more abundant material and see it in more detail. Some important corrections to previously presented Rhodian stamped amphora handles made by Nicolaou (2005) and by the present author are also significant and have been taken into account.[5]

THE ANALYSED MATERIAL

Several scholars have already discussed the problems posed by the lack of publication of a huge part of previously excavated material as well as by the disproportion between both the stamped Rhodian handles and unstamped amphora fragments as shown in publications and also by the lack of details concerning Rhodian amphora stamps shown in old publications.[6] However, it is worth mentioning here some numbers to underline these problems concerning Cyprus. Only around 200 Rhodian unstamped amphorae or their fragments from the whole island have been published or mentioned in papers, while around 4,200[7] stamped handles (of which 408 belong to whole amphorae or their upper parts[8]) have been presented. Furthermore, over 260 unstamped amphorae and 38 or 39 stamped ones from the Kyrenia wreck that were recently discussed by Lawall should be added to this general number.[9] Due to the above-mentioned problems, the present paper is concerned with the result of the analysis of already published stamped amphorae handles, while the unstamped pieces are mentioned only where available. Of the unpublished finds, 97 Rhodian stamped handles from the site of *Maloutena* in Paphos were taken into account.[10]

The analysed material comes mainly from the public and private buildings and graves,[11] found during regular as well as rescue excavations, and also by field surveys throughout the island and underwater research nearby (Map). Moreover, 126 stamped Rhodian handles of unknown origin in Cyprus, belonging to different collections on the island, have also been taken into account, though only in general remarks. In the later part of this article, the material is discussed according to three main regions.

The regional divisions were based on various factors: the extent of the archaeological investigation in different areas, the availability of published Rhodian amphorae, the natural division of Cyprus resulting from the topography of the island, the distribution of natural resources, such as copper and wood, as well as the varying histories of development of different areas at the end of the Classical period and through the Hellenistic period. The first region is the north-eastern and eastern coast of the island, centred on Salamis, with other sites located in the Karpas Peninsula. The second is the south coast and the areas deeper inside the island with the main sites of Kition, Idalion, Amathus and Kourion. The third region includes western Cyprus with Marion-Arsinoe, Palaepaphos, with its main town being Nea Paphos. From the central part of the island and northern Cyprus (except for the amphorae from the Kyrenia wreck) hardly any Rhodian amphorae have been published.[12]

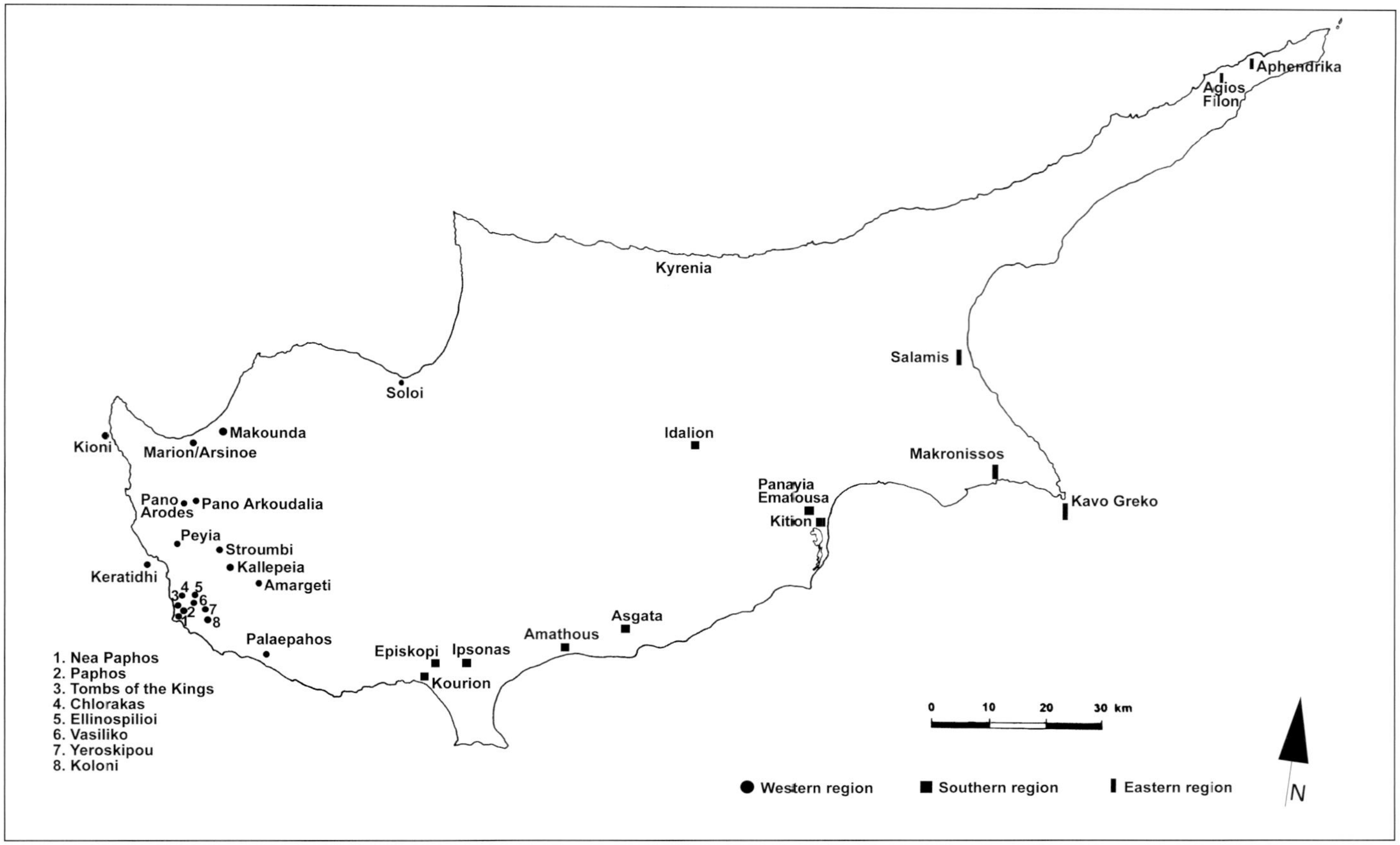

Map of distribution of Hellenistic Rhodian amphorae in Cyprus.

1 Cf. Salles 1993a, 179; Papuci-Władyka 1995, 231-232; Connelly 2010, 175.

2 Cf. Calvet 1972; Sztetyłło 1976; Calvet 1993; Nicolaou 2005; Sztetyłło 2010; it is discussed in more detail by C. Barker, in this volume.

3 Calvet 1972; Calvet 1982; Sztetyłło 1985; Μιχαηλίδης 1990a; Młynarczyk 1990; Lund 1993b; 1999a; Nicolaou 2005; Lund 2006.

4 It was proposed by G. Finkielsztejn in 1995 and 2001a. He dated Period I to *c.* 304-235 BC, Period II to *c.* 234-199 BC, Period III to *c.* 198-161 BC, Period IV to 160-146 BC, Period V to *c.* 145-108 BC, Period VI to *c.* 107-88/86 BC, Period VII to *c.* 85 to Augustus. However, work on its clarification and detailing is still in progress, cf. Lawall 2002; Badoud 2003; Finkielsztejn 2004; Lawall 2011; Lund 2011a.

5 While writing my PhD (Jagiellonian University, Kraków, in progress) on Cypriot trade during the Hellenistic period in the light of amphora finds.

6 Lund 1999a, 188; Barker in this volume.

7 This number should not be taken literally. I counted 3810 stamped handles of certain Rhodian origin and a further 376 handles with worn or illegible stamps of probable, but not necessarily Rhodian origin (not defined in source publications).

8 They constitute 204 pairs, but some of them are worn. On large group of Rhodian eponym – fabricant pairs excavated in Cyprus see: Μιχαηλίδης 1990a, Nicolaou 2005 and Barker in this volume.

9 Lawall 2011, 674; I wish to express my thanks to Dr. M. Lawall for sending me this article before it reached general circulation.

10 They were excavated by the Polish Archaeological Mission of the Warsaw University during the years 2007-2009 and were studied by the present author, cf. Dobosz forthcoming a; forthcoming b. A work on the large number of unstamped shards of Hellenistic amphorae from this site is in progress. Furthermore, amphorae excavated by Polish expedition of the Jagiellonian University, Krakow, within the framework of the *Paphos Agora Project*, will be also taken into consideration in my thesis as far as it will be possible.

11 Cf. Barker in this volume.

12 D. Pilides (2007) mentioned stamped amphora handles found on the Hill of Agios Georgios, in Nicosia, but without any further information and Nicolaou & Empereur (1986, 516 no. 2) published one complete stamped Rhodian amphora from Ambelikou, today in the collection of The Cyprus Museum.

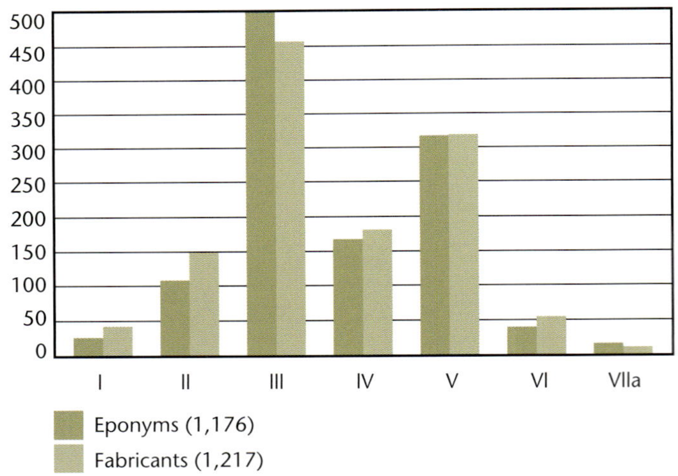

Fig. 1. Chronological distribution of Rhodian amphora stamps found in Cyprus (total number 2,393).

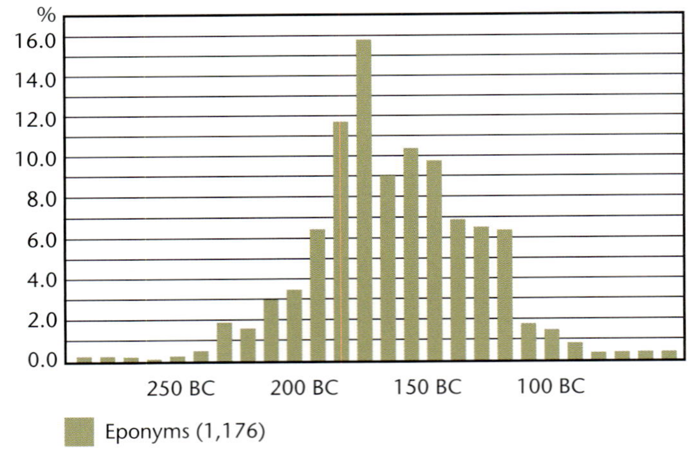

Fig. 3. Chronological distribution of Rhodian amphora stamps of eponyms found in Cyprus (total number 1,176).

Date BC	*East*	*East % (± std error)*	*South*	*South % (± std error)*	*West*	*West % (± std error)*	*Collections*	*Total*	*Total % (± std error)*
299-290	0.3	0.7% ± 2.3	1.0	0.6% ± 1.1	1.0	0.1% ± 0.2	1.0	3.3	0.3% ± 0.3
289-280	0.3	0.7% ± 2.3	1.0	0.6% ± 1.1	1.0	0.1% ± 0.2	0.0	2.3	0.2% ± 0.3
279-270	0.3	0.7% ± 2.3	1.0	0.6% ± 1.1	1.1	0.1% ± 0.2	0.0	2.4	0.2% ± 0.3
269-260	0.0		0.0		1.3	0.1% ± 0.3	0.0	1.3	0.1% ± 0.2
259-250	0.0		0.0		3.0	0.3% ± 0.4	0.0	3.0	0.3% ± 0.3
249-240	0.0		0.0		6.3	0.7% ± 0.6	0.0	6.3	0.5% ± 0.4
239-230	1.8	3.4% ± 5.1	4.0	2.3% ± 2.3	14.7	1.7% ± 0.9	2.0	22.4	1.9% ± 0.8
229-220	2.3	4.4% ± 5.8	3.0	1.7% ± 2.0	13.8	1.6% ± 0.8	0.0	19.0	1.6% ± 0.7
219-210	4.0	7.8% ± 7.5	7.0	4.0% ± 3.0	22.0	2.5% ± 1.0	2.0	35.0	3.0% ± 1.0
209-200	4.0	7.8% ± 7.5	7.0	4.0% ± 3.0	30.0	3.4% ± 1.2	0.0	41.0	3.5% ± 1.1
199-190	8.0	15.7% ± 10.2	8.0	4.6% ± 3.2	56.0	6.3% ± 1.6	4.0	76.0	6.5% ± 1.4
189-180	4.3	8.5% ± 7.8	18.0	10.3% ± 4.6	108.0	12.2% ± 2.2	7.0	137.3	11.7% ± 1.9
179-170	7.3	14.4% ± 9.8	16.3	9.3% ± 4.4	157.3	17.8% ± 2.6	4.3	185.3	15.8% ± 2.1
169-160	4.3	8.5% ± 7.8	13.7	7.8% ± 4.1	78.7	8.9% ± 1.9	9.7	106.3	9.1% ± 1.7
159-150	5.0	9.8% ± 8.3	28.0	16.0% ± 5.5	83.0	9.4% ± 2.0	6.0	122.0	10.4% ± 1.8
149-140	1.3	2.6% ± 4.5	22.7	13.0% ± 5.1	83.3	9.4% ± 2.0	7.0	114.3	9.7% ± 1.7
139-130	4.7	9.1% ± 8.1	16.3	9.3% ± 4.4	54.7	6.2% ± 1.6	5.0	80.7	6.9% ± 1.5
129-120	1.0	2.0% ± 3.9	10.0	5.7% ± 3.5	60.0	6.8% ± 1.7	6.0	77.0	6.6% ± 1.4
119-110	2.0	3.9% ± 5.4	7.0	4.0% ± 3.0	61.0	6.9% ± 1.7	5.0	75.0	6.4% ± 1.4
109-100	0.0		1.3	0.8% ± 1.3	16.7	1.9% ± 0.9	3.1	21.2	1.8% ± 0.8
99-90	0.0		1.7	0.9% ± 1.5	14.7	1.7% ± 0.9	1.4	17.7	1.5% ± 0.7
89-80	0.0		1.6	0.9% ± 1.4	7.3	0.8% ± 0.6	0.8	9.7	0.8% ± 0.5
79-70	0.0		1.6	0.9% ± 1.4	2.3	0.3% ± 0.3	0.4	4.3	0.4% ± 0.4
69-60	0.0		1.6	0.9% ± 1.4	2.3	0.3% ± 0.3	0.4	4.3	0.4% ± 0.4
59-50	0.0		1.6	0.9% ± 1.4	2.3	0.3% ± 0.3	0.4	4.3	0.4% ± 0.4
49-40	0.0		1.6	0.9% ± 1.4	2.3	0.3% ± 0.3	0.4	4.3	0.4% ± 0.4
Total	**51**	**100%**	**175**	**100%**	**884**	**100%**	**66**	**1,176**	**100%**

Fig. 2. Number, percentage and confidence level of Rhodian eponym stamps from the three regions of Cyprus as well as from the collections dated to different decades. Figs. 3, 7, 9, 11 are based on this data. All confidence levels (also in Fig. 5a) are given for 95% of chance that the proportion of stamps in each decade fell within the range indicated.

THE CHRONOLOGICAL DISTRIBUTION OF RHODIAN AMPHORA STAMPS IN CYPRUS

Of the above-mentioned group of *c.* 4,200 Rhodian stamped amphora handles found all over Cyprus, 2,393 examples are identified, of which 1,176 belong to eponyms and 1,217 to, fabricants. The rest of these handles are either unclassified, too worn for restoration, or not published in sufficient detail. The fact that the number of the eponym and fabricant stamps in each period (using the lower Rhodian chronology of the eponyms) is similar suggests that this group is representative (Fig. 1).

Since the chronology of Rhodian eponyms is much more precise than that of the fabricants, let us study the eponym stamps in more detail. While its final refinement is still in progress (cf. note 1), the eponym stamps are analysed here according to decades (Fig. 2).[13] As Fig. 3 shows, the earliest Rhodian stamped amphorae most probably came to Cyprus in the first decade of the 3rd century BC.[14] It seems that they were not very common in Cyprus until the last four decades of the 3rd century BC compared to their number later on, since in each decade they constitute not even 1% of the whole group. This proportion would change, however, if we also take into consideration the amphorae from Kyrenia wreck (especially the unstamped ones) and some other stamped handles of early Rhodian amphorae found in the eastern and the southern part of the island, concerning which it is unclear whether their stamps are those of eponyms or fabricants.[15] Assuming that the earliest stamped amphorae constitute *c.* 10% of the total number of Rhodian amphorae of this date and also that the stamped amphorae in the later decades of Period I constitute *c.* 40-50% of the whole production at that time,[16] the number of Rhodian amphorae dated to Period I found in Cyprus should be multiplied. Since nearly all of Rhodian amphorae dated to the 2nd century BC were stamped,[17] the proportion between early Rhodian amphorae and these of the 2nd century would differ from what Fig. 3 shows. The number of stamped Rhodian amphorae steadily increased on the island over the last four decades of the 3rd century BC (in 200s it reached *c.* 3.5% of the whole group). From the beginning of the 2nd century the increase is more rapid, peaking in the 170s BC (*c.* 15.8%). Two of the three eponyms whose stamps occur the most frequently in Cyprus are dated to 170s: Αἰνησίδαμος II[18] (30 items) and Καλλικρατίδας II[19] (32 items).[20] In the next three decades the number of Rhodian stamps in Cyprus is much lower (it changes from *c.* 15.8% in 170s to *c.* 9% in 16Cs, *c.* 10.4% in 150s and *c.* 9.8% in 140s BC) and remains at a similar level in each of the decades. However, these numbers could change slightly if we also take into account the unpublished stamped Rhodian amphorae from the Tombs of the Kings, among which examples dated to the Period V (*c.* 145-108 BC) dominate.[21] It is also worth mentioning that the most frequently appearing single eponym in Cyprus, Παυσανίας III (34 items) is dated to the 150s.[22] There is a further decrease from *c.* 9.8% in 140s to c. 6.8% in 130s and similar number appears in each of the next two decades (*c.* 6.5% in 120s and *c.* 6.4% in the decade of 110s BC). From the last decade of the 2nd century on, the number of stamped examples is low, but again, very few Rhodian amphorae after the mid 1st century BC (or even earlier?) received stamps, therefore the actual quantity of Rhodian amphorae in Cyprus at that time differs from what Fig. 3 shows. The unstamped Rhodian amphorae dated to early Roman period found on many sites in Cyprus prove the continuation of the trade between these two centres,[23] although they do not play as significant a role as in most of the Hellenistic period.

THE QUANTITATIVE DISTRIBUTION OF RHODIAN AMPHORA STAMPS IN DIFFERENT REGIONS OF CYPRUS

Out of the total number (2,393) of identified Rhodian stamps found in Cyprus, 2,267 examples are of known origin and can be attributed to the three regions discussed

13 Cf. Lund 2011b, 287.
14 According to recent suggestions about the early Rhodian chronology proposed by Lawall 2011; cf. also Finkielsztejn 2001a.
15 Cf. Calvet 1972, 1982.
16 Cf. Finkielsztejn 1995, 382-383.
17 Garlan 2000, 177; cf. also Lund 2011a, 271.
18 179/177 BC: Finkielsztejn 2001a, 192, or 178/177 BC: Lund 2011a, 278.
19 175/173 BC: Finkielsztejn 2001a, 192, or 176/175 BC: Lund 2011a, 278.
20 These eponyms are also among the most frequent in general, cf. Lund 2011b, 285.
21 Barker in this volume.
22 152 BC: Finkielsztejn 2001a, 192, or 158/157 BC: Lund 2011a, 278.
23 Cf. Jacobsen 2006, 317-319; Kaldeli 2009, 380-384.

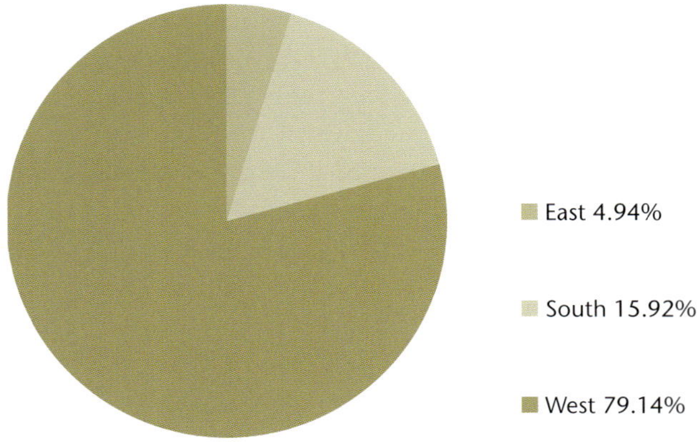

Fig. 4. Quantitative distribution of Rhodian stamps in three regions of Cyprus (total number 2,267).

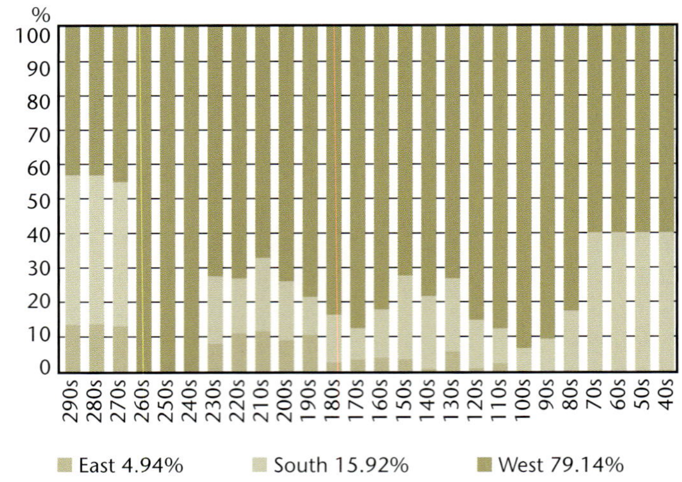

Fig. 5b. Chronological distribution of Rhodian amphora stamps of eponyms in three regions of Cyprus (total number 1,110).

Date BC	*East*	*South*	*West*	*Total*	*East %* (± std error)	*South %* (± std error)	*West %* (± std error)	*Sum %*
299-290	0.3	1.0	1.0	**2.3**	14.3% ± 4.94	42.9% ± 8.55	42.9% ± 8.55	100%
289-280	0.3	1.0	1.0	**2.3**	14.3% ± 4.94	42.9% ± 8.55	42.9% ± 8.55	100%
279-270	0.3	1.0	1.1	**2.4**	13.8% ± 4.77	41.4% ± 8.26	44.8% ± 8.75	100%
269-260	0.0	0.0	1.3	**1.3**			100.0% ± 17.71	100%
259-250	0.0	0.0	3.0	**3.0**			100.0% ± 17.71	100%
249-240	0.0	0.0	6.3	**6.3**			100.0% ± 17.71	100%
239-230	1.8	4.0	14.7	**20.4**	8.6% ± 1.29	19.6% ± 1.96	71.9% ± 3.74	100%
229-220	2.3	3.0	13.8	**19.0**	11.8% ± 1.58	15.8% ± 1.82	72.4% ± 3.75	100%
219-210	4.0	7.0	22.0	**33.0**	12.1% ± 1.21	21.2% ± 1.60	66.7% ± 3.60	100%
209-200	4.0	7.0	30.0	**41.0**	9.8% ± 0.98	17.1% ± 1.29	73.2% ± 2.66	100%
199-190	8.0	8.0	56.0	**72.0**	11.1% ± 0.79	11.1% ± 0.79	77.8% ± 2.74	100%
189-180	4.3	18.0	108.0	**130.3**	3.3% ± 0.32	13.8% ± 0.65	82.9% ± 2.83	100%
179-170	7.3	16.3	157.3	**181.0**	4.1% ± 0.30	9.0% ± 0.45	86.9% ± 1.38	100%
169-160	4.3	13.7	78.7	**96.7**	4.5% ± 0.43	14.1% ± 0.76	81.4% ± 1.34	100%
159-150	5.0	28.0	83.0	**116.0**	4.3% ± 0.39	24.1% ± 0.91	71.6% ± 1.25	100%
149-140	1.3	22.7	83.3	**107.3**	1.2% ± 0.22	21.1% ± 0.89	77.6% ± 1.69	100%
139-130	4.7	16.3	54.7	**75.7**	6.2% ± 0.57	21.6% ± 1.07	72.2% ± 1.63	100%
129-120	1.0	10.0	60.0	**71.0**	1.4% ± 0.28	14.1% ± 0.89	84.5% ± 1.77	100%
119-110	2.0	7.0	61.0	**70.0**	2.9% ± 0.40	10.0% ± 0.76	87.1% ± 2.22	100%
109-100	0.0	1.3	16.7	**18.1**		7.3% ± 1.27	92.7% ± 2.29	100%
99-90	0.0	1.7	14.7	**16.3**		10.1% ± 1.57	89.9% ± 2.26	100%
89-80	0.0	1.6	7.3	**8.9**		18.3% ± 2.86	81.7% ± 6.04	100%
79-70	0.0	1.6	2.3	**3.9**		40.6% ± 6.43	59.4% ± 5.15	100%
69-60	0.0	1.6	2.3	**3.9**		40.6% ± 6.43	59.4% ± 5.15	100%
59-50	0.0	1.6	2.3	**3.9**		40.6% ± 6.43	59.4% ± 7.77	100%
49-40	0.0	1.6	2.3	**3.9**		40.6% ± 6.43	59.4% ± 7.77	100%

Fig. 5a. Number, percentage and confidence level of Rhodian eponym stamps from the three regions of Cyprus dated to different decades. Fig. 5b is based on these data.

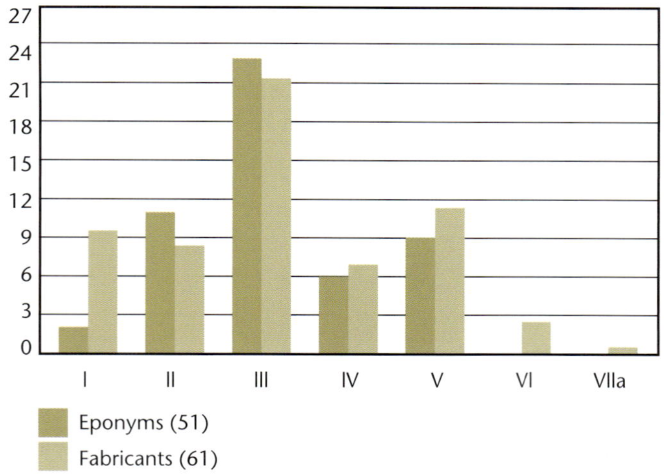

Fig. 6. Chronological distribution of Rhodian amphora stamps found in eastern Cyprus (total number 112).

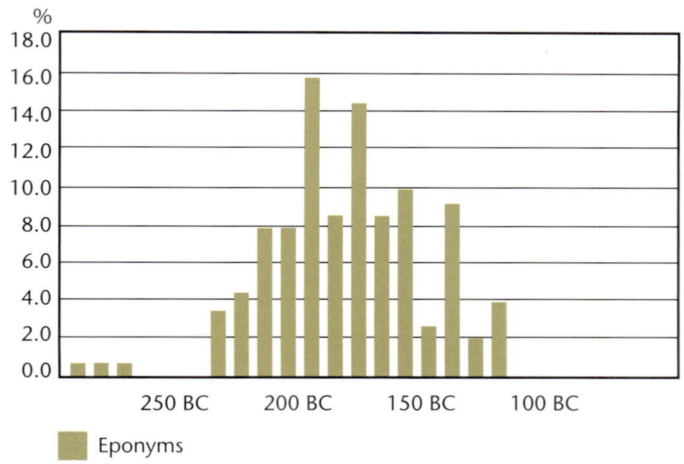

Fig. 7. Chronological distribution of Rhodian amphora stamps of eponyms found in eastern Cyprus (total number 51).

in this paper (Fig. 4).[24] The stamps found in the western part of the island constitute the most numerous and dominant group of 1,794 examples (*c.* 79.14%), while the stamps from the south are fewer – 361 examples (*c.* 15.92%) and a group of 112 examples (*c.* 4.94%) from the eastern region is the smallest one.

Following the proportion of eponym stamps from different regions to their total number in each decade (Fig. 5a-b) an equal percentage (*c.* 43%) of the stamps in the west and in the south can be observed in the first three decades of the 3rd century BC. Only *c.* 14% of all Rhodian stamps imported to Cyprus in each of these decades reached the eastern region of the island. All of the eponym stamps dated to the next three decades were found in the west, but a presence of fabricant stamps in other regions proves that trade with Rhodes continued there as well. In each decade from the 230s until the 80s BC more than *c.* 67% (oscillating between 67%-93%) of eponym stamps appeared in the western part of the island. The south and the east shared the rest of them until the end of the 110s, but always with a dominant percentage in the southern region. The eastern part flourished only between 230s and 190s, when around one third of the whole group of eponym stamps imported to the east and to the south reached this region in each decade. Between the 190s and the end of 110s the percentage of eponym stamps in the east decreases, and after 110s none of these stamps were found in the east.

Still, some fabricant stamps dated to this time appear in Salamis (cf. Fig. 6). During the first three decades of the 1st century BC, Rhodian eponym stamps appeared only in the west and in the south, with a much higher percentage in the former region. After the 80s BC this proportion changed and eponym stamps in the south constituted *c.* 41% of the whole group, while in the west it was *c.* 59%.

THE CHRONOLOGICAL DISTRIBUTION OF RHODIAN AMPHORA STAMPS IN DIFFERENT REGIONS OF CYPRUS

Eastern Cyprus

Stamped Rhodian amphora handles found in eastern region of Cyprus constitute a rather small group of 51 eponym stamps and 61 fabricant stamps. Most were found in Salamis. Due to the small sample size and also unequal quantities of stamps of eponyms and those of fabricants, especially in the Period I (Fig. 6),[25] this collection should be studied more carefully since it may be not quite representative.

Stamped Rhodian amphorae probably appear in this region at the beginning of the 3rd century BC (Fig. 7). From then until the end of this century they seem to appear

24 126 examples (66 of eponyms and 60 of fabricants) of unknown origin in Cyprus gathered in various collections were omitted here.

25 There may be, however, some confusion between eponyms and fabricants in this period.

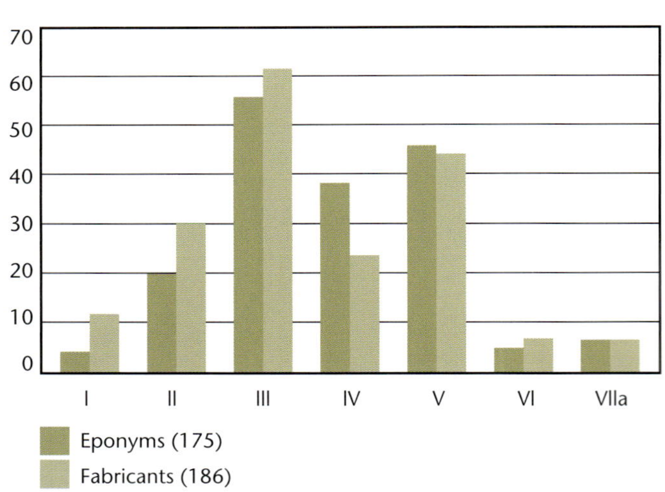

Fig. 8. Chronological distribution of Rhodian amphora stamps in southern Cyprus (total number 361).

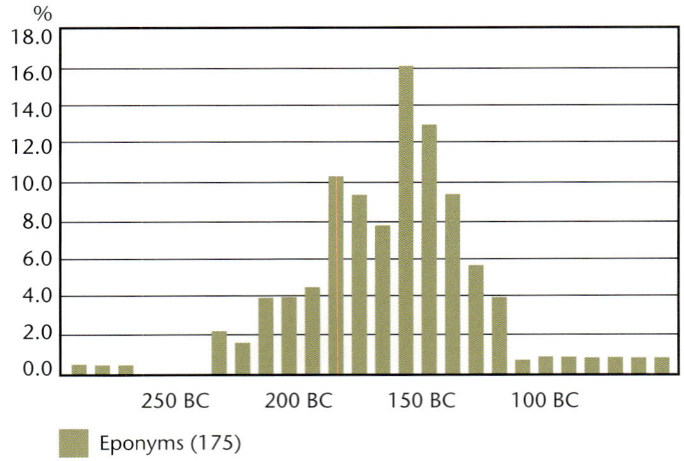

Fig. 9. Chronological distribution of Rhodian amphora stamps of eponyms found in southern Cyprus (total number 175).

there in a greater ratio to the total number known from this region than elsewhere, as can be noticed from the proportion of eponym stamps, which constitute 25.5% of the whole group of eponym stamps in the east, 13.7% in the south, and 10.6% in the west (Fig. 7, 9 ,11), and it is also shown by the number of producer stamps in Periods I and II, which are 18 out of 61 (29.5%) in the east, 42.5 out of 186 (22.8%) and 131.5 out of 910 (14.5%) on the west (Figs. 6, 8, 10). The largest number of Rhodian stamps occurred in the eastern region in the 190s BC, therefore slightly earlier than elsewhere on the island (cf. below). It decreased in the 180s, but again was very high in the 170s. The next decline is seen in the second half of the 2nd century apart from an increase in the 130s BC. From the end of the 2nd century BC, Rhodian stamps are very sporadic in the eastern region, and stamps of the eponyms are not found at all.

Southern Cyprus

Of the stamped Rhodian amphora handles from the southern region, 361 are published (248 come from Kition), and further examples from Amathus[26] and Kourion[27] are only mentioned. Apart from these, there are many unstamped fragments dated mainly to the 2nd and the 1st century BC, which come from Panayia Ematousa.[28] Of the 361 published examples, 175 belong to eponyms and 186 to fabricants. The number of the eponym and fabricant stamps in different chronological periods is not as discordant as in the group of the examples found in the eastern part of the island (Fig. 8). The differences are noticeable mainly in Periods I-II and also IV and they could raise a slight doubt about the representativeness of this collection.

Stamped Rhodian amphorae first appear in the southern region at the same time as elsewhere on the island, i.e. at the beginning of the 3rd century BC (Fig. 9). Until the end of this century, their ratio to the total number known from this region is smaller than it is in the eastern part but larger than it is in the west (cf. above). In the 190s they still constitute only 4.6% of the whole group from this region. During the next three decades, Rhodian stamps occur in higher number (10.3% in the 180s, 9.3% in the 170s and 7.8% in the 160s), but they reach a peak only in the 150s BC (16%), therefore later than in other regions, and continue at a high level in the next two decades (13% in the 140s and 9.3% in the130s). From the 120s BC their percentage decreases. In the 1st century BC they are not very common, however the ratio of eponym stamps to the total number of eponym stamps known from this region is higher than elsewhere (5.5% in the south, 3.5% in the west, and they do not occur in the east at all).

Western Cyprus

Rhodian amphora stamps found in the western part of Cyprus constitute the largest collection on the island with a quantity of 1,794 pieces (79.14% of the group from the

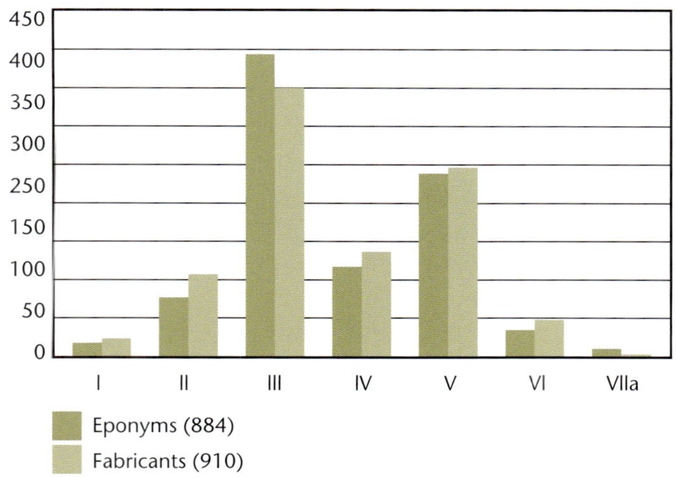

Fig. 10. Chronological distribution of Rhodian amphora stamps found in western Cyprus (total number 1,794).

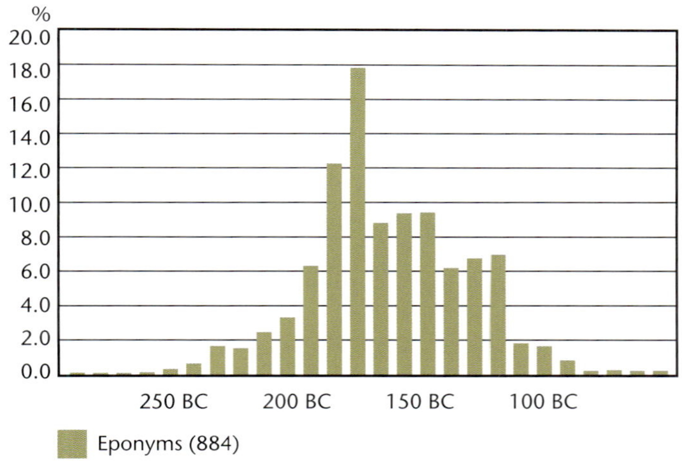

Fig. 11. Chronological distribution of Rhodian amphora stamps of eponyms found in western Cyprus (total number 884).

whole island), of which 884 are eponym stamps and 910 fabricant stamps. 1581 examples of this group were found inside the walls of ancient Nea Paphos. They certainly constitute a representative group, especially for the town of Nea Paphos (Fig. 10). It is hardly surprising that the chart showing their distribution is very similar to the one showing the general distribution of Rhodian stamps in the whole Cyprus (Figs. 1, 10).

As elsewhere on the island, they most probably occur in this region at the beginning of the 3rd century BC. Until the end of this century their ratio to the total number of Rhodian stamps known from this region is lower than elsewhere (cf. above). During the first three decades of the 2nd century BC their percentage raises gradually (6.4% in the 190s, 12.35% in the 180s and 17.9% in the 170s). They occur in the highest number in this region in the 180s and the 170s, therefore later than in the east, but earlier than in the south. During the next decades their percentage decreases twice, in 160s (to 8.9%) and in 130s (to 6.2%). In the last decade of the 2nd century they are much more sporadic, and during the 1st century their percentage is very low (1.7% in the 90s and from the 70s only 0.3%).

TRADE BETWEEN RHODES AND CYPRUS

An extension of the Ptolemaic domination over Cyprus (*c.* 312-310 BC) designated the beginning of transitional period on the island, during which its organization changed from kingdoms (which had functioned there since the Bronze Age) to 'united' cities governed from one capital, and economic and cultural changes also took place. According to the traditional opinion, this transformation was rather rapid and invasive, not only in the area of politics, but also in the administrative and economic areas.[29] Recently, however, various researchers have argued that these changes occurred as a process, which took a large part of the 3rd century BC, and in which local societies also participated.[30]

A process of general changes that filled this period in Cyprus is also noticeable from the picture traced by amphorae. Before the first Rhodian examples reached Cyprus, locally made amphorae played a dominant role there, while those originating in other places, for example Samos, Thasos, Chios or Levant were in the minority.[31] The

26 Marangou 2009, 362 fig. 7.
27 Grace 1979, 179 note 4.
28 About 50 of them are mentioned by Jacobsen 2006, 317-319.
29 Cf. Vessberg & Westholm 1956, 223-237; Jehasse, 1978, 8-9.
30 E.g. Borowicz 2009; Papantoniou 2012; Keen, forthcoming.
31 Cf. Jacobsen 2006, 305 and Table 4. The best evidence for the trade relations of Cyprus in the 4th century BC are finds from the Mazotos wreck; however as its excavator, S. Demesticha (2009, 395) remarks: "it remains the only tangible evidence of systematic wine trade between Chios and Cyprus before Hellenistic times".

chronological distributions of Rhodian amphora stamps just discussed show that Rhodes-Cyprus trade links were established at the beginning of the 3rd century BC, during the short period of control over Cyprus by the Antigonid dynasty (306-294 BC). These early Rhodian amphorae are attested all over Cyprus. The examples found in Kyrenia ship constitute an important closed context of early Rhodian amphorae. Their appearance on the island at that time proves the beginning of changes in the picture of its trade and economy. At first, they coexisted with the examples of still functioning local production and also of other centres.[32] Cypriot production of Classical and early Hellenistic types seems to have petered out during the 3rd century to the beginning of the 2nd century BC[33] and the number of Rhodian amphorae, as in other places,[34] was gradually increasing, especially from the years between 240 and 190 BC. The decline in local production, however, should not be seen only in reference to Rhodian imports, since there had always been Aegean imports and there is no evidence that Rhodian amphorae exceeded the import needs once fulfilled by the Aegean in general.[35] In the 2nd century BC Rhodian amphorae occur on the island in the vast majority. The growth in their number in the 180s BC is substantial in Cyprus; however, it was not as rapid as was seen in the general group of wide range of centres importing Rhodian amphorae showed by Lund.[36] The peak of Rhodes-Cyprus trade contacts is generally placed between 180 and 170 BC, although it differs according to the region of Cyprus. The data are most reliable for the western part, where stamped Rhodian handles are published in the largest number.

The decrease in their number from the 160s BC is much more noticeable in Cyprus than in other centres in general,[37] and Rhodes itself,[38] where it is barely visible. However, the fluctuation in their quantities on the island in the next decades, showing a slight growth in the 150s and a slight decrease in the 140s is similar to that experienced in other places outside the island. Research conducted by Lund indicates that the opening of a free port in Delos in 166 BC did not necessarily affect general export of Rhodian amphorae,[39] and there is a possibility that it even flourished in the second half of the 2nd century BC, if the evidence from Alexandria is reliable.[40] In the 160s, a turbulent time began in Cyprus due to its involvement in the military expeditions of Antiochus IV against Egypt; an antagonism between Ptolemy VI Philometor and his brother Ptolemy VIII Euergetes II caused instability in the rule of Egypt. As observed by Ino Nicolaou: "this quarrel had some repercussions in Cyprus, and may have affected the flow of imports to the island".[41] A slight decrease in the number of Rhodian amphorae in Cyprus is noticeable again in the 130s BC, and it is followed by almost equal numbers in the next three decades. In the second half of the 2nd century BC (and especially at the end of this century) a production of amphorae imitating Koan and Knidian examples had begun in Cyprus.[42] Very soon, in late Hellenistic and early Roman periods, these locally made amphorae[43] and other examples of both western and eastern origin, were replacing Rhodian ones in Cypriot markets.[44] As in other places, a decline in Cypriot trade contacts with Rhodes began in the last decades of the 2nd century BC, and although Rhodian amphorae also occur in Cyprus during the Roman period,[45] they did not play an important role in its market anymore.

As mentioned above, it might be possible that commercial links between Rhodes and Alexandria flourished in the second half of the 2nd century BC, which could be implied by increasing number of Rhodian amphorae in this city at that time.[46] It has been suggested that Cyprus, and especially Nea Paphos, "was a linchpin in trade relations" between these two places.[47] Although such a position of Cyprus could be confirmed by its dependence on Egypt during the Hellenistic period and also by natural conditions, for example, winds propitious for a navigation from Rhodes to Alexandria through Cyprus,[48] the growth in the number of Rhodian amphorae in the second half of the 2nd century BC is not noted in their chronological distribution, neither on the island nor in its western region (Figs. 3, 11). It seems that even if we take into consideration their increasing number during the Period V in the Tombs of the Kings in Nea Paphos, their general configuration would not change much. One could suggest that the examples traded to Alexandria through Cyprus might flow only through the Paphian harbour and not enter deeper into the city itself. However, fewer Rhodian amphora stamps found in this harbour area presented by Nicolaou (2005) may be dated to Period V (Fig. 12) than in other places. Thus, they do not confirm this supposition. As Lawall has noted,[49] they could also simply pass Paphos, and not be off-loaded there at all, even if the ships stopped at Paphos on the way to Alexandria; or simply fewer jars were stopping at Paphos, since Alexandria generated more demand and reward for such imports. However, most of the collection of Rhodian amphorae from Alexandria has not been published yet. Also, the examples found in the Paphian harbour comprise only a limited group collected from a single place and not from the whole area of the harbour, therefore further research in this area could shed a wider light on this problem. The question of Alexandria, Nea Paphos and the Rhodian wine trade can be discussed now only with much conjecture, and a further discussion of this topic should be undertaken in the future, especially since the role of Cyprus' Hellenistic capital as a linchpin between Rhodes and Alexandria trade relations seems probable.

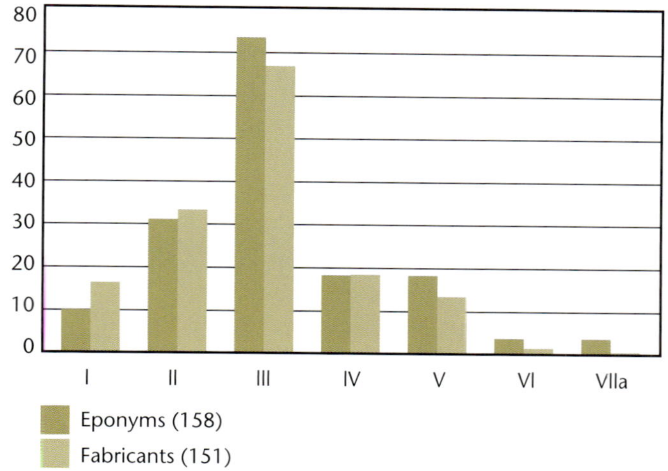

Fig. 12. Chronological distribution of Rhodian amphora stamps found in Nea Paphos harbor (total number 309).

THE ROLE OF THE DIFFERENT REGIONS OF CYPRUS IN ITS TRADE RELATIONS WITH RHODES

The charts presented above show that the quantitative and chronological distribution of Rhodian amphorae in the different regions of Cyprus was not consistent. But since the sample of the excavated material (published or at least mentioned) is quite small, and the archaeological work done in different places on the island is not equally advanced, we should not compare literally the number of Rhodian amphorae occurring in these regions. However, if we note that from the end of the 3rd century BC, Nea Paphos was the capital of the island, it seems that the predominance of this material in the western part of Cyprus over the rest of the island is not accidental. It could be supported by the fact that at places like Salamis, Kition, Kourion or Amathous, which were active during the Hellenistic period and which have been excavated quite satisfactorily, the number of these amphorae is generally much lower.[50]

Although the early Rhodian amphorae occur all over the island, it seems that during the 3rd century BC and through the 190s the greatest ratio of these early amphorae to the total number known from a single region is seen in the east. Also, the highest number of stamps appears in this region earlier than elsewhere in the 190s BC, emphasizing that this was the heyday of Salamis. It is not surprising if we remember that Ptolemy I Soter I designated the last king of Salamis, Nicocreon, to be the first *strategos* of the island, and at that time his city became a capital of Cyprus. Salamis held this position until the end of the 3rd century BC when Nea Paphos took over this role.[51] At the beginning of the 3rd century Nea Paphos was a young town with a developing harbour,[52] but judging from the number of

32 Deshayes 1963, 210-212; Calvet 1972, 11.
33 Calvet 1986, 597; Jacobsen 2006, 306-309.
34 Cf. Lund 2011b, 288.
35 I am indebted to Dr. M. Lawall for this observation.
36 Lund 2011b, 288.
37 Lund 2011b, 288.
38 Lund 1999a, 195, Fig. 9. The chart is based on the 'higher' chronology, but if the data would be lowered to the G. Finkielsztejn's chronology, a decrease in 160s is rather small.
39 Lund 2011b, 288-289.
40 Cf. Finkielsztejn 1995; Finkielsztejn 2001b.
41 Nicolaou 2005, 9.
42 Hayes 1991, 85.
43 They are defined as a Cypriot production on the base of the similarity of their clay to that of the local Plain Ware. A lack of kiln finds where they could have been produced in Cyprus and also, of their proper petrographic or neutral activation analysis leaves the question of their production centre unclearly specified (cf. Jacobsen 2006, 303ff, 309).
44 Hayes 1991, 88, 90; Jacobsen 2006, 305-306; Kaldeli 2009, 377-379.
45 Cf. Kaldeli 2009, 381-384.
46 Lund 1993, 368; 1999a, 201; 2011b, 288-289.
47 Lund 1999a, 201.
48 Murray 1995, 39-40.
49 I am also grateful for this observation.
50 Cf. Calvet 1972; Grace 1979; Calvet 1982; Calvet 1993; Salles 1993a; Marangou 2009.
51 Młynarczyk 1990, 121.
52 Hohlfelder 1995, 194.

Rhodian stamps dated to this period found there it seems that it was already an important commercial centre. However, a ratio of the early stamps to their total number from this region, which is lower than anywhere else, shows that it developed later than other cities on the island. Still, the actual number of Rhodian stamps in the west was growing during the last four decades of the 3rd century, and exceeded the number of stamps in the other regions of the island, showing an increasing position of Nea Paphos as a trade partner of Rhodes. In the south, at Amathus, a construction of a harbour was undertaken at the end of the 4th century BC but it is not clear whether it was planned as a military or a trade harbour as well as if it was properly finished at all.[53] The harbour in Kition lost its military function with the fall of the kingdom at the end of the 4th century and its buildings were probably destroyed at that time. Its reconstruction was undertaken at the beginning of the 3rd century and since then it was probably used for trade transactions.[54] A high ratio of Rhodian stamps of the 3rd century to the total number of Rhodian stamps known from this region proves its cities, especially Kition, were active as a trade centres at that time. The fluctuation of Rhodian stamps in this region (collected mainly from Kition) suggests however, that it played an important role as a trade partner of Rhodes, much later.

During the 2nd century a dominant position of Nea Paphos on the island as a commercial partner of Rhodes is very clear. A peak point of this relation is placed during the 180s and the 170s. Since then, a decrease of the number of Rhodian amphorae in western part of the island can be observed, however they remain much more numerous there than in other regions during the whole 2nd century. To this century the most intensive period of commercial links between southern region of Cyprus and Rhodes is also dated, falling in the 150s and 140s. The number of Rhodian stamps declines there gradually from the 140s BC to the end of the 2nd century. In Salamis after the 190s BC, Rhodian amphorae occur rather irregularly with very low quantities in some decades, showing its unstable position in trade contacts with Rhodes, and also its decreasing role as a commercial centre.

The declining number of Rhodian amphorae in the whole of Cyprus after 110 BC shows that trade links between these two islands were no longer very intensive, even though they continued into the Roman period, which can be observed especially in the southern region. Nea Paphos kept its position as a prosperous economic centre, where locally produced amphorae and those originating in different centres of the Roman world took over the previous, dominant position of Rhodian amphorae in the market.

53 Empereur 1995; Raban 1995, 160-161.
54 Yon 2007.

ACKNOWLEDGEMENTS

I would like to express my thanks to the editors of this volume for inviting me to write an article and for their valuable help and advice in writing this paper.

Early Roman Amphorae from Cyprus as Evidence of Trade and Exchange in the Mediterranean

BY ANTHI KALDELI

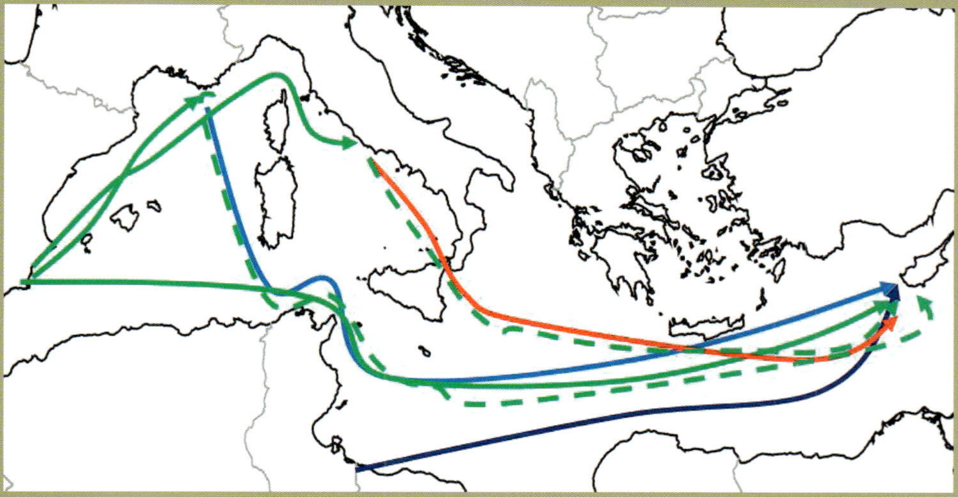

Early Roman Amphorae from Cyprus as Evidence of Trade and Exchange in the Mediterranean

BY ANTHI KALDELI

INTRODUCTION

The purpose of this article is to examine the character of trade and exchange in the eastern Mediterranean, as well as between the eastern and western Mediterranean, in the early Roman period (1st century BC – early 3rd century AD), as evidenced by the amphorae imported to Cyprus. It is needless in this volume to underline either the importance of the study of amphorae for the reconstruction of trading activities or the previous lacuna in research concerning the economics of the eastern part of the Roman Empire,[1] which resulted in the disparity between the two halves of the Empire. Only fairly recently has systematic work in the form of excavations and surveys in eastern Mediterranean areas produced new amphora types and begun to clarify the economics of a number of sites.[2] Nevertheless, despite the increasing information, there has been no attempt to synthesize these data in order to elucidate aspects of trade. Furthermore, emphasis is still primarily put on the identification of amphorae dating to the late Roman period, while many issues involving the production of early Roman amphorae, such as the variants of established types, imitations and the traits of newly identified types, still need to be more widely addressed.

The emphasis put on the archaeological study of early Roman trade to date, especially in regards to the commercial exchanges occurring within the western part of the empire, has revealed that it was fundamental to the Roman empire, as it provided the means to accomplish the political strategy of economic exploitation of its territories. Despite the past focus on the study of the archaeological record deriving from the western Mediterranean, it still became evident that trade acquired a Pan-Mediterranean character, which encouraged regional interaction and promoted socio-cultural unity and economic expansion within the empire, especially as it was facilitated by a uniform currency and a common market. This unparalleled expansion of trade is also supported by new data from the afore-mentioned research currently conducted in eastern Mediterranean areas. It is useful to our discussion to remember that past research on the character of Roman economy had favoured a variety of explanations ranging from ideas developed from modern economics,[3] deterministic approaches, and interpretations stressing agriculture as the dominant form of economic activity.[4] Although the economic and political importance of trade in the development of the Empire is now widely accepted among archaeologists and economic historians, the lack of a synthesis of data deriving from the eastern Mediterranean still prevents an in-depth understanding of the character of trade. In other words, despite the advances in research, our limited knowledge on the mechanisms engaged in the distribution networks that operated in the eastern Mediterranean discourages a holistic approach of the extent of these exchanges, and their true impact on the overall economic endeavours, as the character of trading activities remains to a large degree unknown.

This paper aims to contribute towards such an understanding, firstly, through presenting the early Roman amphorae imported to the cities of Nea Paphos and Amathous and, secondly, by tackling the complexity of the trade patterns operating in the eastern Mediterranean. Thus, it is intended to highlight the central role of Cyprus in the examination of early Roman trade patterns, chiefly through the application of a consistent methodological framework that enables us to explore the patterns underlying the data. The focus on Cyprus is not arbitrary, as the island (annexed by Rome in 58 BC), due to its centrality in eastern networks, offers a starting point for the investigation of trade and exchange in the broader region. Its active involvement in maritime activities is attested by the large number of harbours and anchorages along the coasts, identified by archaeological investigation and listed by Strabo.[5] The line of enquiry followed in this paper, as outlined in the following section, comprises the use of quantitative data, in association with other available information, for an in-depth understanding of long-distance trade and exchange networks in the study period.

THE METHODOLOGICAL FRAMEWORK

The tasks involved in order to address the objectives described above are the identification of the areas with which parts of the island were commercially linked, the examination of the mechanisms by which the amphorae were exchanged, and the volume of these exchanges. For a meaningful interpretation these issues are examined within the broader economic, socio-political and ideological context that developed after Rome's annexation of the eastern Mediterranean. The focus on amphora assemblages from Nea Paphos and Amathous is imposed, on the one hand, by the absence of adequate, published, quantifiable data elsewhere, and, on the other, by the need to achieve a broader understanding of the exchange networks that operated in different parts of the island .[6] The sites from Nea Paphos include the House of Orpheus[7] and the Theatre[8]. The sites from Amathous involve the Agora[9] and the site of Amathous-Palaea Lemesos.[10]

Key to addressing the objectives is the research model, comprising a theoretical and methodological framework, developed to link the theoretical framework to the data by means of quantification, model-building and statistical analysis.[11] A basic component of the research model was the collection and study of a representative sample from all stratified contexts from each site, based on elaborate sampling techniques,[12] in order to avoid bias in the process of analysis. In brief, analysis included the identification, sourcing, and quantification of known and unknown types from each period, based on morphology and fabrics. For the examination of distribution, data from each city were aggregated. The models that were tested statistically were based on the observation of patterns resulting from such quantification. Particularly useful in this process was the information from published sites from Cyprus and other Mediterranean sites, thus contributing towards a synthesis of the available information. The brevity of this paper, however, discourages at present a detailed discussion of ideas generated from data deriving from other regions, and imposes the rather concise presentation of the patterns primarily represented in Cypriot assemblages.

The statistical techniques, included in the methodological framework, are regression analysis and correlation, used to test hypotheses or to suggest further ideas.[13] In other words, given the complexity of the processes underlying the data, both techniques are used in an 'exploratory' way, as the objective is to explore the patterns responsible for the character of the archaeological record.[14] Regression is used to identify and describe the relationship between the dependent variable, quantity of the amphorae based on their origin, and the independent variable, distance from that point of origin. The quantities of the amphorae reaching the cities under study are thereby analyzed in relation to the distance from their place of origin. Quantity is estimated in percentages of amphorae imported from different areas in each studied assemblage, and distance in approximate kilometres is calculated in straight-line. The origin, where the x axis crosses the y axis, is taken to be Nea Paphos or Amathous, accordingly. The underlying assumption, for the purposes of the present study, is that the further the place of origin, the smaller the quantity should be reaching the island.

---

1 Abadie-Reynal 1992, 361.
2 Cf. Reynolds 1995; Rauh & Slane 2000; Eiring & Lund (eds.) 2004; Maxfield & Peacock 2006.
3 Cf. Rostovtzeff 1957.
4 Finley 1973; Jones 1974; Greene 1986.
5 Leonard 1995a, 227-242; Leonard & Demesticha 2004.
6 The study does not include data from the northern area of the island, due to the current political situation. It is attempted, nevertheless, to advance hypotheses on the networks that involved the northern coasts of the island, as suggested by data analysis.
7 The excavation of the House of Orpheus is under the direction of Professor Demetrios Michaelides, University of Cyprus, to whom I wish to express my gratitude for granting me permission to study the material, as well as for his constant help and invaluable support.
8 The excavation of the Theatre in Paphos, at the so-called Fabrika site, is directed by Prof. Richard Green, and recently co-directed also by Dr. S. Gabrieli and Dr. C. Barker, University of Sydney. I am indebted to them for granting me permission to study the material and thankful for kindly accepting me as part of the project study group.
9 The site of the Agora in Amathous was excavated by the late Dr. Loulloupis, former director of the Department of Antiquities of the Republic of Cyprus. I am grateful for granting me permission to study the material while working on my MA and Ph.D. Thesis.
10 The so-called site of "Amathous-Palaea Lemesos" has been excavated by Dr. P. Flourentzos, former director of the Department of Antiquities of the Republic of Cyprus, to whom I wish to express my gratitude for allowing me to study and publish the amphorae from this excavation.
11 Cf. Orton 2000 and Kaldeli 2007; for a more detailed account on the research model and the theoretical and methodological framework, including the use of statistical techniques, see Kaldeli 2007. I wish to express my gratitude to my supervisors, Professor Clive Orton and Professor Ruth Whitehouse for their support and invaluable advice throughout the Ph.D.; the development of the methodological framework would not have been feasible without the constant advice, support and knowledge of Prof. C. Orton. I am also thankful to the examiners of the thesis, Professor D.P.S. Peacock and Senior Researcher J. Lund for the advice and their ideas, which have been incorporated in my post-doctoral research.
12 Orton 2000, 30-32.
13 Shennan 1997, 131, 132, 139.
14 Orton 1980, 15.

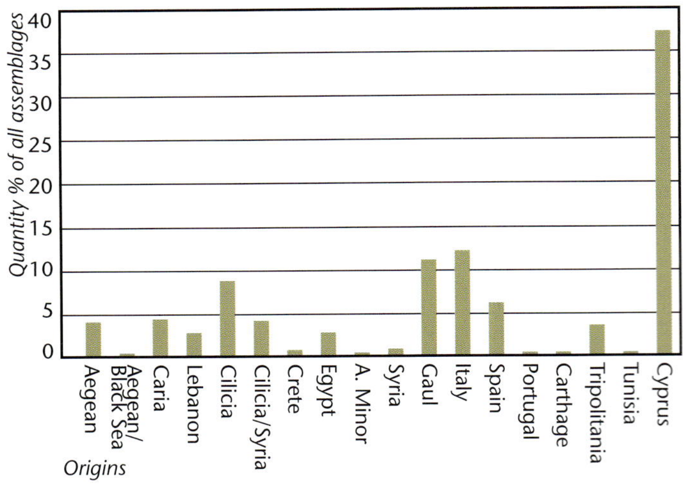

Fig. 1. Quantity (%) of early Roman amphorae from Nea Paphos (all sites) based on their origins.

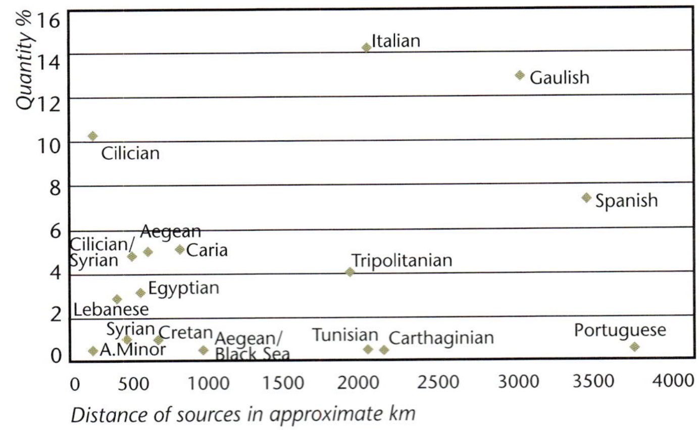

Fig. 2. Regression analysis of the quantity (%) of early Roman amphorae imported to Nea Paphos (all sites) and approximate distance (km) of the region of origin.

Correlation analysis here examines the spatial processes of direct exchange and redistribution, by exploring the quantitative relationships between the amphorae based on their origin. Because of the differences in the quantities of amphorae from various sources, between the assemblages, rank correlation was used, each rank representing the quantity of amphorae from each site. However, following an initial filtering of the ranks, not all data could form part of the final analysis. To facilitate 'reading' the correlation tables, I note here that a correlation coefficient between amphorae from two different sources is considered to be strong, when it exceeds .600; when it rates to around .500 it is considered to be moderate, and below this number it is considered weak, albeit still statistically significant.

EARLY ROMAN AMPHORAE IMPORTED TO CYPRUS

Analysis revealed a vast range of early Roman amphora types from a number of western, eastern and probable local sources in both cities under study. The more common types imported to Nea Paphos include the Dressel 2-4 amphora, the Gauloise 4, Gauloise 5 and Gauloise 1 amphorae from Gaul, the Beltrán III, Beltrán IIA and IIB amphorae, the Dressel 16, and N. African amphorae, including Tripolitanian amphorae. Other common types include the Pinched-Handle amphora, Beirut amphorae and amphorae from other eastern sources, such as the Pseudo-Cos en cloche amphora, the 'Rhodian' and the Cretan 1 amphora, as well as many previously unidentified types, which will not be discussed in this paper.

Among the amphorae imported to Amathous are, again, the Dressel 2-4 amphora, the Beltrán I, IIA, IIB, IVA and IVB, the Gauloise 4, Tripolitanian amphorae, the Pamphylian and the Pinched-Handle amphora, the Pseudo-Cos en cloche and the 'Rhodian' amphora. The types identified by Hayes are also encountered in the study assemblages, and especially in Nea Paphos.[15] Worthy of note are also the local or eastern imitations of western amphorae, and in particular the imitations of the Dressel 2-4 type, evidenced in the large number of specimens of Sub-Koan tradition in all assemblages under study.[16] These types are not included in the tables presented here or in the discussion, as they are part of an on-going, large-scale, project, aiming at establishing their morphology and identifying their place of origin.[17] The analysis and publication of the various imported types noted above, including the description of the petrographic traits and of their fabrics, is in progress, as part of this on-going project.

The import of these amphorae reveals Cyprus's engagement in pan-Mediterranean trade networks and the expansion of exchange activities in the eastern Mediterranean basin. However, despite the superficial similarity in the types circulated in Nea Paphos and Amathous, their different quantities attest to the complexity characterising long-distance exchange networks and the

		AEGEAN	CIL.SYR	CILICIAN	GAULISH	ITALIAN	SPANISH	TRIPOL
Kendall´s tau_b	**AEGEAN**							
	Correlation Coefficient	1.000	.037	.518**	-.448**	-.187	-.115	.216
	Sig. (2-tailed)	.	.803	.000	.002	.193	.430	.149
	N	37	37	37	37	37	37	37
	CIL.SYR							
	Correlation Coefficient	.037	1.000	.180	.048	.032	.131	.052
	Sig. (2-tailed)	.803	.	.211	.737	.824	.368	.728
	N	37	37	37	37	37	37	37
	CILICIAN							
	Correlation Coefficient	.518**	.180	1.000	-.125	-.132	.043	-.014
	Sig. (2-tailed)	.000	.211	.	.365	.340	.760	.924
	N	37	37	37	37	37	37	37
	GAULISH							
	Correlation Coefficient	-.448**	.048	-.125	1.000	.223	.283*	-.282*
	Sig. (2-tailed)	.002	.737	.365	.	.106	.042	.049
	N	37	37	37	37	37	37	37
	ITALIAN							
	Correlation Coefficient	-.187	.032	-.132	.223	1.000	.341*	-.021
	Sig. (2-tailed)	.193	.824	.340	.106	.	.015	.883
	N	37	37	37	37	37	37	37
	SPANISH							
	Correlation Coefficient	-.115	.131	.043	.283*	.341*	1.000	.120
	Sig. (2-tailed)	.430	.368	.760	.042	.015	.	.407
	N	37	37	37	37	37	37	37
	TRIPOL							
	Correlation Coefficient	.216	.052	-.014	-.282*	-.021	.120	1.000
	Sig. (2-tailed)	.149	.728	.924	.049	.883	.407	.
	N	37	37	37	37	37	37	37

Fig. 3. Correlation analysis of the early Roman amphorae imported to Nea Paphos based on their origins.

variability of the economic trends of the island. The contexts in which these amphorae were found suggest that trade had boomed between the late 1st and late 2nd century AD, also suggested by the amphorae studied by Hayes.[18] The decision to concentrate on the analysis of the quantities of amphorae in relation to their area of origin, and not to the quantities of the various types themselves, is imposed by the fact that certain types, such as the Dressel 2-4 amphora, were produced in areas other than their original sources; a study focusing on the quantities of the amphora types, therefore, could provide misleading outcomes as to the character of trade and exchange networks.

DISTRIBUTION MODELS AND STATISTICAL ANALYSIS

Nea Paphos

The quantification of amphorae from Nea Paphos, based on their sources, has shown that western products were primarily imported from Italy, followed by products from Gaul, Spain, Tripolitania and Portugal (Fig. 1). From the east, products were imported from Cilicia, the Aegean and Caria, Lebanon and Egypt. Thus, the model concerning

15 Hayes 1991.
16 Kaldeli 2009.
17 The project is entitled "Roman Amphorae from Cyprus: evidencing production, trade and exchange in the eastern Mediterranean" (ROMACY project) and is conducted at the University of Cyprus. The author is the chief researcher of the project, in collaboration with Prof. D. Michaelides (coordinator), Professor C. Orton, Dr. S. Demesticha and Dr. V. Kassianidou. Part of the project consortium is the University of Southampton (Professor D. Williams, Professor D.P.S. Peacock), the CNRS Demokritos Institute (Dr. V. Kilikoglou), the CNRS/Univ. of Aix-en-Provence (Professor M. Bonifay and Dr. C. Capelli) and the National Museum of Denmark (Senior Researcher J. Lund). The project is co-financed by the European Development Funds and the Republic of Cyprus through the Research Promotion Foundation.
18 Hayes 1991.

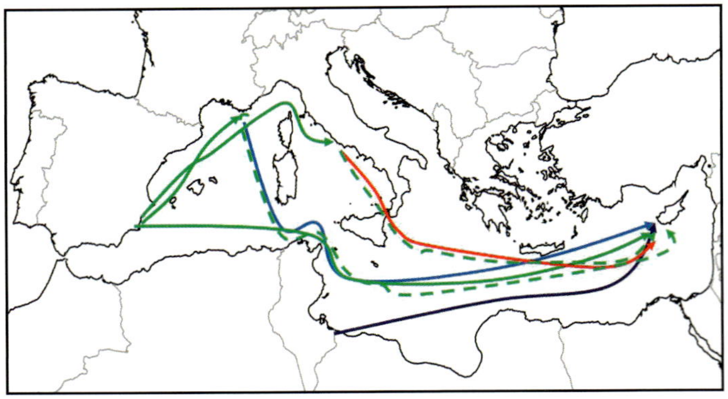

Fig. 4. Distribution patterns of early Roman western amphorae from the region of origin to Nea Paphos, as suggested by statistical analysis.

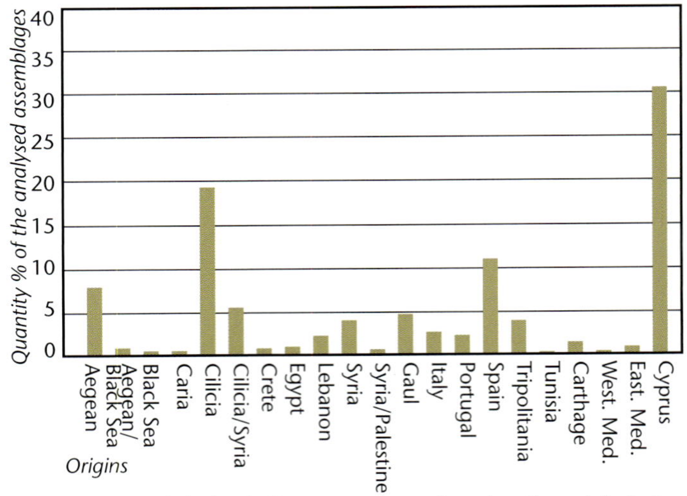

Fig. 5. Quantity (%) of early Roman amphorae from Amathous (all sites) based on their origins.

the distribution of western amphorae, based on these observations, suggests the existence of direct exchanges with Italy, Gaul, and Spain.

Interestingly, the relationship between the quantities of these imports and distance from their place of origin, identified in regression analysis, is suggestive of such direct links (Fig. 2). In other words, the 'negative' relationship between quantity of imports and distance from their region of origin implies that the closer the source, the greater was the quantity of the amphorae reaching the city. Despite this outcome, nevertheless, it is important to investigate whether these patterns are the result of redistributive mechanisms.

According to the research model, correlation analysis was applied to the data for the examination of such a possibility (Fig. 3). The relationships revealed between Spanish and Italian amphorae, and Spanish and Gaulish amphorae, albeit not strong, suggest the occasional redistribution of Spanish goods to the East on ships transporting products from Gaul and Italy. Nevertheless, the fact that none of these correlations are strong shows that Spanish amphorae were predominantly distributed directly. The lack of correlation between amphorae from Italy and Gaul suggests that Gaulish products imported to Italy were primarily consumed within the centre of the empire, leaving no surpluses for regular exchange beyond. Concerning the N. African products, represented in analysis by Tripolitanian amphorae, the lack of any correlations may be suggestive of direct distribution to Nea Paphos. This pattern may show that N. African products were not only distributed northwards,[19] but that other mechanisms may have also been responsible for their distribution, although perhaps to a lesser extent.

The map provided here serves to demonstrate the trade routes through which products from throughout the western Mediterranean were distributed to Nea Paphos (Fig. 4). Given the complexity of trade and exchange in the Roman world, these identifications should not be taken to imply their uniqueness, as other processes must have also been involved in their distribution. They rather comprise the more common mechanisms engaged in the distribution of these amphorae. Furthermore, direct links with the west are supported by the lack of correlations with amphorae from eastern sources, which could have acted as redistribution points. The only correlation between Aegean and Gaulish imports is negative, suggesting competition rather than redistribution.

The model for the distribution of eastern amphorae is more straight-forward. The small distances involved in the region suggest the operation of both direct and re-distributional trade from neighbouring areas. The frequent, concurrent, operation of both processes is suggested by the moderate, but statistically significant, correlation between Aegean and Cilician amphorae (Fig. 3). In particular, in this case the greater quantity of Cilician imports could suggest that Aegean amphorae, apart from being traded directly,

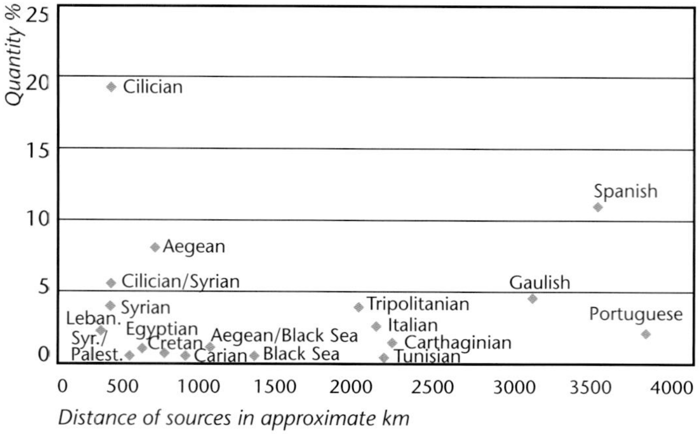

Fig. 6. Regression analysis of the quantity (%) of early Roman amphorae imported to Amathous (all sites) and approximate distance (km) of the region of origin.

were also occasionally redistributed with Cilician products.

Amphorae from the Levantine coast, as suggested by the lack of correlation with imports from the broader Cilicia/Syria region, apart from direct journeys, could have also been redistributed to Nea Paphos from Cypriot cities situated on the south of the island. Such an idea is also supported by the frequency of amphorae from the Levant in Amathous (see the following section). These ideas extend from the complex processes operating in the eastern Mediterranean basin. Moreover, they are intended to investigate the variability in the processes underlying the exchange of products among eastern regions, especially given the long tradition in both, production and exchange in the broader area. It is essential to note that if a region produced less, it would have exported less – a trend that would be apparent in the quantification of data and in the overall percentage of imports in the study assemblages. A smaller production output, however, would not necessarily imply the non-existence of direct distribution links, but rather a smaller frequency of such interactions.

Amathous

The amphorae that circulated in Amathous during the early Roman period, as attested by the aggregated data from the two sites under study (Fig. 5), derived from the same sources as observed in Nea Paphos. An interesting aspect, nevertheless, is the different quantities in which products from various sources appear, in relation to Nea Paphos. A striking difference occurs in the quantity of Spanish amphorae, followed by Gaulish, Italian and N. African amphorae. Another interesting aspect is the greater quantity of amphorae from the northern Levant, such as Cilician and Syrian amphorae, and from the Aegean. The divergence in the quantities of amphorae imported from the above regions, in relation to the quantities of imports to Nea Paphos, therefore points to the operation of diverse exchange mechanisms.

The general trends observed in regression analysis (Fig. 6), concerning the distribution of western amphorae to Amathous, show that the further the source the greater the quantity. Had Italian, Gaulish and Spanish amphorae been predominantly distributed from Nea Paphos, the pattern would be similar, as there should be a fall-off trend of the products directed from Nea Paphos to Amathous. Thus, the model put forward, based on the patterns resulting from quantification and also portrayed in regression analysis, proposes that this unexpected outcome could be the result of redistributive mechanisms from the north-eastern areas of the Levant, with which Amathous shared strong commercial links. For the investigation of this possibility, emphasis was put on the correlations observed between the western and eastern imports. Considering, however, the possible role of eastern areas in such a redistribution of western products, it was considered essential first to examine the mechanisms involved in the distribution of eastern amphorae to this southern Cypriot city. As with data from Nea Paphos, eastern amphorae in Amathous could have also been distributed directly or redistributed from neighbouring areas. Again, the differences in the quantities of imports from different areas could be the result of each region's production output (Fig. 6); yet, it is interesting to observe that the amphorae produced in the Aegean appear in a larger quantity than the amphorae produced in the opposite Levantine coastland, despite the greater distance separating the Aegean and the south coast of Cyprus.

Concerning the distribution trends of eastern amphorae, correlation analysis has revealed relationships between Aegean and Cilician amphorae, as well as between Cilician and Syrian amphorae. The first relationship suggests the redistribution of Aegean amphorae via Cilicia, whose

19 Fulford 1989, 171.

products were imported to Amathous in large amounts (Fig. 7). Empereur and Picon have in the past demonstrated that the Aegean, and Rhodes in particular, mostly supplied Asia Minor.[20] Another suggestion is that through this route, leading to Antioch, Aegean amphorae could be traded to northern areas of Cyprus, which probably acted as stops for these ships. Such links are demonstrated by imports at the north-western area of Kioni.[21] One can also easily imagine continuous exchanges between the north coast of Cyprus and the opposite Cilician coast, separated by a very short distance. It is, therefore, possible that Aegean and Cilician amphorae could also reach Amathous and other areas through intra-regional trade, perhaps also via Salamis. The moderate, but statistically significant, correlation between Cilician and Syrian amphorae suggests that amphorae from areas in close proximity could have also been distributed together, and reinforces the complexity of the long-established exchange networks operating in the eastern Mediterranean basin.

Among the western products only Spanish amphorae formed part of correlation analysis (Fig. 7), as a result of the unusually high quantity in which they are represented in the assemblages from Amathous. In particular, correlations resulted between Spanish amphorae and amphorae from Cilicia, amphorae from the broader Cilicia/Syria region and the Aegean. The first two correlations point to their extensive redistribution from south Asia Minor. The correlation with Aegean amphorae possibly reflects the sea route uniting the Aegean with the Iberian peninsula, as well as their common redistribution from the northern Levant. The same route was probably followed by N. African amphorae, as suggested by the correlations between Tripolitanian amphorae and amphorae from Cilicia, the Aegean, and indeed Spain. The correlation with Egyptian amphorae may suggest sparse redistribution with Egyptian products. The outcomes of this analysis and the differences observed in the quantity of imports from different sources, between the two cities, certainly reflect the complexity of the exchange networks operating in this part of the Empire, as well as the complexity of the trade patterns in which Cyprus was involved. The possible factors underlying these differences, especially in regards to the distribution patterns of western amphorae between Nea Paphos and Amathous, are discussed in the following section.

DISCUSSION

Despite the small distance separating Nea Paphos and Amathous, the patterns revealed through the analysis of the amphora assemblages from each city have pointed to the operation of different exchange processes and, most importantly, to the involvement of the two cities in different trade networks. This became particularly evident in the different quantities of products imported from western areas. Despite the superficial similarity in the typology of the amphorae circulating in both cities, the application of a solid methodological framework – firstly involving the sampling processes, which aimed at avoiding bias in the selection and analysis of data from different sites, secondly, quantification and, thirdly, the exploratory use of statistical techniques – has demonstrated significant differences. In sum, analysis has pointed to the operation of networks passing through the West and the North coast of the island, while other networks linked the south-eastern coasts of Cyprus with the opposite Levantine coastland.

The exchange network existing between Cyprus and the western part of the Empire predominantly involved Nea Paphos, the capital of Roman Cyprus. The analyses discussed here show that the city shared strong commercial contacts with major ports across the Mediterranean. Its commercial links to the West, and in particular Rome, as evidenced by the large quantity of Italian amphorae, and to the East, suggest its centrality in the maritime exchange networks occurring in the eastern Mediterranean. Products, as revealed by statistical analysis, were distributed either directly or redistributed from areas other than their sources, thus portraying the complexity of distribution mechanisms characterizing Roman trade.

Amathous, on the other hand, was primarily involved in eastern exchange networks. The regional focus of the commercial endeavors of this southern city is attested by the supremacy of imports from eastern sources, and in particular the northern Levant. Moreover, the different and unusual quantities of amphorae from a number of western sources, in relation to those from Nea Paphos, have suggested the redistribution of western goods along with eastern products from the neighboring regions, with which this city shared strong commercial links. This trend, moreover, should not exclude the possibility of intra-regional redistribution of imported products from Nea Paphos to other Cypriot cities, including Amathous, particularly given the complexity of exchange. However, as the patterns underlying the data

		AEGEAN	CIL.SYR	CILICIAN	EGYPT	SPANISH	SYRIAN	TRIPOL
Kendall´s tau_b	**AEGEAN**							
	Correlation Coefficient	1.000	.616*	.706**	.510	.719**	-.370	.609*
	Sig. (2-tailed)	.	.024	.006	.083	.008	.178	.029
	N	10	10	10	10	10	10	10
	CIL.SYR							
	Correlation Coefficient	.616*	1.000	.440	.455	.902**	.551	.573*
	Sig. (2-tailed)	.024	.	.100	.138	.001	.053	.048
	N	10	10	10	10	10	10	10
	CILICIAN							
	Correlation Coefficient	.706**	.440	1.000	.369	.545*	.510	-.616*
	Sig. (2-tailed)	.006	.100	.	.199	.039	.058	.024
	N	10	10	10	10	10	10	10
	EGYPT							
	Correlation Coefficient	.510	.455	.369	1.000	.604*	.035	.606
	Sig. (2-tailed)	.083	.138	.199	.	.046	.911	.054
	N	10	10	10	10	10	10	10
	SPANISH							
	Correlation Coefficient	.719**	.902**	.545*	.604*	1.000	.500	.519
	Sig. (2-tailed)	.008	.001	.039	.046	.	.076	.070
	N	10	10	10	10	10	10	10
	SYRIAN							
	Correlation Coefficient	-.370	.551	.510	..035	.500	1.000	.251
	Sig. (2-tailed)	.178	.053	.058	.911	.076	.	.390
	N	10	10	10	10	10	10	10
	TRIPOL							
	Correlation Coefficient	.609*	.573*	-.616*	.606	.519	..251	1.000
	Sig. (2-tailed)	.029	.048	.024	.054	.070	.390	.
	N	10	10	10	10	10	10	10

Fig. 7. Correlation analysis of the early Roman amphorae imported to Amathous based on their origins.

suggest, other, inter-regional, mechanisms were more prominent and frequent. The differences in the exchange networks in which the two cities were involved are not surprising, considering the island-specific traits of Cypriot economy, and the long tradition of diverse economic orientations of different parts of Cyprus, which seem to have continued to affect the overall economy of the island. Still, one should not interpret this variability in Cypriot exchange networks based solely on historic traits and geographical features, which influenced regional patterns; as exchange occurred within an Empire, it is pertinent to consider the character of distribution mechanisms within the conditions that had developed after Rome's annexation of Cyprus and the eastern Mediterranean.

It is within this Roman context that we must examine the suggestion put forward in the above analysis, i.e. that western products were mainly traded to the capital of the island directly, and not via a nearer exporting area. The political role of Nea Paphos, as the seat of the administrators, which shared strong links with the political rulers in Rome, may justify this pattern suggested by statistical analysis. In addition, the existence of an advanced harbour "for all winds" at the site,[22] further reinforces the potency of the city to participate actively in the long distance maritime trade networks that had developed between the two halves of the Mediterranean during the early Roman period. Based on these identifications, and building on the distribution mechanism of the *annona* and its impact on economic structures, it could be suggested that Nea Paphos was a stop for ships travelling from Italy to Egypt for the transfer of

20 Empereur & Picon 1989, 243.
21 Leonard 1995b, 144, 149.
22 Leonard 1995a, 232.

the *annona*, and a stop on the route of their return voyage; an assertion expressed in relation to late Roman trade and supported by the prevailing winds and currents.[23] It is therefore possible that the patterns observed were largely the result of the broader economic organisation of this part of the empire, created to facilitate the exploitation of the region.

These issues relate to the political integration of the Roman economy, and to topics, such as economic rationalisation under the Roman Empire. Although they cannot be addressed in the present paper, they can certainly provide a basis for further research in the future. A related idea that requires further investigation, extending from the patterns observed in amphora distribution, is that Nea Paphos collected and redistributed, along with local products, the goods and taxes paid in kind by eastern areas not located along the regular route of the ships transporting the *annona* from Egypt to the West. Such regional nodes are common in core-periphery systems.[24] It is important to note that it is not only trade that flourished during this period in Cyprus, but also local production. This economic aspect was not limited to everyday essentials, but also included metals, timber and natural medicaments, which were famous throughout the empire.[25]

The main mechanism underlying exchanges is market exchange, which was the predominant form of exchange in the Roman world. Within the Empire framework, the expansion of these exchanges must be seen as a response to the disequilibrium created by the exploitation of the peripheries by Rome. Money was also raised by intra-regional exchange, and commercial activities between the cities and their hinterland. Analysis of published data from rural areas shows that foreign exchange was mainly conducted by the cities,[26] which then provided the countryside with imports. Likewise, the hinterland provided local products to their centres. Within the Empire, these patterns are the result of urban monopolies with close ties to the ruling elite.

Finally, the development of long-distance trade in the early Roman period was also promoted by the competition between the centres and the establishment of a common identity between the exchanging parties. Despite the debate on the "Romanisation" of the empire,[27] certain values conveyed by the centre were implanted in the societies of diverse socio-cultural background, thus affecting the character of production and promoting exchanges and interactions between the trading agents.[28]

CONCLUSION

The complexity and variability of early Roman trade, as demonstrated in the above analysis, should be further highlighted, as a concluding remark. Cyprus, as shown by the vast amphora types that were imported throughout the early Roman period, was central in the exchange networks that operated in the eastern Mediterranean basin. Most importantly, it has been shown that certain western products were not only traded in the western part of the Empire, as previously believed; on the contrary, data from Cyprus suggest that they were also largely consumed in significant quantities in the eastern part of the Empire. It would thus not be an exaggeration to suggest that the channels of communication with neighbouring areas, owing to the island's strategic position, convey Cyprus a chief role for the examination of the complex exchange mechanisms in this part of the Mediterranean. Hopefully, the future establishment of more concrete typologies of eastern Mediterranean amphorae will provide a better insight into eastern networks and the export of such products to the western part of the Empire.

Furthermore, it is crucial that we approach data from such key areas in conjunction with a concrete methodological framework that would enable the investigation of different economic processes. Most importantly, the development and use of such a framework will contribute towards overcoming the limitations imposed by the variability of the data and the lack of adequate information from different areas of the eastern Mediterranean. On this basis, the analysis of amphorae from Cyprus, and other eastern regions, will contribute greatly to elucidating important issues relating to Roman economy, such as economic organisation, the role of supply and demand, economic integration and the relationship between the Roman economy and traditionally defined market economies.

23 Bakirtzis 1995.
24 Matthews 2003, 144
25 Michaelides 1990b, 122.
26 Cf. Lund 1993a.
27 Freeman 1997, 8-13.
28 Kaldeli 2009.

Roman Amphorae from the Polish Excavations at Nea Paphos, *Maloutena*: An Overview

BY HENRYK MEYZA & DOBIESŁAWA BAGIŃSKA

Roman Amphorae from the Polish Excavations at Nea Paphos, *Maloutena*: An Overview

BY HENRYK MEYZA & DOBIESŁAWA BAGIŃSKA

Almost 50 years of excavations at the site of Maloutena have resulted in the recovery of an enormous mass of amphora fragments, but – as is usual in residential areas at settlement sites – relatively few mendable pieces. Most of the site is covered by a shallow accumulation over the latest monumental structures, which were intensively searched for stone in more recent centuries. The area was until recently used for agriculture. Several rooms have preserved *in situ* groups of transport, storage or domestic amphorae (Fig. 1a), usually accompanied by other forms of vessels used in these three functional spheres.

Two main catastrophic events at the site have helped to preserve pottery *in situ*,: one probably contemporary with the earthquake that hit the neighbouring House of Dionysos in – or after – the time of Hadrian, well-dated thanks to a purse with countermarked coins found by the skeleton of a victim;[1] the other one, the earthquake that destroyed Kourion at the beginning of the middle of the 5th century (though some argue this event is better dated to AD 365.)[2] There were numerous other earthquakes, known from textual sources, both at the beginning of Roman period and during 4th century, resulting in difficulties in identifying the specific one that caused the observed damage.

A number of relatively well-preserved groups found before 2005 were presented at a Roman Crafts and Trade (ROCT) conference in Ghent,[3] but during the next four seasons of excavations more deposits were uncovered in earlier strata, and they will be discussed here, set against an overview of more frequently occurring types. Due to the urgency of excavation (related to shelter construction), the enormous amount of pottery collected could not be studied in detail at the time of excavation.[4] Therefore, the following must be considered a preliminary statement.

THREE SELECTED CONTEXTS

The first group was found below room 16NW of Villa of Theseus, the second in the row of rooms (20-23) of the so-called Hellenistic House north of the western courtyard no. 13 and the great black-and-white mosaic in room 10. Both can be dated to the 2nd century AD. Included here, too, are some new late Roman finds in the North-Eastern House (NEH = northern part of Late Roman insula of the House of Aion).

The first group was a dump in two compartments (1, 2), placed west of the main north-south wall,[5] including a large deposit of broken, but mostly complete, transport amphorae, cooking vessels, jugs and a large plain ware jar (Fig. 1b). A coin of Gordian III, dating to AD 240 was found on top of the deposit in compartment 2 (coin cat. 915), giving a *terminus post* quem for the overlying fill, which preceded floors of Villa of Theseus. Apart from numerous pottery fragments, the deposit consisted of loose light-brown soil, which filled the compartments almost up to top of the preserved walls. The collection included examples of the typical Paphos series of 2nd- to 3rd-century amphorae similar to those found in destruction deposits of the House of Dionysos.[6] The most frequent one is Hayes 1991 Roman Type II in two paste variants: beige and red. Less frequent were Hayes 1991 Roman Type I, i.e. the Sub-Koan one. In the same group occur other amphorae popular in the House of Dionysos: Hayes 1991 Roman Type 3, also known as "pinched-handle" amphorae (of the beige and pink variants), and examples of the Amrit/Tartus type, as well as two Plain Ware examples similar to Lusitanian 9 jars in two sizes (Fig. 13), together with other vessels, the most unusual a Plain Ware, non-coarse pithos.[7]

In rooms 20-23 of the Hellenistic House, the floor layers of the destruction of the beginning of the 2nd century AD were found intact (unless excavated in earlier trial pits of

1 Nicolaou 1990, 144-146.
2 Soren & Leonard 1989, 446; Lichocka & Meyza, 192-194.
3 Meyza forthcoming.
4 Preservation policy of finds at the site has favoured the chronological aspect of pottery, and therefore, apart from evident deposits, body sherds of plain and coarse wares, such as the amphorae, were selected less often for long-term storage.
5 Daszewski & Meyza 2010, 513.
6 Hayes 1997.
7 Daszewski & Meyza 2010 fig. 11.

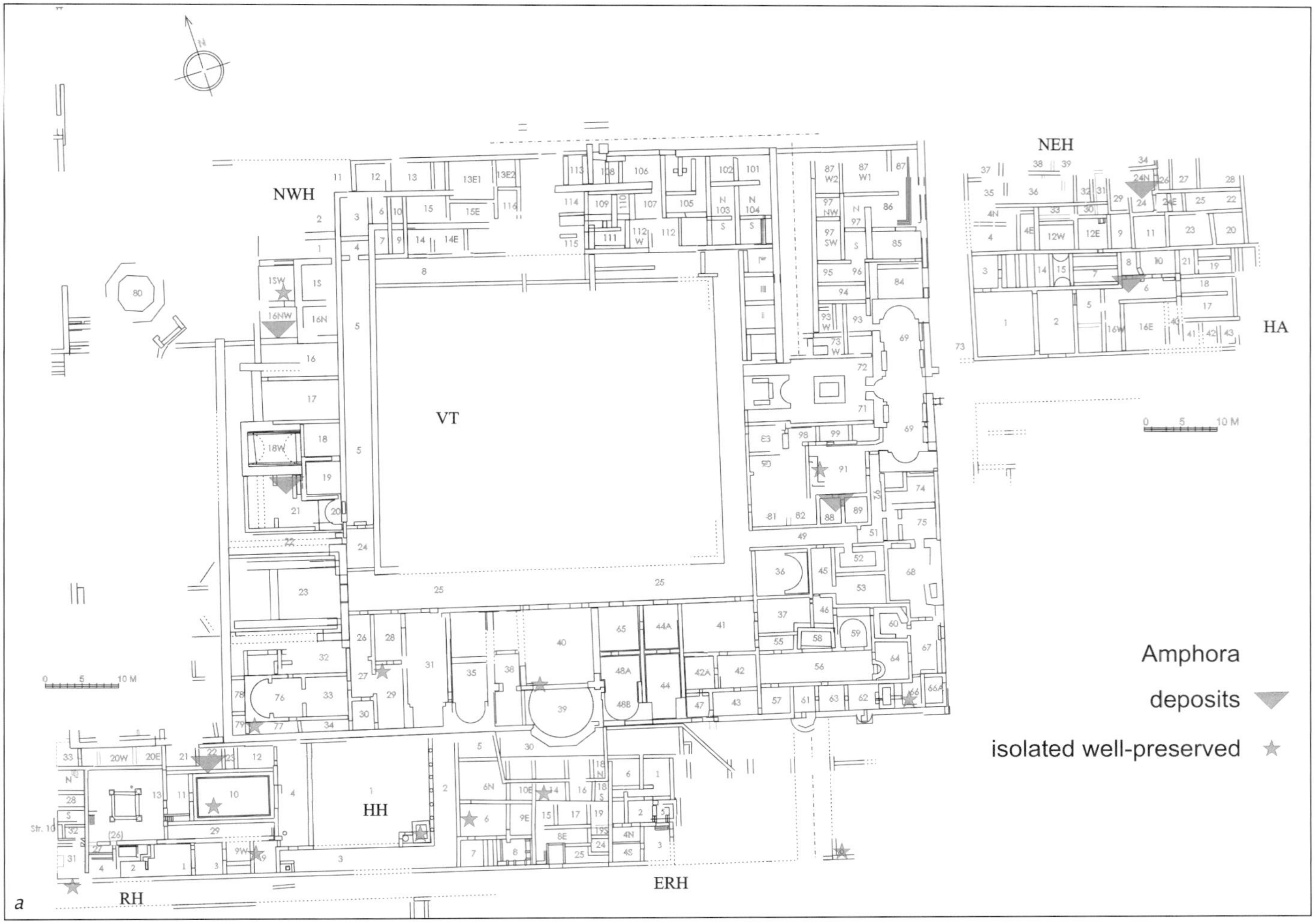

Fig. 1. Main deposits of amphorae

a. General plan of Polish excavations at Kato Paphos – Maloutena, distribution of amphora finds. Drawn by H. Meyza after St. Medeksza, A. Brzozowska, M. Słowińska.

b. Deposit under Villa of Theseus Room 16NW (in compartment 2=deposit I, context 128/07). Photo by J.K. Rądkowska.

c. Part of floor deposit in the so-called "Hellenistic House" Room 22, amphora Pompei V (Fig. 5d=g) in situ. Photo by W. Machowski.

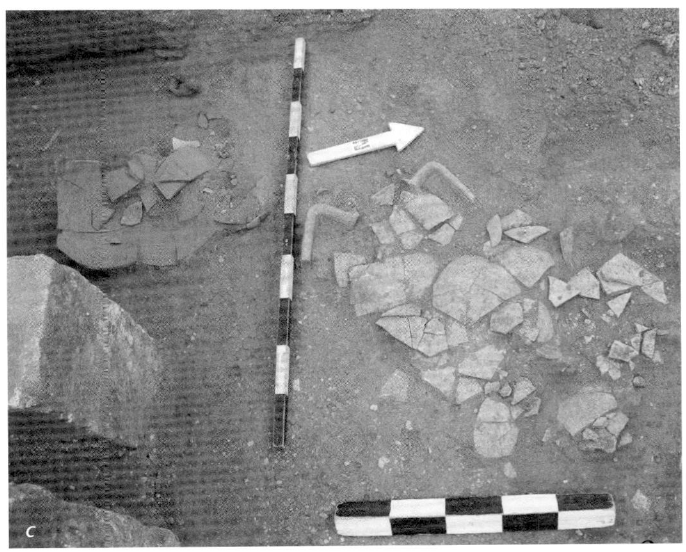

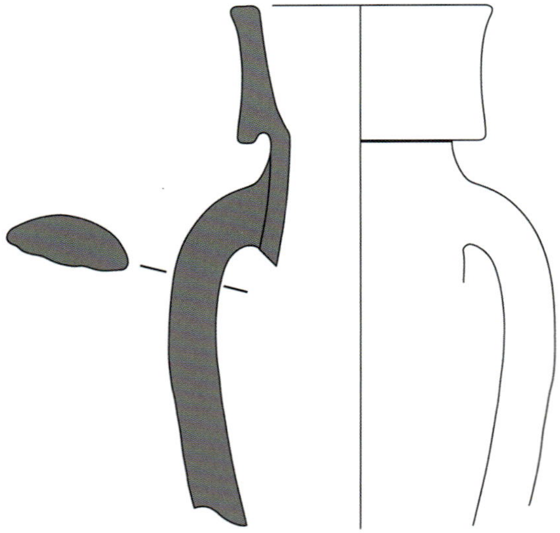

a

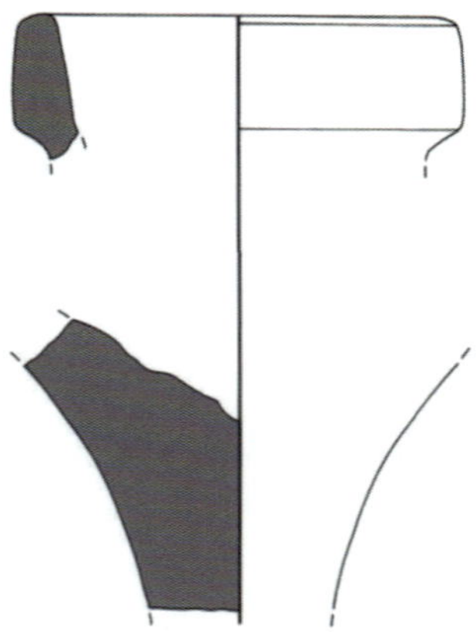

d

Fig. 2. Republican and Early Imperial Italian amphorae

a. Dressel 1B/C, trial pit 3/86, layer II, (Papuci-Władyka 1985, group D.5) drawn by M. Drabot.

b. Dr 6 with a stamp THB on rim found on floor in the so-called "Hellenistic House" Room 21. Photo by K. Woszczyńska.

c. Stamp of the same amphora. Photo by J.K. Rądkowska.

d. Rim and base of another Dr 6 found in adjacent room 20E. Drawn by D. Bagińska.

1976, 1990 and 1995, or shelter foundation trenches in 2003), thanks to their deep location in comparison with the surrounding floors. Several crushed and broken amphorae, including examples of early "pinched-handle" types were found in room 23, a large Dressel 6A occurred in room 21, and a Pompei V amphora in room 22 (Fig. 1c). This material comprises the second group reported here.

Finally, in Room 12 West of the NEH, on Floor I, at 35-50 cm below preserved top of the northern wall of Rooms 7 and 14, we came across a large collection of Late Roman coins (42 pieces), a lead vessel, a lead applique, several complete lamps of the 4th century, including a rare Tripolitanian lamp, a bronze pin and a necklace made of perforated shells, which seem to support the catastrophic character of destruction of this area. Crushed or broken mendable pottery vessels found in some quantity, including a small bowl of Phocaean Red Slip Ware form 9, an African spatheion amphora as well as a krater of uncertain origin, possibly also African, confirm that supposition.[8] Some tiles and small flat stones that probably were used as voussoirs are the remains of collapsed roof.

METHODOLOGICAL CONSIDERATIONS

A typological overview of the relevant material is presented below in a roughly chronological order, with a mixture of types contemporary with the strata of their discovery and residual ones. Such an overview will, due to simple numerical domination, emphasize material found outside the undisturbed *in situ* groups, and it should neither be regarded as comprehensive nor representative in a statistical sense. As mentioned above, the study of this material is still at an early stage.[9] Moreover, the nature of the sample presented here is affected by the fact that the southern part of excavated site was little used after the construction of the Villa of Theseus in the end of the 2nd century. Hence, the destruction strata of the Hadrianic or later earthquakes are least disturbed there. Remains of destruction without much later intrusion can be observed particularly in the northwest and the east parts of the so-called Hellenistic House. It seems that earlier events of similar character have left traces also in some areas and the final construction with remodelling corresponds to the benefaction of Augustus after the 14 BC cataclysm.

CATALOGUE OF FORMS FREQUENT AT PAPHOS, MALOUTENA

Campanian Dressel 1B/C (Fig. 2a)

One large fragment, which can be classified precisely, was found in layer II of the trial pit below room 4E ("corridor") of the North-eastern House, i.e. north of room 13 of the House of Aion proper.[10]

The specimen has thick, vertical collar rim, protruding over neck and a heavy, cylindrical neck, slightly tapering in the middle, all features associated with Dressel 1B amphorae. The handles, however, are long, curved, semi-ovoid in section and ribbed, tapering downwards, features associated with Dressel 1C. In light of this mixture of traits, we describe it as transitional between Dressel 1B and 1C. Several heavy cylindrical toes and more, smaller handle, rim or body fragments have also been found, identifiable as Dressel 1 amphorae by their rough, sandy fabric, fairly thick walls pink brownish in colour with light slip. Inclusions are especially distinctive as they contain much of 'black sand' sharp-edged grains.[11] Some fragments most probably belong to Dressel 1B, as these preserve very heavy concave-cylindrical toes. The Dressel 1B/C fragment was found in a stratum dated between the first half 1st century BC and the third quarter of 1st century AD.[12] Other pieces of that type were found in later, mostly secondary deposits.

In the Eastern Mediterranean, Campanian amphorae have been found in large number at Delos. Jean-Yves Empereur classified examples found there as Dressel 1A and 1C,[13] though in some cases (the examples with cylindrical rims and parallel handles) they may be better classified as 1B. Most published complete amphorae are Dressel 1C.

Dressel 6A (Fig. 2b-d)

Two fragments (and another neck fragment, probably originally more) were found in the Hellenistic House Room 20E in the fill of the robbing trench for the southern wall (F: 38/07:6, Fig. 2d), as well as under the floor level with other Roman pottery in F: 57/07.[14]

A large fragment of rim and neck with handles with a commonly occurring stamp of Titus Helvius Basila (THB) on the rim was found in the so-called Hellenistic House Room 21 in Early Roman stratum below the floor, (F: 90/07, Fig. 2b-c),[15] and another fragment appeared in a disturbed part of the fill in the same room (F: 72/07).

Another rim with the THB stamp was also encountered under room 17 of the Villa of Theseus, i.e. over the street B (F: 104/07:1). A third example was found in a disturbed rubble layer covering courtyard 1 of the so-called Hellenistic House (F: 67+73/11).

An unstamped upper part of a Dressel 6A amphora was collected from slabs covering a channel in street C leading from the Villa of Theseus north wing Room 105N.[16]

Another upper part, also unstamped, was found in the trial pit made in 1992 in insula 9A, south of the House of Aion.[17]

These amphorae of Adriatic origin found in Paphos often carry the stamp of THB, which dates them to the time of Tiberius or (less probably) that of Augustus.[18] A *dipinto* on a Dressel 6A amphora from Magdalensberg with a consular

8 Meyza 2008, 518-519.
9 For other preliminary reports, see Meyza *et al.* forthcoming.
10 Daszewski 1987, 688 fig. 41 (classified as Dressel 1C); Papuci-Władyka 1995, 76, 125 pl. 22 no. 136.
11 Peacock & Williams 1986, 87, 90.
12 Papuci-Władyka 1995, 100; the Dressel 1B/C was found in deeper part of a combined stratum, probably deposited early in the 1st century BC.
13 Empereur 1982 pl. 40.1, middle, 40.2, second from left; 1983; Hadjidakis 2003, 269 fig. 444 compares the two forms B and C, as well as other forms.
14 Daszewski *et al.* 2010, 511 figs. 8-9 (in NW corner); Meyza *et al.* forthcoming.
15 Daszewski *et al.* 2010, 511 fig. 8; Meyza *et al.* forthcoming.
16 Daszewski 1996, 97-98.
17 Daszewski 1993, 86.
18 This stamp is previously known from three other amphorae from our excavations: Sztetyłło 1991, 101 nos. 246-247; Sztetyłło 2010, 157 no. 187. For the dating, see: Hainzmann, M., Instrumentum domesticum inscriptum. Minuskeltexte, http://www-gewi.uni-graz.at/monae/INDOM/INDOM-Minuskel/web-IDOM-min-neu/blocks/x000003.htm = AD 38; Dressel 1879, 50-51. And for the origin and distribution: Lindhagen 2009, 86, 97 and 102.

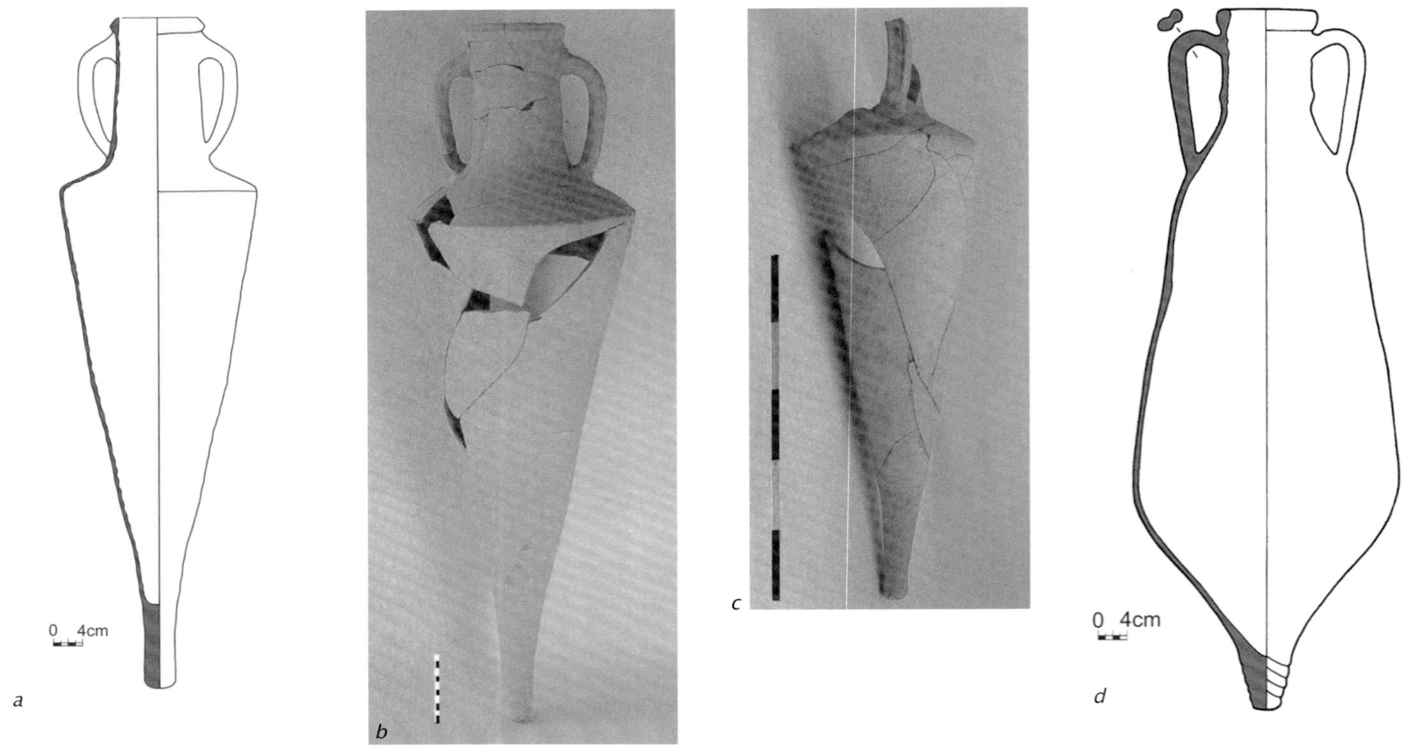

date of AD 38 suggests that Titus Helvius Basila, governor of Galatia under Tiberius and Caligula (AD 33-39) and son of the proconsul of the same name, should be the workshop owner. Of course, numerous occurrences of the stamp at Castro Praetorio make it possible that these amphorae were also produced in times of the father, but not necessarily, since the latest consular dates in the latter deposit are almost contemporary (AD 36, of Sextus Papinius and Quintus Plautius). It seems that earlier specimens, like the Lamboglia 2 amphorae known from Delos, did not reach Cyprus frequently. In Paphos, the best-dated pieces occur below floors covered by 2nd century AD destruction strata.

Hayes 1991 Roman Amphorae type II (Amathus 4, "Carrot amphora", Pompeii 15) (Fig. 3a-c)
Several complete or almost complete examples were found below Room 16NW, west of the main north-south wall in the Villa of Theseus.[19] Large fragments occurred in rooms 20, 21, 22 of the so-called Hellenistic House while smaller pieces come from under VT Room 46, Trench K/9-10 (2002),[20] below VT Room 16N (1995) and in the bedding of the Theseus mosaic (1971). At least two further pieces were found in upper strata.

Large amphorae Roman type II (with a height of 93-100 cm)[21] appear at Maloutena in two paste variants. The first, unknown until now and less frequent, is light buff on the outer surface with a dark beige layer below and reddish body inside or almost uniform with dark beige to pinkish in section, with quite fine clay, most grains around 0.1 mm, brownish, black and few up to 0.5 mm as well as some larger, extruding limestone pieces. Generally this variant has thinner walls (c. 0.7 cm). The second paste variant, occurring in at least eight examples, is dark red (10R 5/6) with light brown to dark grey core. This fabric, known already from the House of Dionysos, contains some quartz sand, mainly around 0.3 mm, reddish grains, isolated larger light grey particles and few limestone inclusions of c. 0.8 mm size. The walls are thicker, 0.9 to 1 cm walls, sometimes bearing traces of pitch. The fabric is hard, and the surface unslipped. In both paste variants the toes are elongated and solid. The ribbed rim of the example published from the House of Dionysos is only one of the forms present at our site. The form differs from an example from Amathous both

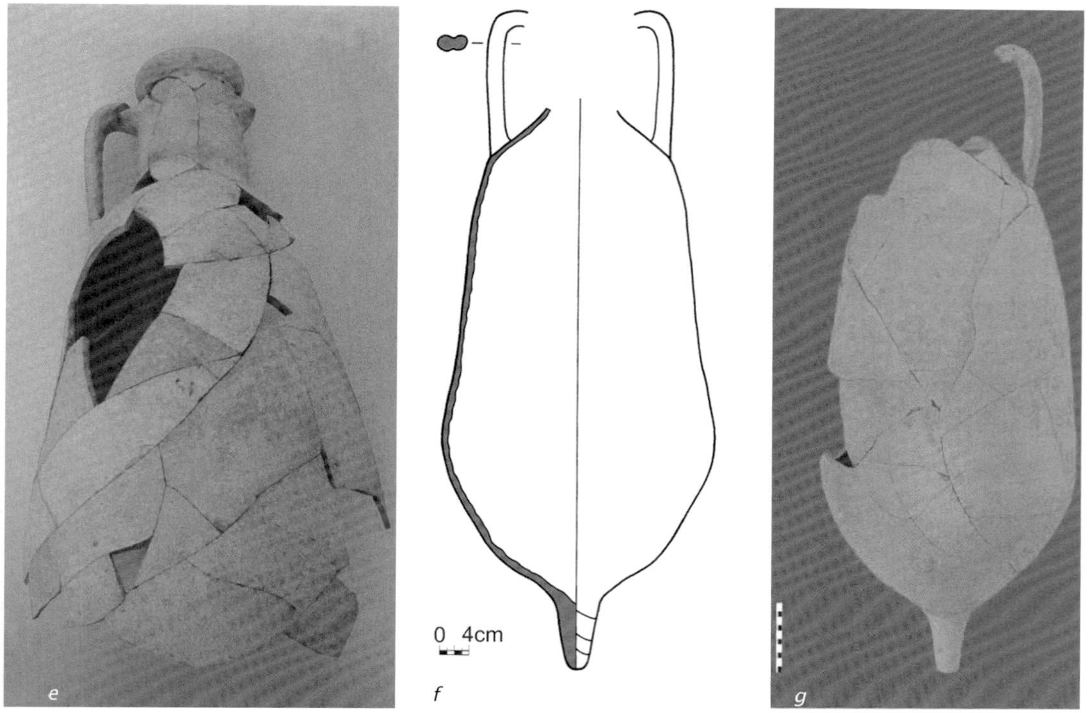

Fig. 3. Paphos House of Dionysos Roman Amphora Types I and II

a. Type II, under VT Room 16NW. Drawn by K. Lach.

b. Same. Photo by K. Woszczyńska.

c. Type II, HH Room 22, fill over floor. Photo by K. Woszczyńska.

d. Type I, HH R. 21, destruction layer. Drawn by K. Kapiec.

e. Same. Photo by K. Woszczyńska.

f. Type I, found under VT Room 16NW, Deposit in "niche 1". Drawn by M. Droste.

g. Same. Photo by K. Woszczyńska.

in the heavier and longer toe and in the form of the handle section.[22] The presence of pitch suggests that this amphora type probably contained wine.

The destruction deposits preceding the mosaic floors in the House of Dionysos, where this form first occurs, were initially dated to early 2nd century AD by a coin group found with an earthquake victim, but now Hayes accepts a later date both for this stratum and the last phase. Numerous finds of this amphora type are associated with the final destruction of the house, after the mosaics were laid.[23] In our excavations at Nea Paphos, the final destruction of the so-called Hellenistic House is dated to the later 2nd century AD. Most probably it is contemporary with final destruction of the House of Dionysos. The Roman Type II amphorae, therefore, date to the 2nd century.

Sub-Koan Amphorae (Hayes 1991 Roman Amphorae type I) (Fig. 3d-g)

Many fragments of Type I amphorae are found at our excavations, particularly in 2nd century destruction layers in the southern and western part of excavated site, but rarely as nearly-complete vessels; one such example was found west of the main north-south wall. The Sub-Koan pieces from Maloutena were most-often produced in porous, gritty, highly calcareous ware with fine dark grains 0.1-0.2, rarely 0.3 mm in size. At the House of Dionysos in Paphos these amphorae were most frequent in the 2nd/3rd-century destruction contexts.[24]

Pseudo-Cos en cloche (Agora M 54; Hayes 1991 Roman Amphorae type VIII)

Isolated fragments or larger amphora parts broken into small fragments were found in the north-western part of the so-called Hellenistic House, around a well-head

19 Daszewski & Meyza, 2010, 512.
20 Meyza 2003, 257.
21 Hayes 1991, 91, 204 fig. 70.12 pl. 24.2 (OΔ 3568).
22 Empereur 1987, 44 pl. 26.4.
23 Hayes 1991, 91, 204-205 figs. 70.12, 70.5 (no. II.3) pl. 24.2; Hayes 1997.
24 Hayes 1991, 90-91, 204 nos. 20, 26 pl. 24.1; 205 nos. 2-3 figs. 70.1-4, from a post-mosaic destruction context in corridors O and Σ.

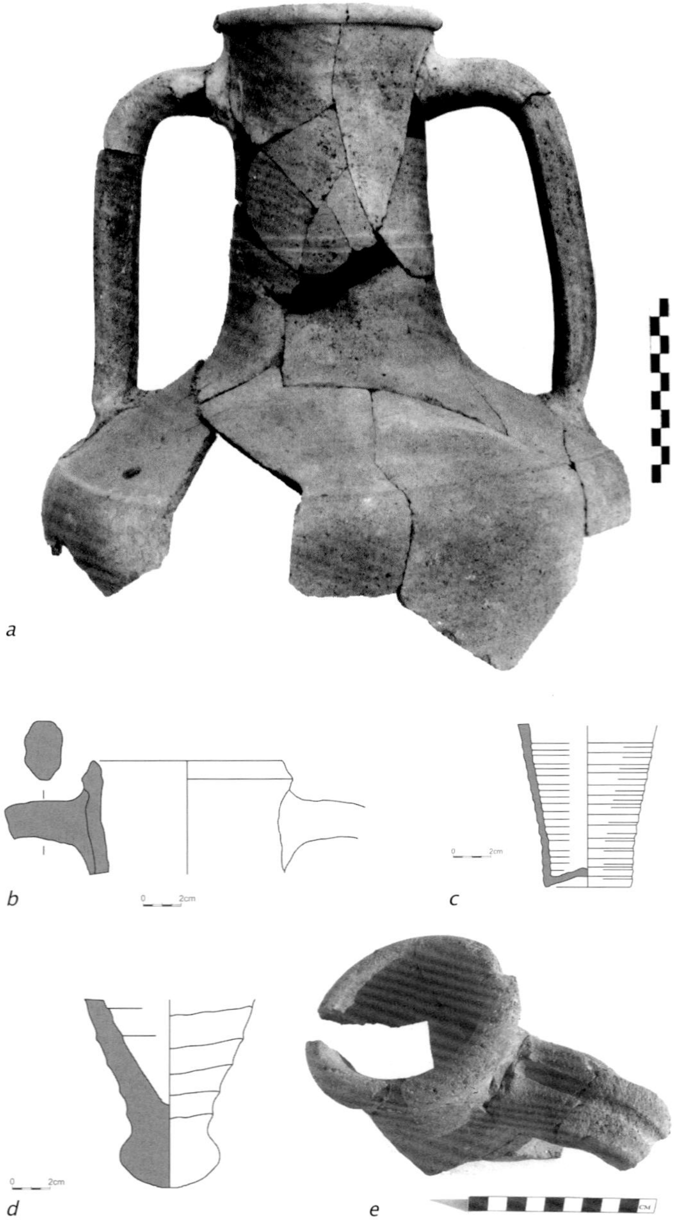

Fig. 4. Various forms:

a. Amrit amphora, Early Roman House, E from Room 1. Photo by W. Jerke.
b. Roman Amphora Type I, trial pit below Theseus mosaic, layer 2, fill below bedding of the mosaic. Drawn by Meike Droste.
c. Beirut amphora form 8, found in trial pit in VT Room 69N/ layer 8, 1977. Drawn by M. Droste.
d. Amrit amphora found in VT N wing Room 102/104. Drawn by K. Hołderna.
e. Amrit? Amphora, HA Room 12E, rubble layer. Photo by W. Jerke.

in the South portico of VT,[25] and in rooms 4 and 12W of the North-eastern house. Of these, the last ones may be residual. Though fragmentary, these amphorae can be identified thanks to characteristic peaked, curved, double-barrelled handles, and convex profile of the neck widening from a narrow mouth to wide upper body set off by a slight bulge at the shoulder. The fabric has sandy inclusions protruding through the wet-smoothed, though lumpy, surface, and is yellowish-buff to reddish yellow (7.5YR 7/6) in colour. Amphorae of this fabric seem to have been produced at a kiln site identified at Yumurtalık in Cilicia; two other production centres are suspected in the same region.[26] The type occurs in cistern 5 of the House of Dionysos in Nea Paphos, filled around AD 100-125.[27] The latest examples appear in a destruction deposit at the Villa Dionysos in Knossos dated c. AD 170-180.[28] Likewise, at our excavations in Paphos the latest occurrences belong to destruction layers of 2nd century AD.

Beirut amphorae (Fig. 4c)
Amphorae of the Beirut series also appear but most are later variants, such as the illustrated bottom of type 8 found below the floors of VT vestibule Room 69.[29] Earlier forms are also present, e.g., the rim and neck of a form Beirut 4.1 amphora,[30] dated to the 2nd century and found in a compartment in SE corner of room 20E of the so-called Hellenistic House.

Our example has a gritty texture, reddish grey with partially grey-brown slip and large elongated chips of black ironstone (up to 2 mm), irregular/angular reddish grains, some large (1mm), fine pores, and smaller (below 1 mm) grey shale and lime bits.

Amrit amphora (Hayes 1991 Roman Amphorae Type IX) (Fig. 4a, d-e)
This amphora type is fairly frequent on our site. Apart from a piece found in a late Roman rubble layer in the North-eastern House Room 12E (Fig. 4e),[31] other fragments were found in destruction strata of the late 2nd century AD. A large fragment of the upper part of this type was found in the so-called Early Roman House (Fig. 4a). A toe was found west of the main north-south wall under VT room 16NW. Heavily built toes, typically showing a solid rounded knob, a marked spiral twist, and traces of ribbing inside are usually particularly well-preserved: examples were found in an Early Roman deposit in R.101SW of the northern wing

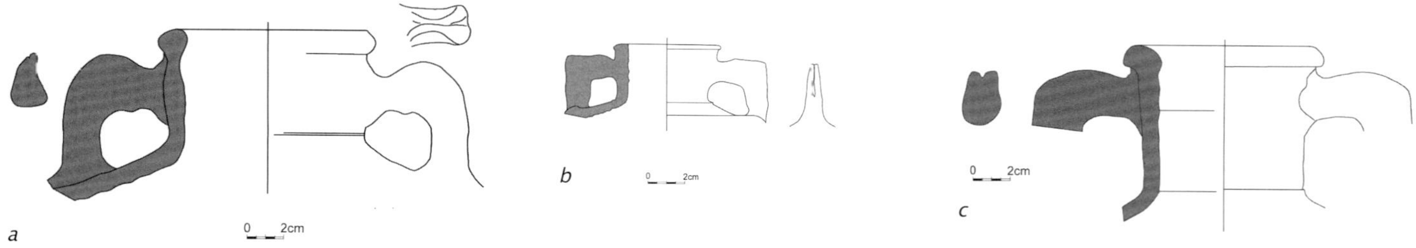

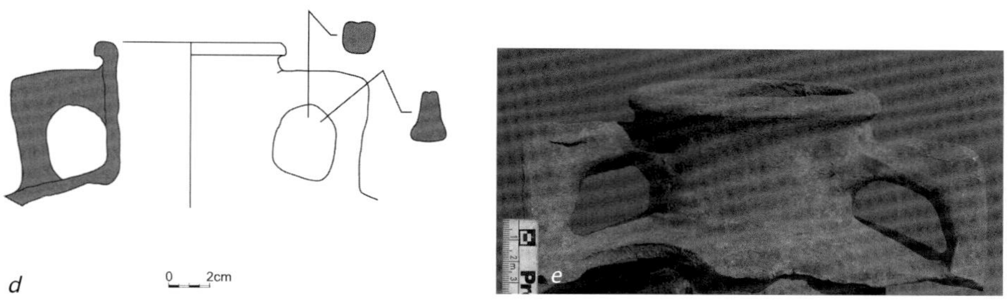

Fig. 5. Pinched-handle amphorae – upper parts

a. Red version found in VT Cistern in central part of Room 69, fill. Drawn by M. Droste.
b. Pink version, found in so-called "Hellenistic House". Drawn by K. Bergmann = e.
c. Buff external surface, reddish section found in Street 9 (Sq 7/81). Drawn by M. Droste.
d. Ware as above, HH Room 12. Drawn by H. Meyza.
e. = b. Photo by H. Meyza.

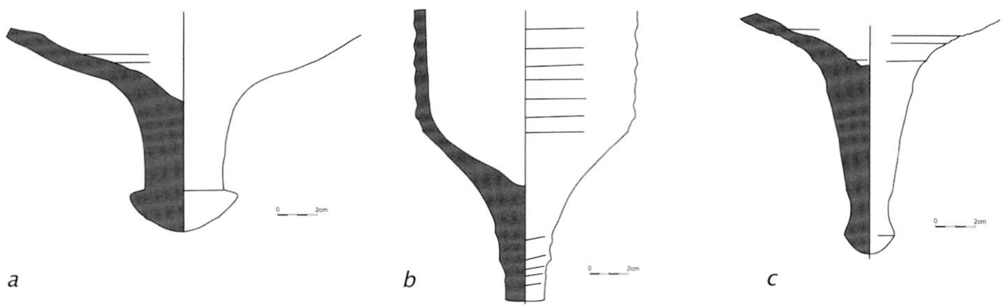

Fig. 6. Pinched-handle amphora bases

a. Dark beige version, found in VT Room 69 central part, fill of the cistern. Drawn by M. Droste.
b. Dark red variant, square 3/77. Drawn by A. Kopacz.
c. Micaceous orange body with beige surface, VT N wing, Room 102/104 Deposit. Drawn by K. Hołderna.

of the Villa (Fig. 4d), in fill below Floor I under R. 16N/95 in the West wing, as well as in enclosure W from dromos to cistern in the so-called Hellenistic House western courtyard (13).

The paste can also usually be identified by macroscopic inspection, as grey inclusions stand out (often up to 1 mm large) and the sherds usually are covered with spots of dark organic stain. The body is usually coated inside with black impermeable tar. A neck of reduced length, but in practically the same paste, was found in the North-eastern House in a Late Roman (5th century) context (Fig. 4e).[32]

Mau 27/28 (Hayes 1991 Roman Amphorae type III; "Pinched-handle" amphorae) (Fig. 5a-e; Fig. 6 a-c)
The pinched handles of this amphora type are as distinctive as its mushroom-shaped toes. The shoulder edge and ribbing (regular wide grooves separated by equally standardized slightly narrower flat bands) are usually diagnostic as well. This is one of the most frequently identified amphora forms at our site, although they occur in many variants of form and fabric. We have not found

25 Meyza 1997, 124 note 4.
26 Empereur & Picon 1989, 231-232.
27 Hayes 1991, 93-94, 195 fig. 68 top: d, pl. 25.3 (without provenance).
28 Hayes 1983, 98, 158.
29 Reynolds 2005, 569 fig. 82 (type 8.1 – AD 551).
30 Reynolds 2000, 388, 394 fig. 19; Reynolds 2005 fig. 71.
31 Lichocka & Meyza 2001, 172-176.
32 The piece is paralleled by finds in Beirut; see Reynolds 2005, 568 fig. 55.

any easily mendable or complete example as the walls are quite thin and break into relatively small fragments; these were not always collected.

The best-preserved examples come from the Villa of Theseus (VT) west wing Room 16NW, west of the main north-south wall; and in the fill over the floor of the so-called Hellenistic House in rooms 21 and 23.[33] Variants of the same form also occur in VT North wing, Room 102/104 Deposit (Fig. 6c). Another set was found in a cistern under the central part of VT Room 69 (Figs. 5a, 6a). Other pieces occurred under the mosaic of the eastern portico of VT (Room 50), in the bedding (5th century AD at latest) of that mosaic, as well as in the fill over North Eastern House Room 12E. The lower part of a late variant (Fig. 6c) was found in the VT Room 87, in a 5th century AD stratum.

A variant with incompletely squeezed handles, found in Hellenistic House room 23, suggests that originally the handles were double-barrelled and that the handles were made as one shaft and grooved only in later examples.

In 1996, Daszkiewicz and Schneider analysed 14 samples using XRF-WD and petrographic study of thin sections. They identified at least three different groups of pastes divided preliminarily into six provenance groups.[34] It is still unclear whether the buff/yellowish coloured variant is truly of local production, as Hayes supposed.[35] In the meantime production sites of these amphorae in other pastes were found in Rough Cilicia.

Three main variants of fabric occur in Paphos. First, the variant produced in Cilicia Tracheia[36] has a reddish-yellow (7.5YR 7/6) outer surface, (2.5 YR 6/6) light red inner surface, hard, dense, dark red fabric with limestone and dark inclusions, matt surface with streaky slip. The second is pale yellow (5Y 8/4) in colour, small grained, hard, dense yellowish-green fabric with limestone inclusions, coarse surface without slip. The third has pink (7.5YR 8/4) outer surface, and reddish-yellow (5YR 7/6) inner surface, hard, dense pinkish-orange fabric with hematite, mica and limestone, coarse surface with a pink slip.

Amphorae found in Pompeii show that the earliest version of the type securely pre-dates AD 79. Such amphorae were most common in the pre-mosaic 2nd/3rd century AD destruction layer of the House of Dionysos,[37] and continue through the 3rd century. The late versions, treated by Slane as a separate form, were found at Corinth in a context dated no earlier than AD 292 and a 4th-century context at the Athenian Agora.[38] At Maloutena, these amphorae first seem to occur around the 2nd century AD but continue into the 4th century.

Dressel 20, Dressel 20 *similis* (Fig. 7b) **and Dressel 23a** (Fig. 7a, c)

A classical Dressel 20 of the 1st century AD was found in the Hellenistic House, R. 21, in a disturbed fill, together with a rim of a Dressel 6A amphora. A large upper part of a Martin-Kilcher variant 42/47 (group C)[39] was found in the NW part of the Villa of Theseus in 1966. Another rim and neck, belonging either to Dressel 23D or Tejarillo 1 form, comes from the House of Aion R. 7 fill just above collapsed plaster.[40] The illustrated example of form Dressel 23 was excavated in 1967, and was probably found in R.9 of the villa (Fig. 7a, c). A Dressel 20 imitation (?) was found in VT R.21, 2nd layer, made up of collapse debris dated to 5th century (fig. 7b).

Of the several examples of this form group, the earliest, in spite of its late find context, seems to be the one depicted on Fig. 7b, with its concave rim that is oval in section, and affinity to form Oberaden 83.[41] Its walls are flaking; the fabric is relatively soft and porous and may belong to imitations rather than actual Baetican olive amphorae. The other vessel illustrated belongs to typical Guadalquivir valley products with a hard fabric and thick walls.

The only piece found at Paphos, *Maloutena* providing good dating evidence – is the one from the House of Aion fill over room 7 which must belong to the late 4th century AD at the earliest. It shows a simple rounded rim and ridged handle belonging to a Late Roman series.[42]

Pompeii V (Fig. 7d, f-h)

Fragmented Pompeii type V amphorae occur in the destruction stratum of the so-called Hellenistic House in R. 22 (Fig. 1c, 7d, g). A group of rim and neck fragments was found in VT, most probably in R.98, in a Late Roman context (Fig. 7f, h). These and other fragments show the typical median ribs on the handles, the ovoid body, and rims with shallow hollows on upper and outer face.

The broken example from HH R. 22 should date to the first half of the 2nd century AD.[43] An upper part from the House of Dionysos seems to belong to the late 2nd or early 3rd century AD.[44]

Late Roman 1 (Fig. 8a)

A number of complete – or nearly complete – Late Roman 1 amphorae were found in destruction strata in the Villa of Theseus and the House of Aion.[45] Surprisingly, since Paphos produced this type, Late Roman 1 amphorae are not overwhelmingly frequent. The better-preserved pieces were also made in a non-local fabric, probably Cilician, as far as our knowledge of finds from the Paphos kiln and mainland ones permits us to say.[46] Also, most of them seem to be earlier than the products of known kilns. A detailed study of form and paste variants present at our site has isolated two main fabric types: 1) a hard, porous body with limestone and black inclusions and hematite particles, very pale brown (10 YR 7/4) outer and inner in colour; and 2) light red in colour (2.5YR 6/8), a hard, porous fabric with hematite, quartz, limestone.

A number of production sites of this class of amphorae have been identified in Cilicia and Cyprus. Some petrographic characterisation of these has been done, but a more comprehensive study is needed.[47]

At Paphos, such amphorae occur first in 4th century AD levels, but they are most frequent in layers of "squatter" reoccupation in 6th and 7th centuries AD.

"Gaza" amphorae/Late Roman 4 (Almagro 54)
(Fig. 8b-d)
The better-preserved examples are few: a steep rim, ribbed, thin-walled body with red *dipinto* and twisted handles comes from VT Western enclosure, 6*/76. Another rim, belonging to a wide-bodied amphora (Fig. 8c), was found in a context under VT, Room 32, dated possibly to the 1st/2nd century AD. A later context in the North-eastern House, Room 12E, has provided both round- and steep-shouldered fragments (Fig. 8b, d).[48] Several fragments (a rim, handles and bottom of an amphora similar to the last one, see Fig. 8d) were uncovered in a 2nd- century stratum close to the floor of HH Room 14.

Amphorae of this group are defined by thickened lip or low band rim, accretions of extra clay around the rim and on the shoulder, and ribbing below and around the rounded or concave base. Irregular, looped and twisted handles are also characteristic. These easily recognizable fragments have been identified in a number of contexts. They belong in fact to two main sub-forms, wide bodied (A) and steep shoulder ones (B). Most scholars, apart from Barbara Johnson,[49] view this as a chronological development. Several workshops have been excavated, but fabric descriptions are available only for a few pieces, too few to be used as characterize and identify the jars from particular production sites. Rims of the illustrated wide and medium body pieces (Fig. 8b-c) are unusual by having thickened, out-turned, rounded lip,[50] which, in the standard version, has a concave lid seating or is simply cut. The fabric of these also differs from the typical hard, thick sandy fabric with a little white limestone, drab brown colour (5YR 5/6), sometimes with a greyish core, with grains of quartz, occasionally fossil shell with augite and tourmaline as accessory minerals.[51] Instead, they contain fewer inclusions and the colour is more light orange. The typical Gaza rim (Fig. 8d) seems to belong to Majcherek form 4 (= Late Roman 4C), dated to late 6th century at earliest.[52] These "cigar-shaped" amphorae are very wide-bodied and thick-walled with a conical base. Loop ring handles are attached to the shoulders. There is a wide band of rough ridges on the shoulder, where the handles are attached, and near the base.

The fabric of our specimens is diverse, which reflects both the longevity of the production of the type and its wide production area. The buff-brownish ware of our

---

33 Meyza *et al.* forthcoming.
34 Daszkiewicz *et al.* 1997, 138.
35 Hayes 1991, 91-92 pl. 24.4; for the question of a possible Cypriot production of such amphorae, see Williams & Lund in this publication.
36 Rauh & Slane 2000, 325-328; Rauh 2004, 330-331.
37 Hayes 1991, 91-92 pl. 24.3. In the final destruction layer, above the mosaics, only isolated fragments of this amphora type occurred.
38 Slane 1994, 136-137, 148 note 19, fig. 6.25-26 pl. 34.24; Robinson 1959, 106 no. M 239 pl. 28, found together with coins of early 4th century.
39 Martin-Kilcher 1987, 54 Beilage 1.
40 Lichocka & Meyza 2001, 163 fig. 4.10.
41 E.g. Berni Millet 1998 108 no. 5.6 fig. 19; CEIPAC 17719 at http://ceipac.gh.ub.es.
42 Berni Millet 1998, 53-61 pl. 2; some finds suggest even later date as Bonifay & Piéri 1995, 118-120 (Annexes 2, 3), Carreras Monfort & Williams 2003, 67.
43 Cf. Reynolds 2005, 565 pl. 2 from Beirut.
44 Hayes 1991, 207-208 fig. 71.13
45 These are published in the preliminary report by Daszewski (1970, 141 pl. 23.5).
46 Demesticha & Michaelides 2001, 292; Demesticha 2003, 472 note 11.
47 Reynolds (principal contributor) Late Roman 1/petrology, in Williams & Keay 2005 [2006].
48 Meyza 1995 pl. 8.3-4; Lichocka & Meyza 2001, 174 fig. 11.1.
49 Johnson & Stager 1995, 103.
50 Similar to type Kingsholm 117; Peacock & Williams 1986, Class 66.
51 Peacock & Williams 1986, 199.
52 Majcherek 1995, 169.

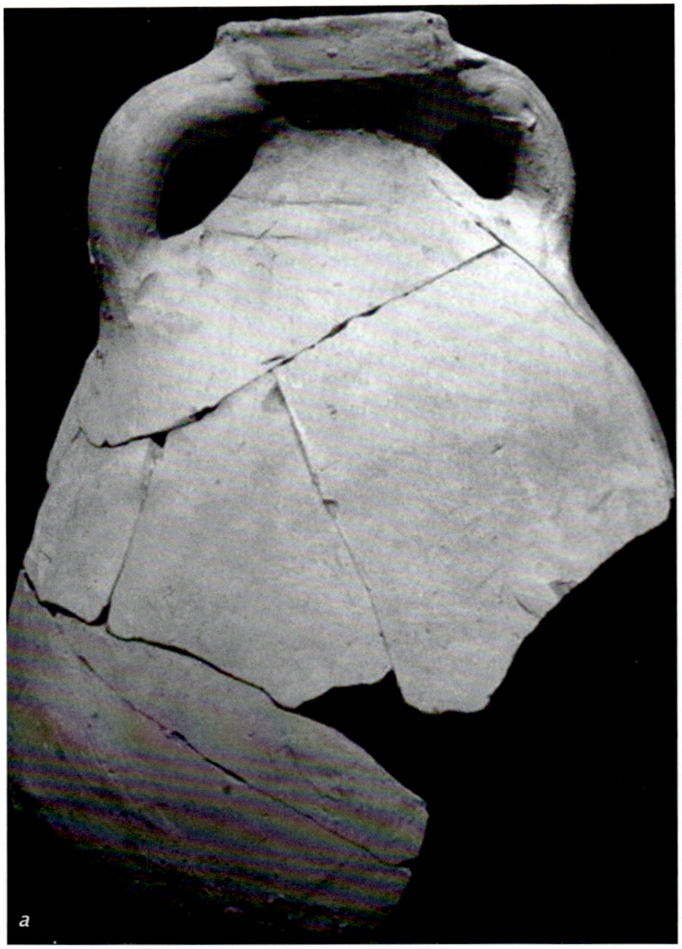

a

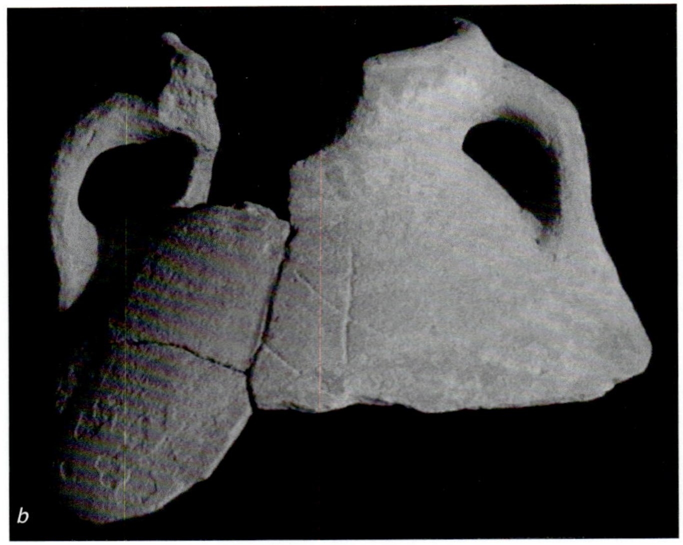

b

Fig. 7. Baetican and Levantine

a. Dr 23, VT NW sector, 1967. Photo by H. Meyza = c.

b. Dr 20?; VT Room 21 SW second layer. Photo by H. Meyza.

c. Dr 23 = a. Drawn by M. Droste.

d. Pompei V, deposit in HH Room 22. Drawn by K. Kapiec=g.

e. Beirut AM 72, HA Room 12E. Drawn by H. Meyza.

f. Pompei V similis, probably VT Room 98. Drawn by K. Hołderna.

g = d. Photo by K. Woszczyńska.

h. A set of Pompei V similis, belonging to the same group, probably VT Room 98. Photo by H. Meyza, rightmost=f.

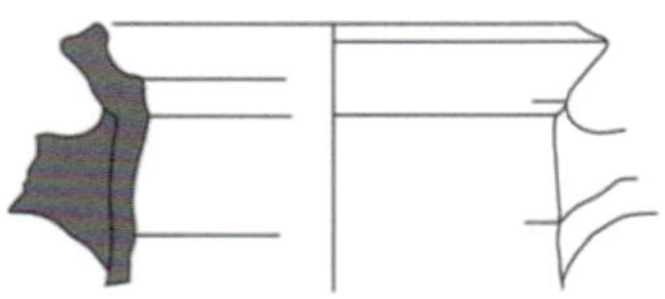

e

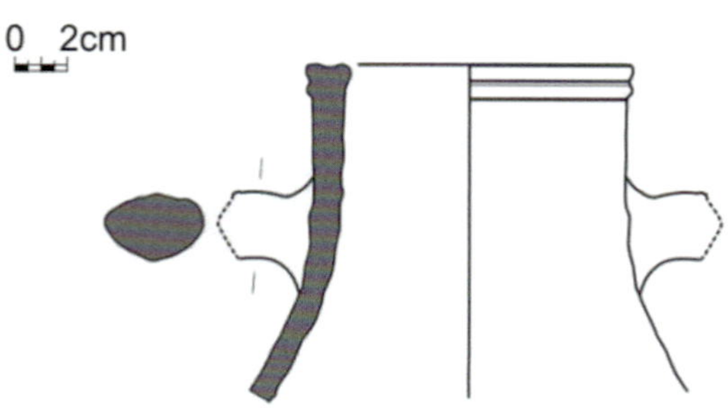

f

g

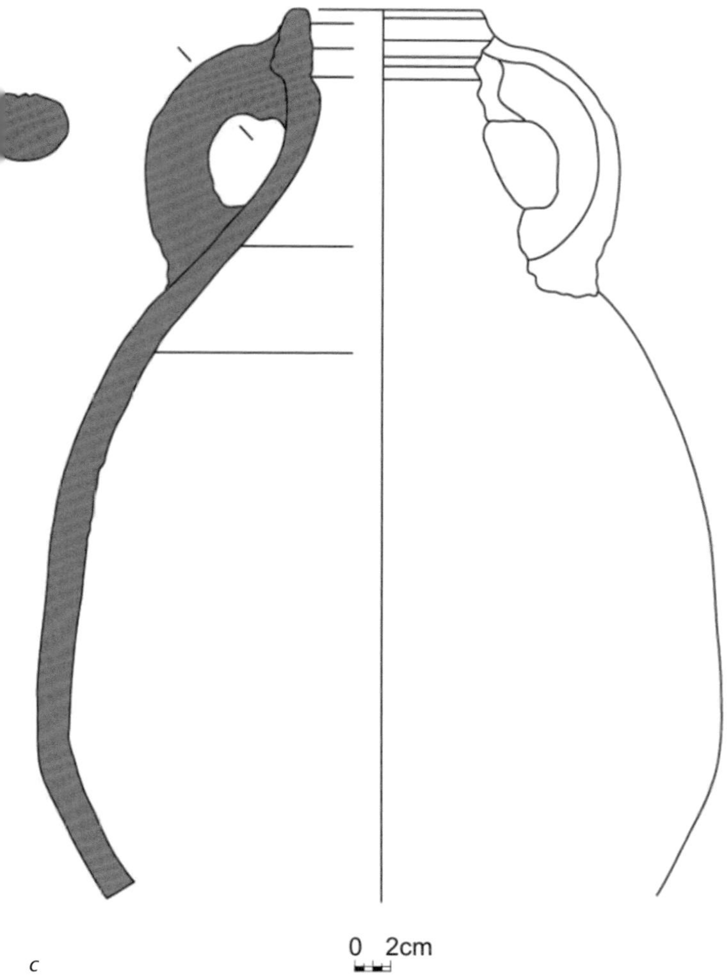

c

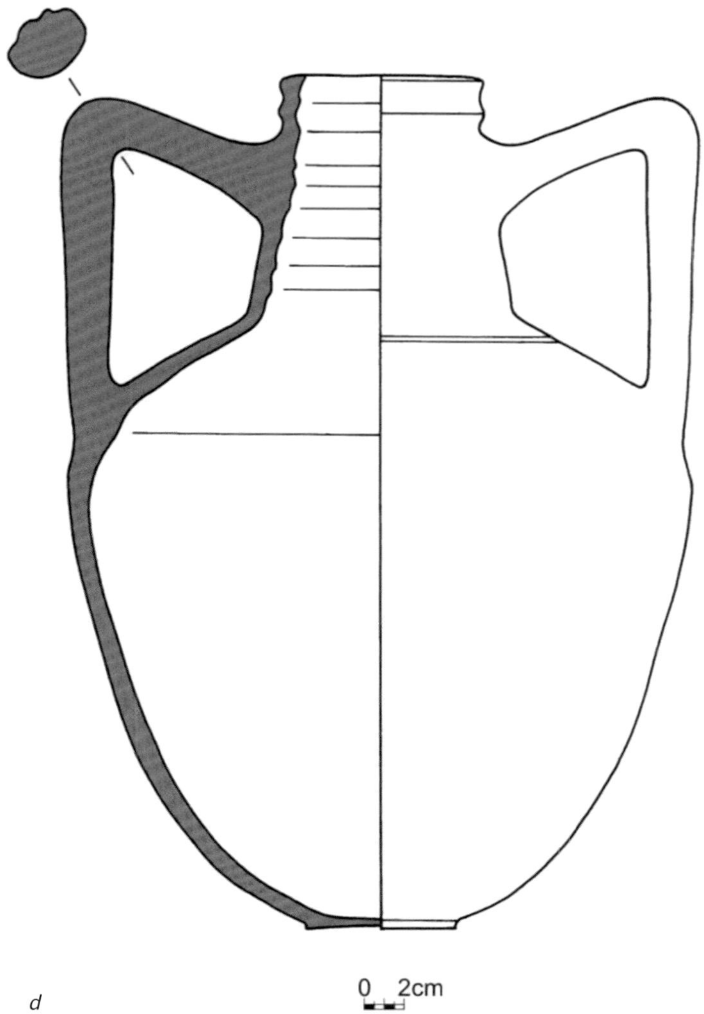

d

h

typical rim macroscopically fits better with Schuring fabric H[53] than with the fabrics described with Peacock & Williams Classes 48 and 49.[54]

At Paphos such amphorae are contextually dated 2nd-5th century AD.

Akko-Ptolemais amphora (Agora M 334) (Fig. 8e-f) These amphorae were found in several late deposits: VT room 40, upper fill (Fig. 8e); North-eastern House room

53 Schuring 1984, 172-174.
54 Peacock & Williams 1986.

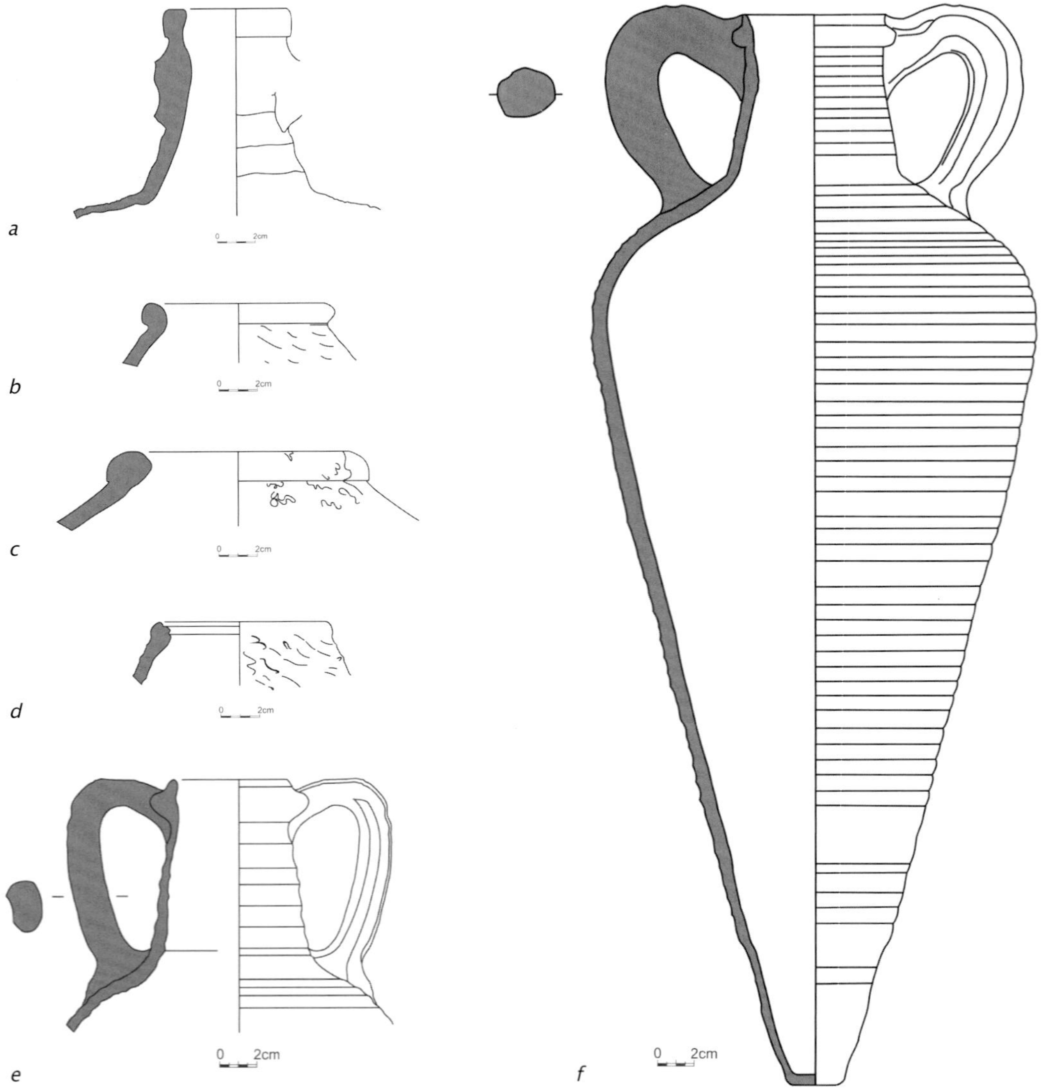

Fig. 8. Levantine amphorae

a. LRA 1, fill of channel round the Villa of Theseus latrine R. 52 and its inlet. Drawn by K. Hołderna.

b. Gaza? Northeastern House, Room 12E, TP 1/90, Meyza 1995, fig. 8: 4.

c. Gaza ? VT, Trench 3/70? = Room 32. Drawn by M. Droste.

d. Gaza, Northeastern House, Room 12E, TP 1/90. Drawn by H. Meyza.

e. Akko-Ptolemais amphora, VT Room 40, upper layer. Drawn by E. Milczarczyk.

f. Akko-Ptolemais Amphora, Northeastern House, Room 24N. Drawn by U. Gorczyca.

24N, pottery deposit (Fig. 8f),[55] which is dated by a coin of Constantius II (350-361 AD) inv. 855, type FelTempReparat; VT room 21, an amphora deposit with another coin, inv 590, uncertain but possibly Byzantine.[56] The fine wares found with the amphorae in VT room 21 included Late Roman D (Cypriot Red Slip Ware) forms H1/3C and 11.

The body of this amphora is carrot-shaped with a small flat base. The neck is high and the rim flanged. The two handles are ridged and stretch from the rim to the shoulder. The complete example is 59.7 cm high, with a horizontal ribbing over practically the whole body and light beige self-slip particularly on upper part. Fragments of one amphora most probably represent a Palestinian product from Akko (Reynolds' 5th century version). [57] Another small amphora fragment, from VT R. 21, preserves only the upper part; the belly (28 cm diameter) has a narrow, sharply protruding flange and is made in dusty, laminating fabric with a many fine quartz grains.[58] In other cases the paste is fine and smooth and includes quite numerous grey grains and fine quartz. According to Paul Reynolds, this is a fabric of Akko-Ptolemais, where kiln sites are known at Horvat Masref, Horvat Uza and at Horvat Eitayim.[59]

a b c

Fig. 9. Mid Roman: Kapitän II, Egyptian

a. Small Kapitän II, deposit in VT Room 21, AR 14/84. Photo by W. Jerke.

b. As above FR 16/84. Photo by W. Jerke.

c. As above FR 15/84. Photo by W. Jerke.

d. Base of large Kapitän II amphora. Drawn by K.Hołderna.

e. Amphora Egloff 172. Drawn by M. Kosznicki.

f. Amfora AE7-3/1 (Majcherek 6). Photo by W. Jerke.

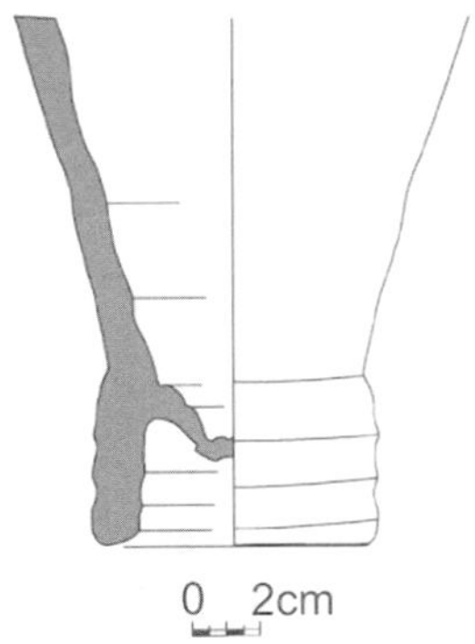

d

f

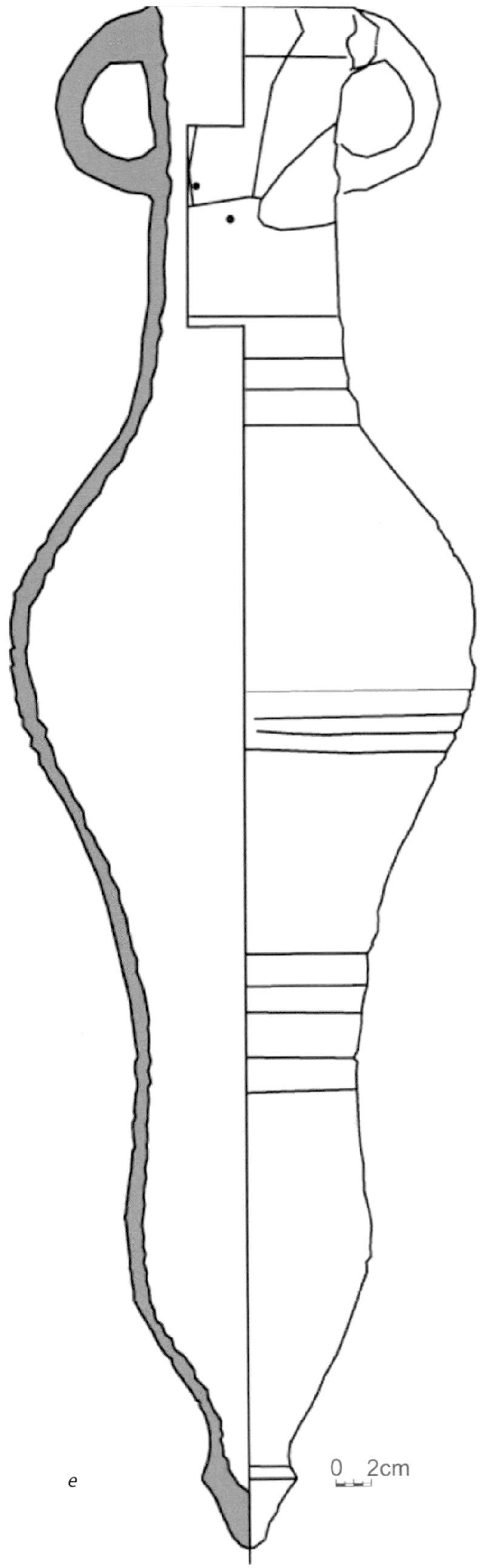

e

55 Daszewski *et al.* 2007, 401 figs. 9-10; Meyza forthcoming fig. 2.
56 Meyza forthcoming fig. 4c.
57 Reynolds 2005, 572 fig. 114.
58 Reynolds 2005, fig. 112.
59 Reynolds 2005, 571.

Fig. 10. Late Roman: Spatheia, Agora 273

a. Cylindrical African amphora, probably from VT R. 77. Photo by H. Meyza.
b. Spatheion 1/African 3C found on floor I of NEH Room 12W. Photo by H. Meyza.
c. Spatheion rim, VT R. 66. Drawn by K.Hołderna.
d. Ag M273 from VT room 21. Photo by W. Jerke.
e. Ag M273 from VT room 21. Photo by W. Jerke.

Kapitän II (Hollow-foot amphorae) (Fig. 9a-d)
This thick-walled amphora with a particularly massive base, heavy handles and thickened rim is often found in 3rd-4th century deposits including VT, R. 21, along the northern wall, where three almost complete miniature examples were found (Fig. 9a-c).[60] According to Kathleen W. Slane, such small versions are later in the series.[61] A base of a large example was found below the eastern part of mosaic of Theseus in TP 3/93.[62] Another fragment was found in the bedding levels under the floors of the Villa Room 46.[63] Most finds come from secondary deposition. Contexts include NEH Room 36, fill of modern pit (rim); fill of VT R. 45, (base, Fig. 9d), and the upper layer above street B (numerous fragments).

The characteristic fabric of these amphorae makes them easily recognizable, even body fragments. In spite of this, even in recent papers, no evidence for its origin has been convincingly presented, and erroneously, the matter is treated as a typological problem.[64] In addition, Grzegorz Majcherek and Tamas Bezeczky have reported another paste, which is much less frequent than the standard fabric.[65] At Paphos only the standard fabric is present, as is the case in Ephesus.[66] The amphora in its basic fabric clearly came from a single production area, if not a single site. The small size of the three illustrated amphorae (heights of 48 cm, 48.9 cm, 47.7 cm) is indicative of their late position in the series, similar to that of Agora M 303, with a preserved height (without the base) of 43.9 cm.[67] In Paphos, many examples of the large version also appear, but none is equally well preserved. The base of one is illustrated (Fig. 9d).

The paste contains quartz, sandstone, mica and black lava fragments, relating to volcanic activity.[68] The volcanic material limits the areas of possible origin and puts in doubt the proposed workshops on lower Danube, as the closest appropriate geological deposits are found in Hungary. Ardeţ turns attention to the occurrence of fragments of such amphorae near the pottery kilns in Romula.[69] It is, however, unclear if the kilns were producing that type of amphora, or if it is an incidental find. Amphorae from Paphos are dated from the 3rd to the early 5th century AD. Dating of the deposit in VT R. 21 with three almost intact examples indicates the terminal date. It is interesting to note that while the Athenian Agora (M 303) piece differs from the standard form (cf. M 237 and M 274) – and hence shows development towards the late (post- 3rd century) form at Novae,[70] our miniature variants do not diverge from the standard shape. None of the complete or fragmentary pieces from Paphos exhibited traces of resin, which was the basis of identifying contents as wine.[71]

Egyptian Kellia 172 (Dixneuf AE3T-2) (Fig. 9e)
Two almost complete amphorae were found in VT in a cistern below the stairs from R.39 to R.40,[72] and in the deposit along the northern wall of VT R.21 (Fig. 9e). The paste is relatively soft and erodes easily; apart from these two complete examples, mostly small fragments of thicker parts (rims, bases and handles) are preserved. The illustrated piece was coated inside the belly with pitch, and the neck was mended in antiquity (two holes across the break). In Paphos, the type first appears in the late 4th century AD; the well-preserved pieces seem to be later, dating to the 5th century.[73]

Late Roman 7 (Majcherek 6; Dixneuf AE7-3/1) (Fig. 9f)
This is a rare form in Paphos. One well-preserved piece comes from the deposit in VT R.21. The amphora is small, missing the base, and has a firing crack along neck, shoulder and upper belly.[74] The form is not standardized to the extent characteristic of Egloff 172. The fabric is a typical Nile Silt.

The form group is dated from the late 4th century AD to the 8th century and is most frequent in the 5th century. The Paphos example dates from the late 5th century.

African 3C/Spatheion 1 (Late Roman 8) (fig. 10a-c)
Nearly complete examples were found in destruction strata of the Late Roman insula of the House of Aion. A further specimen occurred in the fill of a pit with several other amphorae at the south-east corner of House of Aion room 7. The latest finds in this dump were probably fragments of a somewhat dispersed, but mendable, spatheion amphora, located at the bottom of that fill, which otherwise contained mostly earlier material.[75] Another was found on the floor of room 6 in the House of Aion. One was collected in North-eastern House room 12W on Floor I (Fig. 10b).[76] And, finally, a piece found in the fill of the *praefurnium* Room 66 of the VT (Fig. 10c) was dated by the abandonment of the bath in the southeast part of the Villa in 6th century AD.

The Spatheion 1 form, in spite of the noted variation of rim, is very characteristic, and pieces are generally easy to identify, particularly as most of the rims belong to one variant (Bonifay variant A). However, as noted by Simon Keay, the type is not easy to tell apart from some of the less elongated cylindrical and slightly larger amphorae of the form (Late) African 3C.[77] Only the dimensions of the body fragments allow us to identify the possible types

60 Meyza forthcoming fig. 5.
61 Slane 2004, 365 note 14.
62 Daszewski 1994, 109; the amphora base seems to be the latest pottery fragment and was not noted by the excavator.
63 Meyza 2003, 257 note 3.
64 Dyczek 2010, 993.
65 Majcherek 1993, 218; Bezeczky 2005b, 43-45; Sauer 2005, 117-118 nos. WA 17-18/98 Tables 2-3 fig. 1 pl. 3.
66 Bezeczky 2005a, 213-214.
67 Robinson 1959, 112 pl. 311.
68 Peacock & Williams 1986, 193-195.
69 Ardeţ 2004, 331 after Popilian 1997, 7-20.
70 Dyczek 2010, 995.
71 Robinson 1959, 106.
72 Daszewski 1972, 211 fig. 7a.
73 Meyza forthcoming.
74 Majcherek 1992b, 92-97 pl. 6.3-4; Egloff 1977, 113, 115-116 pls. 19.7a, 57.7, 59.7.
75 Lichocka & Meyza 2001, 162 fig. 11. 7.
76 Meyza 2008, 518-519 fig. 2.
77 Keay 1984, 212.

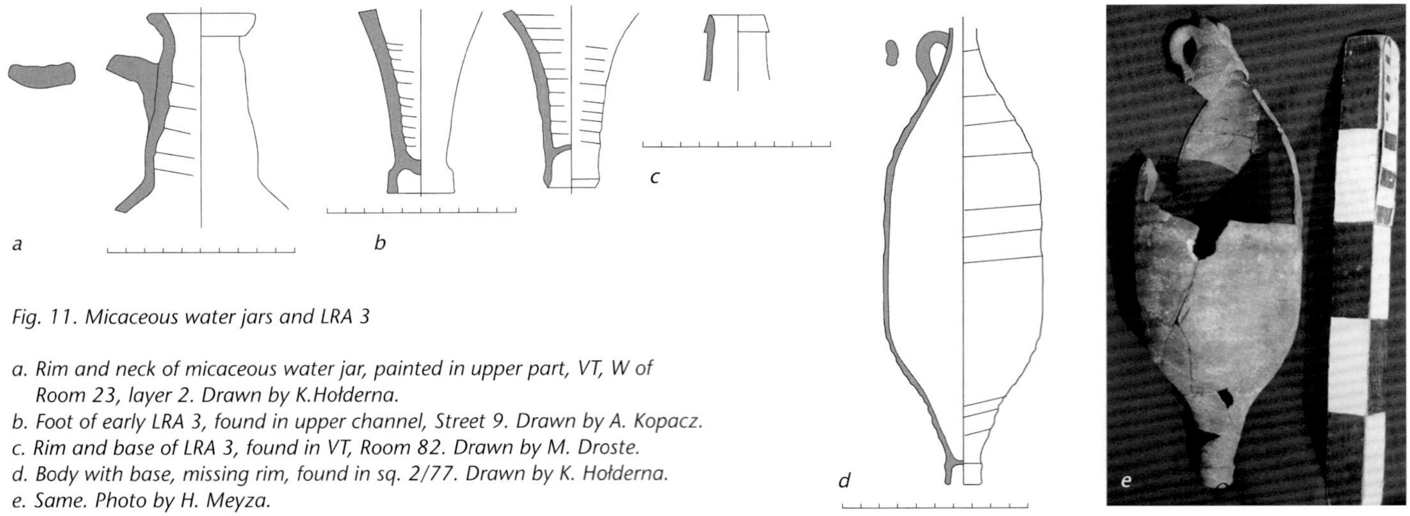

Fig. 11. Micaceous water jars and LRA 3

a. Rim and neck of micaceous water jar, painted in upper part, VT, W of Room 23, layer 2. Drawn by K.Hołderna.
b. Foot of early LRA 3, found in upper channel, Street 9. Drawn by A. Kopacz.
c. Rim and base of LRA 3, found in VT, Room 82. Drawn by M. Droste.
d. Body with base, missing rim, found in sq. 2/77. Drawn by K. Hołderna.
e. Same. Photo by H. Meyza.

represented by a specific piece (Fig. 10a). The paste differs little in all examples, and the surfaces of all these amphorae show traces of vertical smoothing by scraping.

The Tunisian amphora production is relatively well-known thanks to extensive survey work, during which several workshops were identified.[78] Our examples, with a red section, do not exhibit features of the only workshop easily identified by eye, i.e. the one at Salakta. The best-dated piece from Paphos dates to the end of 4th century AD to the middle 5th century AD (Fig. 10b).

Agora M 273 (Fig. 10d-e)
Examples of this type were found in the deposit of VT R. 21, together with two Egyptian amphorae and three small Kapitän II.

The Cypriot version of this type is similar in general shape to Agora M273, but the base is different: a knobbed peg at the end cylindrical stem, much closer to Samos Cistern type. The ribbing of the body and rim seem to be simplified variants of Agora M273 type, but the forms of the neck and handles are closer to the Samos Cistern.[79]

Two nearly complete amphorae with ribbed body differ in proportions, but the more oblong (Fig. 10d) is as wide as Agora M273. The Nea Paphos examples are, therefore, transitional between the Agora M273 and Samos Cistern types. The fabric of our amphorae is coarse, buff-reddish to reddish with lenticular pores and numerous varied inclusions. Reddish and white angular grains, normally around 0.5 mm in size are most frequent, black impurities much fewer. The rough appearance of the surface and similarity to Buff Ware basins suggests local origin.[80] It is certainly of a different fabric from the standard, micaceous Samos Cistern ware.

The deposit against the northern wall of VT R.21 is dated by the presence of Egyptian amphorae form Egloff 172 and Late Roman 7, and Late Roman D ("Cypriot Red Slip Ware") form K1/K3,[81] and the find spot is crucial for the late dating. Room 21 belongs to late phase in the history of the Villa of Theseus. It was added to the west wing after destruction of room 19W, and it seems later even than construction of cellar 18W, also post-dating the destruction. The building of room 21 should therefore be dated in the 6th century AD, but prior to abandonment of the south wing to squatters. Medeksza has placed it in the third (last) sub-phase of the second phase of VT construction.[82]

Agora F65-66/Late Roman 3 (Hayes 1991 Roman Amphorae type VI) (Fig. 11)
At Paphos, a long series of this form was previously found in the House of Dionysos, starting from large-size micaceous water jars of type Agora F65-66 (with one handle and unusually, probably early, two-handled).[83] Similar pieces occur in the destruction layer of the so-called Hellenistic House (Room 9A), and in contexts preceding VT: in strata below the floor in the vestibule R. 69N,[84] and before construction of R. 23 and the early western external

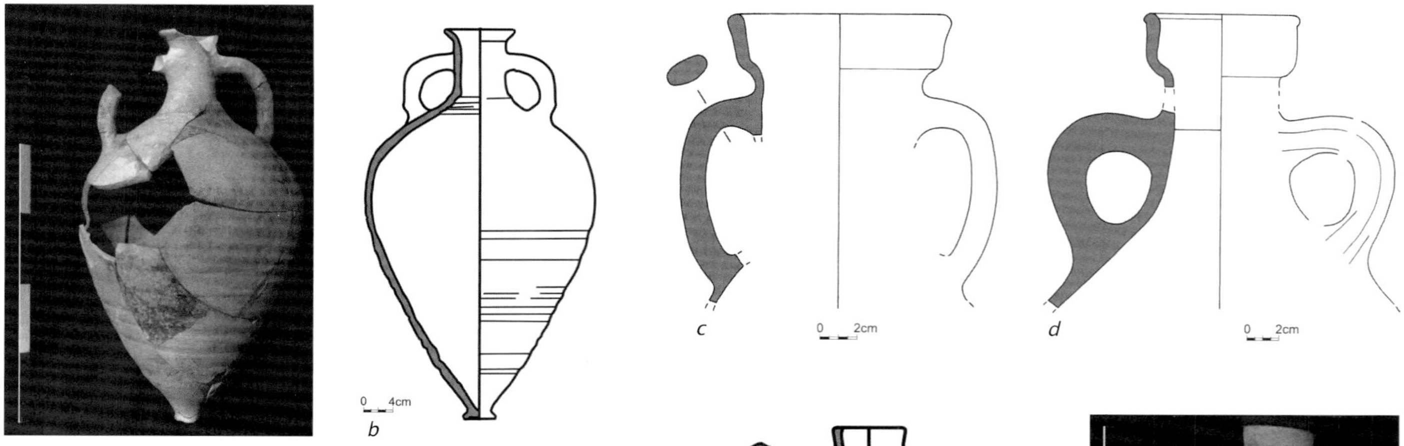

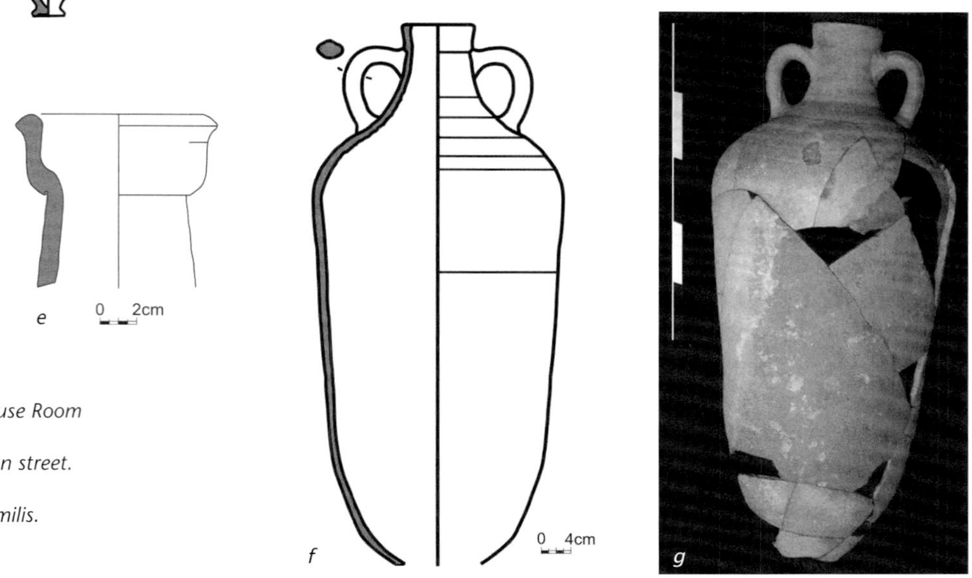

Fig. 12. Uncertain imitation forms and Lusitanian amphorae.

a. Gauloise 5/Spello -style imitation amphora, with grafitto on shoulder. Photo by W. Jerke
b. Same. Drawn by K. Hołderna
c. Table amphora Almagro 51 A/B similis, HH Room 21. Drawn by K. Kapiec.
d. Almagro 51A/B upper part, Northeastern House Room 36. Drawn by A. Mazany.
e. Almagro 51 rim and part of neck, Late Roman street. Drawn by K. Hołderna.
f. Imitation (?) of Cretan amphora, late AC1 similis. Drawn by K. Holderna.
g. Same. Photo by H. Meyza.

78 E.g. Peacock *et al.* 1989.
79 Robinson 1959, 109-110 pls. 29 and 58; Opaiţ 1996, 210-211, Opaiţ 2004b, 302 fig. 24; Williams 1987, 235 fig. 1.
80 The ware seems close to "standard gritted ware" as for instance the jug Hayes 1991, 67 cat. b fig. 73.10.
81 Meyza 2007, 65, 132 no. 18 (context 581).
82 Daszewski 1985, 952–955 fig. 122; 1986, 858 fig. 91; Medeksza 1992 fig. 22; 1998 fig. 7.
83 Hayes 1991, 92-93 fig. 39.26-29; the two handled piece no. 28 has early type of rim and relatively wide neck. The context is not, however unequivocally early, as it belongs to top fill layers (tray 1002 from ΓΞ, East, at depth of 1.00 to 1.50 m).
84 Młynarczyk 1990, 187-188 fig. 25 (floors 3 and 4); Meyza 2007, 127, context 406 (originally marked layer 8, dated to late 1st or early 2nd century AD, with several pieces of Cypriot Sigillata Form P40. The identification of K1 base of Late Roman D ("Cypriot Red Slip Ware") (sherd id: 1157) is doubtful, as the piece is overfired. Młynarczyk has identified it as a Çandarlı L26A/B, which may be correct, as the sherd contains much golden mica.

Fig. 13. Lusitanian 9 similis Plain jars. Drawn by M. Droste, photo by W. Jerke.

wall of VT (Fig. 11a).[85] Both of the principal forms of Late Roman 3, one- and two-handled, are present, with a clear preponderance of examples of the earlier variety, which are better preserved (Fig. 11d-e).[86] The bellies are often cylindrical, and the feet are never of the contracted late version.

At our site in Paphos, the contexts with these forms are dated from the 1st to 5th centuries AD.

Numerous smaller fragments have been noted, as the fabric is easily identified, particularly in case of Late Roman 3. Examples appear in VT R.46 from the substratum of the floor.[87] A large quantity of mica makes it glimmer, contrasting with the dark brown-red background, while in case of Agora F65-66 the mica presence in the lighter paste is not so evident. Nevertheless, it seems that both the earlier and later fabrics were very similar and probably of the same origin. Naturally, the larger F65-66 amphorae have thicker walls, though both forms are thin-walled.

An imitation of a Cretan AC1a amphora (Fig. 12f-g)
This amphora was found in the storage deposit in VT R.88.[88] Its shape resembles late variants of Cretan AC1a, closest to the production of Dermatos, but with a wider neck.[89] This is not, however, an actual Cretan amphora, but a large container with a long cylindrical body, 78.9 cm high without the base. The surface is smooth both inside and around the maximum diameter of belly. At the shoulder/neck there is an oval hole with worn edges, probably made at the same time as the removal of the base.

The paste is hard, beige reddish on the outer surface, reddish inside, with quite frequent lenticular and irregular pores usually c. 1 mm long, in some cases up to 3.8 mm, and has numerous white inclusions, without reaction rims, most about 0.3 mm in size, subangular with matte surface, fewer grey inclusions and some transparent quartz sand.

We are unable to identify the origin of this amphora. The piece is dated by associated coin finds to the last quarter of 4th century AD at the earliest.[90]

Gauloise 4-5/ Spello style (?) (Fig. 12a-b)
A nearly complete, 54.6 cm high amphora was found in the storage deposit in VT R.88.[91] A large graffito of Chi-Rho was scratched on the shoulder. The ovoid body is similar to Gauloise types 4 and 5 but it has a small conical base, out-turned plain, slightly thickened rim, short neck and two handles round in section. In some respects, the form shows a better fit with the Spello amphorae, particularly with a piece published in the Southampton Amphora Database.[92]

The fabric is clean, without inclusions visible to the naked eye, with a buff – beige surface and reddish core. This is similar to the calcareous Gauloise fabric used at several production sites in the Languedoc, Rhone and Arc valleys as well as Provence.[93] The lack of visible inclusions makes the identification with Spello amphorae less probable since their fabric is varied and even the finer examples contain visible inclusions.

The context of the Paphos amphora may be dated at the earliest to the fourth quarter of 4th century AD.

Almagro 51A&B (fig. 12d-e)
Rim and neck fragments were found in late, 5th - 6th

century AD, contexts including the Late Roman street destruction layer, fill in Northeastern House Room 36, as well as fill in the House of Aion Room 7. The rim has a characteristic cup shape with vertical walls and a slightly everted lip set upon a narrower neck slightly contracted upwards. The hard, rough, sandy fabric, although varied, is specific enough to verify the identification. A similar form existed in earlier table amphorae (found together with Pompei V amphora illustrated above). The table variant has thinner walls and a low conical base (Fig. 13).

Such amphorae were produced in Lusitania where they are dated from 3rd to 6th centuries AD. Context dates at Paphos indicate that our examples date late in the series.

CONCLUDING REMARK

The present overview is a preliminary statement – much more research into the collected pottery and a lot of detailed ware study is needed to achieve comprehensive picture of amphora imports and local production in Roman Paphos. A database of fresh break macro photographs and low-magnification portable electronic microscope photographs is under construction. There are numerous better preserved amphora fragments which need to be drawn. Even so, already we are able to document a wide range of imports including Levantine, Egyptian, Aegean, and various types from western Mediterranean sources including Italy, Spain and Africa.

---

85 Daszewski 1986, 860.
86 The exact find spot of illustrated piece is uncertain; for another nearly complete example Lichocka & Meyza 2001, 172 note 82 fig. 11.3.
87 Meyza 2003, 257 note 3.
88 Meyza forthcoming fig. 8ab.
89 Marangou-Lerat 1995, 68-70 nos A10-14 fig. 28 pl. 2.
90 Meyza forthcoming.
91 Reynolds 2005, 567 fig. 44 pl. 6; Arthur & Oren 1998, 201 fig. 5.9. For the deposit, see Meyza forthcoming fig. 9a-b.
92 http://ads.ahds.ac.uk/catalogue/resources.html?amphora2005, Spello: image PEC91.jpg.
93 Laubenheimer & Schmitt 2009, 37-110.

Petrological Analyses of "Pinched-handle" Amphorae from the Akamas Peninsula, Western Cyprus

BY DAVID F. WILLIAMS & JOHN LUND

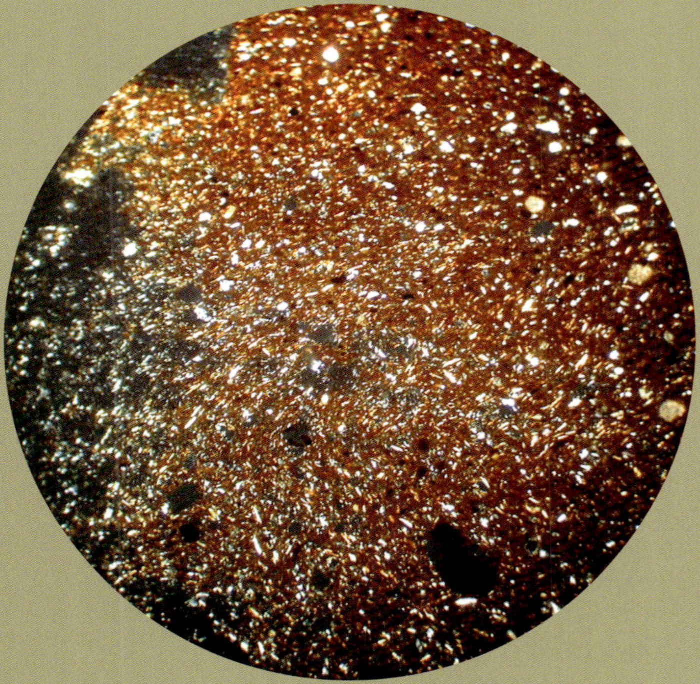

Petrological Analyses of "Pinched-handle" Amphorae from the Akamas Peninsula, Western Cyprus

BY DAVID F. WILLIAMS & JOHN LUND

The present contribution addresses a fundamental issue with regard to the transport amphorae and trade of Cyprus, namely our ability to distinguish between the amphora classes that were produced in Cyprus and those which were imported.

The identification of amphorae produced in Hellenistic and early Roman Cyprus must at present rely on scientific clay analyses and traditional scholarly methods, seeing that no amphora kilns (or indeed pottery kilns) from the periods in question have hitherto been discovered on the island.[1] The amphora kilns identified until now are all of Late Antique date.[2]

The aim of this paper is to publish the petrological results of an amphora class that is quite commonly found in Cyprus (particularly in the western part of the island) during the Roman period.[3] The type is known under several names, e.g., Mau XXVII-XXVIII, Agora G 199, Zemer 41, Mid Roman Amphora 4, Nea Paphos Type III and Cilician Type 1.[4] But here we prefer the descriptive designation "pinched-handle amphora", which John R. Leonard suggested in 1995.[5] As we shall see, evidence from workshop sites in Rough Cilicia shows conclusively that such amphorae were manufactured there. But were they also produced in Cyprus?

To answer this question, 20 amphora sherds from Cyprus which clearly belong to the "pinched handle" form were selected for thin sectioning and study under the petrological microscope (see Appendix 1). This material was recovered during a series of Danish expeditions to the Akamas peninsula in westernmost Cyprus between 1989 and 1993, a project that combined a survey with excavations at selected sites.[6]

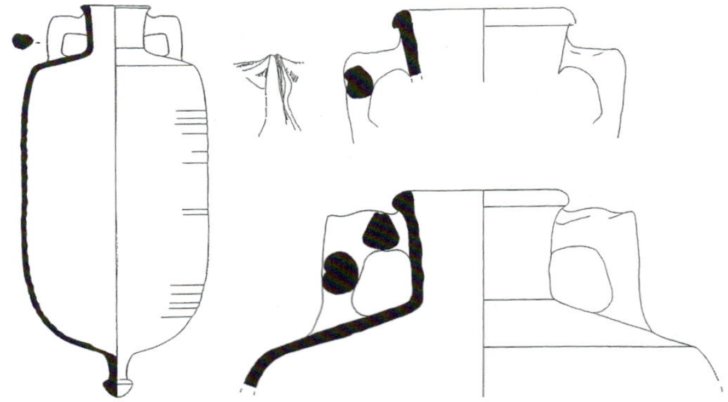

Fig. 1. Completely preserved example of "pinched-handle" amphora after Zemer 1977 pl. 15.41 and the upper parts of two "pinched-handle" amphorae found during the Danish survey and excavations at Ayios Kononas in the Akamas peninsula. Not to scale. After Lund 2000, 566 figs. 1-2.

THE "PINCHED-HANDLE" AMPHORA: A BRIEF INTRODUCTION

The short and right-angled handles, which are grooved and pinched from the sides, constitute the distinctive feature of this class (Fig. 1), which has a cylindrical neck and a gently everted rim. Its cylindrical body ends in an elongated toe, sometimes with a "mushroom" cap.

In the early examples, the neck is fairly tall, and the vertical portion of the handle is taller than the width of the horizontal portion. Later specimens have shorter necks and vertical and horizontal portions of the handles of equal length. They also seem to lose the distinctive mushroom-cap at the base.[7] "Pinched-handle" amphorae are normally between 65 and 75 centimetres high, and capacities are quoted in the literature ranging from 19.3 litres, over 36 and 45.8 litres to allegedly as much as 53 litres. Two late examples were lined with a black resinous substance, which might indicate wine as their contents.[8] In addition, a further pitch-lined top of a an earlier white ware "pinched-handle" amphora was found in 2004 by Cheryl Ward during the Rough Cilicia Survey Project in the harbour of Antiochia ad Cragum (Fig. 2a-b).[9] However, it has recently been suggested that pitch-lining may also have been used for amphorae containing olive oil,[10] and indeed, Leonard has previously mooted the idea that the class might also have carried olive oil and other agricultural products.[11]

The earliest securely dated examples are from Pompeii, hence pre-dating AD 79. In the Athenian Agora, an example was found in Group G, which is dated to the 1st

Fig. 2.a-b. Exterior and interior of a pitch-lined "pinched-handle" amphora found by the Rough Cilicia Survey Project in the harbour of Antiochia ad Cragum in 2004. Photo: Nicholas K. Rauh.

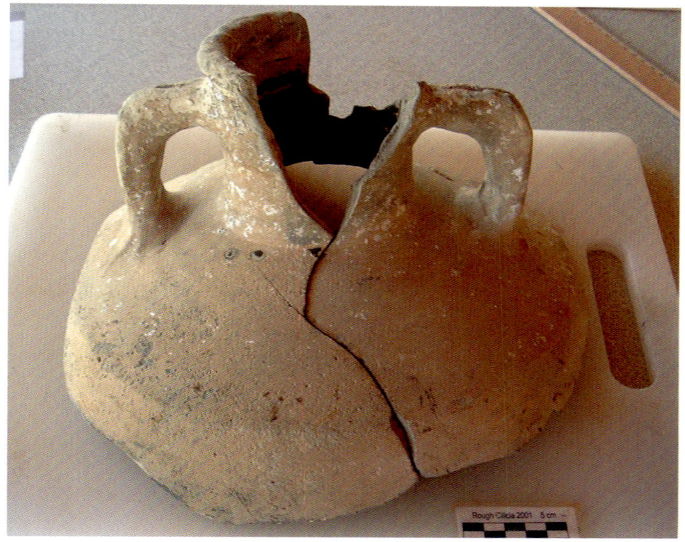

and 2nd century AD.[12] At Anemurium, "sherds appear in Group A1 dating to the Antonine period and earlier".[13] In Cyprus, the type was most common in the 2nd century AD; it is represented in the destruction layer of the House of Dionysos, which according to John Hayes occurred in AD 225 at the latest. It also occurs in a deposit at Corinth with amphorae most likely discarded between about AD 250 and 280,[14] but contexts at Anemurium suggest that the type was still current in the early 4th century AD.[15] The late version (Agora M 239) occurs in a context at Corinth with a date no earlier than AD 292, as well as in an early 4th century context in the Athenian Agora.[16] A coin struck by Maximinus Daia II (AD 304-310) was discovered at the likely kiln site at Syedra in Rough Cilicia.[17]

WORKSHOP SITES IN ROUGH CILICIA

Finds made at four sites in Rough Cilicia have documented that the class was clearly manufactured in that region.[18] Caroline Williams identified a kiln site at Anemurium in 1989,[19] and Nicholas K. Rauh and Kathleen Slane subsequently published evidence of possible kilns at Biçkici and Antiocheia ad Cragum,[20] as well as of a probable kiln site for the late version of the form (Robinson M 239) at Syedra.[21] All four of the likely production sites are situated on the Alanya Massif, which is mainly composed of metamorphic rocks, principally mica-schists, with phyllites, shales/slates and sandstones; the massif is surrounded by calcareous formations.[22]

The clay of the amphorae associated with these sites is

1 Lund 2009.
2 Manning *et al.* 2000; Demesticha 2000; Demesticha & Michaelides 2001; Demesticha 2002; 2003 and 2005; see also Demesticha in the present volume.
3 Lund 2000.
4 Hayes 1991, 91-92; Leonard 1995b, 144-146; Lund 2000; Şenol & Çankardeş-Şenol 2003, 124-125; Reynolds 2005, 564; Marangou & Autret 2011, 359-360; Autret 2012, 255-256. See John Lund, in: Williams & Keay 2005 [2006], and also the contributions by Anthi Kaldeli and Henryk Meyza in the present publication.
5 Leonard 1995b, 144.
6 Fejfer & Mathiesen 1991; Fejfer & Mathiesen 1992a; 1992b and Fejfer (ed.) 1995. The authors are grateful to Jane Fejfer, the field director of the project, for permission to publish the results here.
7 Lund 2000.
8 Robinson 1959, 75 no. L 11 and 106 no. M 239.
9 We are most grateful to Nicholas K. Rauh for drawing our attention to this find and allowing us to publish photos of it.
10 Romanus *et al.* 2009.
11 Leonard 2005, 897.
12 Williams 1989, 93 note 27.
13 Williams 1989, 92.
14 Slane 1994.
15 Williams 1989, 92.
16 Cf. Robinson, 1959, 75 no. L11 Pl. 16; 106 no. M239 Pl. 28; cf. Slane 2004, 36.
17 Rauh 2004, 330; Autret & Rauh 2010.
18 Cf. Autret 2012, 253-254 and 255-256.
19 Williams 1989, 94-95.
20 Rauh & Slane 2000, 323-329; at Biçkici vitrified kiln lining fragments were found and vitrified pieces of amphorae; the evidence for a kiln site at Antiocheia ad Cragum seemed less compelling to Kathleen W. Slane (p. 323-326).
21 Rauh & Slane 2000, 321-323; no surface remains verified the existence of a kiln at the site, but misfired and vitrified material was found, including three pieces of kiln lining.
22 Okay & Özgül 1984.

described as medium-grained with a very gritty texture, and (at Anemurium) full of small white lime particles, small red and dark coloured grits, fine silver mica and silica flakes. It occurs in two colours, presumably produced as the result of different firing conditions. One is orange and the other is dark red with a distinctive purplish tinge.[23]

At Biçkici the fabric was described as fine red micaceous, very fine light red (Munsell 2.5YR 5/8) usually with a buff surface. Fresh breaks are micaceous and still very fine, with a moderate or sparse number of rounded red and black grits just on the edge of visibility.[24] At Syedra and elsewhere a fine-grained, lighter reddish-yellow, micaceous fabric was encountered (2.5YR 6/8), soft to the touch, soapy, micaceous, with small white inclusions. Larger inclusions consist of quartz-mica-schist, muscovite, chlorite, and radiolarian chert.[25]

CYPRUS AS A POSSIBLE SOURCE OF PRODUCTION

In 1977, Hayes suggested Cyprus as a source for the "pinched-handle" amphorae, and he later supported this by noting that one of the two fabrics of the amphorae of this class represented in the House of Dionysos in Nea Paphos "closely resembles the local" Cypriot "coarse buff kitchen wares".[26] Other scholars (including one of the authors of the present contribution) have endorsed this suggestion,[27] adding further arguments in its support.

Małgorzata Daszkiewicz, Henryk Meyza and Gerwulf Schneider, who analysed fourteen specimens from Nea Paphos, concluded that they could be divided into six groups, which are "not all of the same provenance". One of these groups was tentatively related to a workshop in Paphos; however, no geographical source was suggested for the other five.[28] In addition, it has been suggested that the high rate of occurrence of the type in Western Cyprus might be indicative of local production. In the Akamas survey, this was easily the most popular shape in the Roman period. The type comprised nearly 21% of all identified amphorae from the Hellenistic, Roman and Late Antique periods, coming second only to the Late Roman 1 amphorae, which constituted 23%.[29] And finally, the "pinched-handle" amphorae from the kiln sites in Asia Minor are said to contain plentiful mica, whereas mica is not usually present to any great extent (or at any rate rarely mentioned in clay descriptions) in the examples found in Cyprus.[30]

NEW EVIDENCE FROM THE AKAMAS SURVEY

It is now time to adduce the new evidence from the Akamas survey. Of the 20 samples of the pinched-handle form, which were thin sectioned and studied under the petrological microscope, three general fabric groups were established.

1) Micaceous, made up of 15 samples

1A (Fig. 3)

A fine-texture clay matrix containing a groundmass of frequent small flecks of muscovite mica and a few strands of biotite mica. Also present are a scatter of silt-sized and above subangular grains of quartz, some argillaceous material, black iron oxides, the occasional small piece of cryptocrystalline limestone and small fragments of quartz-mica-schist.

No. 1)[31] SAK 101-35N-14 (handle)
No. 2) SAK 101-40N-9 (handle)
No. 3) SAK 778-8N-18 (handle)
No. 4) SAK 778-8S-25 (handle)
No. 5) SAK 778-9N-5 (handle)
No. 6) SAK 778-9S-23 (handle)
No. 7) SAK 783-4-463 (handle)
No. 8) SAK 783-4S-20 (handle)
No. 9) SAK 788-1ON-34 (handle)
No. 10) SAK 788-1IN-25 (handle)
No. 11) SAK 788-11-9 (rim and handle)

1B (Fig. 4)

This appears to be a coarser version of 1A. It contains the same range of non-plastic inclusions as 1A but the size-range amongst the quartz and metamorphic inclusions is larger.

No. 12) SAK 101-8S-26 (handle)
No. 13) SAK 101-31S-18 (handle)
No. 14) SAK 778-8N-6 (handle)
No. 15) SAK 778-8-100 (handle)

2) Limestone-rich matrix (fig. 5)

A groundmass of frequent fine-textured cryptocrystalline limestone, or voids that once held limestone, which has since dissolved out, and with foraminifera scattered throughout. Also present are a few flecks of muscovite mica

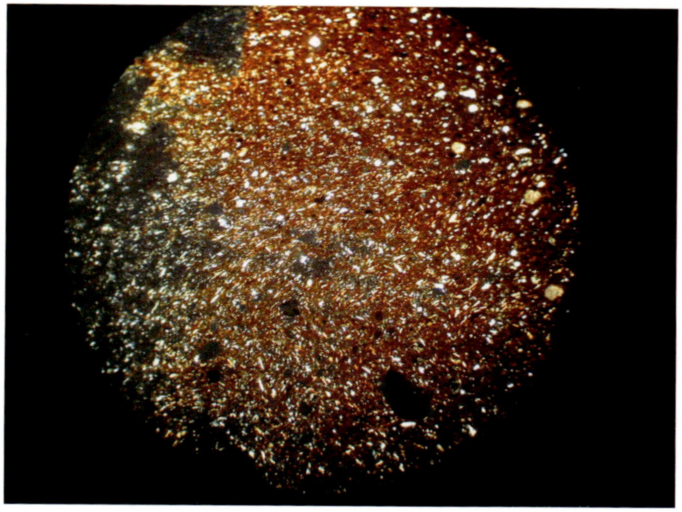

Fig. 3. Photomicrograph of Group 1A. Crossed Polars x 40. The sherd is full of needle-like flecks of mica.

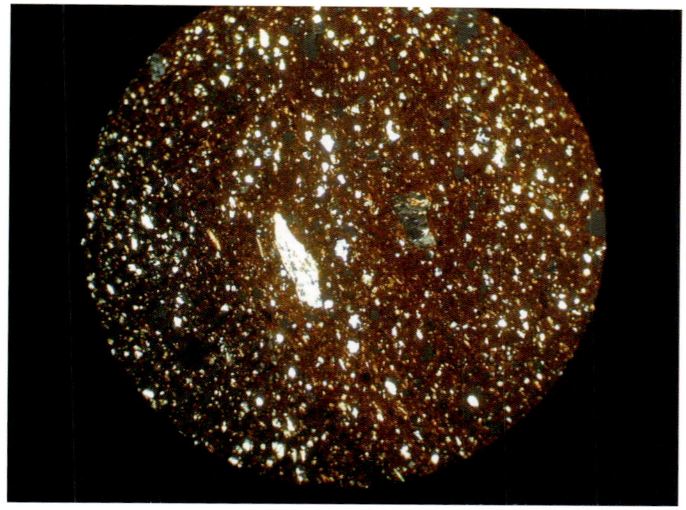

Fig. 4. Photomicrograph of Group 1B. Crossed Polars x 40. A coarser fabric than 1A with a large fragment of quartz-mica-schist roughly in the centre of the picture.

and quartz grains, together with the odd small fragment of fine-textured sandstone, quartzite and metamorphic rocks.

No. 16) SAK 788-9S-3 (handle)
No. 17) SAK 783-2N-70 (handle)
No. 18) SAK 803-2-14 (handle)

3) Radiolarian chert (fig. 6)
Large angular pieces of radiolarian chert are scattered throughout a lime-rich clay matrix, which also includes voids that once held limestone that has dissolved out, and with foraminifera scattered throughout. Also present are small flecks of muscovite mica and a scatter of grains of quartz, average size 0.40 mm and below.

No. 19) SAK 101-9S-6 (handle)
No. 20) SAK 788-9N-27(handle)

GEOLOGY OF THE AKAMAS PENINSULA

Could any of these groups have been manufactured in the Akamas region? The geology of the Akamas peninsula is a varied, complex mosaic. Large parts of it are formed of pillow lavas (basaltic) and a range of basic to ultra-basic rocks derived from the Troodos Igneous Massif, including olivine-gabbros and serpentinite. There are also large parts of the Akamas with sedimentary rocks, such as white reef-limestones and chalks, and yellow to white sandstones. There is very little in the way of metamorphic inclusions in the Akamas or in Cyprus as a whole, although very small outcrops of a hornblende-schist do occur near the Baths of Aphrodite and the village of Neokhorio [metamorphosed local sandstones – Trypa Group].[32]

23 Williams 1989, 91 and 94.
24 Rauh & Slane 2000, 325; Rauh 2004, 331-332.
25 Rauh & Slane 2000, 321 note 2; Rauh 2004, 329-330.
26 Hayes 1977, 100; 1991, 91-92.
27 Lund 2000; however, it was noted in the conclusion that "the true source of these wares", i.e. the non-micaceous "Pinched-handle" amphorae and Cypriot Sigillata, "can only be determined by means of scientific clay analyses or – preferably – the identification of the kilns themselves" (*ibidem* p. 573).
28 Daszkiewicz *et al.* 1997, 138; see also Meyza in the present publication.
29 Lund 2000; see further Leonard & Demesticha 2004, 190 note 6 and 198 figs. 11-13.
30 Leonard 1995b, 145 observed that the "lack of the distinctive mica in the Kioni samples, however, as well as in the Athenian Agora amphorae, must be emphasized and indicates the possible existence of yet another origin for these amphorae", other than Anemurium, that is. Lund (2000, 569-570) suggested that the non-micaceous examples could have been manufactured in Cyprus.
31 The numbers refer to the catalogue in the appendix.
32 Elliott & Dutton 1963, 177; Greensmith 1998, 35-40.

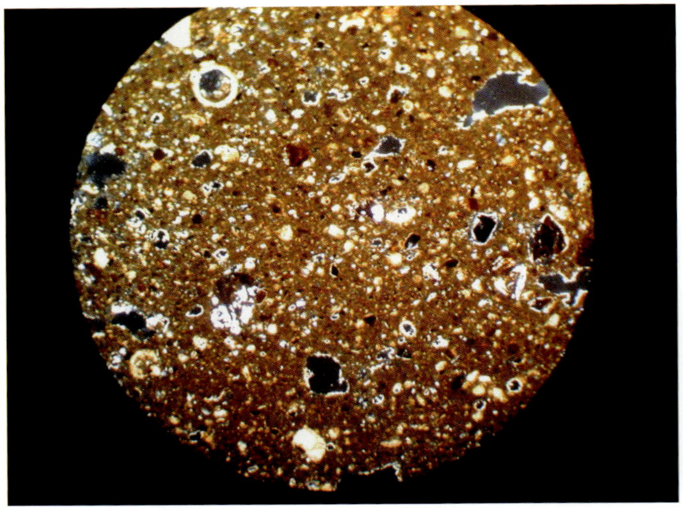

Fig. 5. Photomicrograph of Group 2. Crossed Polars x 40. The lime-rich fabric of Group 2.

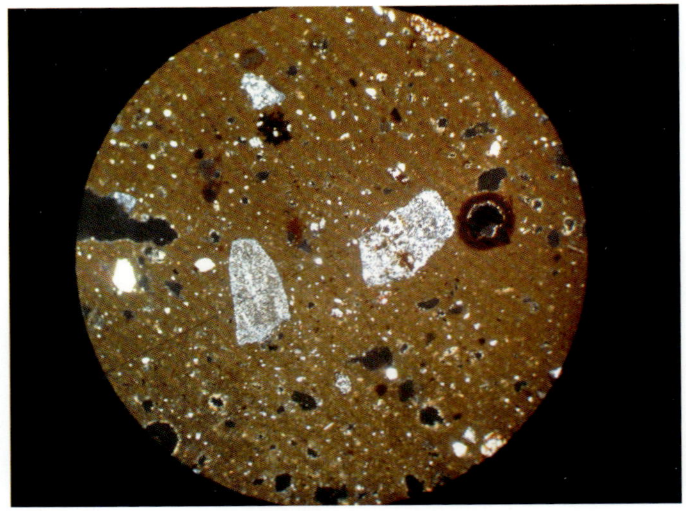

Fig. 6. Photomicrograph of Group 3. Crossed Polars x 40. The large greyish-white inclusions are radiolarian chert.

These small outcrops, however, are unlikely to have been responsible for the micaceous fabric present in Group 1 of the "pinched-handle" amphorae found in the Akamas survey (Nos. 1-15). Moreover, work at Kopetra by Marcus Rautman and his collaborators on a wide range of pottery and roof-tiles from many places in Cyprus did not produce a fabric that contained metamorphic inclusions such as the micaceous fabric above of the "pinched-handle" amphora. Instead, in general terms, most Cypriot fabrics are calcareous-rich and normally contain fragments of basic or ultrabasic rocks from the Troodos igneous complex, or discrete minerals derived from them. Moreover, two kiln "waster" LR1 sherds from Paphos examined by Stella Demestica did not reveal metamorphic inclusions.

Three sherds with a limestone-rich matrix (Nos. 16-18) also contained metamorphic inclusions, so they are probably non-Cypriot as well.

Radiolarian chert occurs both in the Akamas peninsular and western Rough Cilicia. Therefore, on this basis, the origin of Fabric group 3 could be either (Nos. 19-20).

It is difficult to compare directly these petrological results with the chemical analyses undertaken by Gerwulf Schneider at Paphos.[33] A small number of thin sections, however, were also made by Schneider, and these, combined with a reading of the chemical results, show that in general terms three main fabric groupings are relevant to the petrological results presented here. Schneider broadly distinguished a calcareous fabric; a calcareous one, which also contains prominent radiolarian chert; and a non-calcareous, micaceous fabric.

CONCLUSION

The range of fabric variation above shows that "pinched-handle" amphorae were produced at a larger number of kiln sites than those discovered so far in Rough Cilicia. Małgorzata Daszkiewicz, Henryk Meyza and Gerwulf Schneider found that the fourteen specimens they analysed at Nea Paphos could be divided into six groups and concluded that the amphorae in question were "not all of the same provenance".[34] Indeed, it is a well-attested phenomenon that similarly shaped amphorae might be produced at several places. In the Hellenistic period, Rhodian amphorae were not only manufactured on the Island of Rhodes but also in the Rhodian Peraia,[35] and one might also refer to amphorae of the Koan class with double-barreled handles, which were manufactured at numerous places in the Eastern as well as the Western Mediterranean. It is therefore entirely conceivable that the "pinched-handle" amphorae might have been manufactured in Western Cyprus as well as in Rough Cilicia.

However, the vast majority of the "pinched-handle" sherds from the Akamas survey examined in thin section and also visually, could accurately be described as having a micaceous fabric. Moreover, they seem very similar to the fabric descriptions of "pinched-handle" material recovered from the suspected production sites of Biçkici and Syedra in western Rough Cilicia. It is possible that the two pinch-handled sherds with prominent radiolarian chert inclusions might be Cypriot products, but again they might not. Also, it is worth noting that none of the "pinched-handle" sherds from Akamas have fabrics similar to what is thought to be local Late Roman 1 fabric descriptions from Cyprus. If Late Roman 1 took over from locally made Cypriot "pinched-handle" forms, they seem to have been made at different production sites.

The results of this analysis of the examples from the Akamas seem conclusive: 15 (i.e. 75%) of the 20 analysed handles were in all likelihood imports from Rough Cilicia, three calcareous sherds (i.e. 15%) probably had a non-Cypriot source, whereas two (i.e. 10%) – might or might not have been made in Cyprus. Evidently this outcome is strictly speaking only relevant to the situation in the Akamas Peninsula, and further analyses from amphorae found elsewhere in Cyprus are needed to ensure that the results have a general application. Still, the petrological analysis of the examples presented here strongly suggests that the "pinched-handle" amphorae may no longer be used as prime evidence of trade in Cypriot wine.[36] True, it cannot be excluded that some "pinched-handle" amphorae were in fact made in Cyprus, but this new evidence indicates that the vast majority of the "pinched-handle" amphorae found in North-western Cyprus and outside the island contained wine from Cilicia and should be seen as evidence of commercial ties between Rough Cilicia and the places of import.[37] It is not unlikely that they contained Cilician raisin-wine *(passum Cilicium)*, which Pliny the Elder refers to in his Natural History 14.81.[38] The occurrence of imports from Rough Cilicia in the Akamas region and Western Cyprus in general should not come as a surprise, since the available evidence suggests that the two areas constituted a single zone of circulation of pottery (and presumably other goods) in the Roman period.[39]

APPENDIX

Catalogue of the handles submitted for petrological analysis. The descriptions and accompanying profile drawings were made by John Lund during a registration campaign in the Akamas; they are based on examination with the naked eye.

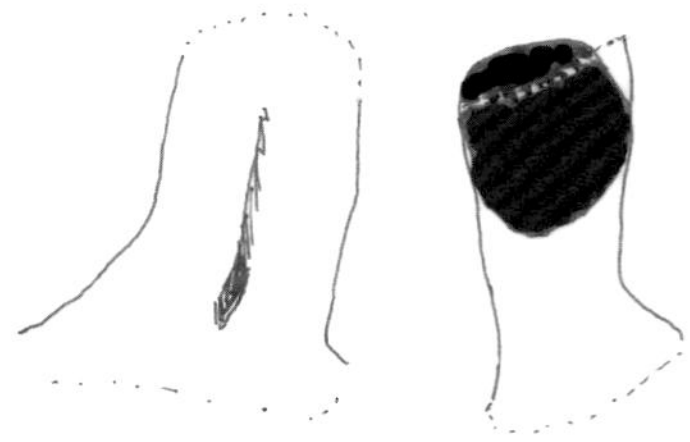

Fig. 7.1-20. Sections of the "pinched-handle" amphorae submitted to petrological analysis, cf. appendix 1.

No. 1 (Fig. 7.1) SAK 101-35N-14.[40] Clay 5YR 5/8 with occasional fine greyish-black inclusions and fine-medium reddish-brown ones. No slip. Surface colour 5YR 5/4 - occasional red grits up to 1 mm.

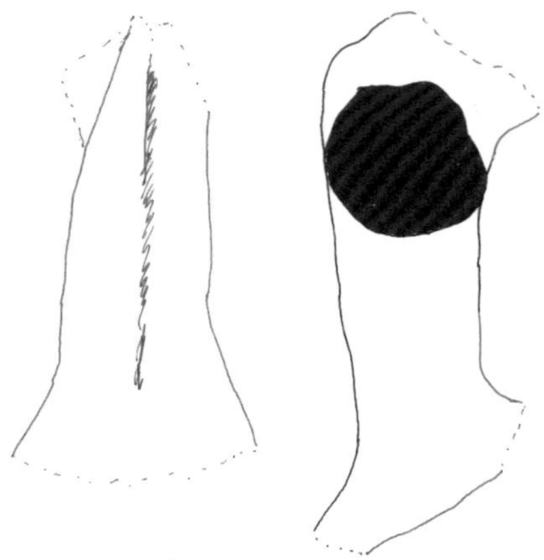

No. 2 (Fig. 7.2) SAK 101-40N-9. Clay 7.5YR 6/6 with occasional fine to medium size rounded yellowish inclusions and a few medium-sized greyish-brown (to reddish) mostly angular inclusions. Also isolated reddish-brown to 1 mm. No slip. Surface colour 7.5YR 6/6.

33 Daszkiewicz *et al.* 1997, 138; see further, Leonard 1995b, 144-145; Lund 2000 569-570.
34 Daszkiewicz *et al.* 1997, 138.
35 Held & Şenol 2010.
36 For instance, Lund 2000.
37 As done by Şenol & Cankardeş-Şenol 2003; Marangou & Autret 2011, 359-360; Autret 2012, 255-256.
38 Williams 1989, 91; Rauh & Will 2002.
39 See Lund 1999b, 10; 2006, 46-47; Autret & Marangou 2011; Autret 2012; Lund forthcoming.
40 When sampled, the number was erroneously read as SAK 101-36-14.

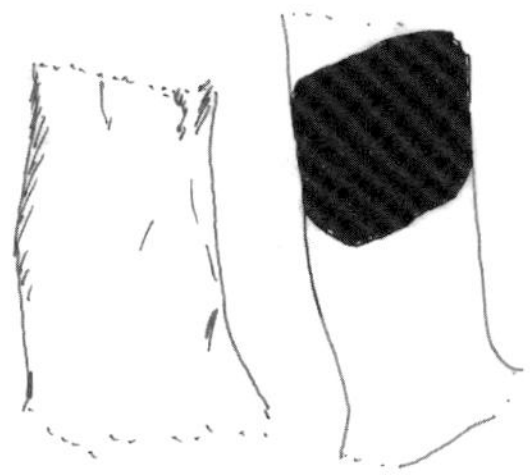

No. 3 (Fig. 7.3) SAK 778-8N-18. Clay 2.5YR 5/8 to 5YR 6/6, clean-breaking with a few fine greyish-black inclusions and occasional fine to medium-sized whitish ones. Isolated angular reddish-brown inclusions up to 1 mm. No slip. Surface colour 5YR 5/6 to 5/4.

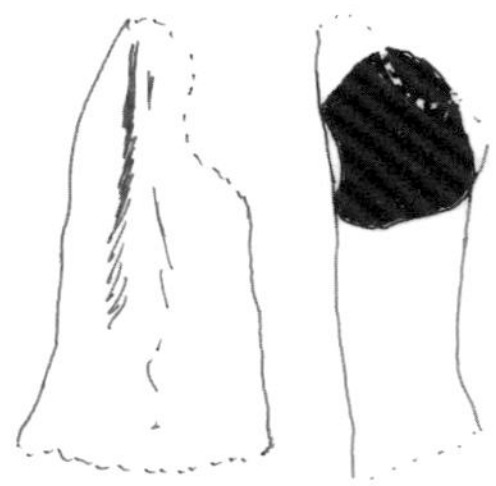

No. 4 (Fig. 7.4) SAK 778-8S-25. Clay 5YR 476-4/4 with occasional fine yellowish white and dark grey inclusions. No slip. Surface colour 5YR 6/6-5/6.

No. 5 (Fig. 7.5) SAK 778-9N-5. Clay 2.5YR 5/4 with occasional medium-sized, often rounded white to greyish-white inclusions. No slip. Surface colour 7.5YR 6/6. Several inclusions in the surface, including milky white ones 2-3 mm. and a few red inclusions.

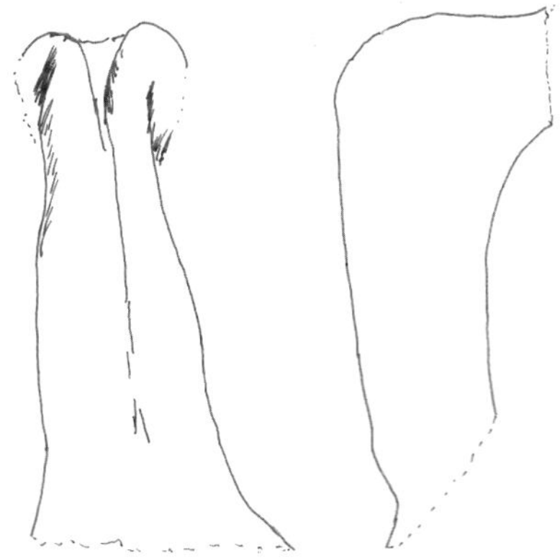

No. 6 (Fig. 7.6) SAK 778-9S-23. Clay pink 7.5YR 7/4; a few tiny light reflecting particles and a few fine greyish black particles and red ones; occasional medium-sized white inclusions and a few medium large reddish grits up to 2 mm. External colour 10YR 7/6 to 6/6.

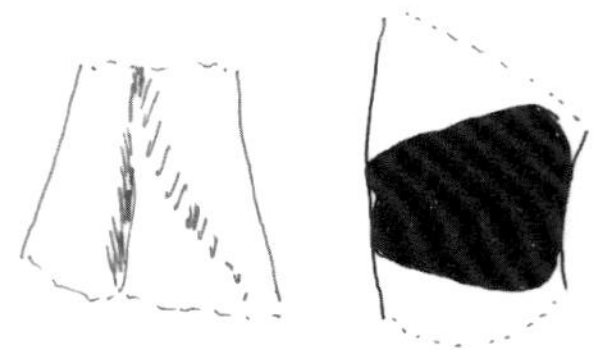

No. 7 (Fig. 7.7) SAK 783-4-463. Clay approximately 7.5YR 7/4-7/6 with occasional rounded medium-sized greyish-black, black and red inclusions. 7.5YR 7/4 to 8/4 on the surface.

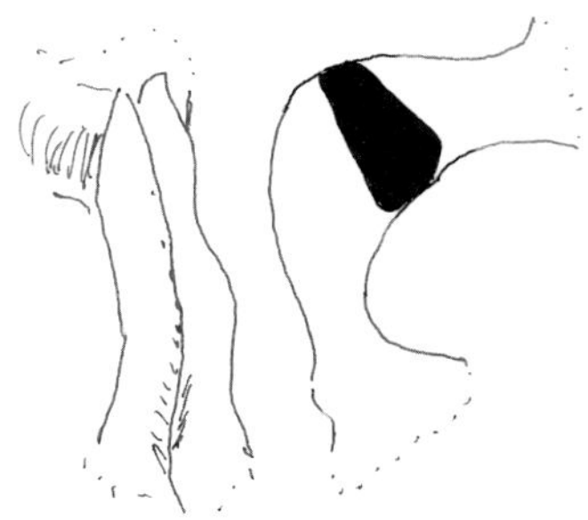

No. 8 (Fig. 7.8) SAK 783-4S-20. Clay 5YR 5/8 with a few fine greyish-black inclusions and occasional fine to medium-sized rounded white-greyish ones; also isolated medium-sized reddish brown as well as light reflecting inclusions. Dull, yellowish red slip 5YR 5/6 to 4/6 and to 2.5YR 5/8 in patches.

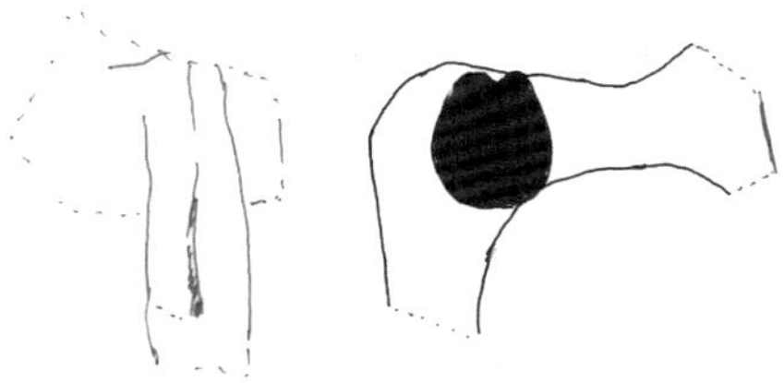

No. 9 (Fig. 7.9) SAK 788-10N-34. Inner d. of mouth: c. 10 cm. Clay c. 5YR 5/6 with occasional medium sized reddish-grey and reddish-brown inclusions, as well as isolated yellowish ones 1 mm. Numerous fine, light-reflecting inclusions: silvery mica? No slip. Surface colour 5YR 5/6-2.5YR 5/8 with a certain amount of inclusions and grits: whitish, reddish-grey.

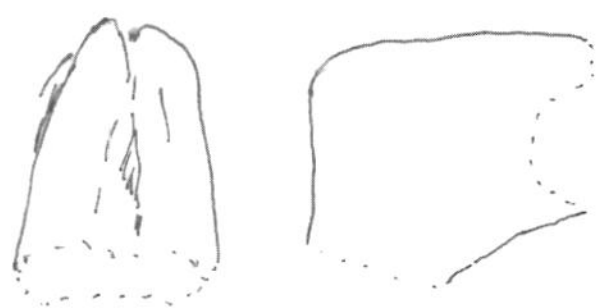

No. 10 (Fig. 7.10) SAK 788-11N-25. Clay 5YR 5/8 to 2.5YR 5/8 with occasional fine yellowish and oblong greyish-black inclusions. Smoothed externally, but no slip: 2.5YR 5/6 to ca. 5YR 6/8.

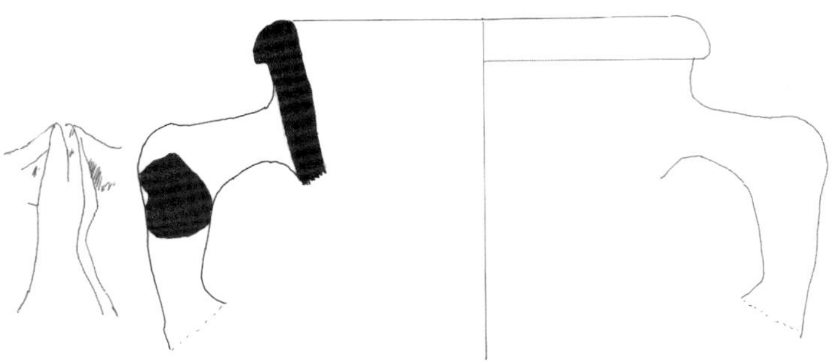

No. 11 (Fig. 7.11) SAK 788-11-9. Inner d. of mouth: 12 cm. Clay somewhat more red than reddish yellow 5YR 6/6-6/8; relatively few inclusions - with a few fine yellowish inclusions and occasional fine greyish-black ones. External colour reddish yellow 7.5YR 6/6.

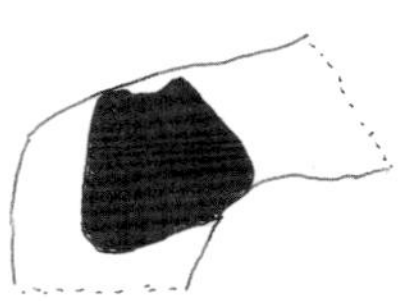

No. 12 (Fig. 7.12) SAK 101-8S-26. Clay 7.5YR 6/4 with a few fine greyish-black inclusions and occasional fine whitish ones. No slip. External colour 7.5 YR 5/4-5/6.

No. 13 (Fig. 7.13) SAK 101-31S-18. Clay 2.5YR 5/8-4/8 with isolated 1 mm large greyish angular grits. No slip. Surface colour 2.5YR 5/6-5/8.

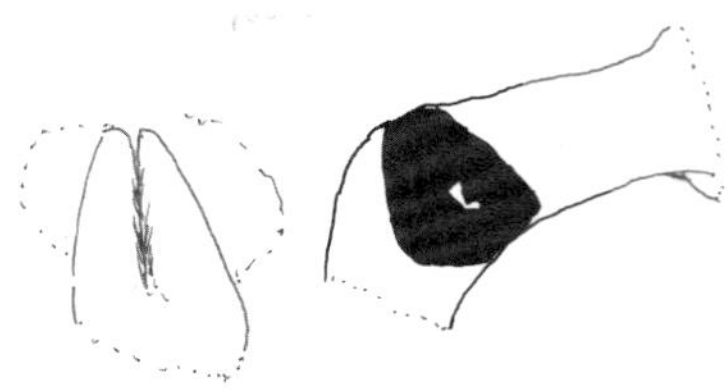

No. 14 (Fig. 7.14) SAK 778-8N-6. Clay 2.5YR 4/6-5YR 5/6 with a few fine yellowish-white inclusions and occasional medium-sized white and yellowish ones also. No slip. Surface colour 5YR 5/6.

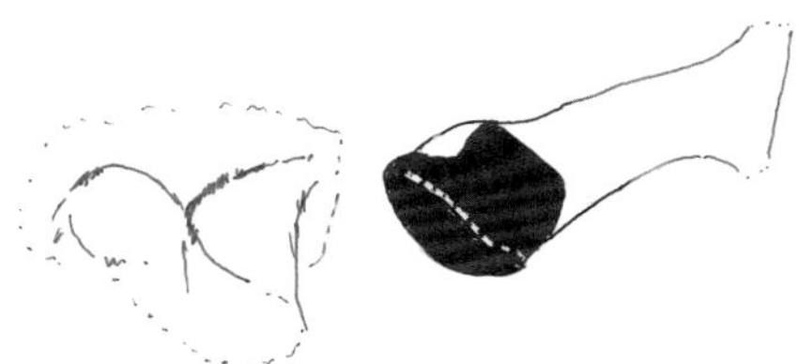

No. 15 (Fig. 7.15) SAK 778-8-100. Clay 2.5YR 5/8 with occasional fine white and greyish-black inclusions; also isolated medium-sized greyish-black ones; a few voids. No slip. External surface fired to 7.5YR 6/4-6/6 at places verging to 5/6.

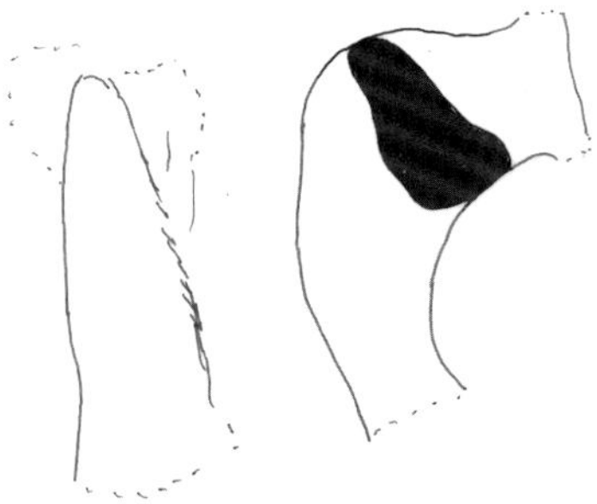

No. 16 (Fig. 7.16) SAK 788-9S-3. Clay 5YR 5/6 with a few fine rounded yellowish inclusions and occasional fine to medium-sized grey ones; numerous fine, light-reflecting inclusions: mica? No slip. Surface colour: 5YR 5/4. Weathered. Also lime particles, up to 2 mm in the surface.

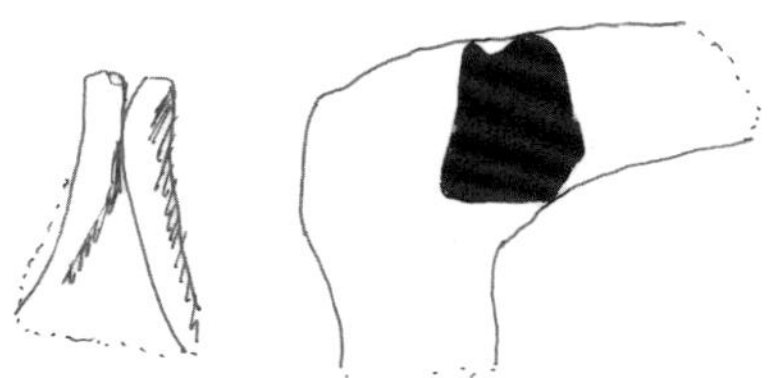

No. 17 (Fig. 7.17) SAK 783-2N-50. Clay yellowish red 5YR 5/6 to light reddish brown 5YR 6/4; in sunlight abundant v. fine light reflecting particles, probably rather quartz than silvery mica? a few fine to medium-size grey and greyish brown inclusions and larger lime and dark red particles (up to 2 mm.), also a few milky white grits and lime – in one case up to 6 mm. External colour light reddish brown to reddish yellow 5YR 6/4 to 5/6.

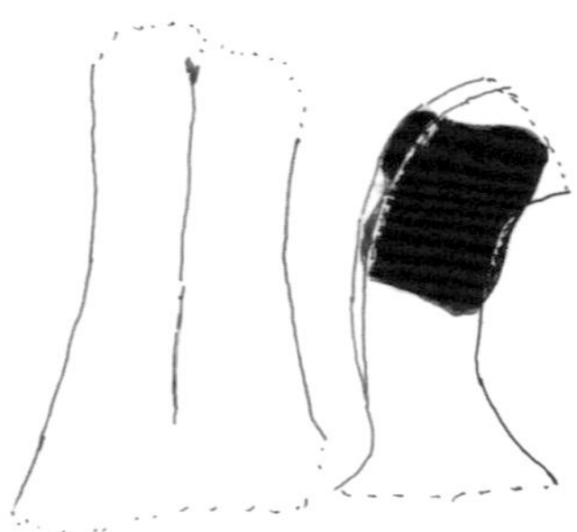

No. 18 (Fig. 7.18) SAK 803-2-14. Clay 10YR 7/4 with a few fine black inclusions and occasional 1-2 mm large grits: white (not lime) and reddish-brown ones. No slip. Surface colour 10YR 7/4 with numerous large grits in the surface.

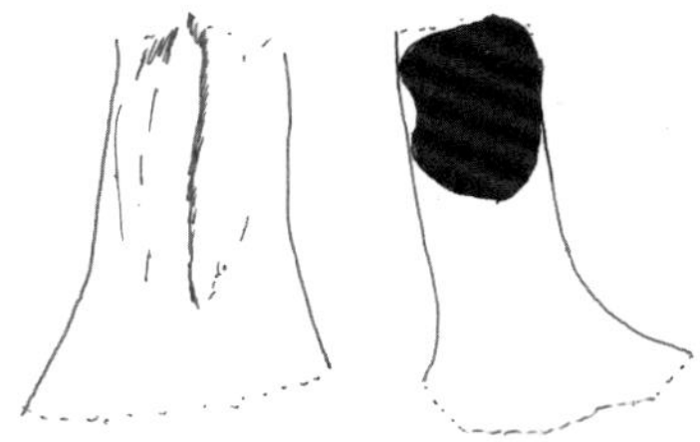

No. 19 (Fig. 7.19) SAK 101-9S-6. Clay 7.5YR 7/6 with a few/ numerous medium-sized greyish-black, mostly angular, inclusions. No slip Surface colour 10YR 8/4.

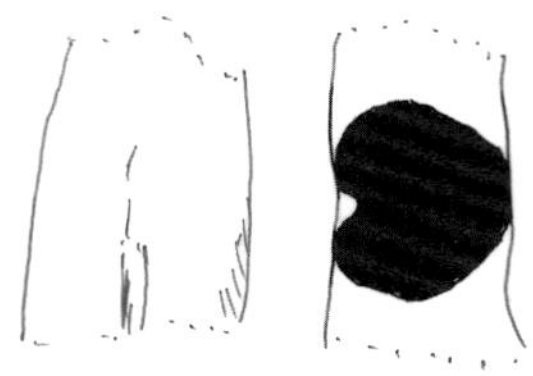

No. 20 (Fig. 7.20) SAK 788-9N-27. Clay 5YR 7/4, with a few/ numerous medium-sized grey and reddish-brown inclusions and occasional medium-sized greyish-black ones; also some voids. Self-slip. Surface colour 10YR 8/3.

Cypriot Amphorae in Ephesus?

BY TAMÁS BEZECZKY

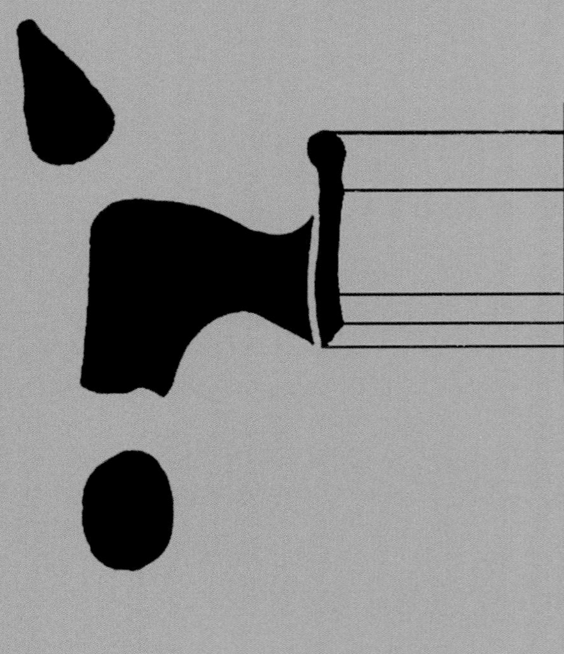

Cypriot Amphorae in Ephesus?

BY TAMÁS BEZECZKY

From Hellenistic times on (or probably even earlier), Ephesus was provisioned with the foodstuffs produced in the Cayster river valley. These little-known farming estates must have been closely related to Ephesus. Inscriptions mention that the temple of Artemis had estates in the Cayster river valley.[1] They also refer to a wine-producing cooperative (συνεργασία). In addition, they describe the way wine was sold in the centre of the city and in the little shops on the road connecting the stadium and the theatre.

During the early Roman period Ephesus had commercial ties with a number of important food producing centres in the eastern Mediterranean region. Amphorae (with their contents) were imported from a range of well-known Greek centres: Rhodes, Kos, Knidos, Chios, Erythai, Crete, and Corinth. During this period, the one-handle jar (Agora F 65-66, J 46-47, M 46-47) was probably used for wine storage and shipment in the vicinity of Ephesus.[2]

The middle Roman period in Ephesus saw the arrival of the amphorae from Cilicia and other eastern Mediterranean amphora types (Kapitän II, Agora M273, Knossos 18). Their exact geographical sources remain undetermined. There are also amphorae from the Black Sea (Zeest 75, 80, 84). Ephesus continued to produce the one-handle jars (Agora M125-126), and certain data refer to the local production of the Kapitän II amphorae.

In the Late Roman/Byzantine period we have amphorae from Cilicia, Chios, Samos, Egypt, Gaza, and Black Sea (Sinopean carrot amphorae) in addition to the large quantities of local amphorae (Late Roman amphora 3, Ephesus 56).[3]

There is little information on the commercial relationship between Ephesus and Cyprus. John W. Hayes published a Koan/Dressel 2-4 amphora, a few one-handle jars and Meander valley Late Roman amphorae 3 among the ceramic finds from the "House of Dionysos" in Paphos.[4] In 1993, John Lund referred to fragments of the same type in the Palaepaphos survey. There are two sub-types among them: the one-handled jar (Mid Roman amphora 3), and the two-handled LR 3. Based on the petrological evidence available at the time, he thought they might have come from the western part of Asia Minor, or perhaps Sardis. Kristina Winther Jacobsen mentioned LR 3 amphorae at Kalavassos-Koperta, but their provenance is not known.[5] If any conclusion can be drawn from this it is that few amphorae produced in Ephesus were shipped to Cyprus.[6]

Potentially two types of amphorae may have been shipped from Cyprus to Ephesus, but since both types were produced outside Cyprus as well, we used Sauer´s petrological data in order to determine their provenance.[7]

The well-known, "pinched-handle" amphora (Agora G 199), which was first identified among the objects found at the Agora in Athens,[8] started to become distributed during the early Roman period. This type of amphora can be found at a number of sites from Italy to northern Africa and the eastern Mediterranean region. It was produced in Rough Cilicia, and apparently also in Cyprus. It has been suggested that the amphorae that do not contain mica were probably produced in Cyprus while those that do were produced in one of the workshops of Rough Cilicia.[9]

Only one pinched-handle amphora (Agora G 199) has come to light in the Ephesus Agora (Fig. 1).[10] Its layer can be dated to the period after the earthquake in AD 23 and before the end of the 1st century AD. The petrological analysis established that it is rich in mica, so it was not produced in Cyprus.

The second type, Late Roman amphora 1 (LR 1), is the best-known amphora of the late Roman/Byzantine period, which can be found all over the Mediterranean.[11] A few fragments were excavated in Ephesus as well. The pieces found at the Agora and at the Terrace House 2 (the excavation of 1999) can be dated the end of the 4th century to the beginning of the 7th century AD. Thirty-three fragments have been found in the Agora and six at the Terrace House 2. In addition, a number of fragments were found during the earlier excavations. Ulrike Outschar thought they were produced in Ephesus.[12] R. Sauer submitted them to petrological analysis, but the results were not published. He has now re-analysed the thin sections of the fragments found earlier (the ones from Church of Mary)[13] as well as the new ones from the Agora.

The upper part of the amphora which was found in the Agora is characteristic of the late period of the type (Fig. 2).[14] All we can say of the handle fragment found at the Church of Mary at this moment is that it was part of a characteristically LR 1 amphora (not illustrated). The fabric of two amphorae is the same as that of the Kourion

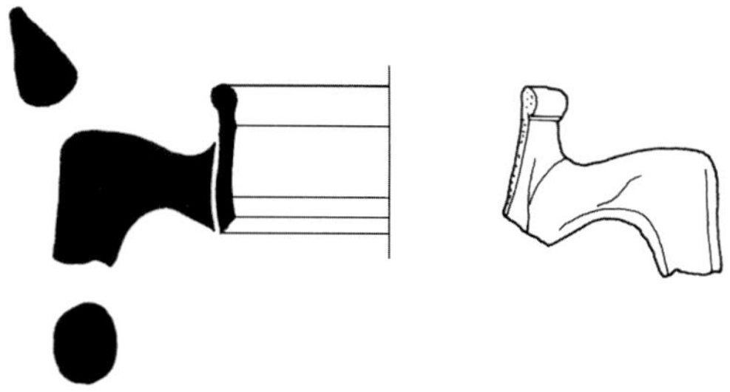

Fig 1. Amphora no. 1.

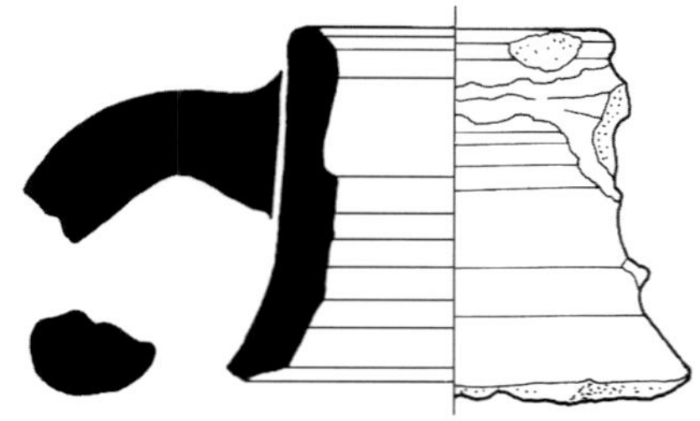

Fig 2. Amphora no. 2.

amphorae described by David Williams.[15] The rest of the LR 1 amphorae[16] in Ephesus have entirely different fabrics. On the basis of the stereo microscopic analysis, they can be classified into four groups. They have not been studied petrologically; they may have been produced in various workshops in Asia Minor (the island of Rhodes and from Ismeler to Seleucia of Pieria on the mainland).[17]

In conclusion may be said that imported amphorae and the foodstuffs in them (wine, olive oil, fish sauce) did not play a significant role in Ephesus. And the evidence for exchange of amphora-borne goods between Cyprus and Ephesus is almost non-existent. The hinterland of Ephesus was able to satisfy local demand.

---

1 Engelmann 2001, 40, IV.4.4 and 41, IV.4.6.
2 Bezeczky 2004, 85-97; *idem* 2006, 287-308.
3 Bezeczky 2005a.
4 Hayes 1991, 92 Type VI and 95, no. 39.
5 Jacobsen 2004, 145.
6 Lund 1993a, 124-125; Peacock & Williams 1986, 188-190.
7 I am grateful to Roman Sauer for allowing me to refer to the results of his analyses.
8 Robinson 1959, 43 pl 8; Lund 2005 [2006].
9 Lund 2000, 569-570.
10 No. 1: Rim, neck, handle fr.; 95/180 (1328); Tetragonos Agora, Trench 95/1; D = 12.5 cm, H = 6.5 cm; light reddish brown (5YR 6/3); Bezeczky 2004, 94-95 no. 35. Petrological description: matrix: very calcareous abundant mica; temper particles: very frequent muscovite, monocrystalline-quartz, limestone, frequent ironoxides, rare brown mica, feldspars, traces of shell fragments and foraminifers, siltstone fragments, crystalline rock fragments, polycrystalline quartz, chert.
11 See Pieri 2005, App. 1, 181-187.
12 Outschar 1993, 51 fig. 2. The petrological analysis does not affirm local production, cf. Sauer 1995.
13 Sauer 1995, EPH 268: matrix: calcareous clay, without mica; temper particles: very frequent limestone grains, serpentinite; frequent chert, pyroxene, rare monocrystalline quartz, feldspar, traces of bioclast fragments (shell fragments and foraminifera, echinid spines), volcanic rock fragments, brownish hornblende.
14 No. 2: Rim, neck, handle fr.; 99/039 (1689); Tetragonos Agora, R-sewer; D = 10 cm, H = 11.5 cm; reddish yellow (5YR 6/6); Bezeczky 2005a, 216 no. 35. Hard fabric, white, black and gray inclusions; Petrological description: matrix: calcareous, no mica; temper particles: very frequent carbonate, frequent monocrystalline quartz, frequent to rare chert, feldspar, plagioclase, pyroxene, serpentinite, brown hornblende, epidote, foraminifers, echinoids, rare crystalline rock fragments.
15 Williams 2005, 166.
16 Bezeczky 2005a nos. 21-22 and 24-25, 217, Pl. 3, Farbtafel XVI.
17 Fulford & Peacock 1984, 22 and 119; Empereur & Picon 1989, 236-243; Demesticha 2000, 549-553; Williams 2005, 162-167; Pieri 2005, 69-85.

Amphora Typologies, Distribution, and Trade Patterns: The Case of the Cypriot LR1 Amphorae

BY STELLA DEMESTICHA

Amphora Typologies, Distribution, and Trade Patterns: The Case of the Cypriot LR1 Amphorae

BY STELLA DEMESTICHA

The economy of Late Roman Cyprus has been approached by various scholars in recent years with the emphasis given to the trade of different commodities as well as to the position of the island on the major sea trade routes of the eastern Mediterranean.[1] These works have shed significant light on the "tranquil obscurity"[2] of the generally accepted prosperity of the island during the Roman period and have provided further documentation to Strabo´s statement that Cyprus was fertile and self-sufficient with regard to specific products (Strabo, 14.6.5). Thus, the active involvement of such an island in the sea-borne trade networks of the eastern Roman Empire is of no surprise to any scholar today. Nevertheless, when the character of this involvement is to be investigated further, it becomes clear that "our understanding of the macro-economic complexity of the eastern Mediterranean is at an early stage".[3]

AMPHORA PRODUCTION ON CYPRUS

Focusing on amphorae – vessels that are fundamentally associated with ancient economies – provides one way to clarify a part of the above-mentioned complexity. Amphora production in Cyprus has been suspected and in some cases documented from the Archaic Period through Late Roman times.[4] The local types and the exported quantities seem to have varied significantly during this long period and explicit evidence for the contents of any of the Cypriot amphora types is still lacking; no systematic scientific analyses have been conducted so far, and local agricultural production cannot illuminate the issue, as both olive oil and wine are mentioned in written sources as local products in abundance, a common phenomenon on Mediterranean islands.[5] Olive oil pressing installations corroborate olive oil production on Cyprus since the Late Bronze Age,[6] and particularly for Late Antiquity.[7] Olive oil production areas are found mainly in the western and northern areas of the island, whereas wine, an important Cypriot agricultural product, has mainly been associated with the southern coast.[8] Still, unlike copper and timber, which were standard Cypriot export products in antiquity, wine or olive oil seem to have been exported in bulk on a less regular basis.[9] It may be that economic factors and mechanisms, in addition to the disposal of a surplus, facilitated the systematic trade of Cypriot wine or olive oil beyond the island, during certain historical times of significant trade activity. Such periods are marked by increased local amphora production, either in distinctive Cypriot shapes, such as the Archaic-Classical basket-handled amphorae,[10] or the Hellenistic "Greek style" ones.[11] The amphora production and trade networks of the eastern provinces of the Roman Empire, especially during the early and the middle periods, are less thoroughly studied. Nevertheless, we know that in Cyprus,[12] as elsewhere, several amphora styles were adopted for the packaging of the local products but none has been distinguished thus far as being widely distributed.[13] This is not the case during the Late Roman period, however, which appears to have been yet another period of distinctive Cypriot amphora production. In this paper I will discuss the association of Cyprus with the production of LR1 amphorae, one of the most widespread Late Roman amphorae during Late Antiquity (4th - 7th century AD)[14], and show that interesting questions may be raised on the role of the island in the politico-economic horizon of this period, which led to the "end of the ancient economy".[15]

PROVENANCE OF THE LR1 AMPHORAE

LR1 amphorae were traded throughout Late Antiquity (4th – 7th century AD) and are today among the most diagnostic Late Roman vessels found in excavations throughout the Mediterranean.[16] In 1989, Jean-Yves Empereur and Maurice Picon published the results of a very extensive survey of amphora production sites during the Imperial period. Among others, they found fifteen kiln sites for LR1 amphorae, located in a broad geographical area, which included north Syria, Cilicia and Cyprus.[17]

Since then, further elements have been added to our knowledge about these kiln sites: Williams published the results of petrographic analysis for four of them: Seleucia and Rhosos in Syria, Yumurtalık and Soles in Cilicia, and Kourion in Cyprus.[18] Reynolds later expressed doubts about LR1 production in Syria (Rhosos and Seleucia)[19] whilst kiln sites found at Elaiussa-Sebaste and Soli-Pompeiopolis have confirmed Cilician production.[20] In addition, another kiln was excavated on the island of Cos, in the Aegean.[21] Concerning the Cypriot sites, archaeological work on the island has also provided more evidence on the matter: production at Kourion has not been associated with a kiln site yet, but excavated wasters in Amathous left no doubt about the existence of a kiln at the city's ancient harbour.[22] Furthermore, a LR1 kiln was excavated in Paphos[23] and another one was surveyed at Zygi-Petrini.[24] All three kilns are dated to the 6th and 7th century AD.[25] Moreover, a large number of LR1 amphorae have been studied from non-stratified layers of excavations at the agoras of Amathous and Kourion.[26] From this material, two more Cypriot fabrics, conventionally named "X" and "ZA", have been distinguished and confirmed by petrographic analysis, but they have not been yet associated with any located kiln site on the island.

LR1 AMPHORA TYPOLOGY

Although a detailed presentation of approaches to LR1 typologies is beyond the scope of this paper, a short reference to the most important is indicative of the specific issues related to their study. Following the increasing number of publications about LR1 amphorae during the past 20 years, it is widely acknowledged that their typology should be revised. Three main approaches of classification may be distinguished thus far:

1. Earlier classifications, which dealt with the LR1 amphorae as one type, without distinguishing variants.[27]

2. Typologies, in which variants within the type are distinguished. These studies were usually based on material richer in numbers than the previous ones, and consequently, acknowledge the clear diversification of the LR1 amphorae morphology. In most of these cases, numbers were used for the classification of the different LR1 variants, found at a specific site or in a particular geographical area.[28]

3. More recent publications, where the established term "LR1", is used as a general identification of the type, which includes several variants or forms.[29]

Despite the increasing number of such studies, it has not so far proved possible to merge the various typological

1 Michaelides 1996; Rautman 2000; Papacostas 2001.
2 Mitford, 1980, 1295.
3 Kingsley & Decker 2001, 14.
4 Calvet 1986; Lund 1993a, 123-124; Grace 1979, 220-223; Jacobsen 2002; Meyza 2004; Leidwanger 2005-2006 [2007].
5 Amouretti 1992, 86.
6 Hadjisavvas 1992.
7 Catling 1972, 14; Louloupis 1975; Christou 1995, 836.
8 Ριζοπούλου-Ηγουμενίδου 1996, 324-325.
9 Karageorghis 1993.
10 Calvet 1986; Jacobsen 2002; Leidwanger 2005-2006 [2007].
11 Grace 1979, 220-223; Meyza 2004.
12 Peacock & Williams 1986, 105-106 Class 10; Lund 1993a, 123-124; Hayes 1991,90-92, types I and III; Lund 2000.
13 Rauh & Slane 2000; Reynolds 2005; 2008.
14 The production of amphorae similar to LR1s continued well after the 7th century, but Cyprus's involvement in this needs to be better investigated (see Armstrong 2009, Demesticha forthcoming b). Thus, it is not included in this paper.
15 McCormick 2002, 115-119; Pieri 2005, 146-199.
16 For the type see Riley 1979, 212-216. The bibliographical references on these amphorae are numerous. For a recent publication with a detailed review of the literature, see Pieri 2005, 69-81, and especially Appendix 1, 181-187.
17 Empereur & Picon 1989, 236-243.
18 Williams 2005, 162-167.
19 Reynolds 2005, 566.
20 The kilns were discovered during public works, hence were not properly documented and excavated (Burragato *et al.* 2007; Ferrazzoli & Ricci 2007, 673; Autret *et al.* 2010, 205).
21 Diamanti 2010a; 2010b; Poulou-Papadimitriou & Didioumi 2010.
22 Empereur & Verlinden 1987; Touma 1989.
23 Demesticha & Michaelides 2001.
24 Manning *et al.* 2000.
25 Demesticha 2003.
26 Demesticha 2002.
27 E.g. Thomas (1959), who studied the amphorae of the eastern Mediterranean imported in Britain (type Bii), Kuzmanov (1973, type XIIIa and b), Scorpan, who classified the Roman amphorae from the Black sea (1977, type VIII), and Peacock & Williams (1986), who divided the main Roman amphorae types from all over the Mediterranean into 66 general "Classes", one of which (Class 44) is the equivalent of the LR1 amphorae.
28 Among the most commonly used ones are those proposed by Egloff for the LR1 amphorae found at Kellia in Egypt (Egloff 1977, 112-113 types 164 - 169), Riley for the same amphorae found at Benghazi in Libya Riley 1979, 212-216 (LR1 and LR1a), and Keay for amphorae from Catalonia, Spain (Keay 1984, 268-278 types LIII A-D.
29 Andrei Opaiţ, for example, divided the amphorae from the Roman Scythia into 5 variants Opaiţ 2004b, 8-10 (LR1/A-E). Likewise, Pieri (2005, 70-76) classified the LR1 amphorae found in Gaul into two "generations" (LR1A and 1B and "sous-modules").

classifications of the type into one scheme that would include the range of the sub-types or variants. This is probably the reason behind the tendency to use only the general typological names (Bii, LR1, Class 44 etc.) in excavation reports thus ignoring the hard work done in many of the more refined typologies of the second and the third group, noted above. Moreover distribution maps, where no distinction is made between the different dates or subtypes, can give a false impression of the spread of these amphorae and hence of Late Roman commerce in general.[30]

In sum, although the areas of provenance and the date range of LR1 amphorae are known today, a great deal more information is required before a full typological syntax can be composed. In this respect, the study of the Cypriot material provides an important insight as it spans the four centuries of the Late Roman period. It comprises local as well as imported examples found in various sites of the island, because Cyprus was a centre of production and consumption. Following Dominique Pieri's classification model of two different generations,[31] I propose in this paper the addition of a third one, departing from published material both from Cyprus and other Mediterranean sites.

The first LR1 amphora generation: LR1/A (4th-5th century AD)[32]

Most scholars acknowledge without dispute the existence of an early phase in the LR1 amphora series.[33] Indeed, the morphological diagnostic features of such amphorae are rather distinctive: an ovoid body covered with grooves, a base that ends in a small knob, a narrow (cylindrical or slightly conical) neck, usually with oblique ridges around the outside, a thickened or folded rim, almost square in section, and two angled handles, grooved and folded, with their horizontal part much longer than the vertical one.

The very wide distribution of these amphorae is well documented, both in the eastern and the western Mediterranean.[34] Their first appearance is securely dated to the middle of the 4th century AD, and is attested in several well-dated contexts.[35] Their rather standardized morphology during this phase, regardless of various sizes and capacities,[36] points toward an enhanced, regional production. Still, our archaeological visibility for this early production phase is limited, as it is not clear which ones (if any) of the known kilns produced specifically these amphorae. Cyprus does not seem to have been among the major LR1/A producers (see below), even if a few Cypriot amphorae of this generation have been found: four at the Agora of Amathous, two at Kourion and one in the sea around cape Kiti (Fig. 1).[38] Moreover, one of the earliest well-dated LR1 amphorae was found at Kourion, in the destruction layers caused by the earthquake of AD 365; it has been considered as Cypriot, i.e. possibly made in a local workshop in Kourion area.[39] Given the above, Cyprus seems not to have been a major amphora producer during the 4th and 5th centuries AD, so Syria and Cilicia (or only Cilicia, if Reynolds' doubts on Syrian production prove correct) should be considered as the most probable providers of the considerable amounts of LR1s found all over the Mediterranean. Indeed, the main morphological links of the LR1/A amphorae with the rim and the handles of a regional, 3rd century AD amphora of Cilician fabric, seem to be very convincing.[40]

The second LR1 amphora generation: LR1/B (end of 5th-6th century AD)

After the middle of the 5th century, changes have been observed in the morphology of LR1 amphorae, mainly in the formation of their neck and rim. These changes are not universal, and they occur in at least three different forms:[41]

Form 1: Keay 1984 LIII B / Opaiţ LRA 2004b 1A3/ Pieri 2005 LR1B and C

Form 2: Keay 1984 LIII B and C/ Opaiţ 2004b LRA 1B1

Form 3: Opaiţ 2004 LRA 1A4, Demesticha 2003, LR1.T1

A distinctive feature of all forms of this generation is that their neck is broader and shorter than the previous ones, often deformed and encircled by a ridge, thus giving the impression of careless manufacture. The rim is either thickened (Form 2) or everted (Form 1 and 3) and the angular handles bear a double groove along the outer face.[42] Their body is oblong to pear-shaped, covered with a spiral ridge, stepped or wavy in section.[43] These morphological differences may be indicative of newly established workshops, still in a period of adjustment, hence an expansion of the type´s territorial zone of provenance, during the 6th century.

Given the lack of studies and excavations of kiln sites, we cannot ascertain chronologically whether the beginning of the greater LR1/B production during the 6th

Fig. 1. LR1/A amphora from Kourion [KOURION 1989, C-D (-8)(-9)], made of X fabric.

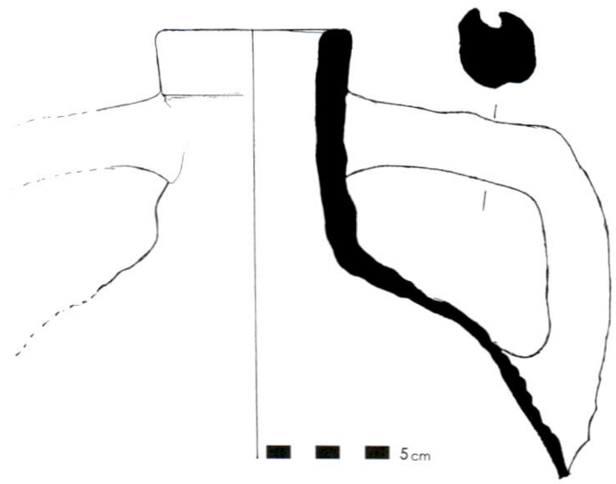

Fig. 2. LR1/B, Form 2 amphora from Kourion [KA1977 K-L (35-36) B=30), made of ZA fabric.

century took place in Cyprus or Cilicia.[44] The description of most of the Form 1 and 2 fabrics, as pinkish buff with fine inclusions, indicates a Cilician provenance.[45] But archaeological evidence from Cyprus shows that this expansion in production was closely connected to the island. A few examples of local LR1/B Form 1 and 2 (Fig. 2) were found in the agora of Amathous. In the same layers, a considerable amount of Form 3s, mainly in X fabric clearly associates this form with the local production (Fig. 4).[46]

The distribution of the different forms of this generation is difficult to trace, because in most of the excavation reports only some images (drawings or photographs) of representative vessels are published. Nevertheless, it is still possible to acquire a picture of the general trends: Forms 1 and 2 were both distributed in the eastern and the western Mediterranean, whereas Form 3 amphorae are mainly found in the east (Table 1).

The third LR1 amphora generation: LR1/C (7th century AD)

The LR1 amphorae of the 7th century AD clearly belong to a different generation, as they show different morphological features: a cylindrical neck, usually higher than the earlier forms, with a neatly formed rim, ending to a distinctive ridge. Their body is rather small and pear shaped, with narrow shoulders (Fig. 4).

Their production is associated with three kiln sites located in the south coast of Cyprus (Paphos, Amathous and Zygi).[47] Dating can be documented only for the Paphos kiln, the sole one excavated on the island so far,[48] whereas the dating of the rest is based on the related chronologies of their products. The abundance of material permits the distinction of five different sizes of the same form (LR1/C i-v)[49], the last three being the most numerous (they are the types that Riley distinguished as LR1a. It is worth keeping in mind that besides Cyprus, LR1 amphora of the third generation were also produced in the Cilician workshop of Elaiussa Sebaste, Soloi and on the island of Cos.[50] Their

30 See for example Pacetti 1995.
31 For the term "generation", see Pieri 2005. For a discussion on amphora classifications, cf. Reynolds 2008 and Demesticha forthcoming a.
32 Pieri 2005, 70.
33 Pensabene 1981, 194; Egloff 1977 type 169; Opaiţ 1984, 317, LRA 1A2; Keay 1984, LIII A; Bonifay & Villedieu 1987; Bonifay & Pieri 1995; Williams 2005, 160.
34 Pieri 2005, 74.
35 Williams 1987, 237; Bass & van Doorninck 1971, type III; Egloff 1977, 113; Pieri 2005, 70-75, type LR1A; Reynolds 2005, 566.
36 See e.g. Pieri 2005, 71, fig. 27.
37 Engvig & Åström 1975, fig. 27 S 29c.
38 Williams 1987, 237.
39 Empereur & Picon 1989, 242; Williams 2005, 166: macroscopically, it resembles the ZA fabric, but it is not exactly the same (in situ observation of the author).
40 Arthur & Oren 1998, 203, fig. 6.1.2; Opaiţ 2010, 1015; Reynolds 2005, 565; 2008, 70-72.
41 For a more detailed description of these forms see Demesticha forthcoming a.
42 Keay 1984, fig. 124.2-5.
43 For an informative image, see Williams 2005, 163, pl.1.
44 Burragato *et al.* 2007.
45 See e.g. Tubb 1986, 55; Pensabene 1981, 197; Abadie Reynal & Sodini 1992, 53; Keay 1984, 558; Fulford & Peacock 1984, 119.
46 For the repertoires of the Cypriot workshops see Demesticha 2003.
47 Demesticha 2003.
48 Demesticha & Michaelides 2001.
49 Demesticha 2003, fig. 3.
50 Burragato *et al.* 2007, 690, figs 2 and 3; Autret *et al.* 2010; Diamanti 2010a.

Area	Site	LRA/B/ Form 1	LRA/B/ Form 2	LRA/B/ Form 3	LRA/C
Aegean	Chios	Garnett & Boardman 1961, 110, nos 22, 24, figs 9, 11.			
	Thasos		Abadie-Reynal & Sodini 1992, 53, no CC210, fig. 23.	Abadie-Reynal & Sodini 1992, 55, fig. 24; Simossi 1991, 284, fig. 10-11.	
	Kythera			Coldstream & Huxley 1973, 172, fig. 52.	
	Cos				Diamanti 2010b, 49-72, fig. 12.1.9.1.
	YassiAda				Bass & van Doorninck 1982, 155-7.
Asia Minor	Goslu Kule, Tarsus			Jones 1950, pl. 210b.	
	Anemurium				Williams 1989, 96, nos 561 and 566, Pls. 56, 57.6
Mainland Greece	Athens			Böttger 1992, 373, no 75	
	Corinth			Williams & Zervos 1983, 29, pl 11.77.	Adamsheck 1979, 116, pl. 27.
	Argos			Aupert 1980, 438, fig. 45, no 322.	
	Torone			Papadopoulos 1989, 100, fig. 12.	
Cyprus	Diorios		Catling 1972, 33, fig. 20.		
	Paphos		Daszewski 1970, 141, pl. XXIII.5.		
	Alassa				Flourentzos 1996, pl. XXX 42, 43.
	Salamis			Diedrichs 1980, 55-56, nos 229, 233.	Diedrichs 1980, 55, nos 211, 212, 221, 225, 234, 235.
	Kalavasos-Kopetra				Rautman 2003, 195, fig. 5.11, nos 142-144.
	Maroni-Petrera				Manning et al. 2002, 53, fig. 6.6, no 97.
	Cape Ap. Andreas				Green 1969, 23-24; 1973, 161, fig. 21.
Egypt		Hayes 1998, pl. 1.			
	Bir Umm Fawakhir	Meyer 1995, 219, fig. 15. a3.			
	Elephantine	Gempeler 1992, 198, fig. 128.1		Gempeler 1992, 198, K759.	
	Firka		Charleston 1955, fig. 89.		
	Kellia			Egloff 1977, 112, Type 164, pl. 57.	Egloff 1977, 112, type 166, Pl. 57.6
	Sinai			Arthur & Oren 1998, 202, fig. 6.	
	Alexandria			Majcherek 1992b, 103.	
	Saqqara			Ghaly 1992, 168, fig. 16 a.b.	
	Nubia (Meroitic Mastaba)			Griffith 1927, 106, Pl. 48.3.	
	Ballana			Emery & Kirwan 1938, 388, pl. III.6.	
	Bosra				
Syria				Joly & Blanc 1995, 119, fig. 4.	

Area	Site	LRA/B/ Form 1	LRA/B/ Form 2	LRA/B/ Form 3	LRA/C
Palestine				Zemer 1977, 76, pl. 23, no 6.6.	Zemer 1977, 76, nos 63-65, pl. XXIII.
	Negev-Tell Fara	Tubb 1986, 55, fig. 2.5			
	Caesarea	Bar-Nathan & Adato 1986, 132, fig. 1.4.	Bar-Nathan & Adato 1986, 132, fig. 1.1.	Magness 1995, 142, fig. 2.1	Adan-Bayewitz 1993, 102, fig. 2.4
	Jalame		Johnson 1988, 212, fig. 7-50.		
	Rehovot-in-the Negev		Rosenthal-Heginbottom 1988, 87, pl. II.		Rosenthal-Heginbottom 1988, 87, pl.III, no 127.
	Tyropoeon Valley, Jerusalem			Crowfoot & Fitzgerald 1929, pl.XXX.29.	
Black Sea	Histria		Scorpan 1977, 277, fig. 12.2.		
	Cernavoda				Scorpan 1977, fig. 39.2; Radulescu 1976, 109, pl XI.1a.
	Troesmis (Bulgaria)			Opaiţ 1984, pl. XV.5.	
	Vratza-Salanovtzi (Bulgaria)			Cancova 1959, 245, fig. 1.8.	
	Crimea			Якобсон 1959, 329, fig. 3.14.	Opaiţ 1984, 319, pl. XV.3; Sazanov 1997.
Adriatic	Butrint	Reynolds 2004, fig. 13. 175; 178-180.	Reynolds 2004, fig.13.183.		
North Africa	Salambo, Carthage		Fulford & Peacock 1984, 119, fig. 34.2.	Fulford & Peacock 1984, 119, fig. 34.1.	
	Bengazi, Libya		Riley 1979, no D377.		Riley 1979, 216, LR1a.
	Ptolemais, Libya			Kraeling 1962, 269, pl. LXII.b.	
Spain	Catalonia	Keay 1984, 268-78.	Keay 1984, 481, 487, 558, figs 119-120		
Italy	Otranto	Arthur 1992, 204, fig. 7.1.			
	Lungo-tevere Testaccio, Rome	Incitti 1986, 588-9, fig. 313.			
	Palatino, Rome	Pensabene 1981, 197.			
	Giacomo degli Schiavoni		Albarella *et al.* 1993, 198, fig. 19.		
France	Marseille	Pieri 2005, pl. 15. 5, 16.1, 2, 4	Bonifay & Pieri 1995, 108-9, LRA1b, fig. 7; Pieri 2005, pl. 14, 15. 1, 17.6	Fiori 1974, 91, pl. III.8; Pieri 2005, pl. 15.1, 8, pl. 16.	

Table 1. Indicative distribution of LR1/B and LR1/C amphorae, based on publications that allow for distinction among the different amphora forms.

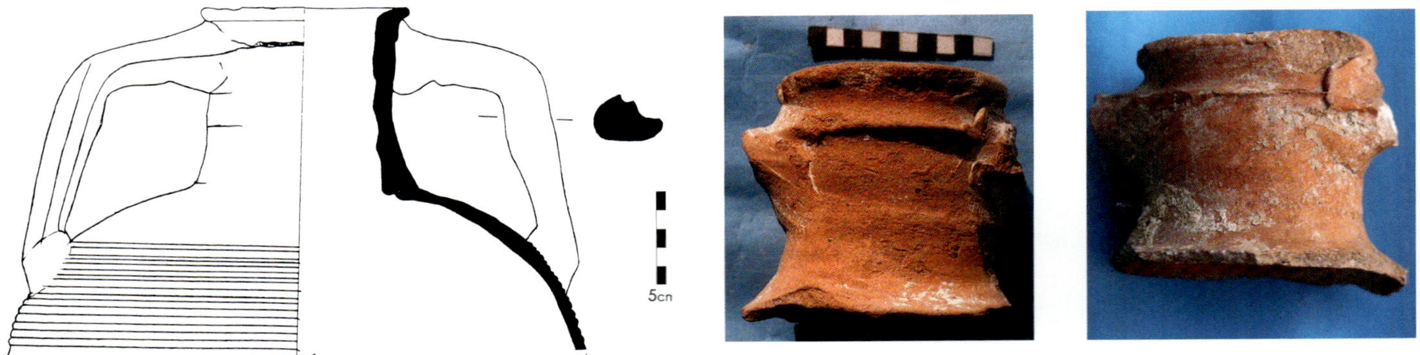

a b c

Fig. 3. LR1/B, Form 3 amphora, made of X fabric
a. from Amathous (AM1988/Baths Room 1. I] .
b. from the site of Agios Georghios Peghias, Paphos [AG93/43].
c. from Amathous (AM1988/FF4/POM XC).

distribution seems to follow the pattern of LR1/B Form 3, i.e. it is rather confined to the eastern Empire (the Black sea, Aegean islands, Palestine and Egypt) without being totally absent from the west.[51]

AMPHORA DISTRIBUTION IN CONTEXT

The first and second LR1 amphora generations (LR1/A and B) had a wide distribution all over the Mediterranean. The first generation was probably much better traded to the west than the second one, as numerous references from the western Mediterranean provinces show, thus creating an impression that they were mostly exported there.[52] Indeed, it is not strange that the Cilicians distributed the products of their province to international markets after the 5th century AD. Antioch was one of the most important cities of the Empire, and it is very probable that it kept its primary position as an economic and administrative centre, for almost a century after the establishment of Constantinople.[53] Merchants from Syria were very active in the western provinces,[54] whereas the traders of neighbouring Cilicia had always played a significant role in naval activities throughout antiquity, as shown, for example, in a fee inscription of the 5th century AD, found at Abydos.[55] In the text, where the taxes paid to Abydos by the merchants bringing food to Constantinople are specified, special privileges are given to Cilician merchants, the only ones identified by their place of origin. The expansion of the LR1/B production centres, in Cilicia itself and on Cyprus, should be interpreted in this context.

The strategic position of Cyprus, being the only large island of the region, was a significant factor that led to its special historical character throughout history. Most sea routes passed through the island, so the Cypriots were inherently involved in commercial activities taking place in the eastern Mediterranean and, especially, in the coastal administrative and commercial centres of the neighbouring mainland. In Late Antiquity, Cyprus belonged for a long time administratively to Antioch and was surely one of its major trading partners, together with Phoenicia, Cilicia and Palestine, as is clearly described in the Seleucia Port Inscription (6th century AD).[56] So the Cypriots had the privilege of participating in established commercial networks and finding ways to disperse their products through those networks.

Following the administrative and trade links of the island, which had always been very close to Cilicia, it was natural for Cypriot potters to manufacture the common amphora shapes of this area in order to ship their products, during the early decades of the period under consideration. Thus, *Optima Cyprus*[57] during Late Roman times could well have been considered as an important *depot* of the Empire, in terms of agricultural production. Indicative of this fact was the *Questura Exercitus*, a praetorian diocese that Justinian created in order to enhance the supply of his army at the Danubian borders (Nov. XLI, VIII cap. V, cp. L. H).[58] According to this, Cyprus was detached administratively from Antioch and formed a new independent diocese, together with Caria and the Aegean islands.

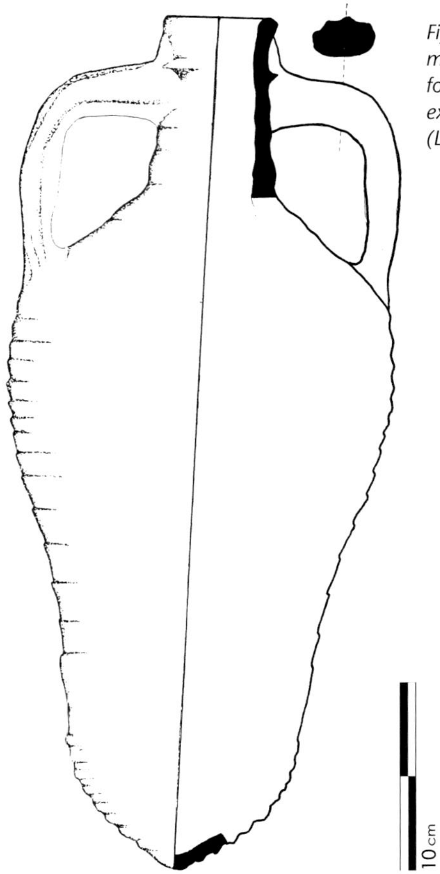

Fig. 4. LR1/C amphora made of Amathous fabric, found during rescue excavations in Limassol (LM1688.i).

The aforementioned different generations of LR1 amphorae provide an interesting insight in the archaeology of these administrative changes in the region: the limited production of the first generation of LR1s seems to be the Cypriot "contribution" to the boost in the diffusion of the oriental wines in the Mediterranean during 4th and 5th centuries AD. During the 6th century, the *Questura Exercitus* created a new status for the island, enhancing its agricultural production.[59] Thus, new workshops were established manufacturing the LR1/B Form 3 amphorae, which bear features of careless forming most probably because of an abrupt raise in demand. Pieri's suggestion that these workshops replaced the Cilician ones, or even that they were established by Cilician potters,[60] should probably be reconsidered for various reasons. The three different forms of the second generation of LR1 amphorae show how the rise in demand led to the contemporary expansion of production in Cilicia, Cyprus and perhaps elsewhere. As explained above, the morphology and the fabrics reported for LR1/B, Forms 1 and 2, indicate than they were produced in Cilicia, whereas the LR1/B Form 3, was produced in Cyprus. The difference in their distribution is also indicative of their parallel function, which served different needs; the 6th century Cypriot LR1s were associated with the *Questura Exercitus* whereas the Cilician ones continued to supply older trade networks and still active but less intense in the West, most probably because of the unstable political and economic situation at the borders of the Empire.[61]

The 7th century is generally characterized as an unsettled period, but as Marcus Rautman has attested "the status of Cyprus both as strategic outpost and agricultural supplier to the late Empire was increased",[62] being a safe point on the perilous sea routes of the eastern Mediterranean. Perhaps this situation enabled the continuity and the augmentation in its surplus export, even when almost all the surrounding commercial world was at war. The typical LR1 amphorae of the third generation are much smaller than the earlier ones, which, amongst other reasons, may be indicative of a recession in demands. The diversification in fabrics and types evidenced by the Yassi Ada wreck,[63] and also by LR1 production in the Aegean (e.g. the kiln at Cos),[64] show that other areas besides Cyprus were also involved in sea borne trade during the middle of the 7th century AD, using a common container to ship their products. As long as the dating of the Cilician workshops remains uncertain, it is difficult to establish the range of sources for the various LR1 amphorae of this generation.

51 Pieri 2005, 76.
52 Pieri 2005, 75.
53 McCormick 2002, 86.
54 Pieri 2005, 157-61.
55 Durliat & Guillou 1984.
56 Dagron 1985.
57 Thomsen 1995, 32.
58 Mitford 1980, 137; Lokin 1986, 7.
59 Lokin 1986; Megaw 1997, 351.
60 See *contra* Pieri 2007.
61 Morrisson & Sodini 2002.
62 Rautman 2000, 330.
63 Alfen 1996, 210-213.
64 Diamanti 2010b; Poulou-Papadimitriou & Didioumi 2010.

CONCLUSIONS

In order to acquire a clear picture of the insights that may be gained from amphora production, especially in the complex economic and administrative horizon of the Late Roman Empire, it is necessary to solve a "jigsaw puzzle" composed of many different pieces. Despite the progress in research, there is still a lot of work to be done before this goal can be achieved: more fieldwork, detailed publications and thorough analysis of the archaeological data of both production and consumption centres. Moreover, factors such as pottery tradition, administration and rules of commerce should be seriously considered in our efforts to understand the patterns of the amphora trade and distribution in the eastern Mediterranean during Late Antiquity.

Towards these ends, the history of the LR1 amphorae, the most common amphora type of that period, is highly important. The detailed typological classification of the Cypriot kiln repertoires – still to be further enhanced – may permit more refined identification of the LR1 amphorae in the trade centres within and beyond the island. Moreover, as amphora production was very sensitive to economic changes, the detailed history of production and export of the three generations of LR1 amphorae may be usefully compared with the main economic and political phases of Cypriot history during Late Antiquity.

ACKNOWLEDGEMENTS

I would like to express my sincere thanks to the following archaeologists for giving me permission to study and publish the amphora material discussed in this paper: Prof. Demetrios Michaelides, Prof. Charalambos Bakirtzis, the late Michalis Louloupis, Dr. Pavlos Flourentzos, Dr. Eleni Procopiou and Dr. Demos Christou. I also thank Mark Lawall for his useful remarks and Bernard Knapp for the corrections in English.

Amphorae and Underwater Survey: Making Sense of Late Roman Trade from Scattered Sherds and Shipwrecks

BY JUSTIN LEIDWANGER

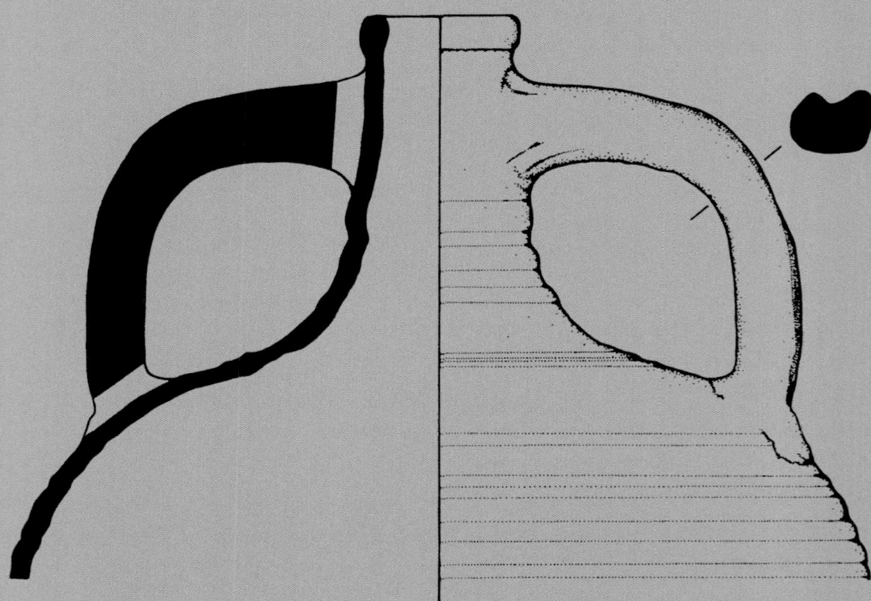

Amphorae and Underwater Survey: Making Sense of Late Roman Trade from Scattered Sherds and Shipwrecks

BY JUSTIN LEIDWANGER

Transport amphorae provide the majority of archaeological material from underwater contexts off Cyprus. Their recording, analysis, and interpretation offer a potentially unparalleled contribution to the study of the island's maritime exchange. In general, shipwrecks provide the most common contexts in which large assemblages of contemporaneous amphorae are found, but off the coast of Cyprus, the number of known ancient wrecks remains relatively small.[1] These amphora cargos provide some of the most detailed evidence for the mechanisms and agents involved with ancient trade. The only fully excavated wreck to date from Cypriot waters, the well-preserved early Hellenistic ship off the island's northern coast near Kyrenia, demonstrates vividly how much can be gleaned from even a single small vessel: the size and scale of a merchant ship, its broad zone of operation, glimpses of the vessel's earlier commercial life, daily routines of its sailors, a possible itinerary for its last voyage, and even a potential cause for its loss.[2]

Recent fieldwork off Cyprus' typically shallow coast has indicated that discrete, well-preserved sites comprising mounds of intact amphorae like that at Kyrenia are the occasional exceptions to more commonly scattered groups of broken jars. Often these poorly articulated assemblages cannot represent the remains of shipwrecks. While some sites can be attributed to port or anchorage activity, others are marked only by carpets of sherds from different periods and depositions not associated with nearby settlements. Such sites necessitate a rather different approach to underwater survey, recording, and interpretation that contextualizes the ceramic evidence alongside shipwrecks (the focus of nautical archaeology) and submerged site remains (the focus of harbour and coastal archaeology). Drawing in part on developments in survey methodology on land, this paper outlines some of the elements of a maritime archaeological approach that addresses the varied types of ceramic contexts and yields socioeconomic insights that complement those of large-scale investigations across regional landscapes. Using case studies from Cyprus' shallow coastal waters, I situate the varied assortment of underwater amphora finds within a broader diachronic study of the island's ancient maritime economy.

MAKING SENSE OF UNDERWATER ARTEFACT SCATTERS

The traditional focus on ships and their cargos as the primary unit of archaeological analysis in the underwater record can lose sight of amphorae within their broader landscape of maritime activity. Looking past the 'wreck site' and toward the individual artefact in this way opens up a different range of methodological challenges as well as interpretative possibilities. A lone amphora, whether on land or underwater, permits the establishment of some economic tie (albeit perhaps indirectly, and assuming the jar can be identified) with an area of agricultural production elsewhere, around the island or farther abroad. Interpretation of the amphora or any other ceramic depends on the ability to identify its form and typological association and to recognize and understand the context of its deposition. Since ceramics in the underwater record represent the remains of activities undertaken as part of life on board ancient vessels, they present a maritime complement to (but not a replacement for) the wide-ranging socioeconomic data derived from terrestrial survey.

On a rudimentary level, ceramic identifications may be complicated by the long-term environmental effects of underwater contexts on the appearance of fabrics. In terms of formal recognition, the submerged material record is at least as advantageous as the survey record on land. Pottery found underwater is generally more intact and often includes significant diagnostic features that allow for easier identification than many comparable survey finds on land, which are frequently heavily worn and often dominated by small body sherds lacking diagnostic elements. Even broken and scattered amphora fragments found in dynamic shallow environments often retain enough diagnostic features for assigning a type, except in instances where marine encrustation renders this impossible. Moreover, routine preservation of sufficiently large fragments could in many instances allow for relatively simple and potentially meaningful quantification in situ by underwater survey.[3]

Visibility issues, which severely affect detection of

materials and have long been a focus of discussion on land,[4] are normally less problematic on the seabed, although alluvial sediments and longshore deposition can at times bury artefacts from view. The relationship between surface finds and subsurface remains, one of the more complex challenges in survey methodology,[5] is likely to be fairly reliable, at least for near-shore deposits where dynamic waters can move, mix, cover and uncover finds continuously, especially during the eastern Mediterranean winter. At times, currents and wave action can also disperse finds from shallow but discrete sites like wrecks or within larger port or anchorage assemblages. Still, in the case of successive seasons of survey in the shallow waters of Avdimou Bay and Dreamer's Bay (see below), quantitative differences were noted in the material record over the course of successive years' visits, but the ceramic assemblages never appeared qualitatively different. Greater or lesser numbers of ceramic finds might be visible on different visits to these sites, but the general character of the assemblages – their chronological and geographical range of materials – were never significantly altered by this changing visibility.

Since the underwater record reflects the breadth of seafaring activities that contribute an archaeological signature, the overall corpus of amphorae, other pottery and artefacts recorded by underwater survey generally matches the range of artefacts from ship assemblages: cargo amphorae, some coarse wares, occasional fine wares, as well as anchors, ship's equipment, etc. For non-shipwreck assemblages, however, the relative proportions of these different categories of material should be altered depending on the particular activities undertaken at or around the sites. For example, shallow reefs where ships tend to founder may reveal higher percentages of amphorae hastily jettisoned to lighten the load. By contrast, casual dumping by vessels at anchor may result in a more complete range of not only cargo amphorae emptied or broken en route, but also worn out shipboard ceramics, tools and other unusable utensils.

When not associated with shipwreck contexts, individual amphorae underwater are most often found at stops like anchorages and harbours, or around reefs, promontories and other navigational hazards.[6] Some of the best evidence for a port town's period of maritime activity is provided by the datable underwater assemblage from its harbour or nearby anchorage. The material assemblages at

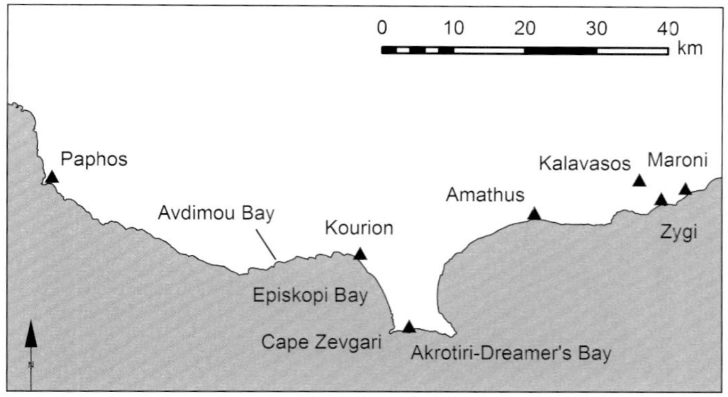

Map of the southern Cyprus showing areas of survey as well as relevant sites and features mentioned in the text.

maritime hazards, on the other hand, reflect the gradual accumulation of debris from passing ships, highlighting the relative intensities and different maritime connections along a particular route. The material records at each of these types of sites merit closer attention.

HARBOUR AND ANCHORAGE ASSEMBLAGES: AKROTIRI-DREAMER'S BAY AND MARONI-*TSAROUKKAS*

The site of Dreamer's Bay, on the south coast of the Akrotiri Peninsula, the southern shore's most conspicuous feature, provides a clear example of the connection between underwater finds from a built harbour and an associated multi-period settlement (Map). The site has long been

1 The exact number of ancient shipwrecks off the coast of Cyprus is not entirely clear. Parker (1992) lists 15, but some of these seem unlikely to be actual wreck sites, and several additional wrecks from recent investigations should be added to this tally. Even with some additions, the number remains small in comparison with some of the more thoroughly explored coastlines of the eastern Mediterranean: i.e. Turkey, Israel, and Greece.

2 Katzev 2005. The recently initiated excavation of the late Classical Mazotos shipwreck off the island's south coast hold much promise for detailed study of another well-preserved site: see Demesticha 2009; 2011.

3 Orton *et al.* 1993, 166-181.

4 Banning 2002, 46-48.

5 Millett 2000.

6 Material can, of course, also be discarded on the open sea, whether in a storm or simply as part of routine activity. This practice may help explain, for example, the phenomenon of the "amphora alley" observed by the survey at Skerki Bank: Foley & Ballard 2004.

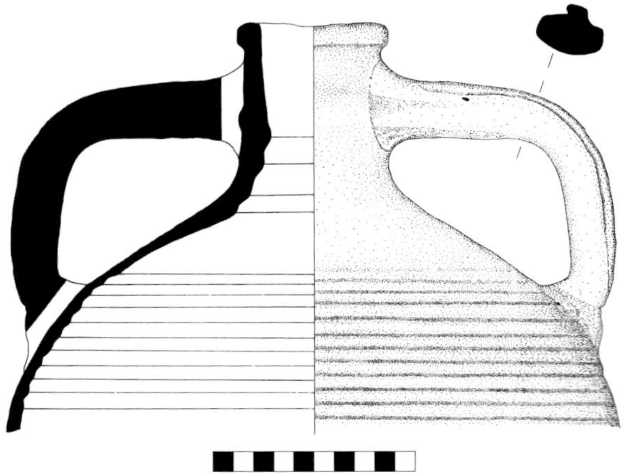

Fig. 1. Early series LR1 amphora (EBS-04-019), probably 4th or 5th century AD, from Akrotiri-Dreamer's Bay.

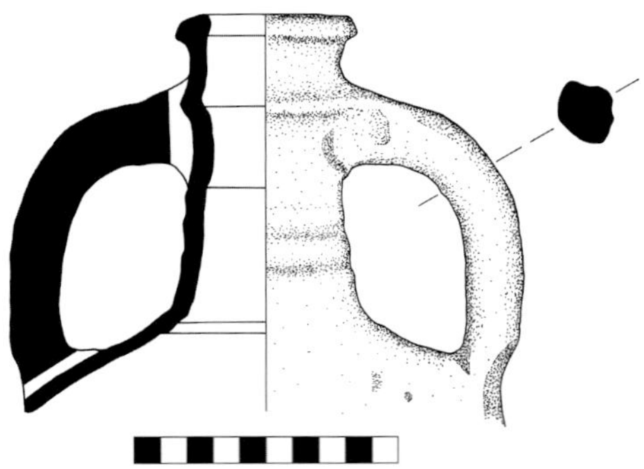

Fig. 2. LR1 amphora (EBS-04-031) from Akrotiri-Dreamer's Bay.

known as a Late Roman settlement on the basis of the predominant surface finds dating from that period. In their more recent analysis of the surface pottery, however, John R. Leonard and Stella Demesticha have noted evidence for earlier Roman occupation, including hints of activity stretching back perhaps as early as the late 4th century BC.[7] No artefact counts were undertaken, but preliminary underwater survey here in 2004-2005 revealed a broadly consistent chronological representation, with ceramic finds spanning from the Hellenistic through the Late Roman period.[8] The later end of this spectrum accounted for the vast majority of finds, particularly in the immediate vicinity of the harbour. Whereas surface survey of the town has detected primarily the last period of occupation with only intermittent traces of earlier activity, the underwater remains confirm that not only was the Late Roman era the last major period of activity, but it was likely also the busiest for local maritime commerce.[9] A few imports from the southern Levant, western Mediterranean, Aegean and Black Sea are outnumbered by various forms of LR1 amphorae, some perhaps from nearby but others almost certainly produced along the island's more distant shores and the neighboring mainland in Cilicia (Figs. 1-4).[10] The probable abandonment of habitation at the settlement toward the end of late antiquity is mirrored by the silence of the underwater ceramic record after the 7th century.

Apart from the elaborate facilities at Dreamer's Bay or the island's capital of Paphos, simple anchorages provide access to exchange on a regular or in some cases a seasonal basis.[11] Typically set apart from major urban areas and generally lacking in built harbour infrastructure, these opportunistic facilities offer material records that provide an index of the economic integration of secondary settlements and even outlying areas.[12] This seems to be the case, for example, at several sites along the coast near Maroni-*Tsaroukkas*, where anchorages saw intermittent use from the Bronze Age through late antiquity. Manning's preliminary snorkel survey in the shallows here brought to light scattered ceramic finds that included LR1 amphorae and other Late Roman pottery. Together with a variety of undated stone anchors, these finds speak to the role of simple maritime shelters.[13] During the particularly prosperous Late Roman period, these anchorages were well-situated to take advantage of traffic up the adjacent Vasilikos and Maroni Valleys.[14] In the Vasilikos Valley, Rautman has demonstrated the vitality of a settlement of perhaps 600 inhabitants at Kalavasos-*Kopetra*, where the rich ceramic repertoire and range of other imports point to the prosperity of a second-tier market town and its probable function as a local redistributive center for satellite villages throughout the valley.[15] Along the coast just west of Tsaroukkas, a kiln for LR1 amphorae at Zygi-*Petrini* speaks to possible models for the packaging and transport of agricultural goods in the vicinity of the anchorage. In addition to meeting the demands of local farmers along the coast, the kiln site may have allowed the fertile valley's

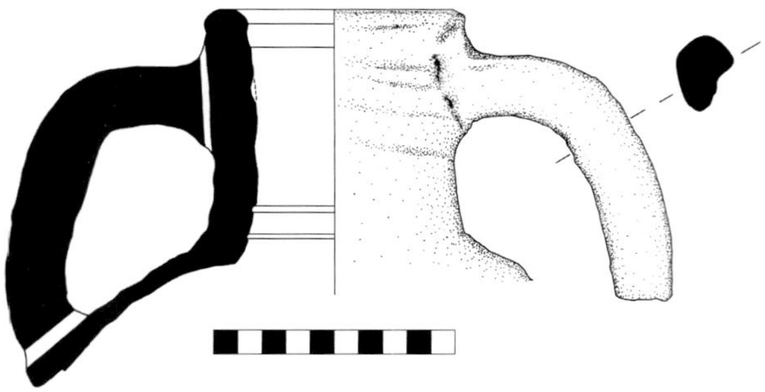

Fig. 3. Late series LR1 amphora (EBS-04-032), probably 6th or early 7th century AD, from Akrotiri-Dreamer's Bay.

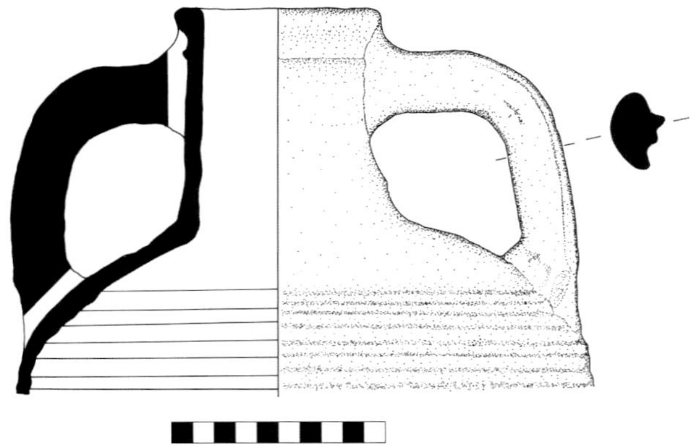

Fig. 4. Late series LR1 amphora (EBS-04-028), probably 6th or early 7th century AD, from Akrotiri-Dreamer's Bay.

agricultural goods to be transported overland or downriver for repackaging in containers suitable for shipment over longer distances by sea. Alternatively, or additionally, empty jars may have been sent up river to sites like Kopetra, where they could be filled with the produce of inland farmers. Systematic documentation of the underwater ceramic record at anchorages along this stretch of coast might yield a quantified material record for comparison with finds from urban centres as well as rural sites identified through survey in the valleys.[16]

ASSEMBLAGES NEAR NAVIGATIONAL HAZARDS: CAPE ZEVGARI

Analyses of ceramic assemblages from harbours and anchorages provide a maritime counterpart to records of long-term maritime trade attested on land at coastal sites. Assemblages near promontories or dangerous rocks and reefs, by contrast, provide another useful gauge of broader trends in the island's economic history. Such evidence avoids the chronological limits imposed by the specific periods of activity associated with harbour or anchorage sites, and provides a complementary and more fully diachronic view of coastal commerce. Several navigational hazards charted on nautical maps of Cyprus and occasionally mentioned as hazards even in antiquity provide opportunities for studying changing patterns of maritime trade through time. For example, early underwater work conducted in the 1970s at Cape Kiti by the team from the Hala Sultan Tekke excavation project brought to light a wide range of amphorae, anchors, and other finds. The dates of this material span from perhaps as early as the Bronze Age through at least late antiquity, overlapping but also far exceeding the chronological

7 Leonard & Demesticha 2004, 198-199.
8 Leidwanger 2005, 269-272; Leidwanger & Howitt-Marshall 2006, 14-15.
9 Leidwanger 2005, 270.
10 Leonard & Demesticha 2004, 189-190 and 199 have raised the possibility of local LR1 production.
11 For the harbour at Paphos, see Hohlfelder 1995.
12 Note the evidence marshaled by Leonard (1995a; 2005), Leonard & Demesticha (2004), and Howitt-Marshall (2003) for a complex network of ports associated not only with major urban areas, but distributed densely along the island's various coast.
13 Manning *et al.* 2002, 118-121.
14 Manning *et al.* 2000; Manning *et al.* 2002, 77-79; Rautman 2003, 241.
15 See Rautman in this volume; 2000; 2003. Imports from abroad include most notably agricultural goods in LR1 amphorae from the mainland of Syria and Cilicia and roof tiles that seem to have been picked up en route along the east coast of the island. Late Roman D (Cypriot Red Slip) wares likewise seem to have been accompanied by another type of bulk roof tile on their short journey around the south coast from the Paphos area, a suggestion now further supported by finds underwater at Dreamer's Bay, where a number of roof tiles were recorded exhibiting the same distinctive form, fabric and signature documented at Kopetra and formerly as well at Kourion: see Leidwanger 2005, 270-271.
16 Manning *et al.* 2000, 237 and 254 fig. 12.1.

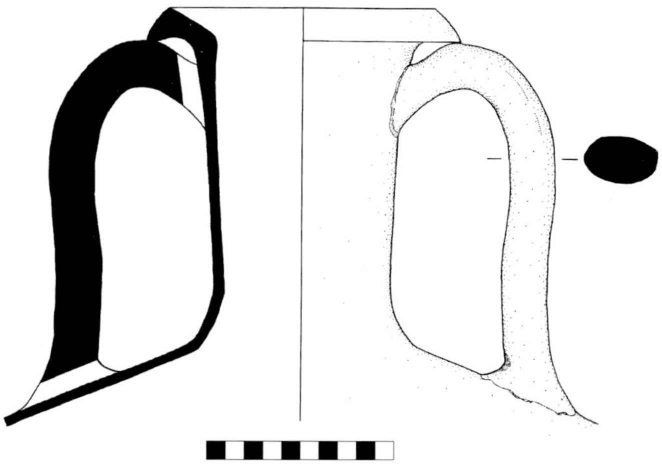

Fig. 5. Late Classical or early Hellenistic eastern Aegean amphora (EBS-03-028) from Cape Zevgari.

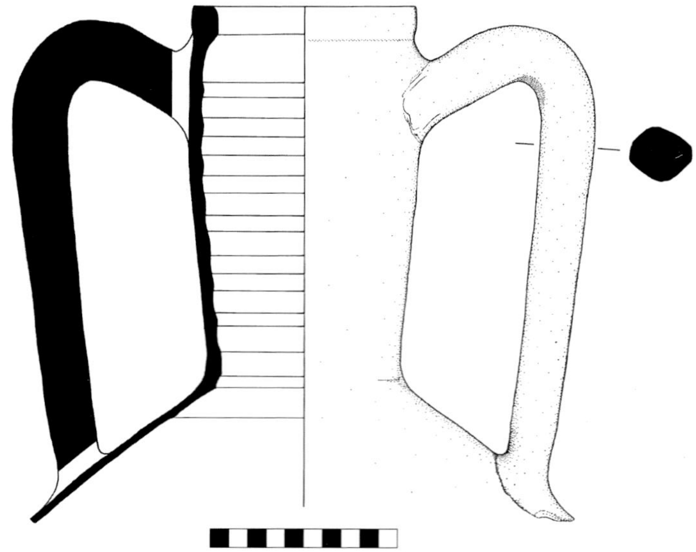

Fig. 6. Rhodian-style amphora (EBS-03-066), probably 3rd century BC, from Cape Zevgari.

bounds of activity attested in the ceramic record at any particular nearby settlement.[17]

Cape Zevgari, located at the southwest tip of the Akrotiri Peninsula, likely served as a landmark for prehistoric and historic sailors passing by the Bronze Age, Greco-Roman, and Medieval sites in the area.[18] Sharp rocks and low-lying reefs here extend for several hundred meters from shore. A trail of torn copper sheathing left behind by a probable 19th-century vessel that came to rest on the seabed just to the east of these reefs attests to the navigational dangers presented by the shallows.[19] The Akrotiri Peninsula's topography has changed somewhat since antiquity. An east-west passage existed until perhaps sometime early in the Roman era, setting off the southern tip (including Dreamer's Bay) as a near-shore island.[20] While this passage through the peninsula would have allowed early mariners the option of avoiding the dangers at Cape Zevgari, it is apparent from earlier finds here and at Dreamer's Bay that ships rounded the cape even before the channel closed.[21]

Recording of the ceramics at Cape Zevgari was undertaken during the summers of 2003 and 2004.[22] Amphorae documented throughout a large area extending southwest for 250 m from the headland provide an index of trade running from the late Archaic or Classical period through at least late antiquity. Elevated levels of deposition are clearly indicated for the Late Hellenistic or Early Roman era as well as the Late Roman period, presumably reflecting increased coastal commerce during these centuries. The most notable early finds include fragments of at least six basket-handle amphorae, probably of late Archaic or Classical date.[23] Scattered remnants of a few mushroom-rim jars, the forms of which are probably eastern Aegean in origin and best situated in the early Hellenistic era (Fig. 5),[24] were recorded along with a considerable number of rims, bases and handles of early Hellenistic through early Roman Rhodian-style amphorae (Fig. 6).[25] Hellenistic and Roman Koan or Koan-style (a.k.a. pseudo-Koan, sub-Koan, Dressel 2-4) jars recognizable by their distinctive bifid handles (Fig. 7) are among the most numerous late Hellenistic or Early Roman types documented in the area.[26] A relative dearth of jars positively attributable to the Mid-Roman centuries (late 2nd to early 4th) is conspicuous, but this is followed chronologically by large numbers of Late Roman ceramics, especially LR1 amphorae representing early and late varieties and a range of subtypes (Figs. 8-10). Other less frequent late finds include LR4 jars from the Gaza/Ashkelon region of the southern Levant and the distinctive carrot-shaped Sinopean-style amphorae.[27] Even later finds are few and outside the scope of the present discussion, but include several Medieval and later glazed sherds.

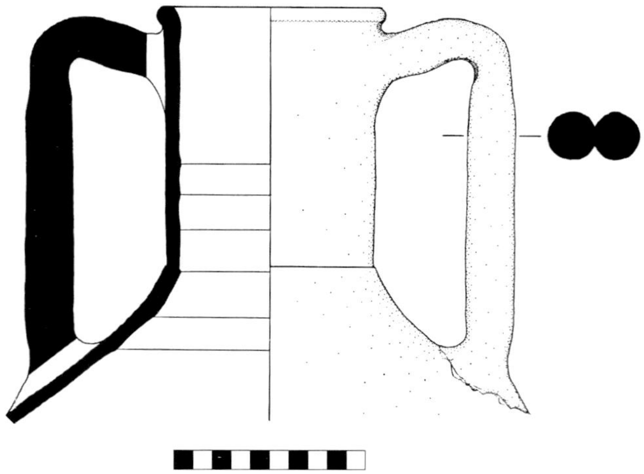

Fig. 7. Koan-style amphora (EBS-03-065), probably 2nd century BC, from Cape Zevgari.

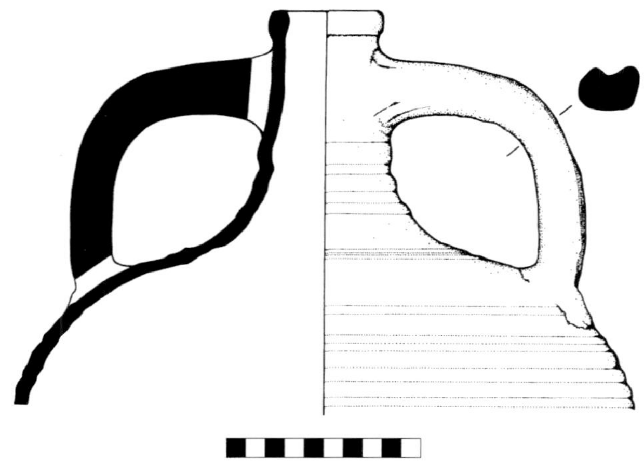

Fig. 8. Early series Late Roman amphora (EBS-03-044), probably 4th or 5th century AD, from Cape Zevgari.

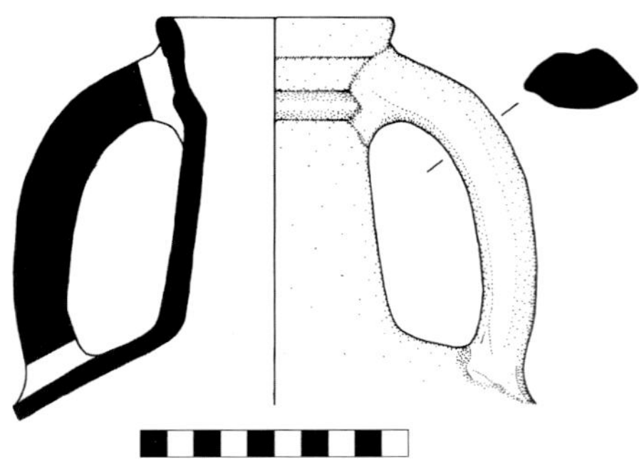

Fig. 9. Late Roman amphora (EBS-03-052) from Cape Zevgari.

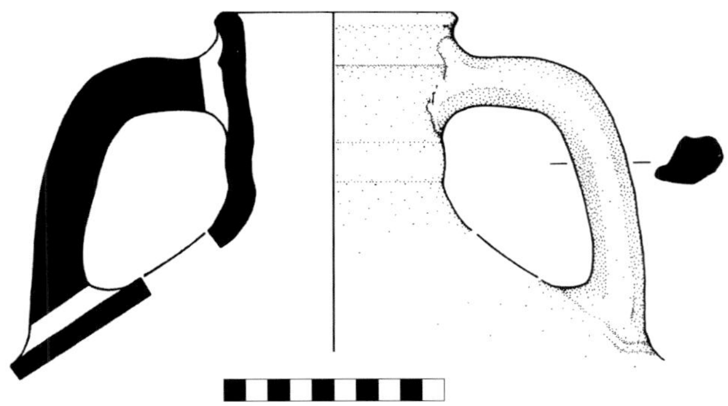

Fig. 10. Late series LR1 amphora (EBS-03-027), probably 6th or early 7th century AD, from Cape Zevgari.

17 Engvig & Åström 1975, 20-21; McCaslin 1978, 130-132 (who also connects the evidence of many of the stone anchors in the area as indication of significant Bronze Age traffic); Engvig & Beichmann 1984, 181-182.

18 See generally Swiny 1982.

19 Thanks to the British Sub-Aqua Club at Akrotiri for sharing the location of this modern wreck with the author, who had the chance to visit the site in the summer of 2003.

20 Leonard 2005, 516-522.

21 Leonard & Demesticha 2004, 191-192 and 198; Leidwanger 2004, 24-25; Leidwanger 2005, 269-272.

22 For a preliminary report, see Leidwanger 2004, 24-26. A comprehensive publication of the ceramic and other finds from Cape Zevgari is currently in preparation.

23 Sagona 1982, 88-90.

24 Lawall 2004, 451-453.

25 Empereur & Hesnard 1987, 18-20; Empereur & Picon 1989, 224-225.

26 Empereur & Hesnard 1987, 22-23; Empereur & Picon 1989, 225-230; Papuci-Władyka 1997, 52-54. These forms, however, can be difficult to date with precision in fragmentary condition.

27 For LR4 jars, see Majcherek 1995; Pieri 2005; for carrot-shaped amphorae produced in the area of Sinope, see generally Kassab Tezgör 2010.

Fig. 11. LR1 amphora in situ from the wreck at Cape Zevgari.

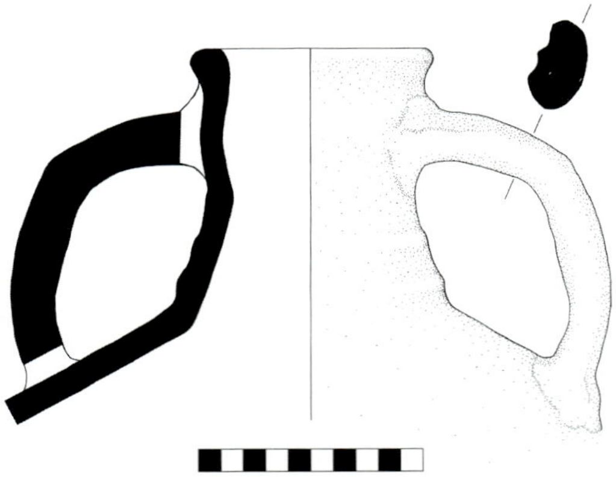

Fig. 12. LR1 amphora (EBS-03-067) from the wreck at Cape Zevgari.

The particularly large assemblages of late Hellenistic or Early Roman amphorae on the one hand, and Late Roman amphorae on the other, merit further attention. The primary aim of artefact study at Cape Zevgari was to sample broadly from the visible ceramic groups on the seabed; such sampling most often yielded materials from these particular periods. The phenomenon cannot be accidental, and the discrepancy between the finds from different periods likely reflects a meaningful pattern in ancient maritime commerce rather than simple vagaries of archaeological survey, like visibility. The wide range of differently dated ceramic forms, moreover, argues against the possibility that the remains represent one or two particularly diverse shipwrecked or jettisoned cargos. Although earlier periods register at a reduced level, such as Archaic/Classical and earlier Hellenistic, no other period approaches the mark of volume or diversity left here by the predominant late Hellenistic/Early Roman and Late Roman amphorae. The contrast between the finds of these two periods and those of the immediately previous and successive eras (especially the Mid-Roman era) is dramatic.

Also of interest to the present study is the primarily regional and local character of the Late Roman ceramics at Cape Zevgari. These suggest an overall picture of late antique ties centered in the eastern Mediterranean rather than long-distance routes. The range of subtypes and fabrics of LR1 jars and their general frequency underscore the island's regional maritime commercial connections with Cilicia and perhaps northwest Syria; the LR4 jars point to another less pronounced but still significant relationship with the southern Levant.

TWO LATE ROMAN WRECKS: CAPE ZEVGARI AND AVDIMOU BAY

Studies of amphorae from harbours, anchorages, and areas of navigational hazards provide opportunities for quantifying and qualifying ancient trade: specifically the activity associated with urban centres and activity along long-term sailing routes. If scattered finds at such sites as Cape Zevgari suggest that the Late Roman period saw a flourishing of maritime exchange, especially on a regional scale, what types of individual ventures defined this commercial network? Two small wrecks, recently recorded in the Episkopi Bay area, allow us to elucidate certain details of the exchange mechanisms at work during late antiquity.

Just west of the dangerous reefs at Cape Zevgari, a small wreck of the 5th or 6th century was recorded at a depth of 5 to 7 m (Map).[28] Strewn across a ledge, the assemblage includes at least 150 LR1 amphorae (Figs 11-12). Only a few largely intact examples were found, and all were too covered in marine concretion to be removed for additional study. The site is located at some distance – perhaps 100 m – from the jettison deposition at the reef, with little archaeological material visible in the intervening area that could connect this group of amphorae to the same overall

Fig. 13. LR4 amphora (EBS-05-035) from the wreck at Avdimou Bay.

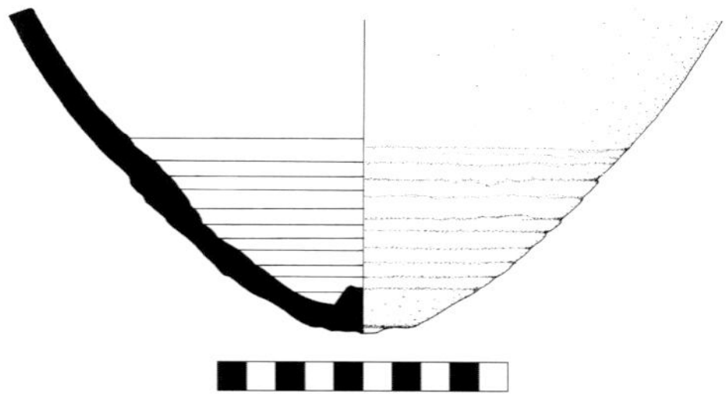

Fig. 14. LR4 amphora base (EBS-05-001) from the wreck at Avdimou Bay.

scatter. The wreck's location suggests that the reef played some role in the sinking of the vessel. If this is the case, a few of the LR1 amphorae from the reef could reflect the vessel's first spill of cargo or jettison in an effort to lighten its load. It seems highly unlikely that a single shipwreck could have accounted for the entire range of forms – separated at times by several centuries – scattered across this large area. The typical LR1 amphora from the Cape Zevgari wreck exhibits a neck that is conical near its base, but bulges slightly where the handles are attached, along with an everted rolled rim with no well-defined lower ridge. The jars are approximately 0.60 m in height and nearly 0.35 m at their greatest width. They display the relatively wide proportions as well as the wide neck (almost 0.11 m in diameter) that point to a date in the 5th or perhaps early 6th century.[29]

A second shipwreck, located in the shallow waters of Avdimou Bay, almost 20 km northwest of Cape Zevgari (Fig. 1), includes the scattered remains of at least 30 LR4 jars from the Gaza/Ashkelon region (Figs. 13-14).[30] The rims are all quite low, though some are marked by a lower groove than others; they are generally thickened, rounded and slightly everted, sometimes flattened on top but otherwise poorly defined. The bases range from shallower with a less defined point to slightly conical. At least two examples of early, narrow-necked LR1 amphorae were recorded among the scatter, as well as three millstones that may have served as ballast, if not as cargo.[31] The circumscribed area and general lack of apparently intrusive materials make it probable that this site represents the remains of a shipwreck or fully dumped cargo rather than casual deposition associated with the anchorage. The assemblage should be dated to the 5th or early 6th century, perhaps best around the mid- to late 5th century.[32] The small size of the site would seem to reflect a modest merchant venture, but the accessibility of the area seems likely to have resulted in some degree of ancient or modern salvage of a site that was initially more extensive.

These two wrecks provide glimpses of merchant vessels that seem quite small and likely operated within a relatively circumscribed area, at least if the surface survey of the more extensive Cape Zevgari wreck is reasonably indicative of the overall character and size of the original assemblage. The cargo of agricultural goods packed in LR1 jars points to traffic with other parts of the island and beyond to the mainland of Cilicia and northwest Syria. In order for the ship to have struck these near-shore reefs, it may have rounded the cape too closely while coasting between the island's many harbours and simple anchorages, perhaps including nearby Akrotiri-Dreamer's Bay. Likewise, the small merchant vessel that came to rest in Avdimou Bay presents a regional exchange network that extended from the island to the southern Levantine coast. It is impossible to determine if the diverse LR4 amphora assemblage points to direct trade or a western coastal circuit of cabotage from Levantine to Cypriot ports, but the pair of LR1 amphorae would seem to indicate an earlier stop. Alternatively, the

28 Leidwanger 2007, 308-311.
29 Pieri 2005, 75-76.
30 Leidwanger 2007, 311-313.
31 Pieri 2005, 70-74.
32 Cf. Majcherek 1995, 168-169 (Forms 3 and 4).

vessel may have been sailing eastward before the seasonal winds and longshore currents from Paphos to the Levant, as Kingsley has proposed for the final voyage of what may be a similar LR4- and LR5/6-laden wreck at Dor (Israel), whose final voyage likewise may have included a Cypriot port.[33]

CONCLUSION: FROM MARITIME MATERIAL ASSEMBLAGES TO ECONOMIC TRENDS IN LATE ROMAN CYPRUS

Each of these three contexts – maritime facilities, navigational hazards, and shipwrecks – provides a window into the transport stage of economic exchange. Through a close reading of different ceramic contexts, these sites complement each other in the development of a model for the trends and mechanisms of maritime trade. In the case of Cyprus, a comparative view of the various maritime ceramic assemblages helps us to investigate the structure and scale of seaborne economic interconnections during antiquity. It also allows us to analyse the potential relationship between the intensity of exchange in different periods – here the Late Roman era in particular – and its occurrence alongside certain patterns of urban and rural settlement, infrastructure development, and the exploitation of the countryside.

Close study of transport amphorae, viewed through the specific cultural processes that create different underwater contexts, provides a basis for comparison among assemblages and with archaeological survey evidence on land. The ceramic record underwater at sites like harbour basins and navigational dangers supplements the general diachronic observations that can be made regarding economic connections and prosperity from assemblages on land. This material record also allows a range of additional insights into a stage of the ancient economy not directly visible in the ceramic consumption trends on land: maritime distribution. Although the essential results of the transport of goods by sea may often be inferred from finds on land (i.e. through the recognition of objects imported from outside the island), the maritime material record serves as a window into the mechanisms behind this commerce and communication. Artefacts in transit recorded at harbours, anchorages, shipwrecks, and other scatters can inform our understanding of the types of ventures, routes and patterns of sailing, the interaction of economic networks, and the scales of exchange that characterized passing seaborne traffic during different periods. Seen in this light, three broad points emerge from the survey evidence that are worth emphasizing regarding Cyprus' Late Roman maritime economy.

First, the island's relative prosperity during the Late Roman period is immediately apparent in the underwater record. This should come as no surprise in light of recent fieldwork on the island,[34] but the maritime record provides additional evidence and new detail. Survey across Cyprus has revealed intensification of settlement in the countryside together with a reasonably high level of prosperity explicitly beyond the largest urban centres, in second-tier towns like Kopetra.[35] Other inland and rural sites testify to some affluence, in part sustained by significant quantities of imports that penetrated well beyond the dozen or so more commercially accessible coastal sites.[36] In the hinterland of Kourion, not far east of Avdimou Bay, the Late Roman period was the densest recorded in the ceramic record, and the majority of farmsteads here seem to have been active into the 7th century.[37] The maritime trends measured at Cape Zevgari – at least with respect to broad intensity of exchange – correlate well with the developments in what Rautman has dubbed the "busy countryside of Late Roman Cyprus".[38]

The maritime material record allows us to contextualize the precise relationship between the prosperity of this era and the economic situation during the periods before and after, a trend that is perhaps less clear overall on land, and certainly controversial. In his demonstration of the potential limitations of uneven survey data, David K. Pettegrew challenges some of the fundamental evidence for the Late Roman settlement "explosion" observed in surveys in Greece and elsewhere in the eastern Mediterranean, including Cyprus.[39] He argues that the differential visibility of body sherds results in over-representation of highly recognizable grooved Late Roman amphorae and other utilitarian wares. Such quantification bias in turn leads to an unwarranted reckoning of the period as one of unprecedented prosperity and settlement boom.[40] Given the extent of preservation of diagnostic ceramics and the relative ease of their identification underwater, quantifying amphorae from maritime contexts on the basis of well-preserved rims, bases or handles can help to yield diachronic economic data that is less subject to biases produced by poor visibility and worn sherds on land. The high degree of diagnostic preservation and generally limited range of ceramic forms found at underwater sites also facilitate their identification and division into narrower periods, allowing the tracking of finer trends in local maritime economic history. In the present case study of Cyprus, the amphorae found underwater are sufficiently diagnostic – and the typologies sufficiently precise – to reveal a discrepancy between the Mid-Roman record and that of the Early and Late Roman periods.[41] In light of this detail, the underwater data set from Cape Zevgari suggests that the exchange in goods by sea around the southern part of the island grew from a low in the Mid-Roman period to a new high during the Late Roman period, starting perhaps in the 4th century. The volume of material in the maritime record also suggests that Late Roman economic activity may have surpassed that of the Late Hellenistic and Early Roman eras. Since populations did not stop making amphorae and consuming amphora-borne commodities during the Mid-Roman period,[42] the dearth of Mid-Roman finds in the underwater record likely reflects the general economic decline during this period visible from regional surveys across the island, a phenomenon that may be related to a temporary retreat from a more widespread Hellenistic and Early Roman settlement.[43]

A second point concerns economic geography and the mechanisms of maritime exchange during this period of prosperity. Kristina Winther-Jacobsen has suggested that "the world around the island had shrunk in the Late Roman period",[44] and this proposition seems appropriate in light of evidence from the present study area. Imports from outside the eastern edge of the Mediterranean are scarce, giving the underwater material record at this corner of the island a decidedly local and regional appearance. But if the Cypriot economic sphere had shrunk in geographical terms during late antiquity, it had apparently also intensified in its regional scope. Both the shipwrecks as well as the scattered material from Cape Zevgari seem to illustrate a Late Roman economic network in which merchant cargos of agricultural staples traveled among the built harbours of larger port towns as well as the simple anchorages that characterized smaller outlying and rural communities along the island's coast. Although occasional imports from outside the region appear, the island's overall economic neighborhood is largely relegated to parts of the nearby coastal mainland, particularly Cilicia and northwest Syria but extending as far as the southern Levant.

A third and final point concerns the particular ventures involved in this exchange. For the short hauls suggested above, small boats probably facilitated the primary exchange of agricultural products across this local and regional Late Roman maritime landscape.[45] Situated some distance from land in difficult waters, the Cape Zevgari wreck provides a general sense of the size and geographic range of one of these small ventures: a ship carrying agricultural goods in something over 150 amphorae all drawn from just a short sail away. Wrecks along the island's other coasts present a broadly similar picture, including as many as five late antique cargos recorded at Cape Andreas, the island's northeast tip opposite the Cilician and northwest Syrian mainland. Mostly comprised of LR1 amphorae, along with roof tiles and occasional (Cypriot?) LR2b/LR13 amphorae, these assemblages seem to represent similarly small wrecks with a decidedly regional scale.[46] The material record preserved in shallow waters centres on coastal maritime activity. Whether a different model characterized offshore ventures cannot be determined until future survey extends into these deeper waters. The assemblages currently available for study appear small in size and restricted in geographical scope of operation.

The underwater record reveals one thin slice of the ancient economy, but these unique contexts offer a useful complement to survey observations made on the basis of

---

33 Kingsley 2002, 85-86.
34 See generally Rautman 2003, 247-255.
35 See Rautman, this volume.
36 Papacostas 2001, 115-121.
37 Swiny & Mavromatis 2000, 438-439.
38 Rautman 2000.
39 For Greece, see Alcock 1993, 37-49; for Cyprus, see Rautman 2000.
40 Pettegrew 2007, based on the Roman ceramic data set of the Eastern Korinthia Archaeological Survey: see Tartaron *et al.* 2006.
41 Continued research into Roman amphora typologies in the eastern Mediterranean is an area of particular interest at present and promises to help refine further these chronological trends: e.g. Reynolds 2005.
42 It is clear from the manufacture and distribution of so-called "pinched handle amphorae" that agricultural products continued to be transported in amphorae: see Williams & Lund, this volume.
43 E.g. in the Vasilikos Valley, see Rautman 2000, 323. For other areas of Cyprus, see Lund 1993a, 140-143; Leonard Jr. 1987, 100; Bekker-Nielsen *et al.* 1995, 22-24.
44 Jacobsen 2004, 144.
45 Horden & Purcell 2000, 142 and 365.
46 Green 1973, 153-163: Sites 12, 16, 17, 24 and 28. Sites 17 and 24 may be two discrete parts of the same wreck, given their proximity, similarity of finds and date.

ceramic assemblages on land. Perhaps most important is the role of the maritime material record in providing a window into the structures and processes that characterized the distribution stage of the ancient economy. Continued study of shipwrecks alongside the interpretation of a broader range of underwater archaeological materials holds considerable potential for expanding knowledge of the economic processes and transport mechanisms involved in the seaborne movement of goods. These issues are more difficult to trace, even indirectly, using quantified data from land survey and excavation, but they are nonetheless crucial to our understanding of the broader contours of the ancient economy.

ACKNOWLEDGEMENTS

The author would like to thank the workshop organizers and volume editors for their invitation to participate in the Athens meeting and their insightful critiques, as well as the workshop participants for their helpful discussion. The investigations described here were undertaken between 2003 and 2005 as part of the Episkopi Bay Survey by kind permission of the Department of Antiquities, Cyprus, and its then Directors, Sophocles Hadjisavvas and Pavlos Flourentzos, to whom many debts of gratitude are owed. These efforts were logistically and financially supported by the Institute of Nautical Archaeology at Texas A&M University, RPM Nautical Foundation, and the Thetis Foundation. All photographs, drawings, and maps were prepared by Troy Nowak, Toby Jones, Joshua Daniel, and the author. Finally, the ideas and text developed here owe much to thought-provoking conversations with, and careful scrutiny and insightful comments by the editors, as well as Elizabeth S. Greene, Thomas Tartaron, and an anonymous reviewer.

Late Roman Amphorae and Trade in the Vasilikos Valley

BY MARCUS RAUTMAN

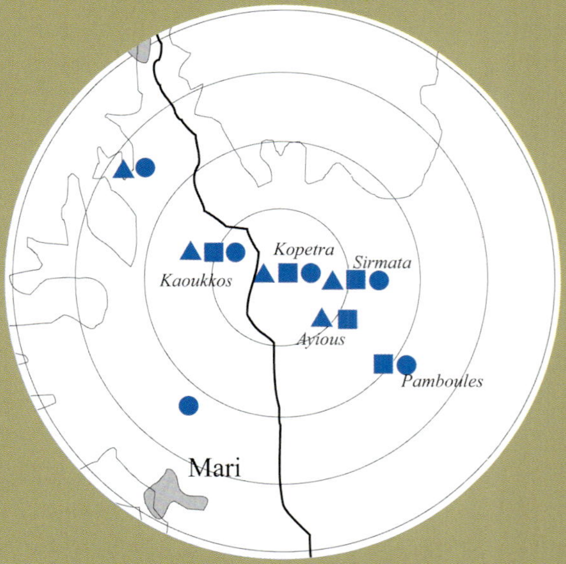

Late Roman Amphorae and Trade in the Vasilikos Valley

BY MARCUS RAUTMAN

Conspicuously located along centuries-old sailing routes, Roman Cyprus held a special place in the economic life of the east Mediterranean. The island's natural wealth was casually assumed by classical authors, who typically regarded it as an incidental stopover on the way to larger provinces on the mainland.[1] Since prehistory the upland valleys and wooded slopes of the Cypriot interior had experienced cycles of pastoral, agricultural, and metallurgical activity, which may have fluctuated in places on a generational, annual, or even seasonal basis. The coastlands, by contrast, were always the island's primary zone of habitation, consumption, and exchange. The cities, ports, and towns of the periphery made up a populous maritime façade that has left behind an abundant and varied material record.

Set against the dramatic backdrop of the Troodos massif, the coastal plain and foothills of south Cyprus hold special potential for exploring long-term patterns of land use and settlement, particularly on the sub-regional level and during early historical times. One of the most extensively explored parts of this area is the Vasilikos valley, which lies about 35 km east of the Akrotiri peninsula. The valley's total catchment encompasses about 150 square km of the eastern Troodos foothills. Pine forests cover much of the upper valley, and at lower elevations give way to small terraces set amid brushy scrub. The uneven topography narrows just above the present village of Kalavasos. Below this strategic point the terrain relaxes into low hills and plateaus, today planted mainly with olives, carobs, and cereals (Fig. 1).

Thirty years ago Ian Todd began systematic, long-term reconnaissance of the Vasilikos valley as far as the large rock-fill dam, built in the 1980s at 150 m asl about 8 km from the coast.[2] Sites were identified by extensive transect survey, selective artifact collection, and in several cases trial excavation. The first volume of the field survey report presents a picture of occupation from earliest times through the Middle Ages, with particularly intense activity occurring in the Neolithic, Late Bronze Age, and Roman periods. Settlement appears especially pronounced along the inland margin of the coastal plain, roughly 80-100 m asl and 2-4 km from the sea. A cluster of Neolithic dwellings occupied the low mound of Kalavasos-Tenta on the river's west bank. Chalcolithic activities were prominent along the nearby ridge at *Ayious* and *Pamboules*. The Late Bronze Age saw the rise of a monumental building complex at *Ayios Dhimitrios*, which acted as a production and distribution center for copper and olive oil.

Settlement in the area may have contracted during the early Iron Age, when the Vasilikos valley came under the sway of Amathus, 20 km to the west, but it apparently rebounded in the 1st and 2nd centuries AD. Thirty-two activity areas of Early Roman date have been identified across plain and valley, and another 25 off-site loci are attested by one or two diagnostic sherds. Most of these sites were distinguished in the field by the presence of worked stone blocks, rooftiles, or fine-ware sherds. Unsurprisingly, amphora fragments were noted at a number of these places. While a few examples of Rhodian and Koan vessels were collected, most surface sherds belong to transport jars of unidentified, east Mediterranean origin. Five new Early Roman settlements stand out in extent and complexity. Three of these are found in the upper valley: at *Arkhangelos, Ayios Kaloyeros*, and around the copper mines at Spilios. Broad scatters have been found about 3 km to the south at *Ayious* and *Pamboules*.

As elsewhere in Cyprus, the 2nd, 3rd, and 4th centuries AD are hard to identify on the ground. Some level of activity presumably exists among the poorly dated local wares, and perhaps the generally scarce imported pottery as well.[3] Despite this uncertainty, it appears that two-thirds of the Early Roman sites saw renewed activity in late antiquity. The VVP has identified a total of 44 significant sites ranging from seasonal encampments and isolated presses to permanent villages. Evidence of expanded activity near *Spilios* is clear from the number of settlements that have been observed in the upper valley around *Arkhangelos* and *Ayios Kaloyeros*. This suggests the renewal of copper mining, a Late Roman phenomenon now receiving attention elsewhere in Cyprus.[4] Another focus of activity developed across the valley above the small settlement of Dhrapia, at a high outcrop of limestone soils. A third area of interest lay at mid-valley, where the related sites of *Ayious, Kopetra, Pamboules*, and *Sirmata* cluster on the eastern bluff. Other

Fig. 1. The central Vasilikos valley, looking north from the Late Roman village site at Kalavasos-Kopetra.

important places, including Sokopra, Mari-*Mesovouni*, and Zyyi-*Petrini*, lie on the coastal plain, their apparent isolation due to erosion and modern development.

Amphorae constitute a key part of this ceramic landscape, even if their testimony is not always clear. Any assessment of archaeological material needs to bear in mind the circumstance and method of collection and recording. Most of the VVP field survey took place during the 1970s and early 1980s with an eye mainly to the area's prehistoric occupation.[5] The state of Roman ceramic studies at the time did not encourage the systematic collection of sherds apart from fine wares, or of amphorae that were not stamped or inscribed or otherwise noteworthy. This is particularly true for the later Hellenistic and Early Roman periods, and few such amphorae were found in clear association with scatters of Cypriot Sigillata and Eastern Sigillata A. Most transport sherds that were collected are fragmentary and in varied Cypriot fabrics.

Late antiquity has greater potential thanks to the increased visibility of more recent material in the plowzone, the standardization of vessel types from the 4th century

1 Michaelides 1996.

2 The pioneering field survey carried out by the Vasilikos Valley Project (VVP) is presented by Todd 2004a, 2004b, and forthcoming. My thanks to Ian Todd for inviting me to study the Roman and Late Roman material from his survey.

3 For the limitations of prevailing ceramic chronologies and possible refinements, see Lund 1993a, 1996; Meyza 2000.

4 For recent investigations of mining landscapes, see Given & Knapp 2003; Kassianidou 2004; Graham *et al.* 2006.

5 Todd 2004a, 47; 2004b, 19-22.

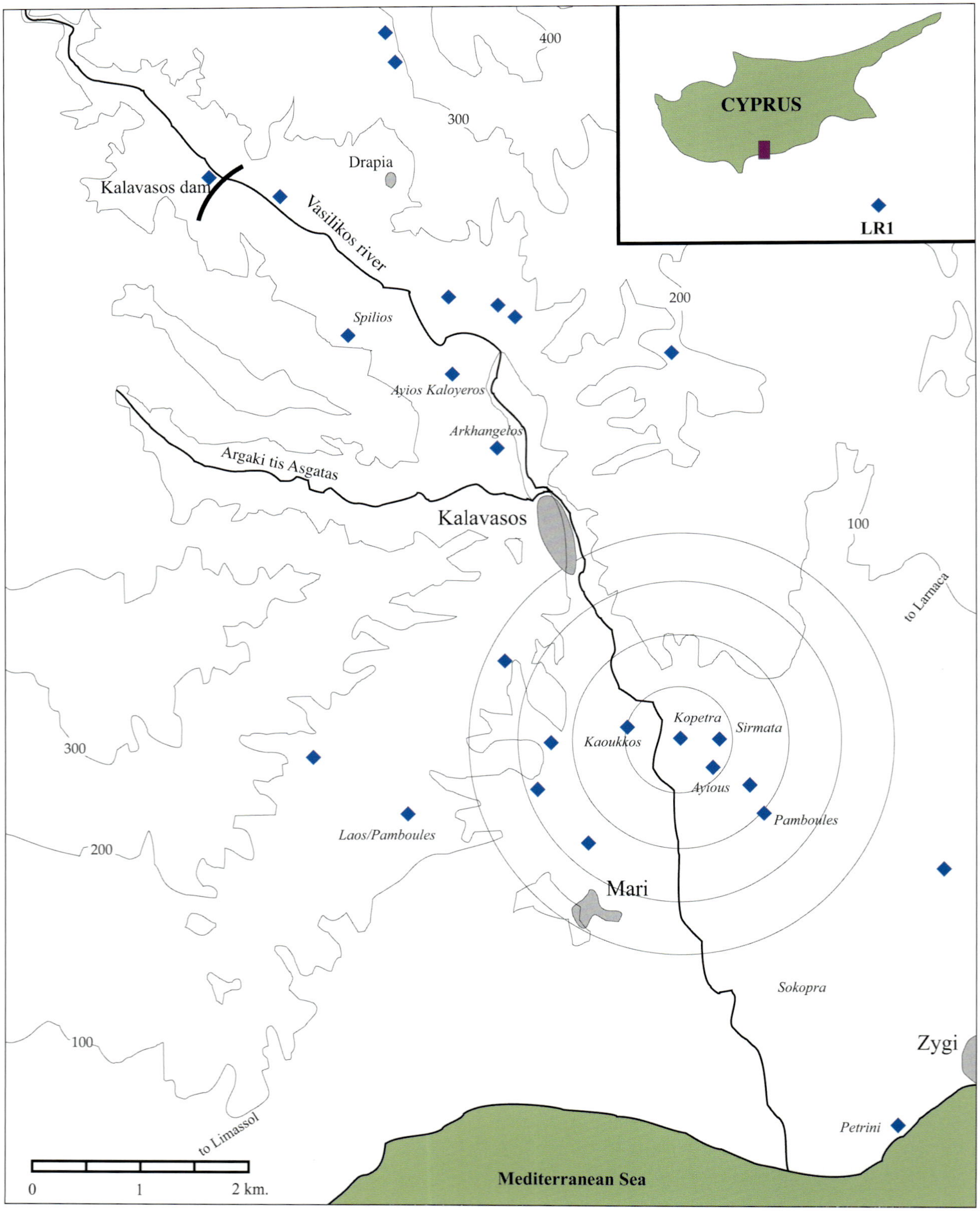

Fig. 2. Vasilikos valley, distribution of LR1 amphora sherds collected by the VVP.

AD, and stratified excavations carried out in 1988-91 at Kalavasos-*Kopetra*.[6] Together with other pottery and rooftiles, the amphorae clearly indicate that the valley saw renewed occupation at this time, which presumably was based on more systematic exploitation of local resources encouraged by expanded economic ties with the mainland. Of 44 significant sites assignable to the 5th to 7th centuries AD, more than 70 percent (30) had identifiable Late Roman amphora sherds, with additional examples noted but not collected. Good correlation exists between amphorae and fine wares, rooftiles, and pithoi as well.

Four vessel types dominate the local picture (Table 1). The most common is the LR1 amphora, the most widely distributed transport jar of late antiquity. LR1 amphorae appear in the three main fabrics observed at *Kopetra*: a dull, gritty fabric with many coarse inclusions, and two sandy fabrics with fine inclusions. Compositional study of the *Kopetra* pottery suggests that about 20 percent of the total, comprising mainly vessels in the coarser fabric, were locally made, while the others came from the mainland.[7] Examples collected by the VVP survey are mainly of imported fabrics, and appear widely distributed across the valley. LR1 amphorae are present at nearly 60 percent of all Late Roman sites, or 87 percent of all sites at which amphora sherds have been noted (Fig. 2).

The second most frequently observed type of amphora is an elongated, carrot-shaped vessel identified as KAmp2 at *Kopetra*. The most distinctive feature of small sherds is the hard, medium-grained red fabric filled with angular inclusions, for which compositional analysis indicates a uniform, off-island source. Examples from the valley are very fragmentary but generally resemble the late Sinope series/Kuzmanov IX amphorae.[8] Similar transport vessels in different fabrics have been reported in the east Mediterranean and Black Sea regions, and production centers have been proposed near Seleucia-Pieria and Sinope. Sherds of this type of amphora were collected by the VVP at 30 percent of all Late Roman sites, or 43 percent of all amphora sites in the valley (Fig. 3).

Two other types of amphora occur in lesser yet still significant quantities. The round-bodied Palestinian LR5 amphora appears in the standard light red, sandy fabric seen at Kopetra and across the Mediterranean.[9] The VVP collected examples at 20 percent of all Late Roman sites, or 30 percent of all amphora sites in the valley. Nearly all of these were found between the environs of *Kopetra* and the sea, with most examples occurring within 2-3 km of the site. A similar presence can be established for the type known at *Kopetra* as KAmp1, a broad globular vessel that belongs to the LR13 series.[10] Two fabrics appear locally: a fine-grained, light red ware of mainland (Aegean?) origin, and a distinctive Cypriot version in a gritty, pale brown fabric. The nine identified examples come from 20 percent of all Late Roman sites, or 30 percent of all amphora sites in the valley. While a few examples have been noted in the upper valley, most KAmp1 amphora sherds occur within sight of *Kopetra*. Other standard transport vessels are represented by several representatives of the sub-Koan series, the pinched-handle MR4, and a few sherds from north Africa.

This uneven scattering of Late Roman amphorae, which were reported to, noted during, or collected by the VVP over the course of 20 years of fieldwork, constitutes the primary data. It is important to note that this summary represents a minimal view of sustained amphora consumption, presumably in the context of habitation, and is based on identifiable sherds found together with other diagnostic material. The distribution of amphorae

	no. sites	*% LR sites*	*% LR amphora sites*
LR1	26	60	87
KAmp2	13	30	43
LR5	9	20	30
KAmp1/LR13	9	20	30

Table 1. Primary types of Late Roman amphorae observed by the Vasilikos valley field survey.

6 The pottery from the Kalavasos-*Kopetra* Project (KKP) is presented in Rautman 2003. For the variable visibility of surface finds see Rautman 2008.

7 For detailed fabric descriptions see Rautman *et al.* 1999; Rautman 2003, 168-171, 267-171; for the wider production of LR1 amphorae see Demesticha 2003, 471-472; Williams 2005; Burragato *et al.* 2007; Ferrazzoli & Ricci 2010.

8 Rautman 2003, 173-174 with references. For recent discussion see Bezeczky 2005a, 210.

9 Rautman 2003, 172.

10 Rautman 2003, 173; for the Cypriot manufacture of LR13 amphorae see Demesticha 2003, 472-473; 2005.

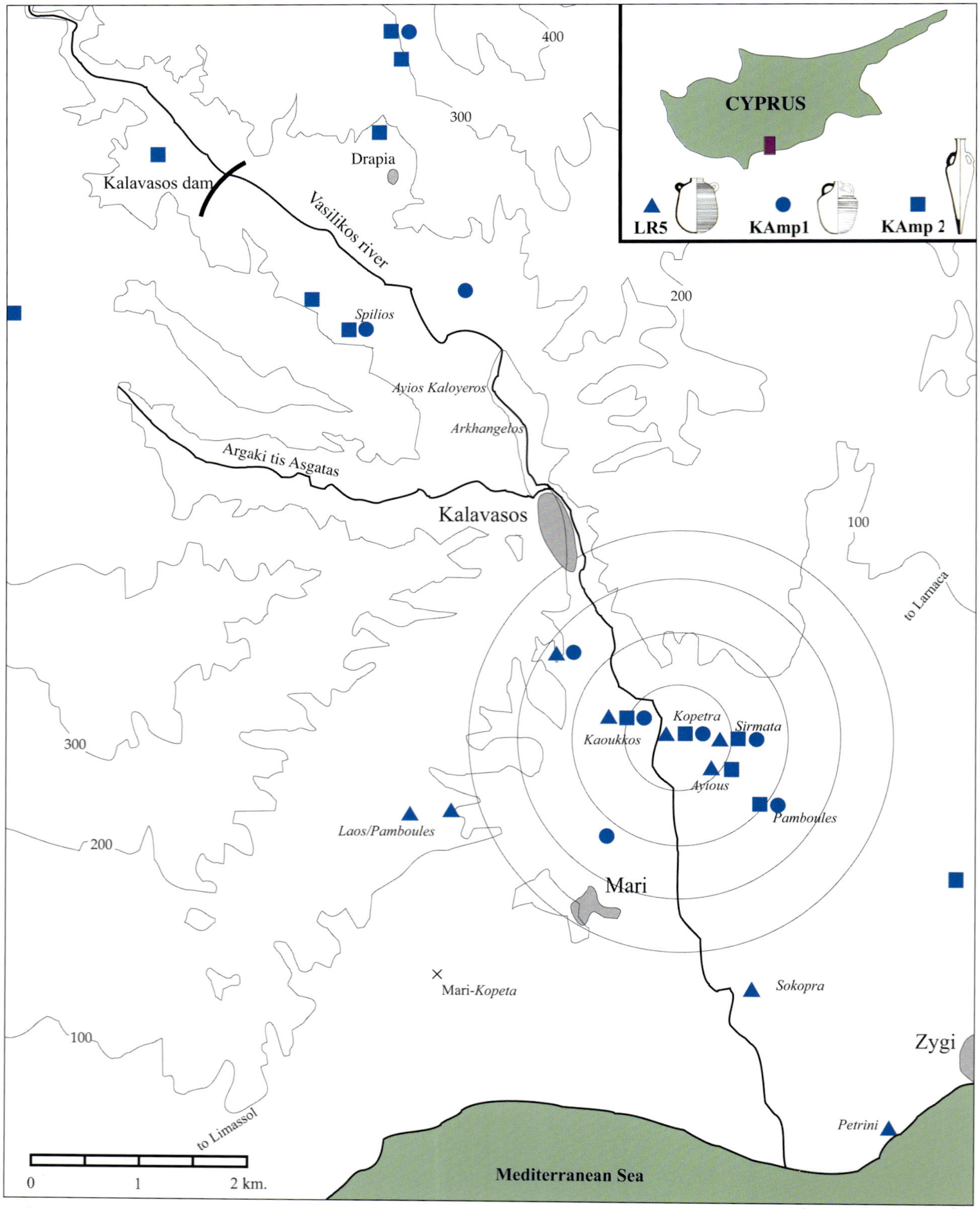

Fig. 3. Vasilikos valley, distribution of LR5, KAmp1, and KAmp2 amphora sherds collected by the VVP.

in Figs. 2-3 includes neither isolated examples nor unverified reports of amphora sherds, which can reflect such transitory activities as the casual reuse of containers by pastoralists.[11] The resulting picture is clearly regional in its makeup, with amphorae from the nearby coastlands of Cilicia and north Syria (LR1 and KAmp2) growing increasingly important between the 5th and 7th centuries AD.[12] The Palestinian LR5 amphorae reinforce the presence of the mainland. All of these vessels probably reached the Vasilikos valley by ships arriving at the port of Salamis-Constantia, before being transferred to smaller craft that sailed along the Cypriot coast. The KAmp1/LR13 amphorae could have followed a similar route, but more likely came from western Cyprus, passing through Amathus or Paphos as port or production center.[13] None of this provides direct information about whether these vessels originally carried oil or wine. The present terrain of the Vasilikos valley appears better suited to cereals and olives than grapes, which might imply a greater local demand for wine in late antiquity. The opportunistic recycling of amphorae for transport and storage, however, complicates the picture.[14]

This broad cross-section of amphora use in the Vasilikos valley gains clarity at Late Roman *Kopetra*. This otherwise anonymous 4-ha habitation site is the largest of several village-size settlements clustering in the central valley, about half way between the copper mines at Spilios and the coast. *Kopetra* lies near the intersection of two key roadways: a natural north-south axis running along the east side of the valley, and the coastal highway joining Amathus and Kition. The nearby sites at *Ayious, Kaoukkos, Pamboules*, and *Sirmata* are not much smaller and have abundant surface pottery as well. Altogether there are about a dozen Late Roman sites lying within a 2-km radius of *Kopetra*. Five years of site-specific survey and excavation by the KKP have documented permanent habitation here as early as the 5th century AD, with significant growth taking place in the late 6th and early 7th centuries AD. Identified buildings include several residential and industrial structures, two churches, and a small monastery.[15]

Late Roman *Kopetra* may have been a place of little account but its amphora assemblage is impressively complex, more so than observed elsewhere in the valley. During six seasons of survey and excavation, the KKP recorded more than 17,000 amphora sherds weighing 530 kg, which amounts to nearly half of all pottery recovered from the site. In addition to the standard 'package' of

	Survey % no.	*Survey % wt.*	*Excav. % no.*	*Excav. % wt.*
LR1	69.9	74.9	83.0	85.6
LR4	0.7	0.9	6.2	3.8
LR5/6	0.3	0.3	4.3	3.8
LR2	0.2	0.1	2.9	3.4
KAmp2	3.9	4.0	1.1	2.1
LR7	0.0	0.1	1.1	0.8
KAmp1/LR13	0.8	0.4	0.9	0.6

Table 2. Primary types of Late Roman amphorae from survey and excavation at Kalavasos-Kopetra (n=17,338).

LR1-7, four or five other fabrics or forms were consistently distinguished. The four main amphora types identified by the valley survey are among the most commonly found at *Kopetra* (Table 2). LR1 is of course the most abundant, constituting at least 70-80 percent of all amphorae. Of other transport vessels, about 4 percent are LR5, about 2 percent KAmp2, and less than 1 percent KAmp1/LR13. The prominence of LR1 is typical of the valley as a whole and the environs of Amathus and Maroni as well.[16] More instructive may be differences between valley and site finds, particularly the presence at Kopetra of types not seen elsewhere: LR4 from Gaza (4-6 percent), LR2 from the Aegean (3 percent), LR7 from the Nile valley (1 percent).[17] All of these vessels are commonly associated

11 As suggested for the Akamas survey finds by Lund 2007, 783-784.

12 Williams 2005; Burragato *et al.* 2007.

13 For production at Amathous see Touma 2001; for the kiln at Paphos see Demesticha & Michaelides 2001; Demesticha 2003; 2005. See Gabrieli *et al.* 2007 for amphorae from the area of the Paphos theater. Anthi Kaldelis, this volume, argues for a northerly route for Aegean shipping.

14 Possible contents are reviewed by Pieri 2005. The practical demands of rural life presented myriad occasions for creatively modifying and reusing amphorae; see recently Peña 2007.

15 Rautman 2003 and 2008.

16 For LR1 amphorae at Amathous, Touma 2001, 49-53; for the Maroni valley, Manning *et al.* 2002, 52-53.

17 Compare Lund 2007, 782, for a similar contrast between (excavated) site finds at Ayios Kononas, and off-site (survey) finds from the vicinity.

with wine, at least in an export setting. Neither LR6 (the gray-fired version of LR5) nor LR7 appears in significant quantities outside their production areas, but LR2 and LR4 amphorae had considerable currency across the east Mediterranean.[18] These vessels were among the largest of contemporary amphorae, a fact that would certainly have limited their overland transport. Of all amphorae that can be assigned a provenance, the clear majority (67 percent of about 12,000 examples) came from the eastern mainland (Cilicia, Syria, and Palestine), probably traveling by ship through Salamis before continuing to the valley. By contrast, amphorae coming from North Africa, the Aegean, and Egypt, and presumably passing through the ports at Paphos or Amathus, amount to 5 percent of the total. It is tempting to see these imported vessels as containing exotic goods deliberately sought by *Kopetra's* inhabitants, which raises the possibility of a speculative commercial market for residential landowners, or perhaps conscription by the church. While some commodities could have been repackaged in smaller, more readily transported barrels, jars, or skins for local distribution, none of these options would be desirable for specialty oil or wine.[19]

The rest of the *Kopetra* assemblage underscores the obvious point that amphorae and their contents make up only part of the larger picture of economic exchange. Fine table wares, for example, constitute 5 percent of all pottery recovered at the site and present a different pattern that clearly looks to the west. Most of the decorated bowls and dishes known as Cypriot Red Slip probably originated in western Cyprus, and the mass-produced red-slipped wares of north Africa, western Asia Minor, and Egypt likely arrived via Paphos.[20] Rooftiles occupy a much larger share of the local market and add a great deal to the total picture. The two main types of tiles used in south Cyprus were made in distinctive yellow and red fabrics, which can be attributed to the environs of Salamis and Paphos, respectively. The strong presence of both tile-making traditions in the 6th and early 7th centuries AD reflects the integration of *Kopetra* and the Vasilikos valley as a whole with wider networks.[21]

In sum, the Vasilikos amphorae were part of a well-developed rural economy that appears closely tied to east Mediterranean exchange networks. In addition to pastoral traditions, production in the valley involved mining and farming, which encouraged the growth of Late Roman settlement around *Spilios* and *Kopetra*. These permanent habitation clusters are prominent but hardly exclusive: significant activity *loci* also include *Palaeodhrapia*, on the upper edge of the limestone hills, and another settlement at Mari-*Koupetra-Loura-Kaphkaloudi*.[22] The valley as a whole presents varied soils suitable for growing cereals on the lower plain, grapes on higher terraces, and olives and kitchen gardens in between. Pastoral economies involved herding goats, sheep, and other animals, to which amphorae contributed at least incidentally. Within the valley *Kopetra* occupied a special place: central located, advantageously sited, and within two hours walking distance of both mines and coast. Its substantial architecture included solidly-built houses and at least three churches, which attests the success of local producers and their investment in multi-seasonal habitation. The presence of elite buildings and goods in a village setting makes clear how *Kopetra* could offer a receptive market for goods traveling from Syria, Gaza, the Aegean, and beyond.

The main impediment to clarifying this picture is the LR1 amphorae. These abundant containers outnumber all other transport vessels combined at every excavation sector at *Kopetra*, at *Petrera*, throughout the Vasilikos and Maroni valleys, and across the island.[23] Their quantities at Kopetra are constant from the 5th century AD and increase from the mid-6th into the 7th century AD. Differentiating fabrics and formal subtypes on the basis of fragmentary surface material is not an easy task. Of the LR1 amphorae at *Kopetra*, almost three-quarters apparently originated on the mainland, which leaves 10-20 percent made somewhere on the island.

One such Cypriot production center may have operated briefly at Zyyi-*Petrini*, a small coastal site near the mouth of the Vasilikos River. Surface finds from *Petrini* qualify this as one of five second-tier settlements in the valley. The eroding shoreline reveals sparse Hellenistic but much Late Roman pottery with plentiful fine wares and amphorae, mainly of LR1 vessels. Among the visible remains are several modest buildings and a recessed, rectangular structure that may have functioned as a kiln. Published ceramics from the unexcavated feature are inconclusive but include vitrified rooftiles of both red and yellow fabrics, and a few charred examples of LR1 sherds of apparent mainland origin.[24] Neutron activation analysis of five LR1 specimens recovered from the context reveals a broad variety of chemical profiles, which present two possible interpretations. On the one hand, most of these amphora sherds might be intrusive, like the rooftiles, and not be kiln wares at all. It is equally plausible, on the other hand, that the sherds reflect production that took place over several seasons. Cluster analysis of the five specimens within a larger dataset of calcareous amphorae and rooftiles shows just how wide this compositional variation could be. The closest comparanda in fact are coarse-fabric rooftiles from *Kopetra*, and LR1 and LR13 amphorae from the Paphos kiln.[25] Such variation would be normal for neighbourhood or seasonal production by a small workshop that sought clays in the shifting fluvial plains of the lower valley.[26]

This evidence suggests the outlines of a sub-regional model of amphora production and use in one Cypriot valley. Agricultural and metallurgical processing took place throughout the area but did not necessarily involve transport vessels. When found in abundance, amphorae are typologically varied and occur together with fine pottery and rooftiles at sites of long-term habitation and consumption. Apart from *Kopetra* itself, millstones, crushing basins, and press weights are not ordinarily accompanied by large quantities of transport vessels. The best known local example of agricultural production is the olive-pressing complex at Mari-*Kopetra*. The site was found during highway construction on the lower plain, about 1 km from the coast, and recorded by the Department of Antiquities on an emergency basis in 1980. Excavation revealed an unusual triple press-bed, ten large weights, and two stone settling tanks, which have been reconstructed in an interpretive display at the Larnaca Archaeological Museum.[27] Sparse contextual finds included a Hellenistic lamp but few transport vessels; for this reason the kiln has been assigned to the Hellenistic period. Late Roman fine wares and dolia found nearby apparently belong to the settlement at *Koupetra-Loura-Kaphkaloudi*, and not the press at Mari-*Kopetra*.[28] Barrels, skins, and other kinds of containers would have been needed for relaying the freshly skimmed oil the short distance to the coast. This would have been the point of sale or shipment at which small coastal centers, like *Petrini*, entered the process.

The Vasilikos amphorae form only a small part of this larger picture and lie more along the axis of consumption than manufacture. The area's material productivity appears most clearly at *Kopetra*, which played a special mediating role in the valley's economic life. Local exports included copper, grain, and oil, all strategic commodities demanded by the new imperial *quaestura* after 534 and with increasing urgency toward 600. In exchange, goods and their containers originating elsewhere reached the valley through unspecified transactions and agencies including market, church, and especially state.[29] Only in the mid-6th century AD, during a time of heightened political and military concern, did this remote island province finally cross the threshold of Constantinopolitan interest. Massive state involvement newly justified the distance and hazard in sailing between the imperial capital and the Near East. Moreover, it stimulated traffic along the island's sheltered south coast, where the valleys of the Troodos supported port cities like Kourion, Amathus, and Kition, but also seaside anchorages at Alaminos-*Latourou Çiftlik*, Avdimou, Dreamer's Bay, and *Petrini*.[30] These forgotten ports-of-call can be seen as local, entrepreneurial responses closely related to the rise of microeconomic centers like *Kopetra*, which between 500 and 600 became the economic and cultural pivot of its environs. Scattered along the coast of south Cyprus, such small places illustrate both the texture of rural lives and the sub-regional connections that joined them to the wider Mediterranean.

---

18 Tomber 2004, 155-160.
19 Brun 2003, 100-106, 166-168.
20 For Egyptian imports see Ballet 1995; Lund 1996; Jacobsen 2004.
21 For localization of tile production see Rautman *et al.* 1999; Rautman 2003, 177-178.
22 Todd 2004b, 118; for *Palaeodhrapia*, Todd forthcoming.
23 Manning *et al.* 2002; Demesticha 2003 and this volume. For aspects of the Cypriot economy in late antiquity see Michaelides 1996; Rautman 2000; Papacostas 2001.
24 Manning *et al.* 2000; Todd 2004b, 143-144.
25 KKP627-631. For the larger dataset, Rautman *et al.* 1999; Rautman 2003, 267-271.
26 Peacock 1982, 25-26.
27 Hadjisavvas 1992, 34-40.
28 Surface finds at these sites are reviewed by Todd 2004b, 117-118.
29 Rautman 2000; 2003, 255-260; Papacostas 2001, 113-115; Metcalf 2009, 229-240.
30 Leonard & Demesticha 2004; Leidwanger 2005.

Supply Mechanisms at Non-agricultural Production Sites. Economic Modelling in Late Roman Cyprus

BY KRISTINA WINTHER-JACOBSEN

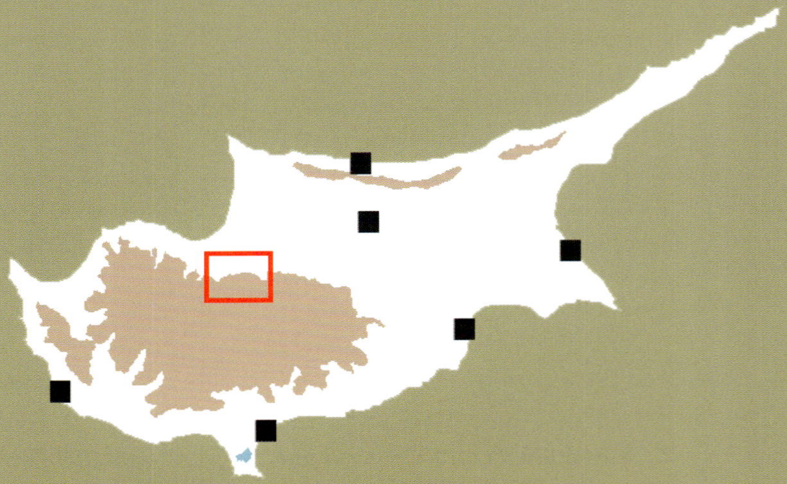

Supply Mechanisms at Non-agricultural Production Sites. Economic Modelling in Late Roman Cyprus

BY KRISTINA WINTHER-JACOBSEN

Even though the increase in survey data seen over the past 20 years has demonstrated a great complexity and variety of scatters of ceramics, this has yet to result in the identification of a greater variety of sites.[1] Rural sites are generally assumed to be residential, and the main classification of sites within the ancient rural landscape is still small settlements contra larger settlements as in Susan Alcock's interpretation of the Greek landscape during the Roman period.[2]

Written sources and ethno-archaeological studies identify a much broader range of rural sites associated not only with agriculture, but with mining, pastoralism, forestry and other human industries.[3] Mining was an important industry in ancient Cyprus and exploiting this rich resource must have affected the use of the surrounding landscape. This article is concerned with supply mechanics at essentially non-agricultural production sites in Cyprus during the Late Roman period. It is less concerned with the actual types and numbers of sites and more with how we use them in economic modelling. The distribution of imported transport amphorae in Cyprus during the Late Roman period indicates that these containers were not restricted to the city-centres but penetrated far into the hinterland.[4] Of course to some extent the hinterland is much better researched and published due to the many large scale surveys carried out on the island.[5] This study is based on data from the Troodos Archaeological and Environmental Survey Project in Cyprus (TAESP), supplemented with comparative data from the University of Liverpool Methana Survey Project in the Saronic Gulf in Greece and from the mining and quarrying sites in the central Eastern Desert of Egypt.[6] With one exception, none of the sites discussed are located on the coast, and they can best be described as hinterland or rural sites. The distributions of imported foodstuff and table wares to tenant farmers on Methana where there were no mines and to imperial labourers in the mines and quarries of the Eastern Desert of Egypt where there was no agriculture each provide clues to provide a deeper understanding of the TAESP landscape.

THE TAESP LANDSCAPE

The TAESP survey area is divided into four ecological zones: the large fertile Karkotis Valley to the west with Skouriotissa, the largest copper mine in Cyprus in the northern end, the central plain including Atsas, Mandres and Koutraphas, Asinou, the mountainous area to the south, and the narrow Lagoudhera Valley running past the copper baring hill Alestos to the east (Fig. 1).

An economic surplus is believed to have been produced by Skouriotissa, the largest copper mine in Cyprus, and a small-scale mining complex to the east in the Lagoudhera Valley and from agriculture in the very fertile Karkotis Valley. Written sources suggest that large-scale mining stopped in the 4th century AD.[7] However, several of the Late Roman sherds found by the enormous slag heap at Skouriotissa were discoloured by slag stains. This new ceramic evidence, which is supported by radio carbon dates of charcoal to be published in the TAESP volume currently under way, suggests that large-scale mining continued at Skouriotissa into the 7th century AD.[8] And yet, although there is a lot of mineral wealth and evidence for related production there is little evidence for trade-goods coming in.

The characteristic combination of ultrabasic minerals and glass from the pillow lavas in the temper suggests that the vast majority of ceramics recorded in the survey area was produced in the near region.[9] I have previously argued that the very low number of imported transport amphorae in the TAESP survey area suggests that the economic surplus, which must have been produced by this region, was not redistributed locally.[10] The pattern of distribution of local and imported transport amphorae is similar in the eastern, southern and central parts of the survey area, which includes a small mining complex in the Lagoudhera Valley (Fig. 1). Transport amphorae were found at all identified sites, although the sites on the Koutraphas Plain appear to have no imported ones. In the fertile Karkotis Valley we found none of the identified local transport amphora types, but imported transport amphorae were found at all identified sites. This includes the area around the Skouriotissa mine where the broadest range of imports came from. Out of more than 30.000 sherds collected only

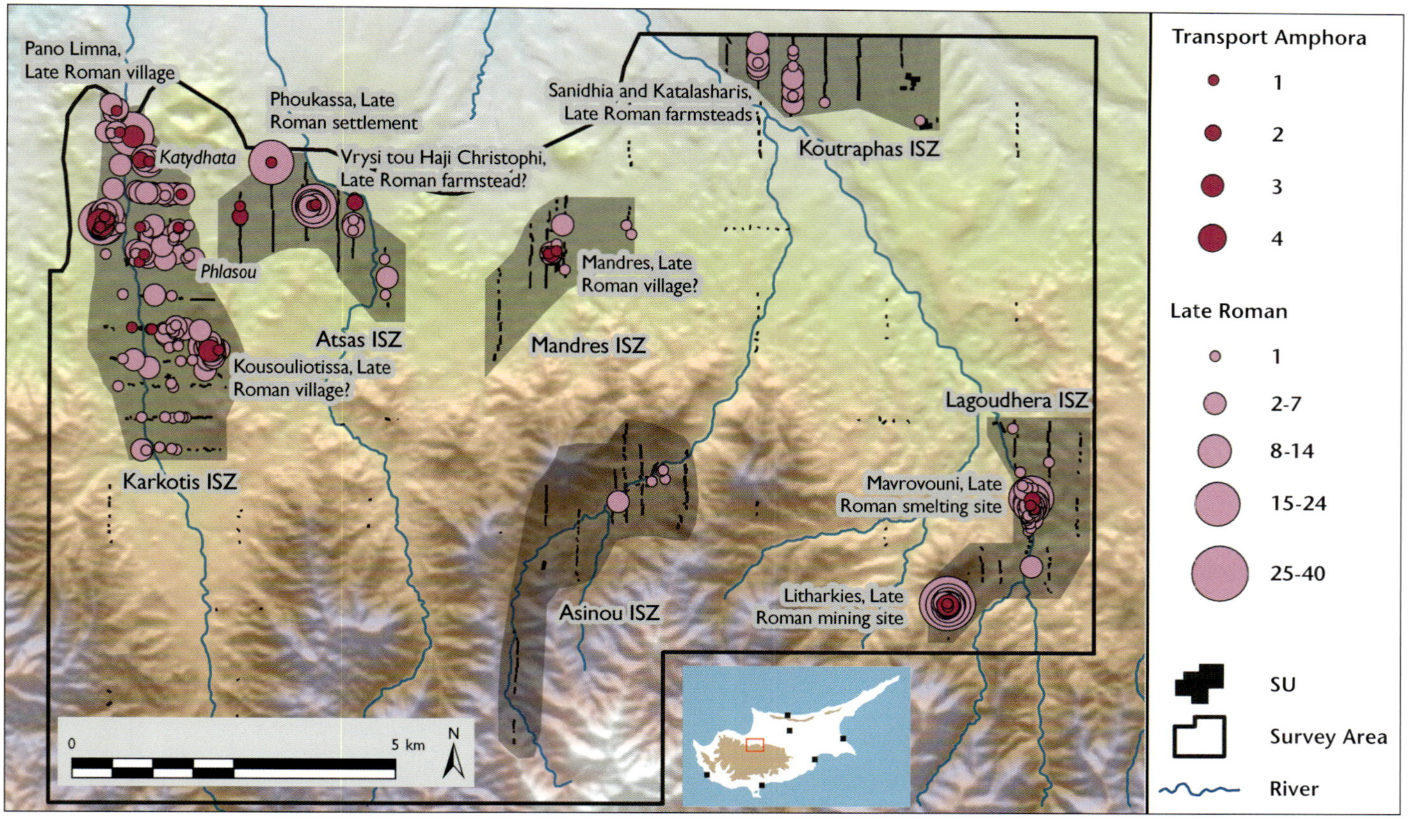

Fig. 1. Distribution map of Late Roman ceramics and Late Roman transport amphorae in the TAESP survey area.

143 came from Late Roman transport amphorae (Table 1). I have not been able to provenance or securely date a bright orange amphora with rare but characteristic large reddish-black particles, possibly iron oxide (Am07). It is the second most common imported amphora type in the area. It is consistently found with Late Roman pottery and should probably be added to this group. The other imports collected represent the standard types of the period: the all dominating Late Roman amphora type 1, as well as a few Late Roman amphora types 4 and 5. Late Roman 1 amphorae were produced along the south coast of Cyprus as well as just across the water from the TAESP landscape on the south coast of Asia Minor, LR4 and LR5 in Palestine.[11] Of course, the transition between the Late Roman and the Early Byzantine period is currently undergoing revision, and some types such as the ubiquitous LR1 clearly continued to be produced in second the half of the 7th and even the 8th century AD.[12]

To summarize, the available resources in the TAESP landscape suggest profitable conditions, but the very sparse distribution of transport amphorae implies little incoming trade in foodstuff. Of course, the link between economic

1 Pettegrew 2001, 189.
2 Alcock 1993.
3 Whitelaw 1994; Murray & Kardulias 2000.
4 Jacobsen 2004.
5 E.g. Sørensen & Rupp 1993; Fejfer 1995; Hadjisavvas 1997; Manning *et al.* 2002; Rautman 2003; Given & Knapp 2003.
6 Mee & Forbes 1997; Tomber 2006; Sidebotham *et al.* 1989; Sidebotham *et al.* 1991; Sidebotham & Wendrich 1996.
7 Eusebius *On the Martyrs in Palestine* XIII.i.
8 Kassianidou forthcoming.
9 Winther-Jacobsen forthcoming a.
10 Winther-Jacobsen forthcoming b.
11 Demesticha 2003; Empereur & Picon 1989, 236-43; Majcherek 1995; Reynolds 2005, 573-574.
12 E.g. Hayes 2007, 437-438; Armstrong 2009.

surplus and import of foodstuff is far from simple. In fact, identifying elite consumption during the Late Roman period is difficult. The tombs are almost devoid of gifts and social hierarchy thus nearly invisible. Metal and glass objects rarely survive on the surface, so all we are left with is architecture and pottery, and in the case of surveys often only pottery. The presence of transport amphorae does reveal access to external networks, but those come in many forms. The simple argument is that the more imported goods are required, the more access to external markets is needed and consequently, the more wealth and connections. But we know market mechanisms to be quite complicated during the Roman period. The goods have somehow to be split into everyday objects and luxury goods, both of which appear to have travelled long distances. Furthermore, it is not only the actual distance, but also the distance from trade routes, which makes some commodities hard to obtain. In this article I look at two different cases, which will allow us a better understanding of the TAESP pattern.

METHANA

The first case is Greek, the landscape of Methana, a peninsula on the south-western side of the Saronic Gulf.[13] Here the survey team from Liverpool identified 27 Roman rural sites mostly of the Late Roman period and mostly interpreted as farmsteads or hamlets. This area was chosen for the rare detailed publication including a catalogue of finds at the identified sites.[14] During the Late Roman period 21 of these sites were equipped with generally high quality pressing installations, which must be associated with an export oriented agricultural production.

Geologically, Methana is characterized by rocks and only small pockets of fertile soil, and yet the pressing installations were all located within an area of about 10 km^2. Lin Foxhall has suggested that the correlation of high quality pressing installations and otherwise very modest accoutrement suggests that sites were not inhabited by landowners, but by tenants.[15] Only one site, MS211, was identified as a possible *villa rustica* of elite occupation. It is an isolated rural site located almost at the centre of the island more than 600m above sea level. The only way the site differed from the other rural settlements in the survey area was the presence of a few fragments of imported transport amphorae dated to the earlier Roman periods: two Early Roman fragments from Spain, one Mid Roman fragment from the Northern Aegean or the Black Sea and one Mid Roman fragment from Africa.[16] Four fragments of imported LR1 amphorae and four fragments of Late Roman amphora type 2 from the Argolid were dated to the Late Roman period. One should not pay too much attention to the actual numbers as they are a grab sample and so have no real statistical relevance. The Late Roman 2 amphora is the dominating transport amphora produced in the near region and unsurprisingly quite common on Methana. Late Roman 1 amphorae were found at three other sites, none of which were associated with anything elite. So it appears that elite interpretation is based on the presence of less than a handful of imported transport amphorae of the Early and Mid Roman periods. On the other hand, imported transport amphorae were generally more common during the Late Roman period and so probably have less elite significance. This is supported by the distribution of imported table wares.

Imported ceramics are sometimes cited by surveys in Greece as status indicators at rural sites e.g. by the Nemea Valley Survey Project, and the Keos survey project.[17] However, it is mostly in cases where there is other evidence typically in the form of architectural remains, marble, column drums, hypocaust bricks, or bits of mosaics. No such architectural evidence was found in the rural Late Roman landscapes of either Methana or TAESP. Furthermore imported table wares collected in these two survey areas cannot be associated with a distribution of special transport amphora types associable with elite occupation, such as the unique North African (and Spanish?) amphorae found in the middle of Methana. The Late Roman transport amphorae recorded are part of the standard Eastern Mediterranean package of this period and they penetrated into the remote corners of Methana. Imported table wares were also found at most Late Roman Methana sites, albeit in very small numbers. Compared to Methana, a wider range of imported table wares were generally collected at the individual TAESP sites, but still in a relatively small number (Table 2). I include Late Roman D Ware (also known as Cypriot Red Slip Ware) among the imported wares, because it was produced on the south coast of Asia Minor, but possibly also on the other site of the Troodos Mountains and had to be shipped to the north coast from where it was distributed into the hinterland.[18] The African Red Slip ware are listed in brackets because since we are dealing with poorly preserved survey finds it is possible they should be dated to the Mid Roman rather than the Late Roman period.

TAESP raw counts	Late Roman transport amphora	Number and type
99.676 sherds counted		
30.719 sherds collected	143 sherds collected	77 LR1 sherds
		2 LR4 sherds
		6 LR5 sherds
		35 local amphorae sherds
		23 others amphorae sherds
		34 Am07 amphorae sherds

Table 1. Number and type of Late Roman transport amphorae collected by TAESP compared to total number of sherds collected.

Site	Imported transport amphorae	Imported table wares
MS211/villa?	LR2, LR1	PRS
MS17	LR2, LR1	PRS
MS101/112	LR2, LR1	(ARS), PRS
MS204	LR2, LR1	PRS, LRD
Vrysi	LR1	(ARS), LRD
Sanidhia	-	(ARS), LRD, PRS
Katalasharis	-	(ARS), LRD, PRS
Mavrovouni	LR1	(ARS), LRD, PRS
Litharkies	LR1	(ARS), LRD, PRS
"Skouriotissa"	LR1, LR4, LR5	(ARS), LRD, PRS, ERS

Table 2. Distribution of Late Roman imported transport amphora and table ware types at Methana and TAESP sites.

To sum up, the rural areas of Methana and the TAESP area both seem to be producing an economic surplus. On Methana, surplus is evidenced by the high quality pressing installations; in the TAESP area, surplus is suggested by the copper mines and the fertile soil. Neither area has evidence for elite occupation in the form of architecture or exotic imports during the Late Roman period. On Methana some food was imported in Late Roman 2 and Late Roman 1 amphorae, but generally finds are modest and farmsteads may have been occupied by tenants.[19] Consequently, the profit would mainly go to absent and presumably urban landowners. In the TAESP area almost no imported transport amphorae were recorded, but a good range of imported table wares were, although the identification of a major LRD production centre just across the water should provide easy access.[20] Both on Methana and in the TAESP area, the most common food import is regional, and extra regional imported foodstuff is exceedingly rare. The near absence of transport amphorae and the lack of evidence for large storage facilities suggest that the food consumed

13 Mee & Forbes 1997.
14 Gill *et al.* 1997.
15 Foxhall 1990.
16 Bowden & Gill 1997, 88.
17 Kosso 2003, Table 3.5.
18 Jackson *et al.* 2012; Meyza 2007.
19 Foxhall 1990.
20 Jackson *et al.* 2012.

in these two areas was locally produced, transported in containers of organic material, and stored by the householders individually from year to year. Consequently, the TAESP area appears to have been agriculturally self-sufficient, so what happened to the profit from the copper production? Was there an absent urban mine owner soaking up the profit as suggested for methana?

MINING EVIDENCE FOR THE ABSENT OWNER

The absent owner *per excellence* was of course the emperor, and imperial mines and quarries tend to be large-scale, as known from Spain and Egypt. Centrally organised, they were in a sense divorced from the local economy, although demands for labour and supplies would certainly influence local economies.[21] Written sources – such as Diodorus and Galen – speak of criminals, captives of war and slaves, who were working in the mines, but this assertion is becoming increasingly controversial.[22] The unfortified living quarters and the testimony from *ostraka* from the Eastern Desert suggest that a large proportion of the workers were free labourers. Generally, large-scale quarrying and mining is believed to have ceased by the Late Roman period; however, this is certainly not the case at Skouriotissa, where mining continued into the 7th century AD.[23] The later emperor Heraclius established a mint in Cyprus based on local metal in AD 609/10 and the metal resources may have been what attracted him to the island.[24] Jonathan Charles Edmondson has suggested that mineral and lithic exploitation was in fact reorganised during the Late Roman period in a way that encouraged small-scale operations, and this is consistent with the decline in centrally controlled large-scale mining, such as imperial ones in Spain and Egypt.[25] The exploitation of the mines in the Lagoudhera Valley may be a case of the new order, but we are unsure if mining in this area may not have started already during the Early Roman period. At 2,200 m^3 the total size of the slag heap in the Lagoudhera Valley equals approximately 4% of the estimated size of the (greatly reduced) 54,000 m^3 slag heap at Skouriotissa. It is tempting to see private local enterprise in the Lagoudhera Valley and centralised organisation in the Karkotis Valley, but is there any evidence besides size and sparseness of transport amphorae?

We do know something about the running of the Cypriot copper mines in Early Roman times. Cyprus was a senatorial province, but there appears to be some doubt concerning the ownership of the Soli mines, one of which was Skouriotissa. In 12 BC King Herod of Judaea paid 300 talents for the rights to Skouriotissa, and he was allowed to keep profits from half of the copper produced.[26] Galen mentions an imperial administrator in relation to his visit to Skouriotissa,[27] and a contemporary inscription (Antonine date: ca. AD 138-192) honours the procurator, possibly the same person.[28] He employed a local company of contractors from three mining villages to work the Soli mines.[29] The Lagoudhera Valley mine may be part of the same set-up, but of course we do not know if this structure of organisation continued during the Late Roman period. The distribution of pottery suggests that the modern villages of Katydhata and Phlasou were occupied in Roman times (Fig. 1), although we have not been able to pinpoint the actual settlements. Sometime during the Medieval period the up to several meters of alluvial sedimentation increased the height of the valley floor and appears to have obliterated any firm traces of settlements *in situ*. Instead we have numerous Hellenistic-Roman tombs in the rocky outcrops along the eastern edge of the Karkotis Valley, especially around Katydhata. Two un-looted tombs of this period located near Evrykhou in the central part of the Karkotis Valley have produced rich jewellery and wonderful glass vessels apart from the more standard ceramic equipment.[30] Oddly enough for an important copper producing area, there were few bronze artefacts and no bronze vessels in the tombs. These tombs may be the only *in situ* remains of a string of once wealthy communities. On the western side of the valley a series of well-preserved treads running along the river have produced no ancient pottery and no likely settlements. Traffic up and down the valley must have run on the eastern side, alongside the tombs and the modern road. However, the absence of evidence for elite living in the central and eastern part of the TAESP area cannot be explained as the product of geomorphological processes.

MINING AND QUARRYING IN THE EASTERN DESERT OF EGYPT

The second case for transport amphora distribution patterns comes from the central Eastern Desert of Egypt, which is certainly the best-preserved and understood quarrying and mining area in the Mediterranean. The data come from the quarries at Mons Claudianus and Mons Porphyrites and the mines at Bir Umm Fawakhir; all located in an area with no or very limited agricultural potential. Not surprisingly the proportional distribution of pottery reveals very high

Amphorae	Scraps	Plain ware	Cooking wares	Jugs	Pipes
2356	196	415	301	49	165

Table 3. Distribution of pottery excavated in two trenches by the Late Roman north gate at Abu Sha'ar Fort (Riley in *Sidebotham* et al. *1989, fig. 19-20).*

percentages of transport amphorae.[31] During the Early Roman period oil, wine, and wheat were part of the official rations and there was obviously an official supply network in the Eastern Desert.[32] The vast majority of the transport amphorae came from the Nile Valley itself, so the network mainly tapped into local resources as appears to have been the case in the TAESP area and on Methana. Relatively few transport amphorae from beyond the Nile Valley were found at Mons Claudianus and Mons Porphyrites. The rare non-Egyptian amphora types were possibly imported for the benefit of special clients. For instance wine was not included in the ration of the imperial *familia* presumably because they had personal access to a wider network. However, no *ostraka* from Mons Claudianus are dated later than the third century and large-scale exploitation appears to have ended by then. Late Roman finds suggest that quarrying did continue during this period, but the organisation of the exploitation may have changed fundamentally. The pottery from the survey at Bir Umm Fawakhir, a Late Roman, gold mining settlement, cannot be quantified, but it is mentioned that here as well most amphorae sherds belong to the Nile Valley types. The imports are mainly LR1 but also a few North African types. Bir Umm Fawakhir is believed to have been the main source of gold to the Eastern Empire during the Late Roman period and so probably under some form of imperial control. At the Late Roman fort at Abu Sha'ar, which guarded the end of the road connecting Mons Claudianus and Mons Porphyrites with the Red Sea, 67% of the raw count of pottery sherds was identified as transport amphorae (Table 3). According to John A. Riley,[33] the vast majority came from the Nile Valley. These presumably had come by land transport from the Nile and not by the Red Sea although Abu Sha'ar is located on the coast.

Interestingly, no Late Roman pottery was found in the excavations of Quseir al-Qadim, the harbour town at the end of Wadi Hammamat, the road connecting Bir Umm Fawakhir with the Red Sea. This suggests that the gold was exported up the Nile.

In brief, even at imperially owned or controlled sites with access to vast resources, local networks appear to have dominated the food supplies, as must have been the case on Methana and in the TAESP area. Army supplies provide a comparison for the non-agricultural production sites, in that they are not self-sufficient either. *Annona militaris* is generally associated with long distance transport such as support of the NW or NE limes with oil and wine.[34] From the 3rd century AD onwards the organisation of army life came increasingly under centralised control, but military provisions were also supplied locally wherever possible.[35] This would certainly be the case at Abu Sha'ar.

CONCLUSIONS

The Late Roman period reveals a wider dissemination of imported transport amphorae and table wares into remote rural areas compared to earlier periods; however, actual numbers in the TAESP area are small. And yet, the TAESP area was not cut off from the extra-regional world. The tables wares found in the survey area are mainly Late Roman D Ware from just across the sea, Pisidia/Pamphylia

21 Edmondson 1989, 96.
22 Diodorus III.12-13; Galen *De temp. Fac. Simp. Med.* 9.
23 Kassianidou forthcoming.
24 Papacostas 2001, 111.
25 Edmondson 1989.
26 Josephus XVI.4.5.
27 Galen *De Temp. Fac. Simp. Med.* 9.
28 Mitford 1950, 13.
29 Michaelides 1996, 144; Mitford 1980, 1298, 1327 n. 177.
30 Nicolaou 1984; Jacobsen 2007b.
31 Tomber 2006, 209, Riley in Sidebotham *et al.* 1989, 151 and Sidebotham *et al.* 1991, 602.
32 Veen with Hamilton-Dyer 1998.
33 Sidebotham *et al.* 1989, 150-151.
34 E.g. Demesticha 2005; Karagiorgou 2001.
35 Junkelmann 1997, 83-85.

in Asia Minor, and south-western Cyprus (if we accept that Late Roman D was also produced in this area), Phocaean Red Slip Ware from western Asia Minor, but also African Red Slip Ware and Egyptian Red Slip Ware. However, in the TAESP area the access to imported table wares was not associated with access to imported foodstuffs. The pattern suggests a centralized economy where surpluses produced were not redistributed in the rural areas producing it. The people who worked the land may have been tenants as suggested by Lin Foxhall at Methana.[36] The broad phenomenon of tenancy is known from literary sources of the Roman period, although I know of no written or epigraphical evidence from Cyprus.[37] I suggest that the surplus of the agriculture was absorbed in the cost of copper production and that although local contractors and labourers were most probably involved even during the Late Roman period, the profit mainly went to the absentee owners of the mines.

Articles on Late Roman Cyprus speak of the prosperity of the province during this period.[38] Apart from the testimonies of the written sources,[39] the evidence is the construction of public buildings and richly decorated houses in the urban centres and the most diffused settlement pattern in the ancient history of the island. The assumption of rural wealth is based on the diffused settlement pattern frequently associated with small churches.[40] During the Late Roman period the church grew very powerful and no doubt accumulated great wealth. According to Richard Alston,[41] the special status of the city in the ancient world was eroded in the Late Roman period because Christianity developed alternative centres of authority and wealth in the monasteries mainly located outside the urban centres. Consequently, the establishment of the church as a powerbase broke the close link between the elite and the city. In Cyprus this may have produced rural sites such as Kalavasos-*Kopetra*,[42] Cape Drepano,[43] and to a lesser extent Ayios Kononas,[44] but we have identified no such sites in the TAESP area. Of course in the Post-Roman period church building was often associated with personal patronage, e.g., the early 12th century Church of Panagia Phorbiotissa of Asinou in the TAESP area. The church was probably originally constructed as a family chapel for Nicephoros Magistros, who later died there in AD 1115.[45] As such they cannot be used as evidence for the general dissemination of wealth in the rural hinterland.

Were the elite settlements all located in the Karkotis Valley and hence now obscured by alluvial sedimentation? Or were the owners absent, settled in the urban centre of Soli, where a great basilica was built during the Late Roman period, or even further away? A man named Ioannis single-handedly paid for the rebuilding of the basilica in Soli in 655 after its destruction in an Arab raid.[46] Did his wealth come from the mines? Years ago Mitford published a mid first-century AD inscription from Soli from a burial enclosure set up by a man named Apollonios.[47] He was an important man in the city serving, among other distinctions, as censor and the inscription also mentions connections to the Roman proconsul. However, first among his distinctions is listed his high priesthood in the imperial cult, and next his captaincy in the local police force. Mitford wondered why the police captaincy should be so prominent. One possibility is that the wealth of the Soli mines has something to do with that. According to Alfred Michael Hirt private contractors were commonly involved in the imperial quarries at least into the third century AD, but the evidence of private involvement in imperial mines is sparse.[48]

Careful analysis of the distribution of survey pottery, especially of transport amphorae, has a lot to offer economic models. From the three areas investigated it is plain to see that even if they were all closely linked with the economy of the Roman world at large providing it with food, minerals and stone, local and regional food stuffs dominated their own supplies completely. Although the export productions should have stimulated local economies it would appear that the profits mainly went to absent owners. The evidence suggests that the local economy in the TAESP area may have been based on a system of tenants and other contractors.

36 Foxhall 1990.
37 E.g. Grey 2007.
38 E.g. Bakirtzis 1995; Michaelides 1996; Papacostas 2001; Papageorghiou 1993; Rautman 2003.
39 E.g. John Lydus *De Mag.* 2.29.
40 Rautman 2000, 318.
41 Alston 2001, 366.
42 Rautman 2003.
43 Bakirtzis 1995.
44 Fejfer & Mathiesen 1995.
45 Stylianou & Stylianou 1997.
46 Papageorghiou 1993, 43.
47 Mitford 1950, 201-205.
48 Hirt 2010, 261.

Bibliography

Bibliography

The abbreviations of journals are in accordance with Project Dyabola, Realkatalog des Deutschen Archäologischen Instituts, Rom.

Abadie-Reynal, C 1992
The Siena Amphora Conference: Part 2: Amphores romaines d'Orient, *JRA* 5, 361-366.

Abadie-Reynal, C. & Sodini, J.P. 1992
La céramique paléochrétienne de Thasos: Aliki, Delkos, fouilles anciennes. Athènes & Paris.

Абрамов, А.Р. 1993
Античные амфоры. Периодизация и хронология, *Боспорский сборник* 3, 4-135.

Adamsheck, B. 1979
Kenchreai, Eastern Port of Corinth IV: The Pottery. Leiden.

Adan-Bayewitz, A. 1986
The Pottery from the 'Late Byzantine Building' and its implications, in: Levine, L.I. & Netzer, E. (eds.), *Excavations in Caesarea Maritima 1975, 1976, 1979, Final Report,* Qedem 21. Jerusalem, 90-129.

Adiego Lajara, I.-J. 2007
The Carian Language, Handbook of Oriental Studies Section 1, The Near and Middle East 86. Leiden.

Albarella, G., Ceglia, A. & Roberts, J. 1993
S. Giacomo degli Schiavoni (Molise): An Early Fifth Century Deposit of Pottery and Animal Bones from Central Adriatic Italy, *BSR* 61, 157-200.

Alcock, S.E. 1993
Graecia Capta: The landscapes of Roman Greece. Cambridge.

Alfen, P.G. van 1996
New light on the 7th-c. Yassi Ada shipwreck: capacities and standard sizes of LRA1 amphoras, *JRA* 9, 189-213.

Alpözen, T.O., Berkaya, B. & Özdaş, A.H. 1995
Commercial amphoras of the Bodrum Museum of Underwater Archaeology. Maritime trade of the Mediterranean in ancient times, Bodrum Museum of Underwater Archaeology Publication no. 2. Bodrum.

Alston, R. 2001
The City in Roman and Byzantine Egypt. London.

Amouretti, M.-C. 1992
Oléiculture et viticulture dans la Grèce antique, in: Wells, B. (ed.), *Agriculture in Ancient Greece. Proceedings of the Seventh International Symposium at the Swedish Institute at Athens, 16-17 May, 1990.* Stockholm, 77-86.

Amphores romaines 1989
Amphores romaines et histoire économique: dix ans de recherche. Actes du colloque de Sienne, 24-26 mai 1986, Collection de l'École française de Rome 114. Paris & Rome.

Αναγνωστοπούλου-Χατζηπολυχρόνη, E. 2004 [2006]
Σωστική ανασκαφή στην αρχαία Μένδη, *AErgoMak* 18, 133-140.

Ardeţ, A. 2004
The Roman Province of Dacia: Aspects of Commerce in Light of Amphoras, in: Ruscu, L., Ciongradi, C., Ardevan, R, Roman, C. & Găzdac, C. (eds.), *Orbis Antiquus. Studia in honorem Ioannis Pisonis.* Cluj-Napoca, 330-341.

Ariel, D.T. 1990
Imported Stamped Amphora Handles, in: Ariel, D.T., *Excavations at the City of David Directed by Yigal Shiloh, 2. Imported Stamped Handles, Coins, Worked Bone and Ivory, and Glass,* Qedem 30. Jerusalem, 13-98.

Ariel, D.T. 2005
Stamped Amphora Handles and Unstamped Amphora Fragments from Acre (Akko), *'Atiqot* 50, 181-193.

Ariel, D.T. 2007
A Stamped Amphora Handle and a Herodian Coin, in: Barako, T.J. (ed.), *Tel Mor: The Moshe Dothan Excavations Directed by 1959-1960,* IAA Reports 32. Jerusalem, 259-261.

Ariel, D.T. & Finkielsztejn, G. 1994
Stamped Amphora Handles, in: Herbert, S.C. (ed.), *Tel Anafa I.i. Final report on ten years of excavation at a Hellenistic and Roman settlement in northern Israel,* JRA Supplementary Series 10. Ann Arbor, 183-240.

Ariel D.T. & Finkielsztejn G., 2003
Amphora Stamps and Imported Amphoras, in: Kloner, A. (ed.), *Maresha Excavations Final Report I: Subterranean Complexes 21, 44, 70,* IAA Reports 17. Jerusalem, 137-151.

Armstrong, P. 2009
Trade in the east Mediterranean in the 8th Century, in: Mango, M.M. (ed.), *Byzantine Trade, 4th-12th Centuries: The Archaeology of Local, Regional and International Exchange. Papers of the Thirty-eighth Spring Symposium of Byzantine Studies, St John's College, University of Oxford, March 2004*, Society for the Promotion of Byzantine Studies 14. Farnham, 157-178.

Arnaud, P. 2005
Les routes de la navigation antique: itinéraires en Méditerranée. Paris.

Arthur, P. 1992
Amphorae for bulk transport, in: D'Andria, F. & Whitehouse, D.B. (eds.), *Excavations at Otranto II: The Finds.* Lecce, 197-217.

Arthur, P. 1998
Eastern Mediterranean amphorae between 500 and 700: a view from Italy, in: Saguì, L. (ed.), *Ceramica in Italia: VI - VII secolo. Atti del Convegno in onore di John W. Hayes, Roma 11-13 maggio 1995.* Firenze, 157-184.

Arthur, P. & Oren, E.D. 1998
The North Sinai survey and the evidence of transport amphorae for Roman and Byzantine trading patterns, *JRA* 11, 193-212.

Aston, A.D. 2007
Amphorae, Storage Jars and Kegs from Elephantine A Brief Survey of Vessels from the Eighth-Seventh Centuries BC to the Seventh-Eighth Centuries AD, in: Marchand & Marangou (eds.), 419-445.

Aubert, C. 2004
Le commerce antique en Phénicie d'aprés les amphores locales et importés de Beyrouth, in: Eiring & Lund (eds.), 31-42.

Aupert, P. 1980
Objets de la vie quotidienne à Argos en 585 ap. J.-C., Études Argiennes, BCH Supplément 6. Athènes & Paris, 395-457.

Autret, C. 2012
Cyprus and Cilicia: Amphora Production, Trade and Relations in the Early Roman Era, in: Georgiou, A. (ed.), *Cyprus: An Island Culture: Society and Social Relations from the Bronze Age to the Venetian Period.* Oxford, 251-267.

Autret, C. & Rauh. N. 2010
Roman Amphora Production in Western Rough Cilicia, in: Aydinoğlu & Şenol (eds.), 109-122.

Autret, C., Yağci, R. & Rauh, N.K. 2010
A LRA 1 Amphora Kiln Site at Soli-Pompeiopolis, *ANMED Anadolou Akdenızı Arkeoloji Haberleri* 8, 203-204.

Aydinoğlu, Ü. & Şenol, A.K. (eds.) 2010
Olive Oil and Wine production in Anatolia during Antiquity. International Symposium Proceedings 06-08 November 2008, Mersin, Turkey/Uluslararası Sempozuyum Bildireleri 06-08 Kasım 2008, Mersin, Türkiye. İstanbul.

Badoud, N. 2003
Remarques sur la chronologie des éponymes amphoriques rhodiens, *REA* 105/2, 579-587.

Badre, L. & Gubel, E. 1999-2000
Tell Kazel, Syria. Excavations of the AUB Museum, 1993-1998. Third Preliminary Report, *Berytus* 44, 123-203.

Bagnall, R.S. 1976
The administration of the Ptolemaic possessions outside Egypt, Columbia Studies in the Classical Tradition IV. Leiden.

Bakirtzis, C. 1995
The Role of Cyprus in the Grain Supply of Constantinople in the Early Christian Period, in: Karageorghis & Michaelides (eds.), 247-253.

Balandier, Cl. 2000
The defensive organisation of Cyprus at the time of the city-kingdoms (8th c.-end of the 4th c. B.C.), *RDAC*, 163-177.

Balandier, Cl. 2002
La défense des territoires à Chypre de l'époque archaïque aux invasions arabes (VIIIe s. av. n.è. – VIIe s. de n.è.), *DialHistAnc* 28, 175-206.

Ballard, R., Stager, L., Master, D., Yoerger, D., Mindell, D., Whitcomb, L., Singh, H. & Piechota, D. 2002
Iron Age Shipwrecks in Deep Water off Ashkelon, Israel, *AJA* 106, 151-168.

Ballet, P. 1995
Relations céramiques entre l'Egypte et Chypre à l'époque gréco-romaine et byzantine, in: Meyza & Mlynarczyk (eds.), 11-25.

Ballet, P., Finkielsztejn, G., Çankardeş-Şenol, G. & Şenol, A.K. 2012
Amphores importées, in: Ballet, P. & Poludnikiewicz, A. (eds.), *Tebtynis V, La céramique des époques hellénistique et impériale, campagnes 1988-1993*. Le Caire, 157-172.

Banning, E.B. 2002
Archaeological Survey, Manuals in Archaeological Method, Theory and Technique. New York.

Barako, T. 2008
Amphoras Through the Ages, in: Stager, L.E., Scholen, J.D. & Master, D.M. (eds.), *Ashkelon 1, Introduction and Overview (1985-2006), Final Reports of the Leon Levy Expedition to Ashkelon*. Winona Lake, Indiana, 429-461.

Barker, C. 2002a
Rhodian amphorae stamps, in: Raptou, E., Stylianou, E. & Vassiliou, E., A Hellenistic Tomb in Pegeia (P.M. 3534), *RDAC*, 215-216.

Barker, C. 2002b
Three new eponym-fabricant combinations on Rhodian amphorae from the 'Tombs of the Kings' at Nea Pafos, *RDAC*, 189-200.

Barker, C. 2004
The Use of Rhodian Amphorae in Hellenistic Graves at Nea Paphos, Cyprus, in: Eiring & J. Lund (eds.), 73-84.

Barker, C. forthcoming
Stamped Amphora Handles, in: Green, J.R. et al., *The Theatre of Nea Paphos: Final Excavation Report*, 1995-2006.

Bar-Nathan, R. & Adato, M. 1986
Byzantine Pottery (Stratum 5), in: Levine, L.I. & Netzer, E. (eds.), *Excavations at Caesarea Maritima 1975, 1976, 1979: Final Report*, Qedem 21. Jerusalem,160-175.

Bass, G.F. & Doorninck Jr., F.H. van 1971
A Fourth-Century Shipwreck at Yassi Ada, *AJA* 75, 27-37.

Bass, G.F. & Doorninck Jr., F.H. van 1982
Yassi Ada: Volume I, A Seventh-Century Byzantine Shipwreck, Ed Rachal Foundation Nautical Archaeology Series. College Station, Texas.

Bekker-Nielsen, T. 1993
Centres and Road Networks in Hellenistic Cyprus, in: Bilde, P., Engberg-Pedersen, T., Hannestad, L., Zahle, J. & Randsborg, K. (eds.), *Centre and Periphery in the Hellenistic World*. Aarhus, 176-191.

Bekker-Nielsen, T. 1995
The Road System, in: Fejfer, J. (ed.), *Ancient Akamas I*. Aarhus, 87-132.

Bekker-Nielsen, T. 2001
The Ancient Road from Amathous to Central Cyprus, *RDAC* 2001, 247-254.

Bekker-Nielsen, T. 2004
The Roads of Ancient Cyprus. Copenhagen.

Bekker-Nielsen, T., Crabb, P., Fejfer, J., Hannestad, L., Hannestad, N., Hayes, P.P., Leonard, J.R. & Thomsen, O. 1995.
Introduction, in: Fejfer (ed.), 15-25.

Benson, J.L. 1973
The Necropolis of Kaloriziki, Studies in Mediterranean Archaeology XXXVI. Göteborg.

Ben-Tor, A. & Portugali, Y. 1987
Tel Qiri. A village in the Jezreel valley, Qedem 24. Jerusalem.

Ben-Tor, A., Portugali, Y. & Avissar, M. 1983
The third and fourth seasons of excavations at Tel Yoqne'am, 1979-1981, *IEJ* 33, 30-54.

Berlingò, I. 1995
Importazione Corinzie nella Siritide, in: *Corinto e l'Occidente*, 417-430.

Berni Millet, P. 1998
Las ánforas de aceite de la Bética y su presencia en la Cataluña. Barcelona, Col·lecció Instrumenta 4. Barcelona.

Bezeczky, T. 2004
Early Roman food import in Ephesus: Amphorae from the Tetragonos Agora, in: Eiring & Lund (eds.), 85-97.

Bezeczky, T. 2005a
Late Roman Amphorae from the Ephesian Agora, in: Krinzinger, F. (ed.), *Spätantike und mittelalterliche Keramik aus Ephesus*, AForsch 13. Wien, 203-223.

Bezeczky, T. 2005b
Roman Amphorae from Vindobona, in: Krinzinger (ed.), 35-107.

Bezeczky, T. 2006
Consumer behaviour in Ephesus in the first century BC, in: Malfitana *et al.* (eds.), 287-308.

Bîrzescu, I. 2009
Funde aus Milet. XXI. Drei Typen archiascher Reifenamphoren aus Milet, *AA*, 121-134.

Bîrzescu, I. 2012
Histria XV: Die archaischen und frühklassischen Transportamphoren. Bucarest.

Boardman, J., Edwards, I.E.S., Hammond, N.G.L. & Sollberger, E. (eds.) 1991
The Assyrian and Babylonian Empires and other States of the Near East, from the Eighth to the Sixth Centuries B.C., Cambridge Ancient History 3.2. Second Edition. Cambridge.

Böttger, B. 1992
Die kaiserzeitlichen and spätantiken Amphoren aus dem Kerameikos, *AM* 107, 315-381.

Bonifay, M. & Piéri, D. 1995
Amphores du Ve au VIIe s. à Marseille: nouvelles données sur la typologie et le contenu, *JRA* 8, 94-120.

Bonifay, M. & Tréglia, J.-C. (eds.) 2007
LRCW 2: Late Roman Coarse Wares, Cooking Wares and Amphorae in the Mediterranean. Archaeology and Archaeometry, BAR International Series 1662. Oxford.

Bonifay, M. & Villedieu, F. 1989
Importations d'amphores orientales en Gaule (Ve-VIIe siècle), in: Déroche, V. & Spieser, J.-M. (eds.), *Recherches sur la céramique byzantine, Athènes, 1987,* BCH Supplément 18. Paris, 17-46.

Borowicz, S. 2009
System ekonomiczny Cypru w okresie późnoklasycznym i wczesnohellenistycznym w świetle produkcji i dystrybucji ceramiki, Ph.D. Thesis, Jagiellonian University, Kraków.

Bourriau, J. & French, P. 2007
Imported Amphorae from Buto Dating from c. 750 BC to the Early 6th Century AD, in: Marchand & Marangou (eds.), 115-133.

Bowden, H. & Gill, D. 1997
Late Roman Methana, in: Mee & Forbes (eds.), 84-91.

Брашинский, И.Б. 1967
Новые данные о торговых связях Ольвии в Самоссом, *KSIA* 109, 22-26.

Briese, M.B. & Vaag, L.E. (eds.) 2005
Trade Relations in the Eastern Mediterranean from the Late Hellenistic Period to Late Antiquity: The Ceramic Evidence, Acts from a Ph.D.-seminar for young scholars, Sandbjerg Manorhouse, 12-15 February 1998, Halicarnassian Studies 3. Odense.

Brixhe, C. with the collaboration of Gonca Çankardeş-Şenol 2012
Timbres amphoriques de Pamphylie, Études alexandrines 23. Alexandrie.

Brun, J.-P. 2003
Le vin et l'huile dans la méditerranée antique. Viticulture, oléiculture et procédés de transformation. Paris.

Buhl, M.-L. 1983
Sukas VII: The Near Eastern Pottery and Objects of Other Materials from the Upper Strata, Publications of the Carlsberg expedition to Phoenicia, Det Kongelige Danske Videnskabernes Selskab Historisk-filosofiske skrifter. Copenhagen.

Burragato, F., di Nezza, M., Ferrazzoli, A.F. & Ricci, M. 2007
Late Roman 1 amphora types produced at Elaiussa Sebaste, in: Bonifay, & Tréglia (eds.), 689-700.

Cabrera Bonet, P. & Santos Retolaza, M. (eds.) 2000
Ceràmiques jònies d'època arcaica. Centres de producció i commercialització al Mediterrani occidental, Monografies emporitanes 11. Barcelona.

Callaghan, P.J., Johnston, A., Hayes, J.W. & Jones, R. 2000
Iron Age Pottery from Kommos, in: Shaw, J. & Shaw, M. (eds.), *Kommos IV: The Greek sanctuary.* Princeton, 210-335.

Calvet, Y. 1972
Salamine de Chypre III: Les timbres amphoriques (1965-1970). Paris.

Calvet, Y. 1978
Timbres amphoriques de Salamine (1971-1974), *RDAC*, 222-234

Calvet, Y. 1980
Anses d'amphores et marques, in: Argoud, G., Cullot, O. & Helly, B. (eds.), *Salamine de Chypre XI: Une residence byzantine 'l'huilerie'.* Paris, 36-37.

Calvet, Y. 1982
Kition-Bamboula I: Les timbres amphoriques. Paris.

Calvet, Y. 1986
Les amphores chypriotes et leur diffusion en Méditerranée orientale, in: Empereur & Garlan (eds.), 505-514.

Calvet, Y. 1993
Les timbres amphoriques, in: Salles (ed.), 61-80.

Calvet, Y. & Masson, O. 1988
Un nouveau timbre amphorique à légende syllabique de Kition, *CETCyprCah* 10, 23-26.

Calvet, Y. & M. Yon 1977
Céramique trouvée à Salamine, fouilles de la ville, in: Gjerstad, E. (ed.), *Greek Geometric and Archaic Pottery found in Cyprus*. Stockholm, 9-21.

Cancova, J. 1959
Amphores du Moyen Age en Bulgarie, *Bulletin de l'Institut archéologique bulgare* 22, 243-262.

Cankardeş-Şenol, G. 2000
İskenderiye (Mısır) Kurtarma Kazılarında Ele Geçen Hellenistik Dönem Amphora Mühürleri, Ph.D. diss., T.C. Ege Üniversitesi, Izmir.

Cankardeş-Şenol, G. 2001
Stamped Amphora Handles from the Necropolis of Gabbari, *Nécropolis 1*, Études alexandrines 5. Alexandrie, 397-408.

Cankardeş-Şenol, G. 2006
Klasik ve Hellenistik Dönem'de Mühürlü Amphora Üreten Merkezler ve Mühürleme Sistemleri. Istanbul.

Cankardeş-Şenol, G. 2007
Stamped Amphora Handles Found in the Rescue Excavations of CEAlex in Alexandria, in: Marchand & Marangou (eds.), 33-56.

Cankardeş-Şenol, G. forthcoming
Proto-Knidian Amphora Exportation to Alexandria/Egypt, Hellenistic Ceramics in Anatolia (4th to 1st century BC.), in: *Colloqvia Anatolica et Aegaea. Congressus Internationales Smyrnenses III, International Workshop, October 12-14, 2010, Izmir, Turkey.*

Cankardeş-Şenol, G. & Alkaç, E. 2007
IV.6. Amphora Mühürleri: Rhodos, Knidos, Kıbrıs ve Lokal Üretimler, in: Durugönül (ed.), 297-473.

Cannavò, A. 2010
The Cypriot Kingdoms in the Archaic Age: A Multicultural Experience in the Eastern Mediterranean, Bollettino di archeologia on line [http://151.12.58.75/archeologia-] (2011) edizione speciale, B.3.5., 37-46.

Canoğlu, E. 2011
Amphora Mühürlerinden Hareketle Klasik ve Hellenistik Dönemlerde Thasos ve Doğu Akdeniz Ticari İlişkileri, MA thesis, Ege Üniversitesi, Izmir.

Carlson, D.N. 2004
Cargo in context: The morphology, stamping, and origins of the amphoras from a fifth-century B.C. Ionian shipwreck, Ph.D. diss., University of Texas, Austin.

Carlson, D.N. & Lawall, M.L. 2005/2006 [2007]
Towards a Typology of Erythraian Amphoras, *Skyllis* 7, 32-39.

Carreras Monfort, C. & Williams, D.F. 2003
Spanish olive oil trade in late Roman Britain: Dressel 23 amphorae from Winchester, *JRomPotSt* 10, 64-68.

Catling, H.W. 1972
An Early Byzantine Pottery Factory at Dhiorios in Cyprus, *Levant* 4, 1-82.

Cavagnera, L. 1995
Anfore commerciali, in: Orlandini, P. & Castoldi, M. (eds.), *Ricerche archeologiche all'Incoronata di Metaponto: scavi dell'Universitá degli Studi di Milano. Istituto di Archeologia 3: L'oikos greco del saggio S. Lo scavo e i repeti*. Milano, 41-54.

Cesnola, A.-P. di 1881
Lawrence-Cesnola Collection: Cyprus Antiquities Excavated by Major Alexander Palma di Cesnola, Member of the Biblical Archæological Society, &c., &c., 1876 to 1879. London.

Cesnola, A.-P. di 1882
Salamina (Cyprus). The History, Treasures, & Antiquities of Salamis in the Island of Cyprus. London.

Cesnola, L.P. di 1903
A Descriptive Atlas of the Cesnola Collection of Cypriote Antiquities in The Metropolitan Museum of Art, New York Volume Three. New York.

Charleston, R.J. 1955
Roman Pottery. London.

Чистов, Д.Е. (ed.) 2012
Материалы березанской (Нижнебугской) античной археологической експедиции, Том 2. Исследования на острове Березань в 2005-2009 гг. Санкт-Петербург.

Christou, D. 1995
Chronique des fouilles et découverts archéologiques a Chypre en 1994, *BCH* 119, 799-838.

Çokay-Kepçe, S. 2006
The Karaçalli Nekropolis near Antalya. Antalya.

Coldstream, J.N. & Huxley, G.L. 1973
Kythera: Excavations and Studies conducted by the University of Pennsylvania Museum and the British School at Athens. London.

Collombier, A.-M. 1987
Céramique grecque et échanges en Méditerranée orientale: Chypre et la côte syro-phénicienne (fin VIIIe – fin IVe siècles av. J.-C.), *Studia Phoenicia* 5, 239-248.

Connelly, J.B. 2010
Cyprus in the Age of Empires, in: Hadjisavvas, S. (ed.), *Cyprus. Crossroads of Civilizations.* Nicosia, 173-178.

Conrad, D. 1989
Notes on a Stamped Amphora Handle, in: Herzog *et al.* (eds.), 339-340.

Corinto e l'Occidente 1995
Corinto e l'Occidente. Atti del Trentaquattresimo convegno di studi sulla Magna Grecia, Taranto 7-11 ottobre 1994. Taranto.

Costa, E.A. Jr. 1974
Evagoras l and the Persians, ca. 411 to 391 B.C., *Historia* 23, 40-56.

Coulson, W.D.E., Mook, M.S. & Rehard, J.W. 1997
Stamped Amphora Handles from Tel Beersheba, *BASOR*, 47-62.

Coureas, N. 2005
Economy, in: Nicolaou-Konnari, A. & Schabel, C. (eds.), *Cyprus: Society and Culture 1191-1374,* The Medieval Mediterranean: Peoples, Economies and Cultures, 400-1500. Leiden & Boston, 103-156.

Courtois, L. 1980
Examen pétrographique et caractérisation matérielle de quelques céramiques de Tell Keisan, in: Brient, J. & Humbert, J.B. (eds.), *Tell Keisan (1971-1976) une cité phénicienne en Galileé.* Fribourg, 353-360.

Crowfoot, J.W. & Fitzgerald, G.M. 1929
Excavations in the Tyropoeon Valley, Jerusalem. London.

Dagron, G. 1985
Un tarif des sportules à payer aux **curiosi** du port de Séleucie de Piérie (VIe siècle), *Travaux et Mémoires* 9, 435-451.

Daszewski, W.A. 1970
Polish Excavations at Kato (Nea) Paphos. Second preliminary report: seasons 1968 and 1969, *RDAC*, 112-141.

Daszewski, W.A. 1972
Polish Excavations at Kato (Nea) Paphos in 1970 and 1971, *RDAC*, 204-236.

Daszewski, W.A. 1978
Fouilles de Nea Paphos (Mission polonaise), in: Karageorghis, V., Chronique des fouilles et découvertes archéologiques à Chypre en 1977, *BCH* 102, 927-930.

Daszewski, W.A. 1985
Fouilles de Nea Paphos (Mission polonaise), in: Karageorghis, V., Chronique des fouilles et découvertes archéologiques à Chypre en 1984, *BCH* 109, 950-955.

Daszewski, W.A. 1986
Fouilles de la Maison de Thésée et de la Maison d'Aion (Mission polonaise), in Karageorghis, V., Chronique des fouilles et découvertes archéologiques à Chypre en 1985, *BCH* 110, 856–862.

Daszewski, W.A. 1987
La villa de Thésée et la Maison d'Aion (Mission polonaise), in: Karageorghis, V., Chronique des fouilles et découvertes archéologiques a Chypre en 198, *BCH* 111, 683-689.

Daszewski, W.A. 1993
Nea Paphos 1992, *PolAMed* 4, 83-93.

Daszewski, W.A. 1994
Nea Paphos 1993, *PolAMed* 5, 101-110.

Daszewski, W.A. 1996
Nea Paphos excavations 1995, *PolAMed* 7, 91-99.

Daszewski, W.A., with Meyza, H. & Papuci-Władyka, E. 2007
Nea Paphos. Season 2005, *PolAMed* 17, 393-407.

Daszewski, W.A. & Meyza, H. with Machowski, W., Papuci-Władyka, E., Rądkowska, J.K. & Wasilewska, O. 2010
Nea Paphos. Season 2007, *PolAMed* 19, 501-514.

Daszkiewicz, M., Meyza, H. & Schneider, G. 1997
A Preliminary Study of Amphorae of the Mau XXVII/XXVIII Type, *PolAMed* 8, 132-138.

Debidour, M. 1986
En classant les timbres thasiennes, in: Empereur & Garlan (eds.), 312-334.

Defernez, C. 1997
La céramique préptolemaïque de Tell el-Herr. Présentation préliminaire, *CahCerEg* 5, 57-70.

Defernez, C. 2001
La céramique d'époque perse à Tell El-Herr: étude chrono-typologique et comparative 1, Cahiers de recherches de l'institut de papyrologie et d'égyptologie de Lille, Supplément 5/1. Lille.

Defernez, C. 2007a
Le mobilier amphorique provenant d'un édifice monumental découvert sur le site de Tell el-Herr (Nord-Sinaï), in: Marchand & Marangou (eds.), 547-620.

Defernez, C. 2007b
La céramique du premier état de la citadelle hellénistique: un ensemble disparate, in: Valbelle, D. & Abd el-Maksoud, M. (eds.), *Tell el-Herr, les niveaux hellénistiques et du Haut Empire*. Paris, 34-38.

Defernez, C. & Marchand, S. 2006
Les imitations égyptiennes des conteneurs d'origine égéenne et levantine (du VIe siècle au début du IIe siècle av. J.-C.): un exemple d'innovation technique secondaire, in: Mathieu, B., Meeks, D. & Wissa, M. (eds.), *L'apport de l'Égypte à l'histoire des techniques. Méthodes, chronologies et comparaisons, Colloque international IFAO, Le Caire, 15-17 septembre 2003*, IFAO Bibliothèque d'étude 142. Le Caire, 63-100.

Demesticha, S. 2000
The Paphos Kiln: Manufacturing Techniques of LR1 Amphoras, *ReiCretActa* 36, 549-554.

Demesticha, S. 2002
Οι Κυπριακοί αμφορείς της Ύστερης Ρωμαϊκής Περιόδου, Ph.D. diss., Πανεπιστήμιο Κύπρου.

Demesticha, S. 2003
Amphora production on Cyprus during the Late Roman Period, in: Bakirtzis, Ch. (ed.), *VIIe Congrès International sur la Céramique Médiévale en Méditerranée, Thessaloniki, 11-16 Octobre 1999, Actes*. Athènes, 469-476.

Demesticha, S. 2005
Some thoughts on the production and presence of the Late Roman Amphora 13 on Cyprus, in: Briese & Vaag (eds.), 169-178.

Demesticha, S. 2009
Questions on trade: The case of the Mazotos Shipwreck, *CahCEC* 39, 387-402.

Demesticha, S. 2011
The 4th-century-BC Mazotos Shipwreck, Cyprus: a preliminary report, *IntJNautA* 40, 39-59.

Demesticha, S. forthcoming a
Late Roman Amphora Typology in Context, in: LRCW 4. Late Roman Coarse Wares, Cooking Wares and Amphorae in the Mediterranean, BAR International Series.

Demesticha, S. forthcoming b
Amphora and trade networks, in: *Proceedings of the 1st International Workshop Byzantium in Transition: The Byzantine Early Middle Ages 7th to 8th Centuries, Nicosia 28-30 October 2011.*

Demesticha, S. & Michaelides, D. 2001
The Excavation of a Late Roman I Amphora Kiln in Paphos, in: Villeneuve & Watson (eds.), 289-296.

Deshayes, J. 1963
Mission Jean Bérard 1953-55: La nécropole de Ktima, Institut français d'archéologie de Beyrouth, Bibliothèque archéologique et historique LXXV. Paris.

Diamanti, C. 2010a
Stamped Late Roman/Proto-Byzantine amphoras from Halasarna of Kos, *ReiCretActa* 41, 1-8.

Διαμαντή, Χ./Diamanti C. 2010b
Εντόπια παραγωγή και εισαγωγή αμφορέων στην Αλάσαρνα της Κώ (5 ος -7ος αι.)/Local Production and Import of Amphoras at Halasarna of Kos Island (5th - 7th c.). Αθήνα.

Diederichs, C. 1980
Salamine de Chypre IX: Céramiques hellénistiques, romaines et byzantines. Paris.

Dietler, M. 1999
Consumption, cultural frontiers, and identity: anthropological approaches to Greek colonial encounters, in: *Confini e frontiera nella grecità d'Occidente. Atti del Trentasettesimo convegno di studi sulla Magna Grecia, Taranto 3-6 ottobre 1997.* Taranto, 475-501.

Dietler, M. 2005
Consumption and Colonial Encounters in the Rhône Basin of France: A Study of Early Iron Age Political Economy, CNRS, Monographies d'Archéologie Meditérranéenne 21. Paris.

Dietler, M. 2007
The Iron Age in the Western Mediterranean, in: Scheidel, W., Morris, I. & Saller, R. (eds.), *The Cambridge Economic History of the Greco-Roman world.* Cambridge, 242-276.

Dixneuf, D. 2011
Amphores égyptiennes. Production, typologie, contenu et diffusion (IIIe siècle avant J.-C. – IXe siècle après J.-C.), Études alexandrines 22. Alexandrie.

Dobosz, A. forthcoming a
Rare Greek amphora stamps found in Nea Paphos in Cyprus. Preliminary presentation, in: *Analysis and Uses of Greek Amphora Stamps International Congress, French School in Athens, University of Rennes 2 – Haute Bretagne, Athens, February 3-5, 2010,* BCH Supplément.

Dobosz, A. forthcoming b
Stamped amphora handles, in: Meyza *et al.* forthcoming.

Docter, R. 2000
East Greek Fine Wares and Transport Amphorae of the 8th – 5th century BC from Carthage and Toscanos, in: Cabrera Bonet & Santos Retolaza (eds.), 63-88.

Domingo, C. de & Johnston, A.W. 2003
A petrographic and chemical study of east Greek and other archaic transport amphorae, *Eulimene* 4, 27-60.

Dothan, M. 1971
Ashdod II-III: The Second and Third Seasons of Excavations 1963, 1965 Soundings in 1967, *'Atiqot English Series* 9-10. Jerusalem.

Dressel, H. 1879
Di un grande deposito di anfore rinvenuto nel nuovo quartiere del Castro Pretorio, *BCom* 7, 36-112.

Dupont, P. 1982
Amphores commerciales archaiques de la Grèce de l'Est, *PP* 37, 193-208.

Dupont, P. 1998
Archaic East Greek Trade Amphoras, in: Cook, R.M. & Dupont, P., *East Greek Pottery.* London, 142-190.

Dupont, P. 1999
La circulation amphorique en mer Noire à l'époque archaïque. Spécificité et problèmes, in: Garlan, Y. (ed.), *Production et commerce des amphores anciennes en Mer Noire. Colloque international organisé à Istanbul, 25-28 mai 1994.* Aix-en-Provence, 143-161.

Dupont, P. 2000
Amphores 'samiennes' archaïques: Sources de confusion et questionnements, in: Cabrera Bonet & Santos Retolaza (eds.), 57-62.

Dupont, P. 2006
Amphores "samiennes" archaïques de mer Noire (approche archéométrique), in: Solovyov, S.L. (ed.), *Greeks and Natives in the Cimmerian Bosporus 7th-1st centuries BC. Proceedings of the International Conference October 2000, Taman, Russia,* BAR International Series 1729. Oxford, 41-50.

Dupont, P. 2010
Erythraea 1ère partie. Les amphores 'samiennes' et 'protothasiennes' de Zeest: La piste nord-ionienne?, in: Kassab Tezgör, D. & Inaishvili, N. (eds.), *PATABS I. Production and trade of amphorae in the Black Sea. Actes de la Table Ronde internationale de Batoumi et Trabzon, 27-29 Avril 2006,* Varia Anatolica 21. Istanbul & Paris, 39-43.

Durliat, J. & Guillou, A. 1984
Le tarif d'Abydos (vers 492), *BCH* 107, 582-598.

Durugönül, S. (ed.) 2007
Nagidos, Results of an Excavation in an Ancient City in Rough Cilicia, Adalya Supplementary Series 6. Istanbul.

Dyczek, P. 2001
Roman Amphorae of the 1st-3rd centuries AD found on the Lower Danube. Typology. Warsaw.

Dyczek, P. 2010
Kapitän II amphorae from Novae – between East and West, in: Menchelli *et al.* (eds.), 993-999.

Edmondson, J.C. 1989
Mining in the Later Roman Empire and Beyond: Continuity or Disruption? *JRS* 79, 84-102.

Egloff, M. 1977
Kellia III: *La poterie copte. Quatre siècles d´artisanat et d´échanges en Basse-Egypte, Recherches suisses d´archeologie copte.* Genève.

Eiring, J. & Lund, J. 2004
Introduction, in: Eiring & J. Lund (eds.), 11-14.

Eiring, J. & Lund, J. (eds.) 2004
Transport Amphorae and Trade in the Eastern Mediterranean. Acts of the International Colloquium at the Danish Institute at Athens, September 26-29, 2002, Monographs of the Danish Institute at Athens 5. Aarhus.

Elaigne, S. 2004
Les indices des échanges dans l'Orient hellénistique d'apres les données de la céramique, in: le Dinahet, M.-T. (ed.), *L'Orient méditerranéen de la mort d'Alexandre au 1er siècle avant notre ère.* Nantes, 392-409.

Elgavish, J. 1968
Archaeological excavations at Shikmona. Field report no. 1. The levels of the Persian period. Seasons 1963-1965 [Hebrew]. Haifa.

Elliott, G. & Dutton, R. 1963
Know Your Rocks: an introduction to geology in Cyprus. Nicosia.

Emery, W.B. & Kirwan, L.P. 1938
The Royal Tombs of Ballana and Qustul. Cairo.

Empereur, J.-Y. 1982
Les amphores de Délos, Mémoire de 4ème année, Athènes, Manuscript in Delos excavation house, Archive of French School in Athens.

Empereur, J.-Y. 1983
Un cour remplie d'amphores à l'Est du Lac Sacré, in: Rapports sur les travaux de l'École française en Grèce en 1982, *BCH* 107, 882-886.

Empereur, J.-Y. 1987
Les amphores, in: *Études Chypriotes VIII, La nécropole d'Amathonte Tombes 113-367 II: Céramiques non chypriotes.* Nicosie, 42-43

Empereur, J.-Y. 1995
Le Port Hellénistique d`Amathonte, in: Karageorghis & Michaelides (eds.), 131-138.

Empereur, J.-Y. & Garlan, Y. (eds.) 1986
Recherches sur les amphores greques. Actes du colloque international organize par le centre national de la recherché scientifique, l`Universitaté de Rennes II et l`École Française d`Athenés, Athénes, 10-12 Septembre 1984, BCH Supplément XIII. Athénes.

Empereur, J.-Y. & Hesnard, A. 1987
Les amphores hellénistiques, in: Lévêque, P. & Morel, J.-P. (eds.), *Céramiques hellénistiques et romaines, Centre de recherches d'histoire ancienne* 70. Paris, 9-71.

Empereur, J.-Y. & Picon, M. 1989
Les régions de production d'amphores impériales en Méditerranée orientale, in: *Amphores romaines*, 223-248.

Empereur, J.-Y. & Verlinden, C. 1987
The underwater excavation at the Ancient port of Amathus in Cyprus, *IntJNautA* 16, 7-18.

Engelmann, H. 2001
Inschriften und Heiligtum, in: Muss, U. (ed.), *Der Kosmos der Artemis von Ephesos*, ÖAI Sonderschriften 37. Wien, 33-44.

Engvig, O.T. & Åström, P. 1975
Hala Sultan Tekke II, The Cape Kiti Survey: An Underwater Archaeological Survey, Studies in Mediterranean Archaeology XLV: 2. Göteborg.

Engvig, O.T. & Beichmann, M. 1984
Underwater activities and the situation at Cape Kiti, Cyprus, *OpAth* 15, 181-186.

Ersoy, Y.E. 1993
Clazomenae: The Archaic Settlement, Ph.D. diss., Bryn Mawr College.

Ersoy, Y.E. 2004
Klazomenai: 900-500 BC. History and settlement evidence, in: Moustaka, A., Skarlatidou, E., Tzannes, M.-C. & Ersoy, Y. (eds.), *Klazomenai, Teos and Abdera: Metropoleis and Colony: Proceedings of the International Symposium held at the Archaeological Museum of Abdera: Abdera, 20-21 October 2001.* Thessaloniki, 43-76.

Ettlinger, E., Hedinger, B., Hoffmann, B., Kenrick, Ph.M., Pucci, G., Roth-Rubi, K. Schneider, G., von Schnurbein, S., Wells, C.M. & Zabehlicky-Scheffenegger, S. 1990
Conspectus formarum terrae sigillatae italico modo confectae, Materialen zur Römisch-Germanischen Keramik 10. Bonn.

Fantalkin, A. 2001
Meẓad Ḥashavyahu: Its Material Culture and Historical Background, *TelAviv* 28, 3-165.

Fantalkin, A. 2006
Identity in the Making: Greeks in the Eastern Mediterranean during the Iron Age, in: Villing & Schlotzhauer (eds.), 199-208.

Fejfer, J. (ed.) 1995
Ancient Akamas I: Settlement and Environment. Aarhus.

Fejfer, J. & Mathiesen, H.E. 1991
The Danish Akamas-Project: The First Two Seasons of Work (1989 and 1990), *RDAC*, 211-223.

Fejfer, J. & Mathiesen, H.E. 1992a
Ayios Kononas. A Late Roman/Early Byzantine Site in the Akamas, in: Åström, P. (ed.), *Acta Cypria 2*, Studies in Mediterranean Archaeology and Literature, Pocketbook 117. Jonsered, 67-83.

Fejfer, J. & Mathiesen, H.E. 1992b
The Danish Akamas Expedition (1991), in: Danish Classical Archaeological Fieldwork 1990-1991, *ActaHyp* 4, 381-383.

Fejfer, J. & Mathiesen, H.E. 1995
The site of Ayios Kononas, in: Fejfer (ed.), 73-86.

Ferrazzoli, A.-F. & Ricci, M. 2007
Elaiussa Sebaste: Produzioni e consumi di una citta della Cilicia tra V e VII secolo, in: Bonifay & Tréglia (eds.), 671-688.

Ferrazzoli, A.F. & Ricci, M. 2010
Un centro di produzione delle anfore LR1: Elaiussa Sebaste in Cilicia. Gli impianti, le anfore, in: Menchelli *et al.* (eds.), 815-826.

Finkielsztejn, G. 1990
Catalogue des anses estampillées de Samarie, fouilles de 1931-1933, 1935 (partiel), in: *Amphores et timbres d'amphores importées en Palestine à l'époque hellénistique: orientations de recherches et premiers résultats* III, AIBL-EBAF. Jerusalem (unpublished manuscript).

Finkielsztejn, G. 1995
Chronologie basse des timbres amphoriques rhodiens et évaluation des exportations d'amphores, *ActaHyp* 6, 279-296.

Finkielsztejn, G. 2000
Les amphores importées au Levant sud à l'époque hellénistique et la révision de la chronologie des timbres amphoriques rhodiens, *E' Επιστημονική Συνάντηση για την Ελληνιστική Κεραμική. Χρονολογικά προβήματα – κλειστά σύνολα – εργαστήρια, Χανιά 1997.* Αθήνα, 207-220.

Finkielsztejn, G. 2001a
Chronologie détaillée et révisée des éponymes amphoriques rhodiens, de 270 à 108 av. J.-C. environ. Premier bilan, BAR International Series 990. Oxford.

Finkielsztejn, G. 2001b
Politique et commerce à Rhodes au IIe siècle a. C.: le témoignage des exportations d`amphores, in: Bresson, A. & Descat, R. (eds.), *Les cités d`Asie mineure occidentale au IIe siècle a.C.* Bordeaux, 181-196.

Finkielsztejn, G. 2004
Establishing the Chronology of Rhodian Amphora Stamps. The Next Steps, in: Eiring & Lund (eds.), 117-121.

Finkielsztejn, G. forthcoming a
The Amphoras and Amphora Stamps, in: Tsuf, O. (ed.), *The final report of the J. Kaplan excavations in Jaffa.*

Finkielsztejn, G. forthcoming b
Stamped Amphorae from King Herod's Circus at Caesarea, in: Porat, Y. (ed.), *The final report of the excavations of King Herod's Circus at Caesarea.*

Finley, M.I. 1973
The Ancient Economy. Berkeley.

Fiori, P. 1974
Le mouillage antique du Cap Gros, *CahASubaqu* 3, 81-102.

Flemming, N.C. 1978
Holocene Eustatic Changes and Coastal Tectonics in the Northeast Mediterranean: Implications for Models of Crustal Consumption, *Philosophical Transactions for the Royal Society of London. Series A, Mathematical and Physical Sciences* 289, 405-458.

Flourentzos, P. 1986
Tomb groups from the necropolis in Ay. Omologites, Nicosia, *RDAC*, 150-163.

Flourentzos, P. 1996
Excavations in the Kouris valley II: The Basilica of Alassa. Nicosia.

Flourentzos, P. (ed.) 2007
Proceedings of the International Archaeological Conference From Evagoras I to the Ptolemies. The transition from the Classical to the Hellenistic Period in Cyprus, Nicosia 29-30 November 2002. Nicosia.

Foley, B.P. & Ballard, R.D. 2004
Amphora Alleys I and II, in: McCann, A.M. & Oleson, J.P. (eds.), *Deep-Water Shipwrecks off Skerki Bank: The 1997 Survey,* JRA Supplementary Series 58. Portsmouth, 183-194.

Foxhall, L. 1990
The Dependent Tenant: Land Leasing and Labour in Italy and Greece, *JRS* 80, 97-114.

Foxhall, L. 1997
Ancient Farmsteads, Other Agricultural Sites and Equipment, in: Mee & Forbes (eds.), 257-268.

Foxhall, L. 1998
Cargoes of the heart's desire: The character of trade in the Archaic Mediterranean world, in: Fisher, N. & Wees, H. van (eds.), *Archaic Greece: New Approaches and New Evidence.* London, 295-309.

Foxhall, L. 2005.
Village to city: staples and luxuries? Exchange networks and urbanization, in: Osborne, R. & Cunliffe, B. (eds.), *Mediterranean Urbanization 800-600 BC,* Proceedings of the British Academy 126. Oxford, 233-248.

Foxhall, L. & Forbes, H.A. 1982
Sitometreia: The Role of Grain as a Staple Food in Classical Antiquity, *Chiron* 12, 41-90.

Fraser, P.M. 1972
Ptolemaic Alexandria I. Oxford.

Fraser, P.M. & Matthews, E. 1987
A Lexicon of Greek Personal Names I: The Aegean Islands, Cyprus, Cyrenaica. Oxford.

Freeman, P. 1997
'Romanisation' – 'Imperialism': What are we talking about? in: Meadows, K., Lemke, C. & Heron, J. (eds.), *TRAC 96. Proceedings of the Sixth Annual Theoretical Roman Archaeology Conference hosted by the Research School of Archaeology and Archaeological science, the University of Sheffield, March 30th and 31st 1996.* Oxford, 8-13.

French, P. & Ghaly, H. 1991
Pottery chiefly of the Late Dynastic period, from excavations by the Egyptian Antiquities Organisation at Saqqara, 1987, *CahCerEg* 2, 93-124.

Fulford, M.G. 1989
To East and West: the Mediterranean Trade of Cyrenaica and Tripolitania in Antiquity, *LibSt* 20, 169-191.

Fulford, M.G. & Peacock, D.P.S. 1984
Excavations at Carthage: the British Mission, I,2: The Avenue du Président Habib Bourgiba, Salammbô: The Pottery and Other Ceramic Objects from the Site. Sheffield.

Gabrieli, R.S., Jackson, M.P.C. & Kaldeli, A. 2007
Stumbling into the darkness: Trade and life in post-Roman Cyprus, in: Bonifay & Tréglia (eds.), 791-801.

Gantès, L.-F. 2007
Les amphores commerciales, grecques, levantines et égyptiennes découvertes à Naucratis: une révision récente, in: Marchand & Marangou (eds.), 143-155.

Garlan, Y. 1997
Un nouveau centre de timbrage amphorique: Ouranopolis, *AErgoMak* 10, 347-353.

Garlan, Y. 1999
Les timbres amphoriques de Thasos. 1 Timbres protothasiens et thasiens anciens, Études thasiennes 18. Athènes & Paris.

Garlan, Y. 2000
Amphores et timbres amphoriques grecs. Entre érudition et idéologie, MémAcInscr nouvelle série XXI. Paris.

Garlan, Y. 2004 [2006]
Η προέλευση της 'ομάδας Παρμενίσκου' από τη Μένδη, *AErgoMak* 18, 141-148.

Garlan, Y. 2006
Interprétation des timbres amphoriques 'à la roue' d'Akanthos, *BCH* 130, 263-291.

Garnett, R. & Boardman, J. 1961
Underwater Reconnaissance off the Island of Chios, 1954, *BSA* 56, 102-113.

Gascoigne, A.L. 2007
Amphorae from Old Cairo: a Preliminary Note, in: Marchand & Marangou, 161-174.

Gates, M.-H. 1994
The 1992 Excavations at Kinet Höyük (Dörtyol/Hatay), *Kazı Sonuçları Toplantısı* 15.1. Ankara, 193-200.

Gempeler, R.D. 1992
Elephantine X: Die Keramik römischer bis früharabischer Zeit, Archäologische Veröffentlichungen 43. Mainz am Rhein.

Georges, P.B. 2000
Persian Ionia under Darius: The Revolt Reconsidered, *Historia* 49, 1-39.

Γεωργίου, Γ. 2005
Η άγνωστη Δένεια. Ένα ταφικό σύνολο των Ιστορικών Χρόνων, *RDAC*, 117-147.

Ghaly, H. 1992
Pottery Workshops of Saint-Jeremia (Saqqara), *CahCerEg* 3, 161-171.

Gill, D., Mee, C.B., & Taylor, G. 1997
Artefact Catalogue, in: Mee & Forbes (eds.), 282-343.

Giudice, F., Pafumi, S., Malfitana, D., Sgarlata, M. & Guzzetta, G. 1993
Paphos, Garrison's Camp. Campagna 1989, *RDAC* 1994, 279-327.

Giudice, F., Pafumi, S.P., Malfitana, D., Bruno, G.A. & Guzzetta, G. 1994
Paphos, Garrison's Camp. Campagna 1990, *RDAC*, 215-268.

Giudice, F., Oliveri, R.A., Pafumi, S.P., Privitera, A., Giudice, E., Malfitana, D., Narbone, G., Bruno, G.A. & Guzzetta, G. 1996
Paphos, Garrison's Camp. Campagna 1991, *RDAC*, 171-267.

Given, M. & Knapp, A.B. 2003
The Sydney Cyprus Survey Project: Social Approaches to Regional Archaeological Survey, Monumenta Archaeologica 21. Los Angeles.

Given, M., Knapp, A.B., Noller, J. & Kassianidou, J.(eds.) forthcoming
The Troodos Archaeological and Environmental Survey Project, Cyprus II. The TAESP Landscape, Levant Supplementary Series. London.

Gjerstad, E. 1946
Decorated metal bowls from Cyprus, *OpArch* 4, 1-18.

Gjerstad, E. 1948
The Swedish Cyprus Expedition, IV.2: Cypro-geometric, Cypro-archaic and Cypro-classical periods. Stockholm.

Gjerstad, E. 1960
Pottery types, Cypro-Geometric to Cypro-Classical, *OpAth* 3, 105-122.

Gjerstad, E., Lindros, J., Sjöqvist, E. & Westholm, A. 1935
The Swedish Cyprus Expedition, finds and results of the excavations in Cyprus, 1927-31 II. Stockholm.

Göransson, K. 2007
The Transport Amphorae from Euesperides. The Maritime Trade of a Cyrenaican City 400-250 B.C., Acta Archaeologica Lundensia, Series in 4° no. 25. Lund.

Gordon, J.M. 2012
Between Alexandria and Rome: A Postcolonial Archaeology of Cultural Identity in Hellenistic and Roman Cyprus, Ph.D. diss., University of Cincinnati.

Grace, V.R. 1948
Rhodian Jars in Florida, *Hesperia* 17, 144-147.

Grace, V.R. 1950
The Stamped Amphora Handles, in: Goldman, H. (ed.), Tarsus I: Excavations at Gözlü Kule. Princeton, N.J., 135-148.

Grace, V.R. 1971
Samian Amphoras, *Hesperia* 40, 52-95.

Grace, V. 1979
Kouriaka, in: Karageorghis, V. *et al.* (eds.), *Studies Presented in Memory of Porphyrios Dikaios.* Nicosia, 178-188.

Graham, A., Jacobsen, K. Winther & Kassianidou, V. 2006
Agia Marina-*Mavrovouni.* Preliminary report on the Roman settlement and smelting workshop in the central northern foothills of the Troodos Mountains, Cyprus, *RDAC*, 345-367.

Grandjean, Y. 1992
Contribution à l'etablisement d'une typologie des amphores thasiennes, le material amphorique du quartier de la porte du Silene, *BCH* 116, 541-584.

Gratien, B. 1996
Tell El-Herr (Nord Sinai). Étude stratigraphique de la céramique, *CahPEg* 18, 51-105.

Gratien, B. 1997
Tell el-Herr sondage stratigraphique, *CahCerEg* 5, 71-73.

Gratien, B. & Soulié, D. 1988
La céramique de Tell el-Herr, campagnes 1986 et 1987. Etude préliminaire, *CahPEg* 10, 23-54.

Grayson, A. K. 1991a
Assyria: Tiglath-pileser III to Sargon II (744-705 B.C.), in: Boardman *et al.* (eds.), 71-102.

Grayson, A. K. 1991b
Assyria: Sennacherib and Esarhaddon (704-669 B.C.), in: Boardman *et al.* (eds.), 103-141.

Green, J.N. 1969
Cape Andreas expedition 1969. Oxford.

Green, J.N. 1970
Cape Andreas Expedition Report, 1969, Report-Department of Maritime Archaeology, Western Australian Museum 270. Oxford.

Green, J.N. 1973
An underwater archaeological survey of Cape Andreas, Cyprus, 1969-70: a preliminary report, in: Blackman, D.J. (ed.), *Marine Archaeology. Proceedings of the Twenty-Third Symposium of the Colston Research Society held in the University of Bristol April 4th to 8th, 1971.* London, 141-178.

Greene, E.S., Lawall, M.L. & Polzer, M.E. 2008
Inconspicuous Consumption: The Sixth-Century B.C.E. Shipwreck at Pabuç Burnu, Turkey, *AJA* 112, 685-711.

Greene, E.S., Leidwanger, J. & Özdaş, H. 2011
Two early Archaic shipwrecks at Kekova Adası and Kepçe Burnu, Turkey, *IntJNA* 40, 60-68.

Greene, K. 1986 [1990]
The Archaeology of the Roman Economy. London [Berkeley].

Greensmith, T. 1998
Geologists' Association Guide no. 50: Southern Cyprus. London.

Grey, C. 2007
Contextualizing Colonatus: The Origo of the Late Roman Empire, *JRS* 97, 155-175.

Griffith, F.L. 1927
Oxford Excavations in Nubia. XLIX. The Church on the Meroitic Mastaba-Field, Annals of Archaeology and Anthropology 14, 57-116.

Gubel, E. 2006
Notes on the Phoenician Component of the Orientalizing Horizon, in: Riva, C. & Vella, N.C. (eds.), *Debating Orientalization: Multidisciplinary Approaches to Processes of Change in the Ancient Mediterranean,* Monographs in Mediterranean Archaeology 10. London, 85-93.

Gunneweg, J. & Perlman, I. 1991
The Origin of "Loop-handle Jars" from Tell Keisan, *RBi* 98, 591-599.

Hadjicosti, M. 1993
The late Archaic and Classical Cemetery of Agioi Omologites, Nicosia in the Light of New Evidence, *RDAC*, 173-193.

Hadjidakis, P.J. 2004
Delos. No place of publication cited.

Hadjisavvas, S. 1980a
Paphos – "Vasiliko". A Hellenistic tomb, *RDAC*, 253-259.

Hadjisavvas, S. 1980b
Tombs of the Kings, *Annual Report of the Department of Antiquities of Cyprus* 1980, 35.

Hadjisavvas, S. 1985a
Excavations in the "Tombs of the Kings" – Kato Paphos, in: Karageorghis, V. (ed.), *Archaeology in Cyprus 1960-1985.* Nicosia, 262-268.

Hadjisavvas, S. 1985b
New Evidence from Recent Excavations at the 'Tombs of the Kings', *Πρακτικά του Δευτέρου Διεθνούς Κυπρολογικού Συνεδρίου, Λευκώσια 20-25 Απρίλου.* Λευκώσια, 343-347.

Hadjisavvas, S. 1992
Olive Oil Processing in Cyprus from the Bronze Age to the Byzantine Period, Studies in Mediterranean Archaeology IC. Nicosia.

Hadjisavvas, S. 1996
The economy of the olive, in Karageorghis & Michaelides (eds.), 127-138.

Hadjisavvas, S. with appendices by Lunt, D.A., Parks, D.A., Aviam, M.A. & Stern, E.A. 1997
Agia Napa. Excavations at Makronisos and the Archaeology of the Region. Nicosia.

Hadjisavvas, S. & Karageorghis, V. (eds.) 2000
The Problem of Unpublished Excavations. Nicosia.

Hall, I.H. 1885
The Greek Stamps on the Handles of Rhodian Amphoræ, Found in Cyprus, and now in the Metropolitan Museum of New York, *Journal of the American Oriental Society* 11, 389-396.

Hamilton, R.W. 1934
Tall Abu Hawam. Interim Report, *QDAP* 3, 74-80.

Hannestad, L. 2007
Timber as a trade resource of the Black Sea, in Gabrielsen, V. & Lund, J. (eds.), *The Black Sea in Antiquity: Regional and Interregional Economic Exchanges,* Black Sea Studies 6. Aarhus, 85-99.

Hayes, J.W. 1977
Early Roman Wares from the House of Dionysos, Paphos, *ReiCretActa* 17/18, 96-108.

Hayes, J.W. 1983
The Villa Dionysos Excavations, Knossos: The Pottery, *BSA* 78, 97-169.

Hayes, J.W. 1991
Paphos III: The Hellenistic and Roman Pottery. Nicosia.

Hayes, J.W. 1997
Comment on the pottery evidence, *JRA* 10, 536.

Hayes, J.W. 1998
Handbook of Mediterranean Roman Pottery. London.

Hayes, J.W. 2007
Pottery, in: Megaw, A.H.S. *et al., Kourion. Excavations in the Episcopal Precinct,* Dumbarton Oaks Research Library and Collection. Harvard, 435-475.

Heinen, H. 1984
The Syrian-Egyptian Wars and the new kingdoms of Asia Minor, in: Walbank *et al.* (eds.), 412-445.

Held, W. & Şenol, A.K. 2010
"Rhodian Wine" From Karia: The Production of "Rhodian Wine" on the Karian Chersonesos in the Hellenistic Period, in: Aydinoğlu & Şenol (eds.), 175-183.

Herzog, Z., Rapp, G. & Negbi, O. (eds.) 1989
Excavations at Tel Michal, Israel. Minneapolis.

Heslin, K. 2011
Dolia shipwrecks and the wine trade in the Roman Mediterranean, in: Robinson, D. & Wilson, A. (eds.), *Maritime Archaeology and Ancient Trade in the Mediterranean.* Oxford, 157-168.

Hild, F. & Hellenkemper, H. 1990
Kiliken und Isaurien, Tabula Imperii Byzantini 5. Wien.

Hirt, A.M. 2010
Imperial Mines and Quarries in the Roman world: Organizational Aspects 27 BC-AD 235, Oxford Classical Monographs. Oxford.

Hodos, T. 2006
Local Responses to Colonization in the Iron Age Mediterranean. London & New York.

Hodos, T. 2009a
Colonial Engagements in the Global Mediterranean Iron Age, *CambrAJ* 19, 221-241.

Hodos, T. 2009b
Local and Global Perspectives in the Study of Social and Cultural Identities, in: Hales, S. & Hodos, T. (eds.), *Material Culture and Social Identities in the Ancient World.* Cambridge & New York, 3-31.

Hodos, T. 2010
Globalization and Colonization: A View from Iron Age Sicily, *JMedA* 23, 81-106.

Hohlfelder, R.L. 1995
Ancient Paphos Beneath the Sea: A Survey of the Submerged Structures, in: Karageorghis & Michaelides (eds.), 191-210.

Hohlfelder, R.L. & Leonard, J.R. 1993
Underwater Explorations at Paphos, Cyprus: The 1991 Preliminary Survey, *Annual of the American Schools of Oriental Research* 51, 45-62.

Holladay Jr., J.S. (ed.) 1982
Tell el-Maskhuta: Preliminary Report on the Wadi Tumilat Project 1978-1979, ARCE reports series 6, Cities of the Delta, part III. Malibu.

Hope, V.M. 2007
Death in Ancient Rome: A Source Book, Routledge Sourcebooks for the Ancient World Series. London & New York.

Horden, P. & Purcell, N. 2000
The Corrupting Sea: A Study of Mediterranean History. Oxford.

Houby-Nielsen, S. 2003
The Swedish Cyprus Expedition 1927-1931 and its Relation to Contemporary Prehistoric Archaeology in Sweden, in: Karageorghis, V., Houby-Nielsen, S., Slej, K., Winbladh, M.-L., Fischer, S.N. & Kaneberg, O., *The Cyprus Collection in the Medelhavsmuseet.* Nicosia, 1-12.

Howitt-Marshall, D.S. 2003
Cyprus Underwater Project 2002: A Preliminary Report, *Enalia* 7, 28-37.

Humbert, J.-B. 1991
Essai de classification des amphores dites "à anses de panier", *RBi* 98, 574-590.

Hummel, R. & Shubert, S.B. 1994
Preliminary Report of the 1992 Season at Mendes: The Pottery of the 'Landfill', *Bulletin de Liaison du Groupe International d'Étude de la Céramique Égyptienne* 18, 5-11.

Iacovou, M. 2008
Cultural and Political Configurations in Iron Age Cyprus: The Sequel to a Protohistoric Episode, *AJA* 112, 625-657.

Incitti, M. 1986
Lungotevere Testaccio, *BCom* 91, 560-569.

Ιωαννίδης, Γ.Κ. & Χατζηστύλλης, Σ. (eds.) 2000
Πρακτικά του τρίτου διεθνούς κυπρολογικού συνεδρίου (Λευκωσία, 16-20 Απριλίου 1996), Τόμος Α'. Λευκωσία.

Jackson, M., Zelle, M., Vandeput, L. & Köse, V. 2012
Primary evidence for Late Roman D Ware production in southern Asia Minor: a challenge to 'Cypriot Red Slip Ware', *AnatSt* 62, 89-114.

Jacobsen, K. Winther 1998
Transport Amphorae found 1993-1996, Third Preliminary Report of The Danish Archaeological Excavations at Panayia Ematousa, Aradippou, Cyprus, *ProcDanInstAth* 2, 349-359.

Jacobsen, K. Winther 2002
Cypriot Transport Amphorae in the Archaic and Classical Period, *ActaHyp* 9, 169-184.

Jacobsen, K. Winther 2004
Regional Distribution of Transport Amphorae in Cyprus in the Late Roman Period, in: Eiring & Lund (eds.), 143-148.

Jacobsen, K. Winther 2006
Transport amphorae, in: Sørensen, L. Wriedt & Jacobsen, K. Winther (eds.), *Panayia Ematousa I. A rural site in south-eastern Cyprus,* Monographs of the Danish Institute at Athens 6.1. Athens, 303-337.

Jacobsen, K. Winther 2007a
Transport amphorae in the copper mining industry of Cyprus. Introducing a new type of transport amphorae from Cyprus, in: Bonifay, M. & Tréglia, J.-C. (eds.), 775-779.

Jacobsen, K. Winther 2007b
Pots for the Dead. Pottery and ritual in Cypriote tombs of the Hellenistic and Roman period, in: Malfitana *et al.* (eds.), 389-396.

Jacopi, G. 1929
Scavi nella necropoli di Jalisso, 1924-1928, Clara Rhodos 3. Rhodi.

Jacopi, G. 1931
Scavi nella necropoli camiresi, 1929-1930, Clara Rhodos 4. Rhodi.

Jehasse, L. 1978
Salamine de Chypre VIII. La céramique a vernis noir du rampart méridional. Paris.

Johns, C.N. 1933
Excavations at Atlit 1930-31. The South-eastern Cemetery, *QDAP* 2, 41-104.

Johnson, B.L. 1988
The Pottery, in: Weinberg, G.D. (ed.), *Excavations at Jalame: Site of a Glass Factory in Late Roman Palestine.* Columbia, 137-226.

Johnson, B.L. & Stager, L.E. 1995
Ashkelon: Wine Emporium of the Holy Land, in: Gitin, S. (ed.), *Recent Excavations in Israel. A view to the West. Reports on Kabri, Nami, Mique-Ekron, Dor & Ashkelon,* Archaeological Institute of America Colloquia and Conference Papers No 1. Dubuque, Iowa, 95-109.

Johnston, A.W. 1981
Imported Greek Storage Amphorae, in: Karageorghis, V., Coldstream, J.N., Bikai, P.M., Johnston, A.W., Robertson, M. & Jehasse, L., *Excavations at Kition IV, the Non-Cypriot Pottery.* Nicosia, 37-44.

Johnston, A.W. 1990
Aegina, Aphaia-Tempel XIII. The Storage Amphoras, *AA*, 37-64.

Johnston, A. 1993
Pottery from Archaic Building Q at Kommos, *Hesperia* 62, 339-382.

Johnston, A. 2005
Kommos: Further Iron Age pottery, *Hesperia* 74, 309-393.

Johnston, A.W. 2006
The Delta: From Gamma to Zeta, in: Villing & Schlotzhauer (eds.), 23-30.

Johnston, A.W. & Domingo, C. de 1997
Trade between Kommos, Crete and East Greece: a petrographic study of Archaic transport amphorae, in: Sinclair, A., Slater, E.A. & Gowlett, J.A.J. (eds.), *Archaeological Sciences 1995. Proceedings of a Conference on the Application of Scientific Techniques to the Study of Archaeology, Liverpool, July 1995*. Oxford, 62-68.

Joly, M. & Blanc, P.-M. 1995
Nouvelles données sur la céramique de Bosra, in: Meyza & Młynarczyk (eds.), 111-134.

Jones, A.H.M. 1974
The Roman Economy: Studies in Ancient Economic and Administrative History. Oxford.

Jones, F.F. 1950
The Pottery, in: Goldman, H. (ed.), *Excavations at Gözlü Kule: Tarsus I: The Hellenistic and Roman Periods.* Princeton, 149-296.

Junkelmann, M. 1997
Panis militaris: die Ernährung des römischen Soldaten oder der Grundstoff der Macht, Kulturgeschichte der antiken Welt 75. Mainz am Rhein.

Kaldeli, A. 2007
Roman Amphorae from Cyprus: integrating trade and exchange in the Mediterranean, Unpublished Ph.D. diss., University College London, University of London.

Kaldeli, A. 2009
Trade and the transmission of Roman values to Cyprus, as evidenced by the amphorae, *CahCEC* 39, 365-386.

Karadema, Ch. 2004
Ainos: An Unknown Amphora Production Centre in the Evros Delta, in: Eiring & Lund (eds.), 155-161.

Καραδήμα-Μάτσας, Χρ. 1994
Εργαστήριο παραγωγής αμφορέων στη Σαμοθράκη, *Γ' Επιστημονική Συνάντηση για την Ελληνιστική Κεραμική Χρονολογημένα Σύνολα – Εργαστήρια. Κείμενα. Θεσσαλονίκη, 24-27 Σεπτεμβρίου 1991.* Αθήναι, 355-362.

Karageorghis, V. with appendices by Charles, R.P., Ducos, P., Masson, O. and others 1967
Salamis 3: Excavations in the Necropolis of Salamis I. Nicosia.

Karageorghis, V. with appendices by Helly, B., Masson, O., Charles, R.P., Ducos, P., Demetropoulos, A., Greenwood, P.H., Hadjiouannou, K., Tyler, C., Renfrew, J., Hjelmqvist, H. and others 1970
Salamis 4: Excavations in the necropolis of Salamis II. Nicosia.

Karageorghis, V. with appendices by Helly, B., Hundt, H.J., Marsden, E.W., Masson, O., Hjelmqvist, H., Tyler, C., Talbot, C.J., Greenwood, P.H., Howes, G.J., Demetropoulos, A., Ducos, P. & Western, A.C. 1973
Salamis 5: Excavations in the Necropolis of Salamis III. Nicosia.

Karageorghis, V. 1982a
Cyprus from the Stone Age to the Romans. London.

Karageorghis, V. 1982b
Cyprus, in: Boardman, J. & Hammond, N.G.L. (eds.), *The Expansion of the Greek World, Eight to Sixth Centuries B.C.*, Cambridge Ancient History 3.3. Second Edition. Cambridge, 57-70.

Karageorghis, V. 1993
The History of Wine in Cyprus. A brief survey, in: Vickers, J. (ed.), *Vines and Wines of Cyprus. 4000 Years of Tradition.* Limassol, 31-45.

Karageorghis, V. & Michaelides, D. (eds.) 1995
Proceedings of the International Symposium Cyprus and the Sea, Nicosia 25-25 September, 1993. Nicosia.

Karageorghis, V. & Michaelides, D. (eds.) 1996
The Development of the Cypriot Economy from the Prehistoric Period to the Present Day. Nicosia.

Karagiorgou, O. 2001
LR2: a Container for the Military annona on the. Danubian Border, in: Kingsley & Decker (eds.), 129-166.

Kassab Tezgör, D. 2010
Les fouilles et le matériel de l'atelier amphorique de Demirci près de Sinope, Varia Anatolica 22. Istanbul & Paris.

Kassianidou, V. 2000
Hellenistic and Roman mining in Cyprus, in: Ιωαννίδης, Γ.Κ. & Χατζηστύλλης, Σ. (eds.), *Πρακτικά του τρίτου διεθνούς κυπρολόγικου συνέδριου (Λευκωσία, 15-20 απρίλιου 1996).* Λευκωσία, 745-756.

Kassianidou, V. 2004
Recording Cyprus's mining history through archaeological survey, in: Iacovou, M. (ed.), *Archaeological Field Survey in Cyprus: Past History, Future Potentials. Proceedings of a Conference Held by the Archaeological Research Unit of Cyprus, 1-2 December 2000,* British School at Athens Studies 11. London, 95-104.

Kassianidou, V. forthcoming
Ancient and modern copper production at Skouriotissa Vouppes, in: Given *et al.* (eds.).

Katzev, S.W. 2005
Resurrecting an Ancient Greek Ship: Kyrenia, Cyprus, in: Bass, G.F. (ed.), *Beneath the Seven Seas: Adventures with the Institute of Nautical Archaeology.* London, 72-79.

Keay, S. 1984
Late Roman Amphorae in the Western Mediterranean. A Typology and Economic Study: the Catalan Evidence, BAR International Series 196. Oxford.

Keen, P. forthcoming
Conquest and Consequences: Local Structures and Civic Elites in Ptolemaic Cyprus.

Kerschner, M. & Mommsen, H. 2005
Transportamphoren milesischen Typs in Ephesos. Archäometrische und archäologische Untersuchungen zum Handel im archaischen Ionien, in: Brandt, B., Gassner, V. & Ladstätter, S. (eds.), *Synergia. Festschrift für Friedrich Krinzinger.* Wien, 119-130.

Kingsley, S.A. 2002
A Sixth-Century AD Shipwreck off the Carmel Coast, Israel: Dor D and the Holy Land Wine Trade, BAR International Series 1065. Oxford.

Kingsley, S. & Decker, M. 2001
New Rome, New Theories on Inter-Regional Exchange. An Introduction to the East Mediterranean Economy in Late Antiquity, in: Kingsley, & Decker (eds.), 1-27.

Kingsley, S. & Decker, M. (eds.) 2001
Economy and Exchange in the East Mediterranean during Late Antiquity. Proceedings of a conference at Somerville College, Oxford - 29th May, 1999. Oxford & Oakville.

Knapp, A.B. 2008
Prehistoric & Protohistoric Cyprus: Identity, Insularity and Connectivity. Oxford.

Koehler, C. 1978
Evidence Around the Mediterranean for Corinthian Export of Wine and Oil, in: Arnold III, J.B. (ed.), *Beneath the Waters of Time: The Proceedings of the Ninth Conference on Underwater Archaeology.* Austin, 231-239.

Koehler, C. 1979
Corinthian A and B Transport Amphoras, Ph.D. diss., Princeton University.

Koehler, C. 1981
Corinthian Developments in the Study of Trade in the Fifth Century, *Hesperia* 50, 449-458.

Kopaka, K. & Cadogan, G. 2012
Two Mediterranean island modes, two island archaeologies. Crete and Cyprus: how near, how far? in: Cadogan, G., Iacovou, M., Kopaka, K. & Whitley, J. (eds.), *Parallel Lives: Ancient Island Societies in Crete and Cyprus,* British School at Athens Studies 20. London, 17-33.

Kosso, C.K. 2003
The Archaeology of Public Policy in Late Roman Greece, BAR International Series 1126. Oxford.

Kraeling, C.H. 1962
Ptolemais: City of the Libyan Pentapolis, Oriental Institute Publications 90. Chicago.

Krinzinger, F. (ed.) 2005
Vindobona. Beiträge zu ausgewählten Keramikgattungen in ihrem topographischen Kontext. Wien.

Kuzmanov, G. 1973
Typologie et chronologie des amphores de la haute époque byzantine [in Bulgarian with French abstract], *ArcheologijaSof* 15.1, 14-21.

Landels, J.G. 1978
Engineering in the Ancient World. London.

Laubenheimer, F. & Schmitt, A. 2009
Amphores vinaires de Narbonnaise. Production et grand commerce. Création d'une base de données géochimiques des ateliers, Travaux de la Maison de l'Orient et de la Méditerranée 51. Lyon.

Lawall, M.L. 1995
Transport amphoras and trademarks: Imports to Athens and economic diversity in the fifth century B.C., Ph.D. diss., University of Michigan.

Lawall, M.L. 1997
Shape and Symbol: Regionalism in 5th-century Transport Amphora Production in Northeastern Greece, in: Gillis, C., Risberg, C. & Sjöberg, B. (eds.), *Trade and Production in Premonetary Greece, Production and the Craftsman. Proceedings of the fourth and fifth International Workshops, Athens 1994 and 1995,* SIMA Pocket-Book 143. Jonsered, 113-130.

Lawall, M.L. 1998
Ceramics and Positivism Revisited: Greek transport amphoras and history, in: Parkins, H. & Smith, C. (eds.), *Trade, Traders and the Greek City.* London, 75-101.

Lawall, M.L. 2002
Early Excavations at Pergamon and the Chronology of Rhodian Amphora Stamps, *Hesperia* 71, 294-324.

Lawall, M.L. 2002 [2003]
Ilion before Alexander: Amphoras and Economic Archaeology, *StTroica* 12, 197-243.

Lawall, M.L. 2004
Amphoras without Stamps: Chronologies and Typologies from the Athenian Agora, *ΣΤ΄ Επιστημονική Συνάντηση για την Ελληνιστική Κεραμική, Βόλος 2000, Πρακτικά.* Αθήνα, 445-454.

Lawall, M.L. 2005
Amphoras and Hellenistic Economies: Addressing the (Over)Emphasis on Stamped Amphora Handles, in: Archibald, Z.H., Davies, J.K. & Gabrielsen (eds.), *Making, moving, and managing: The new world of ancient economies, 323-31 BC.* Oxford, 188-232.

Lawall, M.L. 2011
Early Hellenistic Amphoras from Two Closed Contexts: Kerynia Shipwreck and Ephesos Well LB, in: *Ζ' Επιστημονική Συνάντηση για την Ελληνιστική Κεραμική. Αίγιο, 4-9 Απριλίου 2005, Πρακτικά.* Αθήνα, 673-682.

Lehmann, G. 1996
Untersuchungen zur späten Eisenzeit in Syrien und Libanon: Stratigraphie und Keramikformen zwischen ca. 720 bis 330 v. Chr. Münster.

Lehmann, G. 2002
Iron Age, in: Kempinski, A., Scheftelowitz, N. & Oren, R. (eds.), *Tel Kabri: The 1986-1993 Excavation Seasons.* Tel Aviv, 178-222.

Leidwanger, J. 2004
Episkopi Bay Survey, Cyprus, 2003, *INA Quarterly* 31.2, 17-27.

Leidwanger, J. 2005
The Underwater Survey at Episkopi Bay: A Preliminary Report on the 2004 Field Season, *RDAC*, 269-277.

Leidwanger, J. 2005-2006 [2007]
The Cypriot Transport Amphora: Notes on its Development and Distribution, *Skyllis* 7, 24-31.

Leidwanger, J. 2007
Two Late Roman Wrecks from Southern Cyprus, *IntJNautA* 36, 308-316.

Leidwanger, J. & Howitt-Marshall, D.S. 2006
Episkopi Bay and Beyond: Recent Collaborative Fieldwork and New Prospects on Cyprus, *INA Quarterly* 33.2, 13-22.

Leidwanger, J., Özdaş, H. & Greene, E.S. 2012
Sourcing the Cargos of Three Archaic Shipwrecks: Kekova Adası, Kepçe Burnu, and Çaycağız Koyu', *Arkeometri Sonuçları Toplantısı* 27, 393-409.

Leonard Jr., A. 1987
A Brief Survey, in: Soren, D. (ed.), *The Sanctuary of Apollo Hylates at Kourion, Cyprus.* Tuscon, 80-116.

Leonard, J.R. 1995a
Evidence for Roman Ports, Harbours and Anchorages in Cyprus, in: Karageorghis & Michaelides (eds.), 227-246.

Leonard, J.R. 1995b
The Anchorage at Kioni, in: Fejfer (ed.), 133-170.

Leonard, J.R. 2005
Roman Cyprus: Harbors, Hinterlands, and "Hidden Powers", PhD diss., State University of New York at Buffalo.

Leonard, J.R. & Demesticha, S. 2004
Fundamental Links in the Economic Chain: Local Ports and International Trade in Roman and Early Christian Cyprus, in: Eiring & Lund (eds.), 189-202.

Lichocka, B. & Meyza, H. 2001
Seismic Events and the Evidence of Coins and Pottery. The Case of Destruction of the House of Aion in Paphos, *EtTrav* 19, 145-208.

Lindhagen, A. 2009
The transport amphoras Lamboglia 2 and Dressel 6A: a central Dalmatian origin? *JRA* 22, 83-108.

Lokin, J.H.A. 1986
Administration and Juridiction in Cyprus, in the sixth century AD, in: Παπαδόπουλου, Θ. & Εγγλεζάκη, Β. (eds.), *Πρακτικά του Δεύτερου Διεθνούς Κυπρολογικού Συνεδρίου (Λευκωσία, 20-25 Απριλίου 1982), τ. Β' Μεσαιωνικόν Τμήμα*. Λευκωσία, 1-9.

Louloupis, M. 1975
Excavations at Amathous, *Annual Report of the Department of Antiquities of Cyprus*, 29-31.

Lund, J. 1993a
Pottery of the Classical, Hellenistic and Roman Periods, in: Sørensen & Rupp (eds.), 79-155.

Lund, J. 1993b
Rhodian Amphorae as Evidence for the Relations between Late Punic Carthage and Rhodes, *ActaHyp* 5, 359-375.

Lund, J. 1996
From archaeology to history? Reflections on the chronological distribution of ceramic finewares in South Western and Southern Asia Minor from the 1st to the 7th c. AD, in: Herfort-Koch, M., Mandel, U. & Schädler, U. (eds.), *Hellenistische und kaiserzeitliche Keramik des östlichen Mittelmeergebietes. Kolloquium Frankfurt 24.-25. April 1995.* Frankfurt am Main, 105-125.

Lund, J. 1999a
Rhodian Amphorae in Rhodes and Alexandria as Evidence of Trade, in: Gabrielsen, V., Bilde, P., Engberg-Pedersen, T., Hannestad, L. & Zahle, J. (eds.), *Hellenistic Rhodes: Politics, Culture, and Society.* Aarhus, 187-204.

Lund, J. 1999b
Trade patterns in the Levant from ca. 100 BC to AD 200 – as reflected by the distribution of ceramic fine wares in Cyprus, *MünstBeitr* 18.1, 1-22.

Lund, J. 2000
The "pinched-handle" transport amphorae as evidence of the wine trade of Roman Cyprus, in: Ιωαννίδη & Χατζηστύλη (eds.), 565-578.

Lund, J. 2005 [2006]
Agora G 199, in: Keay & Williams (eds.).

Lund, J. 2006
On the circulation of goods in Hellenistic and Early Roman Cyprus: the ceramic evidence, in: Sørensen, L. Wriedt & Jacobsen, K.W. (eds.), *Panayia Ematousa II. Political, cultural, ethnic and social relations in Cyprus. Approaches to regional studies. Monographs of the Danish Institute at Athens* 6.2. Athens, 31-50.

Lund, J. 2007
Transport amphorae as a possible source for the land use and economic history of the Akamas peninsula, Western Cyprus, in: Bonifay & Tréglia (eds.), 781-789.

Lund, J. 2009
The potters of Hellenistic and Roman Cyprus, *Medelhavsmuseet, Focus on the Mediterranean* 5, 165-170.

Lund, J. 2011a
A new sequence of eponyms named on Rhodian amphora stamps in the first half of the second century BC as established through seriation, *ActaArch* 82, 271-290.

Lund, J. 2011b
Rhodian Transport Amphorae as a Source for Economic Ebbs and Flows in the Eastern Mediterranean in the Second Century BC, in: Archibald, Z.H., Davies, J.K. & Gabrielsen, V. (eds.), *The Economies of Hellenistic Societies, Third to First Centuries BC.* Oxford, 280-295.

Lund, J. forthcoming
Connections between Rough Cilicia and North Western Cyprus between about 200 BC and AD 200: the ceramic evidence and its possible implications, in: Hoff, M. (ed.), *Rough Cilicia: New Archaeological and Historical Approaches.* Oxford.

Luraghi, N. 2006
Traders, Pirates, Warriors: The Proto-History of Greek Mercenary Soldiers in the Eastern Mediterranean, *Phoenix* 60, 21-47.

Maarleveld, T. 2010
Fish and "Chips of knowledge": Some Thoughts on the Biases of the Archaeological Record, in: Bekker-Nielsen, T. & Bernal Casaola, D. (eds.), *Ancient Nets and Fishing Gear.* Cadiz & Aarhus, 256-271.

Macalister, R.A.S. 1912
The Excavations of Gezer I-III. London.

Magness, J. 1995
The Pottery from Area V/4 at Caesarea, in: Dever, W.G. (ed.), *Preliminary Excavation Reports: Sardis, Bir Umm Fawakhir, Tell el-`Umeiri, The Combined Caesarea Expeditions, and Tell Dothan, AASOR* 52. Alpharetta, 133-145.

Maier, F.G. 1985
Factoids in Ancient History: The Case of Fifth-Century Cyprus, *JHS* 105, 32-39.

Maier, F.G. 1994
Cyprus and Phoenicia, in: Lewis, D.M., Boardman, J., Hornblower, S. & Ostwald, M. (eds.), *The Fourth Century B.C.* Cambridge Ancient History 6. Second Edition. Cambridge, 297-336.

Maier, F.G. 2007
From Regional Centre to Sanctuary Town: Palaipaphos in the Late Classical and Early Hellenistic Period, in: Flourentzos (ed.), 17-33.

Majcherek, G. 1992a
Amfory rzymskie i bizantyjskie z Aleksandrii (Kom el-Dikka). Studium typologiczne, Ph.D. diss., University of Warsaw.

Majcherek, G. 1992b
The Late Roman Ceramics from Sector "G" – Alexandria (1986-1987), *EtTrav* 16, 81-117.

Majcherek, G. 1993
Roman Amphorae from Marina el-Alemein, *MDIK* 49, 215-220.

Majcherek, G. 1995
Gazan Amphorae: Typology Reconsidered, in: Meyza & Młynarczyk (eds.), 163-178.

Malfitana, D., Poblome, J. & Lund, J. (eds.) 2006
Old Pottery in a New Century. Innovating Perspectives on Roman Pottery Studies. Atti del Convegno Internazionale di Studi Catania, 22-24 Aprile 2004. Catania.

Manning, S.W., Manning, A., Tomber, R., Sewell, D.A., Monks, S.J., Ponting, M.J. & Ribeiro, E.C. 2002
The Late Roman Church at Maroni Petrera: Survey and salvage excavations 1990-1997, and other traces of Roman remains in the lower Maroni Valley, Cyprus. Nicosia.

Manning, S.W., Monks, S.J., Sewell, D.A. & Demesticha, S. 2000
Late Roman Type 1a amphora production at the Late Roman site of Zygi-*Petrini*, Cyprus, *RDAC*, 233-257.

Manning, S.W., Sewell, D.A. & Herscher, E. 2002
Late Cypriot 1A Maritime Trade in Action: Underwater Survey at Maroni Tsaroukkas and the Contemporary East Mediterranean Trading System, *BSA* 97, 97-162.

Marangou, A. 2009
Amphores hellénistiques d`Amathonte, *CahCEC* 39, 347-363.

Marangou, A. & Autret, C. 2011
L'importation des amphores ciliciennesà Chypre à l'époque impériale, in: Διμιτρίου, A. (ed.), *Πρακτικά του Δ' διεθνούς κυπρολόγικου συνέδριου Λευκωσία 29 Άπριλίου – 3 Μαίου 2008, Αρχαίο τμήμα.* Λευκωσία, 358-366.

Marangou, A. & Marchand, S. 2007
Conteneurs importés et égyptiens de Tebtynis (Fayoum) de la deuxième moitié du IV siècle av. J.-C. au Xe siècle apr. J.-C. (1994-2002), in: Marchand & Marangou (eds.), 239-294.

Marangou, A. & Marchand, S. 2009
Le contribution des conteneurs commerciaux à l'histoire des échanges entre Chypre et l'Égypte de l'époque archaïque à l'époque romaine tardive, in: Michaelides *et al.* (eds.), 242-251.

Marangou, A.G. 2000
Life & Deeds: The Consul Luigi Palma di Cesnola 1832-1904. Nicosia.

Marangou-Lerat, A. 1995
Le vin et les amphores de Crète de l'époque classique à l'époque impériale. Athènes.

Markides, M. 1916
Excavations at Ktima, *Annual Report of the Curator of Antiquities* 1915. Nicosia.

Markoe, G. 1985
Phoenician Bronze and Silver Bowls from Cyprus and the Mediterranean, University of California Publications Classical Studies 26. Berkeley, Los Angeles & London.

Marlière, É. 2002
L'outre et le tonneau dans l'Occident romain, Monographies instrumentum 22. Montagnac.

Martin-Kilcher, S. 1987
Die römischen Amphoren aus Augst und Kaiseraugst. Ein Beitrag zur römischen Handels- und Kulturgeschichte. 1: Die südspanischen Ölamphoren (Gruppe 1), Forschungen in Augst 7. Augst.

Masson, A. 2007
Amphore de Chios et amphore à anses de panier découvertes dans la maison VII du quartier des prêtres de Karnak, in: Marchand & Marangou (eds.), 361-367.

Masson, A. 2011
Persian and Ptolemaic Ceramics from Karnak: Change and Continuity, *CahCerEg* 9, 269-310.

Masson, O. 1967
Les inscriptions syllabiques, in: Karageorghis *et al.*, 132-142.

Masson, O. 1982
Un timbre amphorique syllabique de Ras el Bassit-Posideion, *RDAC*, 153-155.

Masson, O. 1983
Les inscriptions chypriotes syllabique: recueil critique et commenté, Études Chypriotes 1, Second Edition. Paris.

Masson, O. 1986
Les anses d'amphores et l'anthroponymie Grecque, in: Empereur & Garlan (eds), 37-44.

Masson, O. 1995
Les écriture antiques à Chypre, in: Chypre, Au coeur des civilisations méditerranéennes, *Dossiers d'archeologie* 205, 62-66.

Master, D.M. 2003
Trade and Politics: Ashkelon's Balancing Act in the Seventh Century B.C.E, *BASOR* 330, 47-64.

Matthews, R. 2003
The Archaeology of Mesopotamia: Theories and Approaches. London.

Mau, A. 1909
Corpus Inscriptionum Latinarum, vol. IV Supplement 2, Inscriptiones parietariae et vasorum fictilium. Berlin.

Maxfield, V.A. & Peacock, D.P.S. (eds.) 2006
Survey and Excavation Mons Claudianus 1987–1993 III: Ceramic Vessels & Related Objects, Institut français d'archéologie orientale, Fouilles de l'IFAO 54. Le Caire.

McCaslin, D. 1978
The 1977 Underwater Report, in: Hala Sultan Tekke 4, Studies in Mediterranean Archaeology XLV: 4. Göteborg, 97-157.

McCormick, M. 2002
Origins of the European Economy: Communications and Commerce AD 300-900. New York.

McFadden, G.H. 1946
A tomb of the necropolis of Ayios Ermoyenis at Kourion, *AJA* 50, 449-489.

Medeksza, St. 1992
Willa Tezeusza w Nea Pafos. Rezydencja antyczna, Prace Naukowe Instytutu Historii Architektury, Sztuki i Techniki Politechniki Wrocławskiej 15. Wrocław.

Medeksza, St. 1998
Willa Tezeusza w Nea Pafos na Cyprze: powstanie i fazy rozwoju, in: Daszewski, W.A. & Meyza, H. (eds.), *Cypr w badaniach polskich*. Warszawa, 25-50.

Mee, C.B. & Forbes, H.A. (eds.) 1997
A Rough and Rocky Place: The Landscape and Settlement History of the Methana Peninsula, Greece. Liverpool.

Megaw, A.H.S. 1997
The Aegean Connections of Cypriot Church-Builders in Late Antiquity, in: Christou, D. (ed.), *Τμήμα Αρχαιοτήτων Κύπρου: Proceedings of the International Archaeological Conference 'Cyprus and the Aegean in Antiquity: from the Prehistoric Period to the 7th century A.D.' Nicosia 8-10 December 1995*. Nicosia, 343-352.

Mehl, A. 1995
Zyperns Wirtschaft in hellenistischer Zeit, *MünstBeitr* 14, 27-49.

Meiggs, R. 1980
Sea-Borne Timber Supplies to Rome, *MemAmAc* 36, 185-196.

Menchelli, S., Santoro, S., Pasquinucci, M. & Guiducci, G. (eds.) 2010
LRCW 3. Late Roman Coarse Wares, Cooking Wares and Amphorae in the Mediterranean. Archaeology and Archaeometry. Comparison between western and eastern Mediterranean, BAR International Series 2185. Oxford.

Metcalf, D.M. 2009
Byzantine Cyprus, 491-1191, Texts and Studies in the History of Cyprus 62. Nicosia.

Meyer, C. 1995
A Byzantine gold-mining town in the eastern desert of Egypt: Bir Umm Fawakhir, 1992-93, *JRA* 8, 192-224.

Meyer, C. 1998
Gold miners and mining at Bir Umm Fawakhir, in: Knapp, A.B., Pigott, V. & Herbert, E. (eds.), *Social Approaches to an Industrial Past: The Archaeology and Anthropology of Mining*. Mobipocket eBooks.

Meyza, H. 1995
Cypriot Sigillata and Cypriot Red Slip Ware: problems of origin and continuity, in: Meyza & Młynarczyk (eds.), 179-183, 186-196.

Meyza, H. 1997
Nea Paphos. Excavating below the mosaic of the southern portico in the Villa of Theseus, *PolAMed* 8, 122-131.

Meyza, H. 2000
Cypriot Red Slip. Development of the Ware (an Attempt at Refinement), in: Ιωαννίδης & Χατζηστύλλης (eds.), 507-529.

Meyza, H. 2003
Nea Paphos Season 2002, *PolAMed* 14, 255-261.

Meyza, H. 2004
Kouriaka again: Amphora Stamps from the Kourion Acropolis Excavations, in: Eiring & Lund (eds.), 273-284.

Meyza, H. 2007
Nea Paphos V: Cypriot Red Slip Ware: Studies on a Late Roman Levantine fine ware. Warszawa.

Meyza, H. 2008
Pottery finds from the House of Aion (northern sector), *PolAMed* 18, 518-523.

Meyza, H. forthcoming
Amphorae and other pots: three deposits from Nea Paphos.

Meyza, H. & Młynarczyk, J. (eds.) 1995
Hellenistic and Roman Pottery in the Eastern Mediterranean – Advances in Scientific Studies. Acts of the II Nieborów Pottery Workshop. Nieborów, 18-20 December 1993. Warsaw.

Meyza, H. & Papuci-Władyka, E. with contributions by Dobosz, A., Lichocka, B., Mazanek, D., Młynarczyk, J., Marzec, E. & Więch, M. forthcoming
Excavations of Nea Pafos, Maloutena in 2007, Interim report, part 1, *RDAC*.

Michaelides, D. 1984
A Roman Surgeon's Tomb from Nea Paphos, *RDAC*, 315-332.

Μιχαηλίδης, Δ. 1990a
Οι ροδιακοί αμφορείς και ένα ταφικό έθιμο της Πάφου, in: *Β' Επιστημονική Συνάντηση για την Ελληνιστική Κεραμεική: Χρονολογικά προβλήματα της ελληνιστικής κεραμεικής, Ρόδος 1989, Πρακτικά*. Αθήνα, 187-194.

Michaelides, D. 1990b
The Roman Period. 30 B.C.-A.D. 330, in: Hunt, D. (ed.), *Footprints in Cyprus: An illustrated history*. London, 120-133.

Michaelides, D. 1996
The economy of Cyprus during the Hellenistic and Roman periods, in: Karageorghis & Michaelides (eds.), 139-152.

Michaelides, D., Kassianidou, V. & Merrillees, R.S. (eds.) 2009 *Proceedings of the International Conference Egypt and Cyprus in Antiquity: Nicosia, 3-6 April 2003*. Oxford.

Michaelides, D. & Młynarczyk, J. 1988
Tombs P.M. 2520 and P.M. 2737 from the Eastern Necropolis of Nea Paphos, *RDAC*, 149-170.

Michaelides, D. & Sznycer, M. 1985
A Phoenician graffito from Tomb 103/84 at Nea Paphos, *RDAC*, 249-256.

Mikrakis, M. 2012
The 'originality of ancient Cypriot art' and the individuality of performing practices in protohistoric Cyprus, in: Iacovou, M. (ed.), Cyprus and the Aegean in the Early Iron Age. The Legacy of Nicholas Coldstream. Nicosia, 371-393.

Millett, M. 2000
The comparison of surface and stratified artefact assemblages, in: Pasquinucci, M. & Trément, F. (eds.) *Non-Destructive Techniques Applied to Landscape Archaeology,* POPULUS 4. Oxford, 216-222.

Mitford, T.B. 1950
New Inscriptions from Roman Cyprus, *Opuscula Archaeologica* 6, 1-95.

Mitford, T.B. 1980
Roman Cyprus, Aufstieg und Niedergang der römischen Welt II.7.2. Berlin, 1285-1384.

Młynarczyk, J. 1990
Nea Paphos III: Nea Paphos in the Hellenistic Period. Warsaw.

Młynarczyk, J. 1992
Fourth Century A.D. Terracotta Lamps from Nea Paphos, in: Åström, P. (ed.), *Acta Cypria 2, Acts of an International Congress on Cypriote Archaeology held in Göteborg on 22-24 August 1991,* Vol. 2. Jonsered, 255-271.

Монахов, С. Ю. 1999
Греческие амфоры в Причерноморье. Комплексы керамической тары VII - II веков до н.э. Саратов.

Монахов, С. Ю. 2003.
Греческие амфоры в Причерноморье. Типология амфор ведуших центров-экспортеров товаров в керамической таре. Каталог-определитель. Москва & Саратов.

Morris, I. 2000
Archaeology as Cultural History: Words and Things in Iron Age Greece. Malden, Ma. & Oxford.

Morris, I. 2003
Mediterraneanization, *MedHisR* 18, 30-55.

Morrisson, C & Sodini, J-P. 2002
The Sixth-Century Economy, in: Laiou, A.E. (ed.), *The Economic History of Byzantium: From the Seventh through the Fifteenth Century,* Dumbarton Oaks Studies 39. Washington D.C., 171-220.

Μπέσιος, Μ., Τζιφόπουλος, Γ.Ζ. & Κοτσώνας, Α. 2012
Μεθώνη Πιερίας Ι: Επιγραφές, χαράγματα και εμπορικά σύμβολα στην γεωμετρική και αρχαϊκή κεραμική από το 'Υπόγειο' της Μεθώνης Πιερίας στη Μακεδονία. Θεσσαλονίκι.

Munro, J.A.R. 1891
Excavations in Cyprus. Third Season's Work: Polis tes Chrysochou, *JHS* 12, 298-333.

Munro, J.A.R. & Tubbs, H.A. 1891
Excavations in Cyprus 1890, *JHS* 12, 59-198.

Murray, P. & Kardulias, P.N. 2000
The Present as Past: An Ethnoarchaeological Study of Modern Sites in the Pikrodhafni Valley, in: Sutton, S.B. (ed.), *A Contingent Countryside: Settlement, Economy, and Land Use in Southern Argolid since 1700.* Stanford, 141-168.

Murray, W.M. 1995
Ancient Sailing Winds in the Eastern Mediterranean: The Case for Cyprus, in: Karageorghis & Michaelides (eds.), 33-44.

Myres, J.L. 1914
Handbook of the Cesnola Collection of Antiquities from Cyprus. New York.

Myres, J.L. & Ohnefalsch-Richter, M. 1899
A Catalogue of the Cyprus Museum with a Chronicle of Excavations Undertaken since the British Occupation and Introductory Notes on Cypriote Archaeology. Oxford.

Na'aman, N. 1991
The Kingdom of Judah under Josiah, *TelAviv* 18, 3-71.

Naso, A. 2005
Funde aus Milet. XIX. Anfore commerciali arcaiche a Mileto: rapporto preliminare, *AA*, 73-84.

Naveh, J. 1962
The Excavations at Meṣad Ḥashavyahu. Preliminary report, *IEJ* 12, 89-113.

Nicolaou, I. 1984
A Hellenistic and Roman Tomb at Evrychou-Phoenikas, *RDAC*, 234-256.

Nicolaou, I. 1990
Paphos II: The Coins from the House of Dionysos. Nicosia.

Nicolaou, I. 2005
Paphos V: The Stamped Amphora Handles from the House of Dionysos. Nicosia.

Nicolaou, I. & Empereur, J.-Y. 1986
Amphores rhodiennes du Musée de Nicosie, in: Empereur & Garlan (eds.), 515-533.

Nicolaou, K. 1966
The Topography of Nea Paphos, in: Bernhard, M.L. (ed.), *Mélanges offerts à Kazimierz Michalowski.* Warszawa, 561-601.

Niemeier, W.-D. 1999
'Die Zierde Ioniens': ein archaischer Brunnen, der jüngere Athenatempel und Milet vor der Perserzerstörung, *AA*, 373-413.

Nys, K. 2008
The Study of Cypriote Iron Age Pottery after the Swedish Cyprus Expedition: Inflation or Deflation of Gjerstad's Legacy? In: Åström, P. & Nys, K. (eds.), *The Swedish Cyprus Expedition 80 Years. Proceedings of the Symposium in Honour of the Memory of Einar Gjerstad Held in the Royal Academy of Letters, History and Antiquities, Stockholm, 28 September 2007,* Studies in Mediterranean Archaeology and Literature, Pocketbook 175. Sävedalen, 67-91.

Nys, K. & Åström, P. with contributions by Sjöquist, K.-E., García Ramón, J.-L. & Olivier, J.-P. 2004
Corpus of Cypriote Antiquities 23. Cypriote Antiquities in Public Collections in Denmark, Studies in Mediterranean Archaeology XX:23. Sävedalen.

Özdaş, H., Kızıldağ, N. & Okan, E. 2012
Ege-Akdeniz bölgesi sualtı araştırması 2010 yılı çalişmaları, *Araştırma Sonuçları Toplantısı* 29, 267-280.

Okay, A.I. & Özgül, N. 1984
HP/LT metamorphism and the structure of the Alanya Massif, southern Turkey: an allochthonous composite tectonic sheet, in: Dixon, J.E. & Robertson, A.H.F. (eds.), *The Geological Evolution of the Eastern Mediterranean.* London, 429-439.

Oliver, A. 1983
Tomb 12 at Episkopi, *RDAC*, 245-256.

Olofsson, M.S. 2003
Four imported transport amphorae from Acquarossa, *OpRom* 28, 73-83.

Opaiţ, A. 1984
Beobachtungen zur Entwicklung der zwei Amphoratypen, *Peuce* 9, 311-327.

Opaiţ, A. 1996
Aspecte ale vieţii economice din provincia Scythia (secolele IV–VI p. Chr) Producţia ceramicii locale şi de import. Bucureşti.

Opaiţ, A. 2004a
Local and Imported Ceramics in the Roman Province of Scythia (4th – 6th centuries AD): Aspects of Economic Life in the Province of Scythia, BAR International Series 1274. Oxford.

Opaiţ, A. 2004b
The Eastern Mediterranean Amphorae in the Province of Scythia, in: Eiring & Lund (eds.), 293–308.

Opaiţ, A. 2010
On the Origin of Carthage LR Amphora 1, in: Menchelli *et al.* (eds.), 1015-1022.

Oren, E.D. 1984
Migdol: A New Fortress on the Edge of the Eastern Nile Delta, *BASOR* 256, 7-44.

Orton, C. 1980
Mathematics in Archaeology. London.

Orton, C., 2000
Sampling in Archaeology. Cambridge.

Orton, C., Tyers, P. & Vince, A. 1993
Pottery in Archaeology. Cambridge.

Outschar, U. 1993
Produkte aus Ephesos in alle Welt?, *Österreichisches Archäologisches Institut, Berichte und Materialien* 5, 46-52.

Pacetti, F. 1995
Appunti su alcuni tipi di anfore orientali della prima eta bizantina. Centri di produzione, contenuti, cronologia e distribuzione, in: Quilici, L. & Quilici Sigli, S. (eds.), *Agricoltura e commerci nell'Italia antica. Atlante tematico di topografia antica, I Suppl.* Roma, 273-294.

Πανάγου, T.M. 2010
Η σφράγιση των αρχαίων ελληνικών εμπορικών αμφορέων κέντρα παραγωγής και συνθετική αξιολόγηση, Unpublished Ph.D. diss., Εθνικό και Καποδιστριακό Πανεπιστήμιο Αθηνών.

Panzeri Pozzetti, P. 1986
Anfore commerciali, in: *I Greci sul Basento. Mostra degli scavi archeologici all'Incoronata di Metaponto 1971-1984.* Como, 134-143.

Papacostas, T. 2001
The Economy of Late Antique Cyprus, in: Kingsley & Decker (eds.), 107-128.

Papadopoulos, J.K. 1989
Roman Amphorae from the Excavations at Torone, *AEphem* 128, 67-103.

Papadopoulos, J.K. & Paspalas, S.A. 1999
Mendaian as Chalkidian Wine, *Hesperia* 68, 161-188.

Papageorghiou, A. 1993
Cities and Countryside at the end of Antiquity and the beginning of the Middle Ages in Cyprus, in: Bryer, A.M.M. & Georghallides, G.S. (eds.), *The Sweet Land of Cyprus. Papers given at the Twenty-Fifth Jubilee Spring Symposium of Byzantine Studies, Birmingham, March 1991.* Nicosia, 27-51.

Papantoniou, G. 2012.
Religion and Social Transformations in Cyprus: From the Cypriot Basileis to the Hellenistic Strategos, Mnemosyne Supplements History and Archaeology of Classical Antiquity 347. Leiden.

Papuci-Władyka, E. 1995
Nea Pafos. Studia nad ceramiką hellenistyczną z polskich wykopalisk (1965-1991). Kraków.

Papuci-Władyka, E. 1997
A Research Report on Hellenistic Pottery: Cos Amphoras, *PraceA* 8, 47-54.

Parker, A.J. 1992
Ancient Shipwrecks of the Mediterranean & the Roman Provinces, BAR International Series 580. Oxford.

Paspalas, S. 1990
The Transport Amphorae and Domestic Pottery from Two Classical Deposits at Torone, MA thesis, University of Sydney.

Peacock, D.P.S. 1982
Pottery in the Roman World: an ethnoarchaeological approach. London & New York

Peacock, D.P.S., Bejaoui, F. & Belazreg, N. 1989
Roman amphora production in the Sahel region in Tunisia, in: *Amphores romaines,* 179-222.

Peacock, D.P.S. & Williams, D.F. 1986
Amphorae and the Roman economy: an introductory guide. London & New York.

Peirce, S. 2001
The Greek transport amphorae, in: Cambitoglou, A., Papadopoulos, J.K. & Tudor Jones, O. (eds.), *Torone I: The Excavations of 1975, 1976, and 1978.* Athens, 495-513.

Pelagatti, P. 1995
Le anfore commerciali, in: *Corinto e l'Occidente,* 403-416.

Peña, J.Th. 2007
Roman Pottery in the Archaeological Record. Cambridge.

Pensabene, P. 1981
Anfore tarde con iscrizioni cristiane dal Palatino, *RiStLig* 47, 189-213.

Petrie, W.M.F. 1886
Naukratis, Part I: 1884-5, Third Memoir of the Egypt Exploration Fund. London.

Pettegrew, D.K. 2001
Chasing the Classical Farmstead: Assessing the Formation and Signature of Rural Settlement in Greek Landscape Archaeology, *JMedA* 14, 189-209.

Pettegrew, D.K. 2007
The Busy Countryside of Late Roman Corinth: Interpreting Ceramic Data Produced by Regional Archaeological Surveys, *Hesperia* 76, 743-784.

Pieri, D. 2005
Le commerce du vin oriental á l´époque byzantine (Ve – VIIe siècles), Le témoignage des amphores en Gaule, Bibliothèque Archéologique et Historique 174. Beyrouth.

Pieri, D. 2007
Les centres de production d'amphores en Méditerranée orientale durant l' Antiquité tardive, in: Bonifay & Tréglia (eds.), 611-625.

Pikoulas, Y. 2007
Travelling by Land in Ancient Greece, in: Adams, C. & Roy, J. (eds.), *Travel, Geography and Culture in Ancient Greece, Egypt and the Near East.* Oxford, 78-87.

Pilides, D. 2007
The Hill of Agios Georgios, Nicosia: From Ledroi to Levkoton? in: Flourentzos (ed.), 131-144.

Popilian, G. 1997
Les centres de production céramique d'Oltenie, in: Pitar, M. (coordination and verification of translation into French), *Etudes sur la céramique romaine et daco-romaine de la Dacie et de la Mésie Inférieure,* Bibliotheca historica et archaeologica Universitatis Temesiensis 1. Timi oara, 7-20.

Pouilloux, J. 1975
Athènes et Salamine de Chypre, *RDAC,* 111-121.

Pouilloux, J. 1976a
L'hellénisme à Salamine de Chypre, *BCH* 100, 449-460.

Pouilloux, J. 1976b
La rencontre de l'hellénisme et de l'Orient à Chypre entre 1200 et 300 av. J.-C., in Pippidi, D.M. (ed.): *Assimilation et résistance à la culture gréco-romaine dans le monde ancient. Actes du VIe Congrès International d'Études Classiques, Madrid 2-6 Septembre 1974.* Bucarest & Paris, 233-240.

Pouilloux, J. 1989
L'époque classique à Chypre, *JSav,* 147-161.

Poulou-Papadimitriou, N. & Didioumi, S. 2010
Nouvelles données sur la production de l atelier céramique protobyzantine a Kardamaina (Cos – Grèce), in: Menchelli *et al.* (eds.), 741-749.

Raban, A. 1995
The Heritage of Ancient Harbour Engineering in Cyprus and the Levant, in: Karageorghis & Michaelides (eds.), 139-190.

Raptou, E. 1996
Contribution to the study of the economy of ancient Cyprus: copper – timber, in: Karageorghis & Michaelides (eds.), 249-260.

Raptou, E. 1999
Athènes et Chypre à l'époque perse (VIe-IVe s. av. J.-C.). Histoire et données archéologiques. Lyon.

Raptou, E. 2001
A classical tomb from Tremithousa (Pafos), *RDAC*, 187-205.

Rauh, N.K. 2004
Pirated Knock-offs: Cilician Imitations of Internationally Traded Amphoras, in: Eiring & Lund (eds.), 329-336.

Rauh, N.K. & Slane, K.W. 2000
Possible amphora kiln sites in W Rough Cilicia, *JRA* 13, 319-329.

Rauh, N.K. & Will, E.L. 2002
"My Blood of the Convenant": What Did the Apostles Drink at the Last Supper?, *Archaeology Odyssey* 5.5, 46-51 and 62-63.

Rautman, M. 2000
The busy countryside of Late Roman Cyprus, *RDAC*, 317-331.

Rautman, M. with contributions by Benson, L., Fox, S.C., Glascock, M.D., Gomez, B., McClellan, M.C., Neff, H., O'Brien, W. & Reese, D.S. 2003
A Cypriot Village of Late Antiquity: Kalavasos-Kopetra in the Vasilikos Valley, JRA Supplementary Series 52. Portsmouth, RI.

Rautman, M. 2008
Site-specific survey in a Cypriot setting: Settlement definition and verification in the Vasilikos valley, in: Vanhaverbeke H., Vermeulen, F., Waelkens, M., Poblome, J. & Brulet, R., (eds.), *Dialogue with Sites. The Definition of Space at the Macro and Micro Level in Roman Times,* Studies in Eastern Mediterranean Archaeology 8. Turnhoutet *al.* (eds.), 11-19.

Rautman, M., Gomez, B., Neff, H., Vaughan, S. & Glascock, M.D. 1999
Amphoras and roof-tiles from Late Roman Cyprus: A compositional study of calcareous fabric ceramics from Kalavasos-*Kopetra*, *JRA* 12, 377-391.

Reisner, G.A., Fisher, C.S. & Lyon, D.G. 1924
Harvard Excavations at Samaria 1908-1910. Cambridge, Massachusetts.

Reyes, A.T. 1994
Archaic Cyprus: A Study of the Textual and Archaeological Evidence. Oxford.

Reyes, A.T. 1997
Notes on the Iron Age Kingdoms of Cyprus, *BASOR* 308, 65-68.

Reynolds, P. 1995
Trade in the Western Mediterranean, AD 400-700: The ceramic evidence, BAR International Series 604. Oxford.

Reynolds, P. 1997-1998 [1999]
Pottery production and economic exchange in second century Berytus. Some preliminary observations of ceramic trends from quantified ceramic deposits from the Anglo-Lebanese AUB-Leverhulme excavations in Beirut, *Berytus* 43, 35-110.

Reynolds, P. 2000
The Beirut amphora type, 1st century BC-7th century AD: an outline of its formal development and some preliminary observations of regional economic trends, *RCRF* 36, 387-395.

Reynolds, P. 2004
The Roman pottery from the Triconch Palace, in: Hodges, R., Bowden, W. & Lako, K. (eds.), *Byzantine Butrint: Excavations and surveys 1994-99.* Oxford, 224-269.

Reynolds, P. 2005
Levantine amphorae from Cilicia to Gaza: a typology and analysis of regional production trends from the 1st to 7th centuries, in: Gurt i Esparraguera, J.Ma., Buxeda i Garrigós, J. & Cau Ontiveros, M.A. (eds.), *LRCW I. Late Roman Coarse Wares, Cooking Wares and Amphorae in the Mediterranean. Archaeology and Archaeometry*, BAR International Series 1340. Oxford, 563-611.

Reynolds, P. 2008
Linear Typologies and Ceramic Evolution, *FACTA* 2, 61-87.

Reynolds, P. 2010
Trade networks of the East, 3rd to 7th centuries: the view from Beirut (Lebanon) and Butrint (Albania) (fine wares, amphorae and kitchen wares), in: Menchelli *et al.* (eds.), 89-114.

Ριζοπούλου-Ηγουμενίδου, Ε. 1996
Η παραγωγή λαδιού κατά τους Νεώτερους Χρόνους στην Κύπρο και οι παραδοσιακοί ελαιόμυλοι, in: *Ελιά και λάδι: Δ΄ Τριήμερο Εργασίας, Καλαμάτα, 7-9 Μαΐου 1993.* Αθήνα, 324-339.

Riis, P.J. 1979
Sukas 6: The Graeco-Phoenician Cemetery and Sanctuary at the Southern Harbour, Publications of the Carlsberg Expedition to Phoenicia 7. Copenhagen.

Riley, J.A. 1979
The Coarse Pottery from Berenice, in: Lloyd, J.A. (ed.), *Excavations at Sidi Khrebish Benghazi (Berenice)* II, Libya Antiqua Suppl. V.2. Tripoli, 91-467.

Rizzo, M.A. 1990
Le anfore da transporto e il commercio etrusco arcaico I. Complessi tombali dall'Etruria meridoniale, Studi di archeologia pubblicati dalla Soprintendenza archeologica per l'Etruria meridoniale 3. Roma.

Roberts, S. 1986
The Stoa Gutter Well a Late Archaic Deposit in the Athenian Agora, *Hesperia* 55, 1-74.

Robinson, H.S. 1959
The Athenian Agora V: Pottery of the Roman Period, Chronology. Princeton.

Romanus, K., Baeten, J., Poblome, J., Accardo, S., Degryse, P., Jacobs, P., De Vos, D. & Waelkens, M. 2009
Wine and olive oil permeation in pitched and non-pitched ceramics: relation with results from archaeological amphorae from Sagalassos, Turkey, *Journal of Archaeological Science* 36, 900-909, doi:10.1016/j.jas.2008.11.024

Rosenthal-Heginbottom, R. 1988
The Pottery, in: Tsafrir, Y. (ed.), *Excavations at Rehovot-in-the-Negev I, The North Church,* Qedem 25. Jerusalem, 78-96.

Rosenthal-Heginbottom, R. 1995
Stamped Amphora Handles, in: Stern, E. (ed.), *Excavations at Dor, Final Report: Vol. 1B. Areas A and B: The Finds.* Qedem 2. Jerusalem, 183-204.

Rosloff, J.P. 1981
INA's 1980 Turkish underwater survey, *IntJNautA* 10, 277-286.

Rostovtzeff, M. 1957
The Social and Economic History of the Roman Empire 2. Oxford.

Rupp, D.W. 1988
The 'Royal Tombs' at Salamis (Cyprus): Ideological messages of power and authority, *JMedA* 1, 111-139.

Ruzicka, S. 1999
Glos, Son of Tamos, and the End of the Cypriot War, *Historia* 48, 23-43.

Sagona, A.G. 1982
Levantine Storage Jars of the 13th to 4th Century BC, *OpAth* 14, 73-110.

Salles, J-F. 1980
Les Niveau 4 (Fer IIC), in: Briend, J. & Humbert, J.-B. (eds.), *Tell Keisan (1971–1976): une cite phénicienne en Galilée.* Fribourg, 136-141.

Salles, J.-F. 1985
Cuvettes et 'mortiers' du Levant au 1er millenaire avant J.-C., in: Huot, J.L., Yon, M. & Calvet, Y. (eds.), *De l'Indus aux Balkans: recueil à la mémoire de Jean Deshayes.* Paris, 199-212.

Salles, J.-F. 1993a
Présentation, in: Salles (ed.), 171-179.

Salles, J.-F. 1993b
La citerne 198, in: Salles (ed.), 261-284.

Salles, J.-F. 1993 (ed.)
Kition-Bamboula IV. Les niveaux hellénistiques. Paris.

Salmon, J.B. 1984
Wealthy Corinth: A History of the City to 338 B.C. Oxford.

Sauer, R. 1995
Produktionszentren spätthellenistischer und römischer Keramik an der W-Küste Kleinasiens, Unpubl. Bericht über die archäometrischen Untersuchungen für das FWF-Projekt Nr. 9280 mit einem Anhang von U. Outschar.

Sauer, R. 2005
Ergebnisse der mineralogisch-petrographischen Analysen von ausgewählten römischen Amphorenproben aus Wien, in: Krinzinger (ed.), 109–142.

SCE II = Gjerstad *et al.* 1935

SCE IV.2 = Gjerstad 1948

Schattner, T.G. 1996
Die Fundkeramik, in: Tuchelt, K. (ed.), *Didyma III.1 Ergebnisse der Ausgrabungen und Untersuchungen seit dem Jahre 1962: Ein Kultbezirk an der Heiligen Straße von Milet nach Didyma.* Mainz am Rhein, 163-216.

Schuring, J. 1984
Studies on Roman Amphorae I-II, *BABesch* 59, 137-180.

Scorpan, C. 1977
Contributions à la connaissance de certains types céramiques romano-byzantins (IVe – VIIe siècles) dans l'espace Istro-Pontique, *Dacia N.S.* 21, 269-297.

Seifert, M. 2000
Archaische Vorrats- und Transportamphoren in Milet, *MünstBeitr* 19, 1-39.

Seifert, M. 2004
Herkunftsbestimmung archaischer Keramik am Beispiel von Amphoren aus Milet, BAR International Series 1233. Oxford.

Şenol, A.K. 2003
Marmaris Müzesi Ticari Amphoraları. Ankara.

Şenol, A.K. 2004
Kıbrıs'da Amphora Üretimi, (Amphora Production in Cyprus), *İDOL Arkeoloji ve Arkeologlar Derneği Dergisi* 23, 10-14.

Şenol, A.K. 2007
A Statistical Essay on the Distribution of Imported Amphorae Finds of the CEAlex Salvage Excavations, in: Marchand & Marangou (eds.), 57-75.

Şenol, A.K. 2009
3.A.2. Kıbrıs Amphoraları, in: Şenol, A.K. (ed.), *AETAM (Arslan Eyce Taşucu Amphora Müzesi)'nde Bulunan Ticari Amphoralar ve Akdeniz'de Ticaretin İzleri.* Silifke, 102-105.

Şenol, A.K. & Aşkın, E. 2007
Amphoralar ışığında kentin ticari ilişkileri, in: Durugönül (ed.), 241-297 and 425 [English summary].

Şenol, A.K. & Cankardeş-Şenol, G. 2003
Commercial Ties of Cilicia by Means of Hellenistic and Roman Amphorae, *Olba* 7, 119-143.

Şenol, A.K. & Kerem, F. 2000
İçel müzesinde bulunan bir gurup ticari amphora, *Olba* 3, 81-114.

Sezgin, Y. 2009
Arkaik Dönem Doğu Yunan Ticari Amphoraları Sorunu, Ph.D. diss., T.C. Ege Üniversitesi, Izmir.

Shennan, S. 1997
Quantifying Archaeology. Second Edition. Edinburgh.

Shipley, G. 1987
A History of Samos: 800-188 BC. Oxford.

Sidebotham, S.E., Riley, J.A. & Hamroush, H.A. 1989
Fieldwork on the Red Sea Coast: The 1987 Season, *JARCE* 26, 127-166.

Sidebotham, S.E. & Wendrich, W.Z. 1996
Berenike 1995. Preliminary Report of the 1995 Excavations at Berenike (Egyptian Red Sea Coast) and the Survey of the Eastern Desert. Leiden.

Sidebotham, S.E., Zitterkopf, R.E. & J.E. Riley 1991
Survey of the 'Abu Sha'ar Nile-Road, *AJA* 95, 571-622.

Simossi, A. 1991
Underwater excavation research in the ancient harbour of Samos: September-October 1988, *IntJNautA* 20, 281-298.

Singer-Avitz, L. 1989
Local Pottery of the Persian Period (Strata XI-VI), in: Herzog *et al.* (eds.), 115-144.

Slane, K.W. 1994
Tetrarchic Recovery in Corinth. Pottery, Lamps, and Other Finds from the Peribolos of Apollo, *Hesperia* 63, 127-168.

Slane, K.W. 2004
Amphoras – Used and Reused – at Corinth, in: Eiring & Lund (eds.), 361-369.

Smith, J.S. 2009
Art and Society in Cyprus from the Bronze Age into the Iron Age. Cambridge.

Soren, D. & Leonard, J.R. 1989
Archeologia sismica a Kourion. Un approcio multidisciplinare in azione per un terremoto del IV secolo d.C., in: Guidoboni, E. (ed.), *I Terremoti prima del Mille in Italia e nell'area mediterranea.* Bologna, 438-449.

Spataro, S. & Villing, A. 2009
Scientific Investigation of Pottery Grinding Bowls in the Archaic and Classical Eastern Mediterranean, *British Museum Technical Research Bulletin* 3, 89-100.

Spencer, A.J. 1996
Excavations at Tell el-Balamun 1991-1994. London.

Stager, L.E., Master, D.M. & Schloen, J.D. (eds.) 2011
The Leon Levy Expedition to Ashkelon. Ashkelon 3: The Seventh Century B.C. Winona Lake, IN.

Stern, E. 1970
Excavations at Gil'am (Kh. Er-Rujm), *'Atiqot* 6, 31-55* [Hebrew].

Stern, E. 1995
Tel Dor: A Phoenician-Israelite Trading Center, in: Gitin, S. (ed.), *Recent Excavations in Israel. A View to the West.* Bloomington, 81-93.

Stern, E. (ed.) 1995
Excavations at Dor, Final report. Vol. IB. Areas A and C: The finds, Qedem Reports 2. Jerusalem.

Stewart, A. & Martin, S.R. 2005
Attic Imported Pottery at Tel Dor, Israel: An Overview, *BASOR* 337, 79-94.

Stylianou, A. & Stylianou, J.A. 1997
The Painted Churches of Cyprus. Second Edition. Nicosia.

Sztetyłło, Z. 1975
Timbres amphoriques grecs des fouilles polonaises à Alexandrie (1962-1972), Travaux du centre d'archéologie méditerranéenne de l'Académie polonaise des sciences 16, *EtTrav* 8, 159-235.

Sztetyłło, Z. 1976
Nea Paphos I: Les timbres céramiques (1965-1973). Varsovie.

Sztetyłło, Z. 1978
Timbres amphoriques greces des fouilles polonaises à Alexandrie (1973-1974), *EtTrav* 10, 260-316.

Sztetyłło, Z. 1984
Les timbres amphoriques, in: Daszewski, W.A., Fouilles polonaises à Kato Paphas, Chantier de Maloutena, *RDAC*, 311-314.

Sztetyłło, Z. 1985
Les contacts commercieux de Nea Paphos, in: Παπαδόπουλου, Θ. & Χαζηστύλλη, Σ. (eds.), *Πρακτικά του δεύτερου διεθνούς κυπριολογικού συνέδριου, Λευκωσία, 20-25 Απριλίου 1982.* Λευκωσία, 335-338.

Sztetyłło, Z. 1990
Timbres céramiques des fouilles polonaise à Alexandrie (1974-1979), *EtTrav* 14, 159-212.

Sztetyłło, Z. 1991
Nea Paphos IV: Pottery Stamps (1975-1989). Varsovie.

Sztetyłło, Z. 1992a
Timbres céramiques des fouilles polonaises à Alexandrie (1979-1982), *EtTrav* 16, 151-177.

Sztetyłło, Z. 1992b
Timbres céramiques des fouilles polonaises à Alexandrie (1982-1987), EtTrav 16, 179-223.

Sztetyłło, Z. 2010
Nea Paphos VI. Pottery Stamps from Nea Paphos (Excavations 1990-2006), PCMA Monograph Series 2. Warsaw.

Swiny, H.W. 1982
An archaeological guide to the ancient Kourion area and the Akrotiri Peninsula. Nicosia.

Swiny, S. & Mavromatis, C. 2000
Land Behind Kourion: Results of the 1997 Sotira Archaeological Project Survey, *RDAC*, 433-452.

Sørensen, L. Wriedt & Rupp, D. (eds.) 1993
The Land of the Paphian Aphrodite Volume 2. The Canadian Palaipaphos Survey Project Artifact and Ecofactual Studies, Studies in Mediterranean Archaeology CIV:2. Göteborg.

Tandy, D.W. 1997
Warriors into Traders: The Power of the Market in Early Greece, Classics and Contemporary Thought 5. Berkeley.

Tartaron, T.F., Gregory, T.E., Pullen, D.J., Noller, J.S., Rothaus, R.M., Rife, J.L., Diacopoulos, L., Schon, R.L., Caraher, W.R., Pettegrew, D.K. & Nakassis, D. 2006
The Eastern Korinthia Archaeological Survey: Integrated methods for a Dynamic Landscape, *Hesperia* 75, 453-523.

Thomas, C. 1959
Imported Pottery in Dark-Age Western Britain, *MedievA* 3, 89-111.

Thomsen, O. 1995
Written Sources, in: Fejfer (ed.), 26-40.

Todd, I.A. 2004a
Field survey in the Vasilikos valley, in: Iacovou, M. (ed.), 43-54.

Todd, I.A. 2004b
Vasilikos Valley Project 9. The field survey of the Vasilikos valley 1, Studies in Mediterranean Archaeology LXXI:9. Sävedalen.

Todd, I.A. forthcoming
Vasilikos Valley Project 10. The field survey of the Vasilikos valley 2, Studies in Mediterranean Archaeology LXXI:10.

Tomber, R. 2004
Polarising and Integrating the Late Roman Economy: the Role of Late Roman Amphorae 1-7, *AncWestEast* 3.1, 155-165

Tomber, R. 2006
The Pottery, in: Maxfield & Peacock (eds.), 3-236.

Touma, M. 1989
La céramique protobyzantine d'Amathonte: remarques sur le matériel trouvé en 1988, *BCH* 113, 871-875.

Touma, M. 2001
Quelques témoignages de la céramique sur les échanges syro-chypriotes à la période byzantine, in: Villeneuve & Watson (eds.), 49-58.

Τρακοσοπούλου-Σαλακίδου, Ε. 2004
Κεραμικοί κλίβανοι Ακάνθου, *AErgoMak* 18, 167-179.

Tubb, J.N. 1986
The Pottery from a Byzantine Well near Tell Fara, *PEQ* 118, 51-65.

Tufnell, O. 1953
Lachish III: Tell ed-Duweir. The Iron Age. London.

Tzochev, C. 2009
Notes on the Thasian Amphora Stamps Chronology, *Archeologia Bulgarica* 13, 55-72.

Veen, M. van der with Hamilton-Dyer, S. 1998
A life of luxury in the desert? The food and fodder supply to Mons Claudianus, *JRA* 11, 101-116.

Vessberg, O. & Westholm, A. 1956
The Swedish Cyprus Expedition IV, 3: The Hellenistic and Roman Periods in Cyprus. Stockholm.

Villeneuve, E. & Watson, P.M. (eds.) 2001
La céramique byzantine et proto-islamique en Syrie-Jordanie (IVe - VIIIe siècles apr. J.-C.), Actes du colloque tenu à Amman les 3, 4 et 5 décembre 1994, Bibliothèque archéologique et historique 159. Beyrouth.

Villing, A. 2006
'Drab Bowls' for Apollo: The mortaria of Naukratis and exchange in the Archaic eastern Mediterranean, in: Villing & Schlotzhauer (eds.), 31-46.

Villing, A. & Pemberton, E.G. 2010
Mortaria from Ancient Corinth: Form and Function, *Hesperia* 79, 555-638.

Villing, A. & Schlotzhauer, U. (eds.) 2006
Naukratis: Greek Diversity in Egypt: Studies on East Greek pottery and exchange in the eastern Mediterranean, British Museum Research Publication 162. London.

Voigtländer, W. 1982
Funde aus der Insula westlich des Buleuterion in Milet, *IstMitt* 32, 30-173.

Walbank, F.W., Astin, A.E., Frederiksen, M.W. & Ogilvie, R.M. (eds.) 1984
The Hellenistic World, Cambridge Ancient History 7.1. Second Edition. Cambridge.

Waldbaum, J. C. 2011
Greek Pottery, in: Stager *et al.* (eds.), 127-338.

Wallerstein, I. 1974
The Modern World System: Capitalist Agriculture and the Origins of the European World-Economy in the Sixteenth Century 1. New York.

Wiesehöfer, J. 1990
Zypern unter persischer Herrschaft, in: Sancisi-Weerdenberg, H. & Drijvers, J.W. (eds.), *Centre and Periphery, Achaemenid History* IV. Leiden, 239-252.

Westholm, A. 1956
Pottery, in: Vessberg & Westholm, 53-81.

Whitbread, I.K. 1995
Greek Transport Amphorae: A Petrological and Archaeological Study, British School at Athens Fitch Laboratory Occasional Paper 4. Athens.

Whitelaw, T.M. 1994
An ethnoarchaeological study of rural land-use in Northwest Keos: insights and implications for the study of past Aegean landscapes, in: Doukelis, P.N. & Mendoni, L.G. (eds.), *Structures rurales et societes antiques. Actes du Colloque de Corfou (14-16 Mai 1992),* Centre de Recherches d'Histoire Ancienne 126. Paris, 165-186.

Will, É. 1984a
The Succession to Alexander, in: Walbank *et al.* (eds.), 23-61

Will, É. 1984b
The formation of the Hellenistic Kingdoms, in: Walbank *et al.* (eds.), 101-119.

Williams, C. 1989
Anemurium: The Roman and Early Byzantine Pottery, Subsidia Mediaevalia 16. Toronto

Williams, C.K., II & Zervos, O.H. 1983
Corinth, 1982: East of the Theatre, *Hesperia* 52, 1-47.

Williams D.F. 1987
Roman Amphorae from Kourion, Cyprus, *RDAC*, 236-238.

Williams, D.F. 2005
Late Roman amphora 1: a study of diversification in: Briese & Vaag (eds.), 157-168.

Williams, D.F. & Keay, S.J. 2005 [2006]
Roman Amphorae: a digital resource, http://ads.ahds.ac.uk/catalogue/archive/amphora_ahrb_2005/index.cfm

Winther-Jacobsen, K. forthcoming a
3.3. Hellenistic-Roman pottery, in: Given *et al.* (eds.).

Winther-Jacobsen, K. forthcoming b
5.3. The Hellenistic-Roman landscape, in: Given *et al.* (eds.).

Wolff, S.R. 2009
Some Notes on Basket-Handled Amphoras, *ErIsr* 29, 137-146 [Hebrew with English summary on p. 287].

Wolff, S.R. 2011
Basket-Handled Amphoras in the Hecht Museum, *Michmanim* 23, 15*-19*.

Yon, M. 2007
Life and death of a Military Port: Kition 4th-3rd cent. B.C. (political reality and cultural impact), in: Flourentzos (ed.), 53-66.

Зеест, И.Б. 1960
Керамическая тара Боспора, *MatIsslA* 83. Москва, Ленинград

Zemer, A. 1977
Storage Jars in Ancient Sea Trade. Haifa.

Zoroğlu, L. 1994
Kelenderis I, Kaynaklar, Kalıntılar, Buluntular. Ankara.

Zoroğlu, L, 1999
Zwei Lekythoi des Klügmann-Malers aus Kelenderis, *AA*, 141-145.

Zoroğlu, L. 2000
Kelenderis Nekropolü, *Olba* 3, 115-141.

Якобсон, А. Л. 1959
Раннесредневековный Херсонес. Очерки истории материальной културы, *MatIsslA* 63. Москва & Ленинград.

List of Authors

List of Authors

DOBIESŁAWA MARIA BAGIŃSKA
Poznań Archaeological Museum
ul. Wodna 27
61-781 Poznań
Poland
slawabag@yahoo.com

CRAIG BARKER
Sydney University Museums
Nicholson Museum/Macleay
Museum/University Art Gallery
The University of Sydney
NSW 2006
Australia
craig.barker@sydney.edu.au

TØNNES BEKKER-NIELSEN
Department of History and
Civilization
University of Southern Denmark
Campusvej 55
5230 Odense M
Denmark
tonnes@hist.sdu.dk

TAMÁS BEZECZKY
FWF Laecanius Project
Institut für Kulturgeschichte der
Antike der Österreichischen Akademie
der Wissenschaften
Bäckerstrasse 13, PF 8
1010 Wien
Austria
t.bezeczky@gmx.at

GONCA CANKARDES-ŞENOL
Ege University
Faculty of Letters, Department of
Archaeology
Bornova 35100, Izmir
Turkey
goncasenol@yahoo.fr

STELLA DEMESTICHA
Archaeological Research Unit
University of Cyprus
P.O. Box 20537
1678 Nicosia
Cyprus
demesticha@ucy.ac.cy

AGATA DOBOSZ
Department of Classical Archaeology
Jagiellonian University, Faculty of
History Institute of Archaeology
Goł bia 11
PL 31-007 Kraków
Poland
aktaje@gazeta.pl

GÉRALD FINKIELSZTEJN
Israel Antiquities Authority
POB 68141 – Talpiot
91680 Jerusalem
Israel
gerafink@yahoo.fr

KRISTIAN GÖRANSSON
Museum of Mediterranean and
Near Eastern Antiquities
Box 16008
10321 Stockholm
Sweden
kristian.goransson@
varldskulturmuseerna.se

ELIZABETH S. GREENE
Department of Classics
Brock University
500 Glenridge Avenue
St Catharines, Ontario L2S 3A1
Canada
esgreene@brocku.ca

ANTHI KALDELI
Archaeological Research Unit
University of Cyprus
P.O. Box 20537
1678 Nicosia
Cyprus
kaldeli@ucy.ac.cy

MARK L. LAWALL
Department of Classics
University of Manitoba
220 Dysart Rd
Winnipeg, MB R3T 2M8
Canada
lawall@cc.umanitoba.ca

JUSTIN LEIDWANGER
Department of Classics
Building 110, 450 Serra Mall
Stanford University
Stanford, California 94305-2145
USA
jleidwa@stanford.edu

JOHN LUND
Collection of Classical and
Near Eastern Antiquities
The National Museum of Denmark
Frederiksholms Kanal 12
1220 Copenhagen K
Denmark
John.Lund@natmus.dk

HENRYK MEYZA
Institute of Mediterranean and
Oriental Cultures
Polish Academy of Sciences
Palac Staszica
ul. Nowy Świat 72
00-330 Warszawa
Poland
hmeyza@zaspan.waw.pl

HARUN A. ÖZDAŞ
Institute of Marine Sciences and Technology
Dokuz Eylül University
Baku Boulevard 100
35340 İzmir
Turkey
harun.ozdas@deu.edu.tr

MARCUS RAUTMAN
Department of Art History and Archaeology
University of Missouri
109 Pickard Hall
Columbia, MO 65211-1420
USA
RautmanM@missouri.edu

AHMET KAAN ŞENOL
Ege University
Faculty of Letters, Department of Archaeology
Bornova 35100, Izmir
Turkey
ahmet.kaan.senol@ege.edu.tr

DAVID F. WILLIAMS
Department of Archaeology, Humanities
University of Southampton
The Avenue Campus, Highfield
Hampshire SO17 1BJ Southhampton
Great Britain
dfw@soton.ac.uk

KRISTINA WINTHER-JACOBSEN
The SAXO-Institute, Classical Archaeology
University of Copenhagen
80 Njalsgade
DK-2300 Copenhagen S
Denmark
kwjacobsen@hum.ku.dk

K. LEVENT ZOROĞLU
Institute of Science and Letters
Department of Archaeology
Selcuk University
42060 Kampus – Konya
Turkey
lzoroglu@gmail.com

GÖSTA ENBOM MONOGRAPHS are published in connection with the research programme "Pots, Potters and Society in Ancient Greece" (2008-2013) at the Collection of Classical and Near Eastern Antiquities, the National Museum of Denmark.

The research programme and its publications are supported by the "Foundation of Consul General Gösta Enbom".

VOLUME 1
POTTERY IN THE ARCHAEOLOGICAL RECORD: GREECE AND BEYOND
Edited by Mark L. Lawall & John Lund.
Aarhus University Press 2011.

VOLUME 2
RED-FIGURE POTTERY IN ITS ANCIENT SETTING
Edited by Stine Schierup and Bodil Bundgaard Rasmussen.
Aarhus University Press 2012.

VOLUME 3
THE TRANSPORT AMPHORAE AND TRADE OF CYPRUS
Edited by Mark L. Lawall & John Lund.
Aarhus University Press 2013.